The Murmuring Deep

THE
Murmuring Deep

REFLECTIONS ON THE
BIBLICAL UNCONSCIOUS

Avivah Gottlieb Zornberg

Schocken Books · New York

Some of the material in this book originally appeared, in slightly different form,
in the following publications: *Rav Chesed: The Haskel Lookstein Jubilee Volume,*
edited by Rafael Medoff (New York: Ktav, 2009); *Longing: Psychoanalytic Musings
on Desire,* edited by Jean Petrucelli (London: Karnac, 2006); *Diaspora: Homelands
in Exile,* by Frederic Brenner (New York: HarperCollins, 2003); and
Psychoanalytic Dialogues: The International Journal of Relational Perspectives,
May/June 2008, Vol. 18, No. 3.

*Owing to limitations of space, all acknowledgments to reprint previously published
material can be found on page 425.*

Library of Congress Cataloging-in-Publication Data
Zornberg, Avivah Gottlieb.
The murmuring deep : reflections on the biblical unconscious /
Avivah Gottlieb Zornberg.
p.   cm.
Includes bibliographical references and index.
ISBN 978-0-8052-4247-8
1. Bible. O.T.—Psychology. 2. Bible. O.T.—Criticism, interpretation, etc.
3. Subconsciousness—Biblical teaching. 4. Individuation (Psychology)—Biblical teaching. 5. Self—Biblical
teaching. 6. Judaism and psychoanalysis. I. Title.
BS1199.P9Z67 2008
221'.6019—dc22   2008020578

www.schocken.com

Book design by Robert C. Olsson

Printed in the United States of America

First Edition

4   6   8   9   7   5   3

Tehom el tehom korei . . .
Deep calls unto deep . . .
—Psalms 42:8

Tehom—subterranean waters, primeval ocean

Hamah—hum, murmur, coo, reverberate, growl, roar, groan, stir, rush; tumult, thrill of compassion, music of lyre, of flutes, sound of a great throng

CONTENTS

INTRODUCTION
Of the Murmuring Deep

Deep calls unto deep . . .

Psalms 42:8

And the mountain blazed in fire to the heart of
the heavens.

Deuteronomy 4:11

If we had a keen vision and a feeling for all ordinary
human life, it would be like hearing the grass grow and
the squirrel's heart beat, and we should die of that roar
which lies on the other side of silence. As it is, the quick-
est of us walks about well wadded in stupidity.

George Eliot, *Middlemarch*

IN THESE ESSAYS I reflect on the dynamics of communication in a
set of biblical narratives. They are informed by the psychoanalytic
understanding that unconscious mental processes are always at
work, affecting consciousness. Communication that takes place
between human beings is never exhausted by what is consciously
and explicitly communicated.

In any vital encounter, much more is transacted than lies within
the field of consciousness. As Hans-Georg Gadamer often remarks,
we "always already" belong to prejudices, wishes, and interests that
close us to certain truths and open us to others. The complex interplay of forgetting and remembering, the traumatic departures from
our own experience, all leave traces in our movements of communion with one another.

By the same measure, they leave traces in the biblical accounts of
what is transacted between people, between people and God, and
between parts of the self. In this book, I am particularly interested in
the ways in which the Rabbis, in midrashic and Hasidic commen-

tary, reflect on these subtle movements of communion. In effect, my subject is the "Rabbinic unconscious," both in the sense of the understandings of unconscious human life that emerge from these reflections and in the sense of the intimate fullness, complexity, and conflict that resonate within these Rabbinic voices.

"Deep calls unto deep" (Ps. 42:8). Communication takes place between depths, abysses, the voices of many waters. The Hebrew word that is rendered by the English "deep" is *tehom*—incomparably richer in association. This *tehom*—unfathomable, void, dense with watery voices—is one metaphor I would like to explore in this introduction. The other is the volcano, also hidden, unknowable, but explosive, repressing and expressing violent energy, heated beyond human imagining. Together, these metaphors communicate the complexity of human unconscious life, the subterranean power that strains against the deceptively solid eggshell of the earth's crust.

THE SPEECH OF RUPTURE

What do human beings have in common? What can we trust in addressing each other? What are the links that make the other imaginable as an interlocutor? And what is the effect of traumatic experience on this sense that communication is possible? How, indeed, does one understand traumatic experience?

If, as Cathy Caruth claims, trauma leaves a "legacy of incomprehensibility," destruction and survival assume a paradoxical relation with each other.[1] For the survivor, the one who *lives past death,* communication becomes both impossible and essential. Because of an impossible history, the traumatized are possessed by an experience that only belatedly they can begin to possess, to register. The gap at the very heart of memory eliminates simple knowledge and communication; it threatens a collapse of witnessing. Yet witnessing is essential, since it is only in the process of testimony that the trauma is for the first time recorded. Does the study of traumatic experience yield understandings for those who, whether with or without apparent traumatic histories, try to speak and listen to one another? Does the volcano's impacted fury become strangely "reticent," in Emily Dickinson's haunting expression, holding its complex secret?

In these essays, I explore enigmas of communication as they are articulated in twelve biblical narratives, and refracted in midrashic and Hasidic readings of those narratives. At their simplest, the questions are: Can we know the other? Can we speak to the other and be heard? Can we hear the other's cry? I read narratives of rupture and reconnection in three kinds of relationships: between self and other, between self and God, and within the self. The first two of these areas represent a classic Jewish understanding of the dual nature of human experience: *bein adam le-chavero* (lit. between man and friend) and *bein adam la-makom* (lit. between man and God) constitute traditional categories of responsibility, social and religious, each with its complex codes of law and sensibility. The third category—*bein adam le-atzmo* (between man and himself)—represents a relatively modern understanding of the complexities of the self.

As Lionel Trilling points out, a new concept of the personal emerged in eighteenth century European culture: "At a certain point in history men became individuals."[2] Banal or absurd as this statement may be, Trilling characterizes the new person as having an awareness of "internal space": imagining himself in more than one role, he supposes himself an object of potential interest to others simply *as* an individual. He lives in private rooms, looks in mirrors of unprecedented brilliance, paints self-portraits, writes autobiographies. He also begins to use the word *self*: "not as a mere reflexive or intensive, but as an autonomous noun referring, the OED tells, to 'that . . . in a person [which] is really and intrinsically he . . . ,' as that which he must cherish for its own sake and show to the world for the sake of good faith."[3]

The private self, the true self, as Trilling shows in his masterful study, becomes more fragmented and paradoxical as the cultural ideal evolves from one of sincerity to one of authenticity. But the individual self is from the outset in an adversarial relationship with society. This tension becomes the central issue of the modern period.

In the history of Jewish thought, it was the Hasidic masters of the eighteenth and nineteenth centuries who for the first time set the issue of the true self in clear focus. Knowing oneself, maintaining communication with oneself, becomes a spiritual ideal, requiring rigorous and transformative work. By and large, however, the Hasidic commentary on the Bible sharpened and deflected the awareness of the individual self that had led an implicit life in classic exegetical sources, particularly in midrashic literature, for many hundreds of years. Moreover, the relation of self and society was not described as inherently conflictual; the three spiritual registers—social, religious, introspective—were seen as three dimensions of the same redemptive movement.

An enigmatic and powerful Hasidic reading of the Joseph narrative, for instance, addresses the most traumatic biblical history of rupture within the family.[4] At its moment of resolution, Judah "draws close" *(Va-yiggash)* to Joseph and makes the speech that cracks Joseph's shell of alienation. In "drawing close" to his unrecognized brother, Judah achieves a critical rapprochement without fully grasping either his own situation or his relationship with Joseph. In other words, he communicates with his brother effectively but unconsciously, interrupting a tragic history of hatred, jealousy, and resentment.

How, asks Sefat Emet, does he achieve this? His speech, after all, contains no revelations; as family spokesman, he neither acknowledges his past violence against Joseph nor confesses his sins against God. The nineteenth-century Hasidic master answers by turning the word *va-yiggash,* Judah's act of *coming close,* under a prism:

> *Va-yiggash*—"And Judah drew close to him": that is, to Joseph. But also, to himself, his true self. And also, to God. The meaning here is that although Judah said nothing new in his speech and had no real claim to make on Joseph, yet since he clarified the truth of the matter, salvation came to him, as we find in the idea that "Truth springs up from the earth."[5]

With startling simplicity, Sefat Emet unfolds Judah's achievement: with his words, he accesses not only Joseph but equally his true self and God. He approaches the other who is the capricious ruler, his innermost self, and the invisible, silent God.[6] He does this by a specific kind of truth-telling—one that *begets* the truth in the very process of speaking—that restores his relationship with the enigmatic others of his life. I would call this a psychoanalytic form of testimony. A *movement—Va-yiggash—*brings him into contact with lost parts of his world. The midrash tells that Truth is shattered into a thousand pieces when God throws it down to earth. Judah's speech testifies to the fragments of truth that he unconsciously composes in the very anguish of brokenness: "What shall we say to my lord, what shall we speak, how shall we justify ourselves?" (Gen. 44:16).

Without being in lucid possession of his testimony, he gives birth to a new realization about himself. Without mentioning God's name,[7] he comes upon an unbidden perception of his history that brings him close to God, and to Joseph: "How can I go back to my father if the boy is not with me, lest I see the evil which will befall my father?" (Gen. 44:34). With these words, Judah accesses a new knowledge: it is now *impossible* for him to witness his father's anguish at the loss of another son. He acknowledges, in fact, that it was *always* impossible to witness that anguish. An unavoidable truth swells into life through his words, a traumatic truth that only now fills its "shape of absence."[8]

These are the final words of Judah's speech. Immediately after this, Joseph reveals himself to his brothers. Unwittingly, speaking a language that testifies to the birth of knowledge, Judah makes contact with Joseph, with himself, and with God.

Moments earlier, he had spoken of his father in fraught terms:

"Your servant my father said to us, You know that my wife bore me two sons. And one left me, and I said, 'Indeed, he has been torn apart!' And I have never seen him since." (Gen. 44:27–28)

Communicating the pathos of the father who after the loss of one son would die of yet another loss, Judah—in passing, as it were—records his father's reference to *my wife* and *two sons*. This is Jacob's most intimate account of his life; for Judah it marks his father's intimate exclusion of him, his mother, and his brothers. The fact that he is capable of registering his father's unconscious repudiation of himself, of acknowledging his father's emotional life, in all its otherness, gives compassionate force to his words. For since

Joseph's departure, Judah has known his own traumatic losses: his own two sons have died (Gen. 38:7,10). With this wound in his life, Judah records the story of his father's loss with a new empathy. Only now, his own language reveals the intimate resonance of traumatic bereavement. At this moment, he experiences his own history in a way that acknowledges its unfathomable quality.

For Judah to come to his true self is to come to God. And to access Joseph is to give voice to the silent God, as well as to something muted in himself. What he affirms unconsciously in his speech is the unknowable heart—of his father, of his God, at his own core. An omnipotent fantasy is relinquished; he speaks with the voice of reticent power that can touch Joseph's unknowable heart.

To this reading, Sefat Emet brings a sensibility honed by a modern awareness of the splits within the self and between the self and others. And yet it is striking that his emphasis on the unconscious aspects of Judah's achievement—accessing God and his own true self—is based on the most traditional readings of the passage, going back to midrashic and medieval commentaries. How could it be otherwise? In any serious examination of Judah's speech at this crisis in the narrative, certain questions demand satisfaction. These are questions about his motivation and rhetorical intention; about the meaning and possibility of communication in conditions of rupture, as well as about the process of reconciliation. Judah's relations with himself and with God are directly connected with his approach to Joseph, even if his words carry no overt reference to God or to his own history.

How is it possible to communicate with the enigmatic and intrusive other—one's brother whom one has wronged, one's God who has impinged grievously on one's life, one's unfathomable self? The otherness of the other cannot be denied. Perhaps, strangely, it can become the ground of what there is in common.

TRAUMATIC ENCOUNTERS

This question and this hypothesis inform the three groups of essays in this volume. In each section, one plane of relationship is central, but profoundly connected with the other two planes.

The first group of essays engages with the nexus of God and the human being. God creates Adam and immediately—sooner than we thought—He speaks to him. This first address, according to the midrash, is a *seduction:*

"And the Lord God took the human and placed him in the Garden of Eden" (Gen. 2:15): He took him with beautiful words and seduced him to enter the Garden.[9]

It is seduction that is constitutive of the human entry into language. Moved, captivated by divine messages that escape his full understanding, Adam lives henceforth with these unconscious transmissions implanted within him. The first act of communication, then, brings the human being to a place beyond conscious choice.[10]

The French psychoanalyst Jean Laplanche describes in similar terms the first relationship of child and parent. The mother unconsciously transmits to her child seductive messages, which intimate aspects of her life that he is incapable of grasping. The child receives the impact of the other in all her beauty; he is dazzled by a light beyond his comprehension. The alienness of the other is registered; its unassimilable, stimulating message is locked within. From now, the child will be haunted, decentered by his unconscious life. In Freud's words, "The ego is not master in his own house."

This internal stranger, the residue of a seduction, of an inspiration beyond understanding, is, I suggest, evoked in a similar way by the midrash on God's seduction of Adam. Something excessive, restless, inspired beyond his means, is implanted in Adam. Like a foreign body within him, it carries him into Eden. He knows himself as the object of God's enigmatic desire. But he knows neither himself nor God. Only after he has eaten of the Tree of Knowledge of Good and Evil can he speak to God in the disjointed ambiguous language that acknowledges the foreigner within. The mastery with which he had named the creatures in the Garden is modulated into the baffled intensity of a new address to God.

Seduction, of course, contains a traumatic element—the break-in from outside, which becomes an inner "foreign body" and now breaks out from within.[11] "Laplanche's essence of the human soul," writes Adam Phillips, "is a traumatic but unavoidable . . . receptivity to the other. . . . Too open, [it] learns forms of closure."[12] This is the "ineluctable narcissistic closure of the apparatus of the soul,"[13] which attempts to master, to translate those seductive messages. Constructing coherent narratives in which the trauma is domesticated is one such form of closure. Psychoanalysis offers an opportunity to reopen the relation to the enigmatic and traumatic other.

Laplanche's myth of human origins illuminates the complex issues of communication with which I engage in these essays. Between God and Noach, or Jonah, or Esther, the human desire to know and to control the Other, to evade uncertainty and affirm mastery, is enacted in many different ways. But acknowledging God means acknowledging the Other within oneself, as well as the enigmatic human other. Moments of shocked encounter with God—the annunciation of the Flood, God's call to Jonah to cry out against Nineveh, the woundingly present absence of God when a holocaust is decreed in Shushan—are answered by human attempts to appropriate the ungraspable experience. Sealed in an omnipotent box, Noach refuses to open himself to the potential retraumatization of language and sexuality; Jonah flees a place and time that is called *standing in the presence of God;* Esther stands in that place where God's absence becomes presence.

In the second section, "Stranger Within," Abraham, Isaac, and Rebecca live through moments when consciousness brushes against its limits. Rebecca achieves pregnancy only to realize that her self, her *"I-ness,"* has been incomprehensibly wounded: " 'Why then *I?'*— and she went to seek God."

In the final section, "Between Self and Other," Jacob, Joseph, and Ruth seek to affirm connections with others across minefields of betrayal and abjection. Ruth returns with Naomi to a place she never left. Haunted by a past that is not hers, she persists in a liminality, a state of being attached and excluded, where what solicits Boaz is an uncanny presence, a stranger's voice that wakes him from dreams and makes a stranger of him. *Who are you?* he asks her—and Naomi repeats the question in the morning: *Who are you, my daughter?* Elusive, Ruth may become the demon of granary floors, or the ancestor of royalty ... *Who are you?* The Ruth that both Boaz and Naomi know partly eludes their grasp.

THE UNTHOUGHT KNOWN

Christopher Bollas writes of the need to form a relation to the "mysterious unavailability of much of our knowledge." His concept of the "unthought known," of "what we know but may never be able to think," comes to mark a fundamental split between this and "what we think we know."[14] Our sense of a person is registered in wordless and diffuse ways, in body knowledge, in relationship. Our sense of ourselves, likewise, of our own basic idiom, our true selves, our inherited disposition, is constantly developing, before it is ever thought. Some parts of this unthought knowledge will become thought; others will never be transferred to consciousness. "By ... developing a limited relation to the unthought known in ourselves, we can then address the mysteries of our existence."[15]

The "unthought known" in human experience evokes mental states beyond our grasp. This is the place where "knowledge unravels from its own self-possession."[16] Both self and other may be known in a way that in a sense dissolves all identity; in that place, we may communicate. "Each analyst who comes to know his patient ... must unknow him."[17] *Who are you?* is a question that never ceases its murmur.

This model of identity and communication I would like to set beside the following passage from Maurice Blanchot's *The Unavowable Community:*

Now, "the basis of communication" is not necessarily speech, or even the silence that is its foundation and punctuation, but the exposure to death, no longer my own exposure, but someone else's, whose living and closest presence is already the eternal and unbearable absence, an absence that the travail of deepest mourning does not diminish. And it is in life itself that that absence of someone else has to be met. It is with that absence— uncanny presence, always under the prior threat of a disappearance—that friendship is brought into play and lost at each

moment, a relation without relation other than the incommen-
surable. . . . Such is, such would be the friendship that discovers
the unknown we ourselves are, and the meeting of our own
solitude which, precisely, we cannot be alone to experience.[18]

Speech and silence are essential to each other, but not to the
"basis of communication." It is the death of the other, her always
potential absence that gives resonance to friendship. This present
absence, this companionate solitude, can be discovered only in life,
in a friendship of this kind. Haunted by imminent vanishings, we
reach out from and to the unknowable. Abraham works through the
impulse to sacrifice his son; but the death that singed him in childhood never leaves him; now it becomes the basis for a different
recognition of his son's place at the margins of death and life.[19]
At the heart of such a relationship there is a question: "incomplete, the word that questions recognizes that it is only a part. . . . The
question puts the sufficient assertion back into the void; it enriches
it with this preexisting void."[20] In the space between two who recognize this void, there is a reaching out, a not-yet of desire. "The relationship with the other . . . is a transcendent relationship, which
means that there is an infinite and, in one way, unsurmountable distance between me and the other who belongs to the other shore."[21]
Where are you? God asks Adam; *Who told you you are naked? Did you
eat? What is this you have done?* A void opens up in Eden. Isaac asks his
son Jacob-Esau: *Who are you? Who are you, my son?* Jacob may answer,
misidentify himself. But the question will ring endlessly in his ears.
Something was reaching out toward him in his father's question.
It put him and his assertions back into the void. No answer will
ever seal that opening shut again. It will draw on the "unthought
known" of his life, and of his mother's life: *Why then I? I have never
known I.*[22]
R. Nahman[23] describes the *challal ha-panui*—the vacated space,
which God leaves when He creates the world. In the kabbalistic
thought of R. Isaac Luria, God withdraws the plenitude of His being
to *make space* for a world. In R. Nahman's version, a similar space
must exist between human beings if they are to imitate God and cre-

ate their own worlds. Sages, *chakhamim,* cannot be of one mind: in their difference, in the distance between them, they both become subjects. The other must be unknowable; his opaqueness makes interchange possible.

From different shores, then, he and I speak. What do we have in common, across this void? Here, God is absent. But He is present, in the void itself. His present absence brings to life the absent presence that Blanchot describes as the basis of communication. Perhaps this is what exists between people, separating and connecting them. The Talmud calls God "the third who is between them."[24] He knows the truth of their relationship, however they may distort it. In a sense, He *is* its truth. "A space reaches out from us and translates the world" (Rilke).

The communality represented by God may be found, I suggest, precisely in the void between people. The abyss of otherness from which we reach out to translate and retranslate the world may be invisible, but it is not inaudible. Murmurings, whisperings, restless cracklings of life animate that space between us and within us. The other is other than me because he is other than himself. As Eric Santner puts it, "The possibility of a 'We,' of communality, is granted on the basis of the fact that every familiar is ultimately strange and that, indeed, I am even in a crucial sense a stranger to myself."[25] Each of us, singular in our own out-of-jointness, may open to the proximity of our neighbor, in his internal alienness.

Lionel Trilling reports ironically on his graduate students: when asked, in a course on modern literature, "to look into the Abyss,"

> . . . both dutifully and gladly, they have looked into the Abyss, and the Abyss has greeted them with the grave courtesy of all objects of study, saying: "Interesting, am I not?"[26]

What has led these students to ignore so glibly the terror of the void? Perhaps, instead of looking into the abyss, they might listen to it, to its desolate murmur. A new apprehension of themselves might, shivering, be born.

. . .

THE MURMURING DEEP

The history of this "murmur" can be traced back to Creation. In Rashi's rendering, this is the first moment:

> In the beginning of the creation of heaven and earth, when the earth was desolate and void and darkness was upon the face of the murmuring deep and God's spirit hovered over the face of the water, God said, "Let there be light." (Gen. 1:1–3)

The first word is spoken by God to a formless void. Indeed, Stephen Frosh[27] suggests that God's motive in speaking the universe into existence is *because* "the earth was desolate and void *[tohu va-vohu]* and darkness was upon the face of the murmuring deep." The "murmuring deep," a poetic translation from the Hebrew *tehom*, represents a non- or prelinguistic sound, menacing, needing to be revoked. Rashi reads *tohu* as expressive of "the *wonder and astonishment* which a person would feel at the *bohu*, the emptiness of it." Strikingly, he inserts a human consciousness into the uncanny void, as though to say, "If a person had been there, he would have been astounded, *aghast* at such absence—at so unbearable a presence of nothingness."

Tohu—the appalling nature of this reality—is echoed in the word *tehom*. Normally translated "the deep"—the dark, watery mass that God's words transfigure—*tehom* is, in the evocative version cited by Frosh, rendered "the *murmuring* deep."[28] This poetic reading conveys some of the complex harmonics of *tehom*: the Hebrew roots *hamam, hamah, hom* cover meanings like *humming, murmuring, cooing, groaning, tumult, music, restlessness, stirring, panic*. A large register of tones and sounds and movements . . .

On the basis of this translation, Frosh draws on Žižek and Lingis to suggest that God's speech interrupts a primal *noise*: "the first creative act is therefore to *create silence*—it is not that silence is broken, but silence itself breaks, interrupts, the continuous murmur of the Real, thus opening up a clearing in which words can be spoken."[29] Speech and silence are created together to counteract the "inconsolably alien" murmur of the deep. Meaningless, vital, this murmur may be the very substance of what human beings share.

Lingis raises the possibility that communication may not, after all, refer solely to the attempt to rescue meaning from the constant interferences that threaten to submerge it, but, on the contrary, to

> the hearing of the noises in one another's voices—the noise of one another's life that accompanies the harkening to the message[.] What kind of communication would that be?
>
> The one who understands is not extracting the abstract form out of the tone, the rhythm, and the cadences—the noise internal to the utterance, the cacophony internal to the emission of the message. He or she is also listening to that internal noise—the rasping or smoldering breath, the hyperventilating or somnolent lungs, the rumblings and internal echoes—in which the message is particularized and materialized and in which the empirical reality of something indefinitely discernible, encountered in the path of one's own life, is referred to and communicated. With this internal noise it is the other, in his or her materiality, that stands forth and stands apart, making appeals and demands.[30]

In this approach, the murmur is the message: the background hum of life—desolate, excessive, neither language nor silence—is what links us to one another. What can be shared, for example, with the dying? Perhaps, Lingis suggests, rather than transmitting clear meanings, the encounter rests on an acknowledgment of an elemental otherness that is related to our own:

> We do not relate to the light, the earth, the air, and the warmth only with our individual sensibility and sensuality. We communicate to one another the light our eyes know, the ground that sustains our postures, and the air and the warmth with which we speak. We face one another as condensations of earth, light, air, and warmth, and orient one another in the elemental in a primary communication. We appeal to the others to help us be

at home in the alien elements into which we stray: in the drift-
ing and nameless light and warmth of infancy, in the nocturnal
depths of the erotic, and in the domain of dying where rational
discourse has no longer anything to say.[31]

Most alone in the presence of the "alien elements into which we
stray," we seek acknowledgment both of our difference and of the
common ground of our being.

In an inspired reading of his materials, Frosh cites Žižek and
Lingis, as well as Levinas and Agamben, to suggest that the ultimate
communion between people rests in the capacity to draw on an elemental life that is experienced as *inhuman*. In this way, he argues,
access to the murmuring deep, the *inhuman* aspect of human aliveness, sustains contact with the other. "Being 'in' a relationship with
another is also a matter of being outside it, sharing in the imperson-
ality that comes from being lived *through* by the forces that constitute
the human subject." This "ground and deep" of human activity may
then be what unites us: accessible when we acknowledge "the excess
of the other—the other's *intrusiveness*, perhaps, as what is essential."

The place of emptiness—the *tohu* or the *tehom*—appalls us, leaves
us aghast; but it may also constitute us as human. Its inchoate murmur moves us to language and silence. Alien to human meanings,
discomfiting, distracting, unfathomable, the murmur of *tehom*
mocks pretension and threatens sanity.[32] At its heart is *tohu*, signifying *Nothing*. Its *nonsilence* is perhaps related to the Psalmist's mysterious *lo dumiyah*:

> My God, My God, why have You forsaken me,
> And are far from my help at the words of my cry?
> O my God, I call by day, but you do not answer;
> And at night, and there is *nonsilence* for me.
>
> (Ps. 22:2–3)

By day, the Psalmist's cry is met with painful silence. But by night,
he is invaded by aggressive sounds of anguish—a wounded bird's
pathetic cry, the rasping of a tool, the creaking of a door—which, in
Andre Neher's words, constitute a "silence more silent than silence.

It is the fall of silence into a deeper stratum of nothingness; it is a shaft hollowed out beneath silence which leads to its most vertiginous depths."[33] This "metasilent" dimension of silence—like the "inhuman" dimension of humanity—has a liminal existence beyond language and silence.

"*Why* have You forsaken me?" the Psalmist cries. This *Why? (lamah)* haunts the metasilent moments of Rebecca ("*Why I?*") and Esther and Job. It threatens and constitutes the human. "*Tohu,*" says the midrash, "refers to Adam, who became a *lamah.*"[34] *Lamah* is also the Aramaic translation of *tohu—Nothing.* What threatens Adam's dignity, his consciousness, and his power of language is this Nothing, the presence of absence. It is a part of him, his unconscious life, in tension with his conscious aspirations.

> It is the general custom that when a king builds a palace in a place of sewers and garbage and stinks, anyone who declared, "This palace is built in a place of sewers and garbage and stinks," would be considered offensive. So if anyone declares that this world is created out of *tohu va-vohu,* emptiness and void—is that not considered offensive? R. Huna in the name of Bar Kafra said: If this had not been written in the sacred text, it would have been impossible to say it: *In the beginning, God created heaven and earth*—Of what were they made? *And the earth was emptiness and void.*[35]

In the radical imagery of the midrash, *tohu va-vohu* constitutes the very foundation of the palace that God builds: like the plumbing system with its stinks. R. Yossi bar Hanina objects: How can one say such things without defacing the beauty of God's creation? The infrastructure of creation, the *tohu va-vohu,* is the void that leaves one aghast. Such subversive truths should not be talked about. But, R. Huna points out, this is written in the Torah itself. It seems that even a reader who is capable of comprehending the paradoxes implicit in this statement would be constrained from *speaking* them. Only the fact that the Torah itself explicitly tells of the relation of world and void makes the words utterable.

What the Sages struggle with here is the *otherness* that is written into the text. We are being asked to respond with a kind of anguish to the traumatizing words: the world is founded on *nothing*. "God created everything out of nothing. But the nothingness shows through" (Paul Valery).

A few pages later, the midrash records another subversive conversation between two sages:

> "I have heard about you, that you are a gifted interpreter: Where was light created?" asked R. Shimeon ben Yehotzadok of R. Shmuel bar Nahman, who replied, "This teaches that God wrapped Himself in light like a garment and His glorious radiance glowed from one end of the world to the other." *He said this in a whisper.* R. Shimeon objected: "But this is a quotation [from Psalm 134], and yet you say it in a whisper!" R. Shmuel answered: "Just as I heard it in a whisper, so I utter it to you in a whisper!"[36]

The enigmatic and audacious answer to the Sage's question is spoken in a whisper—even though it is clearly written in Psalms. R. Shmuel's rationale is subtle: the troubling text may be written for all to see, but if it is spoken between two people, it becomes a *message*: "I heard it from . . . and I utter it *to you*." Such transactions are seductions, in the sense that Laplanche gives the term. In the context of such an address, the quoted verse becomes enigmatically and powerfully meaningful. It is imbued with revelatory force without explicit meaning.[37] Such unconscious transmissions from the other can be traumatic, leaving the receiver haunted, distraught. For this reason, perhaps, they are to be *whispered*—presumably so as to exclude those incapable of comprehending their meaning. But the midrash continues:

> R. Berachiah said: "If R. Yitzhak had not interpreted the verse in public, it would have been impossible to utter it."

R. Berachiah carries the aphorism of the previous midrash further: it is not sufficient that the subversive words appear in the Torah; in order to be spoken aloud, they must already have been discussed and interpreted in a public lecture. Before that happens, the *whisper* is the only way in which the potentially traumatic address can be contained. Now that there has been such a public explanation, R. Berachiah is free to transmit, in a normal voice, R. Shmuel's interpretation.

In this midrashic narrative, dangerous words become unspeakable, despite the fact that they are simply quotations from the Torah. In the first midrash, the danger lies in the *tohu va-vohu*, in the void that the words carry with them: to speak of the rank odor of the abyss underlying Creation is to ruin the beauty of God's work. In the second midrash, too, the notion that must be whispered contains nothingness at its core—the vertigo of *tohu va-vohu*.[38] Perhaps because the void is less explicitly at issue in this midrash, however, its transmission becomes even more insidious. Like the *murmuring void* itself, the whisper is neither speech nor silence. Unlike the murmur, however, the whisper is shaped precisely as a message, an address to the other. Language has clothed itself in light, lucid meaning has been extracted from the uncanny, prelinguistic murmur. But too much *nothing* remains in those words; the residues of the void overwhelm the speaker; he must whisper, as though to attenuate the claim of language to have dispelled the background noise.

What is communicated, then, is both an intentional address to the other and an appeal to hear the internal noise of otherness in which the message is couched. Only after the public interpretation of meaning has tamed the words of their human excess can they be uttered without fear. They have become public coin: unambiguous, impersonal, invulnerable, usable.

It is striking that the whisper—*lechishah*—is considered the medium of prayer—that is, of the *Amidah* prayer: an expression of intimacy with God. The human being cries out to God in a whisper, as though appealing for Him to hear the impossible address. The tone of the prayer is the message: the murmuring deep in the mouth of the speaker. The same word, *lechishah*, can also be an incantation, a spell—any communication that opens the listener to the otherness, the elemental life of the speaker. Whispering to animals *(The Horse Whisperer)* is an *inhuman* form of communication, therapeutic in intent and effect. As this enters human speech, the voice—urgent, sibilant, husky—becomes part of the message.

According to the Zohar, moreover, a whisper is audible in every biblical verse where the word *amar,* "to say" (as opposed to *dibber,* "to speak"), is used. If God created the world in ten *sayings (asarah ma'amarot),*[39] we understand that He *whispered* rather than spoke it into existence. From the murmuring deep to the whisper of God—"Let there be light!"—a continuity becomes imaginable. The nineteenth-century Hasidic master Mei Ha-Shilo'ach offers a profound meditation on the whisper as the only possible mode of communication when the message concerns divine providence.

> "Say to the priests . . . : None shall defile himself for any dead person among his kin . . ." (Lev. 21:1). Since they believe in His providence, those who serve God ["priests"] are especially prone to bitterness at the apparently random suffering in the world. The enigmas of death and loss, expressions of *midat ha-din* [inscrutable divine justice] in the world, trouble them deeply. So "Say to them—*in a whisper*—not to pollute themselves by this bitterness. For God's intentions are always—in spite of appearances—*ba-omek,* in the depths—benign."[40]

The striking element here is the *whispered* message, the good news of providential love in a world haunted by the abyss. The message must be whispered, because it is both seductive and traumatic: it addresses the spiritual being with an intensity that captivates, but it cannot be comprehended. Tuned to a whisper, it minimizes the wound of the unfathomable. It hints at the inexpressible, transgressing the empirical discourse of mourning.

The whisper, then, haunts the margin between inside and outside. "My heart is astir *[rachash]* with beautiful words." (Ps. 45:2). Like *lachash,* the root *rachash* engages with the unthought known; too strident an address would provoke resistance. Intimations of hope, of gratified desire move the heart with subtle turmoil; they can only be whispered, murmured.

.   .   .

LISTENING TO THE ABYSS

In the relationship with the unthought known—the enigmatic other, the inscrutable God, the stranger within the self—a desire is born. The other calls for meaning to be elucidated, for the intrusive murmur to resolve itself into lucid form—"Let there be light!" It asks to be named. *Tehom el tehom korei*—"Deep calls unto deep." (Ps. 42:8). Unfathomable depths call to one another *by name*—they cry, *Tehom!* The profound murmur of life invokes a companion alienness in the other.

What is it to *listen* to that invocation? As Cathy Caruth expresses it, the traumatic experience of the other

> challenges us to a new kind of listening, the witnessing, precisely, of *impossibility* . . . to be able to listen to the impossible . . . is also to have been *chosen* by it, *before* the possibility of mastering it with knowledge. . . . The history of a trauma, in its inherent belatedness, can only take place through the listening of another. . . . This speaking and this listening—a speaking and a listening *from the site of trauma*—does not rely on what we simply know of each other, but on what we don't yet know of our own traumatic pasts.[41]

The ability to "listen through the departures we have all taken from ourselves" mobilizes a depth of experience not yet comprehended.

What Caruth so poignantly suggests is that the listener, barely aware of her own internal voids, is *chosen* to register the yet-to-be-recorded narrative of the other. What links people is the delays, the departures from knowledge, the intrusive hubbub of the abyss. Silently absorbing an unborn pain, the designated listener, like Emily Dickinson's "reticent volcano," guards her secret, dangerous grief.

> The reticent volcano keeps
> His never slumbering plan;

> Confided are his projects pink
> To no precarious man.
> If nature will not tell the tale
> Jehovah told to her,
> Can human nature not survive
> Without a listener?
> Admonished by her buckled lips
> Let every babbler be.
> The only secret people keep
> Is Immortality.[42]

The abyss in the other seduces, persecutes, reveals, inspires. Whether this is God seducing Adam, or Rebecca taking the soundings of her unknown *"I-ness,"* or Boaz inspired to redemption by Ruth's uncanny night beauty—a mystery is implanted, a fascinated relation to the enigma as such. This other comes to "re-open at privileged moments the wound of the unexpected, of the enigma."[43] To be *opened up,* like a wound, implies being surprised, seized, questioned, *dispossessed.* In the thought of Laplanche and of Levinas, this dispossession, the wound of incompleteness inflicted by the other, is potentially redemptive.

When God sends Jonah to *cry out* against Nineveh, he flees God's presence, takes to the sea, and even in the danger of death, which draws prayers from all the sailors, he refuses to *cry out.* His flight is a resistance to *crying out,* to *standing* in the presence of God, in the human place between death and life. If he were to find his voice, it would emerge from the depths of his being: *Mi-ma'amakim k'ratikha*—"From the depths I have called to you, O God!" (Ps. 130:1). Those deep places are the experience of the inhuman humanity he bears; paradoxically, they provide the ground from which prayer, asking, wishing, can emerge. To cry from deep wounds of grief and need, to allow hollow places to open up within him, would be to stand in God's presence.

In flight from those depths, the human being tells a story of water. As Gaston Bachelard suggests, "For certain souls, *water is the matter of despair.*"[44] To contemplate water "is to slip away, dissolve, and die"; such a water reverie yields "strange and dismal murmurs."[45]

The poet who wrote, "The sounding cataract / Haunted me like a passion," comes to hear "the still, sad music of humanity." He also writes of the "beauty born of murmuring sound"[46] that passes into the face of one who learns to speak in response. Jonah, elusive, terrified of uncertainty, finds himself mortally surrounded by the *tehom* (Jon. 2:6) but resists its impact.[47] God's last words challenge Jonah to acknowledge his depths, to utter his cry.

RETICENT VOLCANO

But there is in my heart like a raging fire, shut up in my bones. I weary myself to hold it in, but I cannot. (Jer. 20:9)

If the murmuring void is the ground and deep of human life, the raging fire is its heart. The material imagination, as Bachelard calls it, dreams of different kinds of depth. Meditation on matter—water, fire—leads one inward to dynamic worlds. The fire in Jeremiah's bones—like the volcano in the phlegmatic mountain—is unbearable because it is both foreign to him and yet ineluctably his. It is most inward but its rage is impelled outward. Its force ignores his decision never again to speak of or for God; prophecy erupts from him like deepest pain.

"Vesuvius at home,"[48] the volcanic heart of the Jewish imagination is the smoking mountain at Sinai: "And Mount Sinai was all in smoke, for God had come down upon it in fire; the smoke rose like the smoke of a furnace, and the whole mountain trembled violently" (Exod. 19:18). From the trembling mountain, fire blazes to the very heart of the heavens (Deut. 4:11). Directly mirroring the trembling of the whole people (v. 16), the volcano projects their elemental being. Terror and desire are bound up in fire—overwhelming force pounding up from the earth's core, telling of interior things.

"Volcano blood"[49] is human lava, intimate, reticent:

> On my volcano grows the grass,—
> A meditative spot,
> An area for a bird to choose
> Would be the general thought.

How red the fire reeks below,
How insecure the sod—
Did I disclose, would populate
With awe my solitude.⁵⁰

Emily Dickinson's vision of the unsuspecting bird meditating on the grass—of calm and stable surfaces—is rent apart by her knowledge of the appalling fire within. But another bird is singed by another fire, in the Talmudic narrative about R. Yonatan ben Uziel: "When he sat and studied Torah, any bird flying overhead was burned."⁵¹ *Up high round the volcano, the heat burns the wings off birds: they drop like melons hitting the ground.*⁵²

The great Hasidic master Sefat Emet asks: What then are we to say of R. Yonatan's teacher Hillel, by whose face no bird was singed? Surely his fire was even fiercer than his student's? But his fire blazed inwardly, leaving no sign on his face. Such was the veil on Moses's face when he returned to earth from Mount Sinai: one gesture of his hand and his face reverts to its normal reticence, while the rays of light blaze within.⁵³ Near the veiled face of the volcano, no birds burn.

That fire of Moses, or of the Sages, is understood to be of volcanic but reticent power. If they were to disclose that force, no bird would survive. "Beware of the fiery coals of the Sages, lest you be singed . . . for their hiss *[lachash]* is the hiss of a serpent and all their words are like coals of fire."⁵⁴ But this same fire is mysteriously sweet and joyful, as it was that day at Sinai:

Ben Azzai was sitting and interpreting Torah, while fire flamed around him. His students went and told R. Akiva: Ben Azzai is sitting and interpreting Torah while fire flames around him. He went to him and said: I hear that you have been interpreting Torah while fire flames around you? He said: Yes, yes. He said: Have you been engaged in esoteric matters? He answered: No. But I have been sitting stringing beads with words of the Torah, linking Torah to Prophets and Prophets to Scriptures. And the words were as joyful as when they were given at Sinai, and they were as sweet as they were at that very moment. For were those words not given in fire?—as it is said, "The mountain blazed in fire to the heart of the heavens" (Deut. 4:11).[55]

The flaming fire *(lahat)* makes all space—especially psychic space—unstable. This is Ben Azzai's volcano, active when he is engaged in interpreting Torah. Three times the words are repeated like an incantation, acknowledging the uncanny: *fire flamed around him.* An incandescent energy, the fulfillment of his reticence, erupts as he speaks, stringing the sacred words, blending spaces. He is re-experiencing revelation in all its otherness, as he generates new strings of language from the molten words. The fire of Sinai destroys and re-forms, provoking a rebirth. Its terror and its sweetness and joy—which are love—are disclosed together. The reticent volcano holds the secret—the only secret—of immortality.

PART ONE

Between God and Self

ONE

Seduced into Eden

The Beginning of Desire

DESIRE: THE LAPSE IN SOVEREIGNTY

The official history of desire begins here: "Your desire shall be for your husband, and he shall rule over you" (Gen. 3:16). With these words, God declares Eve's destiny: a melancholy sketch of the relation of power and desire. Desire is associated with vulnerability. To desire is to lose autonomy; the desired other acquires a sovereignty to which one surrenders in spite of the pain that inevitably ensues. Rashi's classic commentary only deepens the shadow: with feminine desire comes a speechlessness, a failure of language, that in itself gives power to the other.

Our starting point, then, yields a dark image of desire as feminine, helpless, wordless. Strikingly, however, at the opposite end of the spectrum, God, too, experiences the halting impact of desire. At the outset of the Creation narrative, His power in will and word are absolute. The template is "God said, 'Let there be. . . . And it was so.'" Unhesitatingly, word becomes act. However, when God approaches the creation of the human being, the pattern changes. For the first time, there is a preamble, a proposition, a desire: "And God said: *Let us* make Adam in our image and after our form. . . . And God created Man in His image, in the image of God He created him, male and female He created them" (Gen: 1:26–27). Whom is God addressing in this preamble? Is it a soliloquy? To whom does the plural, "Let *us* make man in *our* image," refer? Is this the *pluralis maiestatis,* the royal "we"? Or does it refer to other primal beings, angels perhaps, who are mysteriously included in this final project of creation, the human being? Many midrashic accounts would have it so.[1] But then one cannot avoid the impression that God's sovereignty has been compromised. Indeed, Rashi specifically addresses this "debasing" effect: he quotes the midrash that tells of God's humility in consulting with the angels, whose envy and suspicion of the project He attempts to mollify.

The risk entailed in such humility is the loss of God's status as sole Creator. He is willing to risk heretical responses in order to model humility to the reader: the powerful person should solicit the opinion of his inferiors. For such a moral purpose, He is willing to go on record as sharing power with others. The midrashic narrative does not take this lightly: at least at this moment of contemplation before creating Man, God is, imaginably, no longer sovereign, no longer One.[2]

Of course, the breath of scandal is neutralized immediately: "And *He* [singular] created Adam." However, for the first time in the triumphant litany of God's creations, there has occurred a lapse, a suspension of sovereignty. It is only with the idea of the human being that God is moved to this cryptic humility.

It is striking, however, that a parallel moment does occur later, when God decides to create Eve: "*Let Me* make him a helpmate" (Gen. 2:18) Here, of course, God speaks in the powerful singular form. But here, too, as with the creation of Adam, God reflects on a future act; He expresses an intention. And, as we shall see, His intention is not, in fact, immediately implemented. In the end, it is *Adam's* desire for a mate that enables her creation. This desire arises at the end of a chain of events, a "plot," that separates God's reflection from its consummation. In these critical moments when God relates to the creation of Adam and of Eve, desire both informs and inhibits divine omnipotence, in the same way as, explicitly, it erodes Eve's autonomy.

IN GOD'S IMAGE

If we return now to God's project for man, we are confronted by the most eloquent and mystifying of all God's creative words: "Let us make man *in our image, after our form.*"[3] This creature is to be, in some essential way, similar to his creator. This resemblance will give him dominion over the earth's resources. Clearly, man is to hold a special relationship to God; in a sense, he is to be the symbol of God's presence on earth. But how is one to understand such a notion of being *like* God, given that the human being is limited, mortal, and contingent, while God is infinite, eternal, and absolute? One might even say that one of the main needs that man has of God is that He be different, precisely not limited in the ways that man knows himself to be: man requires a God immune to human deficiencies.

Moreover, to compound the mystery, the enigmatic notion of man resembling God is picked up, strangely, by the serpent, in his insidious suggestion to Eve that the Tree of Knowledge yields precisely such a gift—and that God resents man's appropriating this gift: "For God knows that on the day you eat of it your eyes will be opened, and you will become like God, knowing good and evil" (Gen. 3:5). Eating of the Tree will make Adam indeed like God. Thus the serpent.

But God, too, speaks again, at the end of the narrative, of such a resemblance. He is, in fact, moved by this resemblance to expel him from the Garden:

> And the Lord God said: Behold, man has become as one of Us, knowing good and evil. And now, what if he should stretch out his hand to take also of the Tree of Life, and eat, and live for ever. . . . So the Lord God banished him from the Garden of Eden . . . (Gen. 3:22–23).

It seems that the serpent was right: eating of the Tree of Knowledge has indeed made man like God. Even the recurrence of the plural, "one of *Us*," serves to obscure God's unique sovereignty. Only man's mortality still differentiates him; he must therefore be expelled, before his resemblance to God becomes total. How does this enigmatic scenario engage with God's original project of "man in our image"? Is a specific resemblance implied in the divine project? And is man's eventual likeness to God a fulfillment or a subversion of that project?

ADAM IN THE HUMAN IMAGE?

At this point I would like to modulate to a different set of questions: Does Adam resemble us? Is Adam recognizably human? Do we acknowledge ourselves in the figure portrayed in the Torah? And if Adam does not resemble us, does Adam's resemblance to God become irrelevant to human identity as we know it?

I want to suggest that, indeed, in his created condition, Adam is *not* identical with ourselves. Vast areas of the human are alien to him. My project will be to explore some implications of this difference and of the role that the Tree of Knowledge plays in transforming Adam into a recognizable human being.

Essential to this difference is the history of desire. According to a provocative Hasidic reading,[4] it is the postlapsarian man and woman who, paradoxically, become godlike. My project will involve further questions about time and language, the unconscious, and the decentered self, as constitutive of the human and—in a specific sense—of God.

In the obvious sense, Adam is sui generis: his origin and mode of entry into the world are unlike ours. God's hands shape him out of earth;[5] God's breath breathes him to life. Body and soul, substance and energy are generated directly by God.

The early history of Adam is sparse. But one essential detail, obscured in the text, is detected by the midrash. Adam did not originate in the Garden of Eden. "And the Lord God took the man and set him down in the Garden of Eden" (Gen. 2:15).[6] Wherever he was first created, it was not in Eden. He is transplanted by God, moved out of his place, to another place.

SEDUCED INTO EDEN

The midrash addresses the word *Va-yikach*, "God took." In Rashi's version: "He took [captivated] him with beautiful words and seduced him to enter the Garden." Rashi often makes a similar comment when the word "take" has a human object, as though taking by force is inappropriate in moving a human being from one place to another. His comment implies that the only way to move a human being is by language, "beautiful words."

Here, however, the word *pitahu*, "He seduced him," is disturbing. This midrashic translation makes seduction the first human experience—seduction by God. Seduction, too, is constitutive of man's entry into language. The word carries connotations of persuasion but also of deception, of heady promises about which it might be wise to be suspicious. In the book of Proverbs, the *peti* is a simpleton, easily seduced, the opposite of the valued *chakham,* the wise one. The obvious association is with sexuality, with a manipulation of innocence, in which private purposes are masked in captivating but treacherous language.[7] Why would the midrash, and Rashi in his turn, use this word, which, in both Hebrew and English, has such uneasy associations?

We will return to this question of seduction, which, I will suggest, is the essential repressed moment of the narrative. For now, one wonders why Adam needed to be seduced at all. To enter the Garden of Eden would seem to be a prospect of delight, rather than one about which to have reservations. But God apparently has to persuade Adam with glowing rhetoric to make the move. One midrash[8] has Adam anticipate the risks and challenges of Eden: there he will confront and fail a test. In response, God entices him by promising that a future descendant, Abraham, will retroactively redeem the whole apparently woeful narrative. Subtly, the midrash suggests a cautious self-awareness in Adam that God must overcome by non-rational means. In the end, Adam must yield to God's will.

By using the notion of seduction, however, the midrash implies a kind of "unfairness" about God's influence, which overwhelms Adam's judgment. To suggest this is to raise the question of God's credibility. While, ultimately, His plot turns out for human benefit, the midrash conveys a strange indirection in His methods: blandishments that, in the short term, at least, it might be canny to resist.

Seduction creates an awareness of previously unsuspected desire: here, God awakens in Adam a sense of unfathomed depths of self. One who has been seduced, even by God, is no longer entirely innocent, immaculate. A message has been registered, if not fully comprehended.

Midrashic uses of the idiom of seduction abound. God seduces/persuades Moses for seven days at the Burning Bush to accept the mission of liberating the Israelites;[9] Sarah seduces/persuades Hagar to become Abraham's concubine[10] (her persuasive words are, "*Ashrayikh*[11]—Happy are you to merit union with such a holy body!");

God instructs Moses to seduce/persuade Aaron to ascend the mountain to his death[12] ("Happy are you to see your crown given to your son"). At such moments, the unacceptable is imagined as, potentially, desirable; reality is reshaped by language. In most of these cases, the key word in the Torah is "take," translated as "captivate, beguile, seduce." God, who sometimes seduces in this way, is at other times seduced: Isaac's prayer for Rebecca to bear children is "complied with" (nitpateh lo) by God.[13]

Seducing and being seduced, then, are not always illegitimate; nevertheless, they retain an overtone of embarrassment. After all, if one is to respond to the blandishments of the other, one must yield up an important kind of control. This could be a foolish act, or a generous one. Is this surrender, or submission? To assume the role of seducer: Is this insidious domination, or imaginative enlivening of the other, arousing him to possibilities inherent in what is not fully grasped? Is this faith, or gullibility?

ALIEN SEXUALITY?

Adam, then, has different origins from those we recognize as our own. He is seduced into Eden—and then driven out of it. Another dimension of his difference is indicated in the verse that precedes the serpent's seduction: "And the two of them were naked and unashamed" (Gen. 2:25). It is clear that this comment on the first couple, immediately following on the words "and they shall be one flesh" (2:24), communicates a sense of wonder about an unselfconscious sexuality assumed to be alien to the reader. Indeed, Rashi comments on the link between this observation and the serpent's plot:

> "The serpent was cunning [arum—both 'naked' and 'cunning']":
> Why does this belong here, in the context of nakedness? It would have been more logical to follow the reference to nakedness with, "He made for Adam and his wife coats of skin and He clothed them" (Gen. 3:21). But the Torah teaches the serpent's motive for attacking them: he saw them in naked intercourse and he desired her.

Nakedness thus intimates the unself-conscious sexuality of Adam and Eve, which exposes them to the gaze of the serpent. Perhaps what the serpent desires is precisely this innocent sexuality; he desires her in order to spoil her.

In any event, between the two moments of nakedness and clothing, the serpent engenders a new Adam and Eve whom we begin to acknowledge as familiars.

PROVOKING DESIRE

The chain of events holds an inner logic. First, God moves/seduces Adam into Eden. Then He issues a prohibition, banning the Tree of Knowledge. Then He declares, "It is not good for man to be alone. I will make him a helpmate" (Gen. 2:18). Here, one may wonder, is it that, emotionally, loneliness is not good for man? Or is it rather, as Rashi has it, that it is metaphysically not good that man live in a fantasy world of splendid isolation, imagining himself a god? The latter reading translates the text better, and suggests that the dangers of solitariness at least equal its pathos.

In either case, instead of acting on His judgment, God, as we have already remarked, acts indirectly. Animals are created and brought to Adam for naming. In the process of giving them names—that god-like act, in which man knows that his consciousness gives meaning to the world—Adam becomes aware that "for Adam he could not find a helpmate" (Gen. 2:20). Filled with a new longing, born of his perception of himself as part of the natural world ("for Adam" objectifies him as one of the creatures to be named) and yet different in his needs ("a helpmate"), he is ripe for the sleep, the coma, through which God brings him his mate.[14] Naming is thus linked to sexuality, by way of desire. United with his mate, he arouses another desire in the serpent, who then tempts Eve.

Desire is thus the repressed theme of the narrative; this is the force that keeps the chain of events in motion. God provokes Adam's desire before He acts on His own desire to create Eve, who then becomes the agent of destruction. Is desire then to be viewed as the tragic element in the narrative? Untouched by desire, Adam might have reigned alone, immortal, in the Garden. Is this the lost dream of

Eden? Is paradise the primal bliss of the couple uncompromised by the serpent's oblique passion? Yet evidently it is God who sets in motion the events that trigger desire—by banning the Tree of Knowledge, He creates the conditions for desire.

From this perspective, the serpent completes an arc begun by God. What is the serpent's desire? According to Rashi, by seducing Adam (through Eve's agency) to eat the forbidden fruit, the serpent secretly wished to kill him and to possess Eve.[15] We recognize an oedipal motif, a sense of primal taboo.

THE MISSING FACTOR

This oedipal experience is, I suggest, the significant missing factor in the humanity of Adam. More radically than his origin in the earth or his innocent nakedness, his *unparented* condition differentiates him from us. This is, of course, the structural hazard of Creation stories: the first human must appear from "nowhere," just as the mythic hero, founder of a nation, must be cut off from family and culture; he may be raised by wolves, or decisively orphaned, or invoked by divine command to abandon land and father's house. But it is the psychological implications of such a mythic necessity that lie at the heart of the Eden narrative.

Adam is different from us; lacking parents, he lacks the emotional history that is entailed in being born into a family. His history of desire, with its compromising effects, begins as a function of fulfilling God's desire: God seduces him, God lures him to acknowledge his longing for a helpmate, God overwhelms him with sleep to collaborate with desire. According to one powerful midrash, Adam dreams the woman and wakes, pulsing with agitation, to the fulfillment of his dream.[16] His mate emerges from an unconscious state, from a slippage of mastery.

By choosing the route of desire, God effectively brings to an end Adam's virtuoso display, his "naming" power. The Torah subtly suggests the symmetry: "God *brought* the animals to Adam for naming" / "And He *brought* her to Adam." His mate, newborn to him, is presented in the same way as are the other living creatures of his world, for him to name. But in an instant, Adam's wisdom, his godlike power to communicate himself to God,[17] is struck dumb. Instead of producing a name for his mate, as the text invites us to expect, he launches into an enigmatic utterance: "This one, this time, is bone of my bones and flesh of my flesh. This one shall be called Woman *[ishah]*, for from Man *[ish]* she was taken" (Gen. 2:23).

In this resonant declaration, instead of naming her, he defines the radical difference between his relation to her and that of all future couples: "This one, *this time*, is bone of my bones." Seforno reads:

> *Only* this time is my mate part of my very body. Never again will the female human being relate to her mate out of such an identity. Each future woman shall be called *ishah*, even though she will not be part of a man *[ish]*, for this first woman was taken from a man.[18]

In this dramatic passage, Seforno moves decisively away from the midrashic tradition, which reads the verse as a *paradigm* for future couples. Rashi, for example, has Adam celebrate the consummation of his search for a mate; he has *at last* achieved the reunion of bone and flesh, of two who were one, which will remain the ideal marital relationship, enshrined in the language play of *ish/ishah*. Woman will be named *ishah* to mark forever her origin in Man. This primal union will be recaptured in the child who will again unite the flesh of father and mother.

By contrast, Seforno tells of *rupture*: never again such literal union. This relationship, "bone of my bones, flesh of my flesh," is differentiated from all future marital relationships. The woman will—in that future time—be named *ishah* to evoke an uncanny memory of an original "birth," woman *emerging from man,* and of an original relationship charged with incestuous overtones, never to be reenacted.

In Seforno's reading, Adam himself articulates his own difference from us. In the future, the man will seek a mate with whom he can experience a union of true minds. Such a union may even require

leaving one's parents, with whom one is literally "one flesh"; its purpose is to "become one flesh," to achieve harmonious perfection, *as
though* they were both totally one being." Marriage will be transformed from physical or literal oneness—the primal condition of
Adam and Eve—to metaphorical or spiritual union.

THE MEMORY of the primal union may inspire the spiritual-erotic
quest, but its literal enactment now has an aura of taboo. The image
of one flesh becomes seductive, it provokes imagination, precisely
because its physical enactment has become impossible. "One flesh"
is precisely what will never again be; all future unions will be *as if*
they were one being."

The incest taboo begins here, as, indeed, Rashi makes clear in his
midrashic reading of the following verse:

> "Therefore, a man shall leave his father and mother, and cling to
> his wife" (Gen. 2:24): The Holy Spirit declares this, to impose the
> incest ban on all Noach's descendants [i.e., on all human beings].

The movement of leaving one's parents has a sexual meaning: it
is, in the words of Targum Onkelos, "to leave one's parents' bedroom." The oedipal theme is clearly marked here: all future marriages
will involve partners who have negotiated that separation and the
wrenching conflicts it may generate.

Strikingly, Rashi reads in the first encounter of Adam and Eve a
basis for the laws of incest ("*Therefore* a man shall leave his father and
mother"). What is it in the narrative of Adam and Eve that suggests
the wrench of separation from a fantasy of oneness? Surely Adam's
experience offers no paradigm for this separation from the parents?
It is precisely his unparented condition that differentiates him from
us. But it is that very relationship of "incestuous" union, in which
the erotic coincides with the parental, that engenders the taboo.
Adam is united with the one who emerged from his body. From the
heart of his experience, something within him requires that he (or
the Holy Spirit, according to Rashi) repudiate this model of mythic
union.

POSSESSING ONE'S OWN MIND

Here we return to the irreducible difference between Adam and ourselves. Origin, unashamed sexuality, the subordination of Eve to Adam, as part to whole—two bodies with one desire—underlying all these characteristics is the fact that Adam is not, in the Rabbinic idiom, *yelud ishah,* born of woman. This idiom expresses the human existential condition, in the same way as the English idiom "mortal man."[19] From this viewpoint, not having parents means that there is no oedipal separation, no conflict, no personal history, no unconscious desire. Adam and Eve become fully human only when a primal single-mindedness—one with God, one with each other—gives way to the separate minds, the separate desires, of man, woman, and God.[20]

The moment when unconscious desire is born is a moment when one recognizes the abrasive priority of the other, the parental others. This is the stage, Christopher Bollas suggests, "when the child comes to understand something about the oddity of possessing one's own mind."[21]

For Adam and Eve, how does this happen? The fruit of the Tree of Knowledge brings about a change that, significantly, the Torah never calls "sin." But what enters them at this moment that could resemble, in any sense, the impact of parents on the desire-life of the child?

I would like to consider two views of the significance of the moment of transformation, that of Ramban and that of Ha'amek Davar. Ramban, the classic thirteenth-century commentator on the Bible, understands Adam and Eve before the Tree of Knowledge to be acting with unchanging and unemotional purpose, like the stars in their courses. They know neither love nor hate; they are true to their origin and to each other. The fruit of the Tree of Knowledge engenders wish and desire, which in turn enables choice between contraries.

The sense of "good and evil," as opposed to "truth and falsehood," is identified as the experience of love and hate. The "knowledge" *(da'at)* of good and evil that arises in them only now should, Ramban proposes, be more aptly understood as "the *desire* for good and evil." What they ingest, then, is a new intentionality, a sense of each having his/her own mind. With this, they do indeed become like God, capable of free-willed decision, of carrying out desires, for good or ill. For the human being, however, this development is destructive, since it awakens transgressive desires.

In this portrayal of Adam's condition before the Tree of Knowledge/Desire, Ramban emphasizes an essential difference from our present condition. One of the most powerful modes in which we recognize ourselves—the feelings of love and hate—is absent in him.

Emerson conveys something of this paradisal condition in his essay "Nature": As a lover of nature, who retains "the spirit of infancy even into the era of manhood," he evokes the original human equilibrium:

> Standing on the bare ground—my head bathed by the blithe air and uplifted into infinite space—all mean egotism vanishes. I become a transparent eyeball; I am nothing; I see all; the currents of the Universal Being circulate through me; I am part or parcel of God.[22]

Clear of personal loves and hates, the human being is rapt in transcendence. "Part or parcel of God," he is immune to the accidents of pain, death, and mourning. His very vision is brushed clean of the particular, the isolated experience: "I become a transparent eyeball" carries the charge of the ancient mystical trope of the *aspaklaria me'ira*, the clear lens that obtrudes no "mean egotism" between self and world.

DESIRE TIME

The rapturous experience that Emerson describes is charged with associations of paradise, freshly incarnated in the New World. But in that original Eden, how did the lens grow clouded? The shift in consciousness that is marked by incorporating the Tree of Knowledge, or, in Ramban's translation, the Tree of *Desire* for Good and Evil, is the subject of a remarkable discussion by R. Naftali Tzevi Yehudah

Berlin, the nineteenth-century author of *Ha'amek Davar*. In his reading, it is human time, "desire time," that begins at this moment. One kind of temporality is superseded by another.

He focuses on the word for "shame," in the final description of the prelapsarian couple: "And they were both of them naked but they were not ashamed" (Gen. 2:25). The word *yitboshashu* ("they were ashamed"), he notes, derives, strictly speaking, from a different root—*boshesh*—"they were late, delayed."[23] The primal experience of Adam and Eve was without time lag, in a direct, spontaneous, and uninhibited mode of desire: hence, the "shameless" quality. Before eating the fruit of the Tree of Knowledge, the wish for passionate union *(devekut)* with one's mate, or with God, could move unhesitatingly into the act of erotic or mystic union. Eating the fruit induces a new consciousness, a self-consciousness (Knowledge), which impedes, delays the consummation of desire.

At this moment is born *da'at enoshi*—human consciousness. By this, Ha'amek Davar suggests the complexity of human thoughts and associations that set up barriers between the self and the beloved: memories, disappointments, hopes, fears. A dense inner world expresses itself in a time lag that slows and complicates the connection with the other. An inner strangeness inhabits and inhibits one. Achieving union involves *hit'orerut*, a phase of "arousal," so that two separate beings may achieve intimacy. Simplicity is ruled out: this new experience of time fraught with desire becomes the ground of "shame." It tells of a loss, the loss of a primal attunement, an at-one-ness, life in the moment. No longer "part and parcel of God"—nor of each other—Adam and Eve experience the isolation of separate selves, separate desires.

According to the Talmud, it would be a "chutzpah," an act of insolence, to station oneself in the open field and presume to pray to God.[24] Much work, spiritual preparation is needed to achieve the intimacy of prayer. To ignore this delay factor is to deny the reality of human consciousness.

By the term "human consciousness," Ha'amek Davar, I suggest, refers in part to the world of the *unconscious*, to the perplexing inhibitions that fragment and intensify desire. In place of a transparent sense of immediacy to the other, of whom one is "part and parcel," one is troubled by a density of memory, lost, sporadically revisited. Desire is shaped into idioms that resist easy translation. The unconscious, like a foreign body, strangely complicates relationship.

Milan Kundera describes this condition in his novel *Slowness*. There is, he claims, a secret bond between slowness and memory, on the one hand, and between speed and forgetting, on the other. A man walking down the street slows down as a wave of memory overwhelms him; he speeds up when he tries to forget. In Kundera's "existential mathematics," this constitutes the "well-known equation": "The degree of slowness is directly proportional to the intensity of memory."[25]

To eat the fruit of the Tree of Knowledge, then, of the complex (un)consciousness of good and evil, is to lose the confident experience of life in the moment. One rarely knows oneself as continuous, indeed merged with the other. Adam has wished to "give birth" to his mate. But as in all acts of birth, he splits himself forever from physical oneness.[26] Spiritually, too, he moves irrevocably from an effortless attunement with her to a new awareness of split worlds and separate desires. His own time world slows down, becomes fraught with alien, intimate weight.

Emily Dickinson writes of the need to "wonder what myself will say." The self of the future, even the immediate future, has become mysterious. The self is, at the very least, double: one self to think with and one to think about. Beyond that, there is the uncanniness of an imagined future and a remembered past. And beyond that, of an imagined past and a remembered future: the confusions of the life of fantasy and desire.

THE PROVISIONAL SELF

To have a mind of one's own is to become aware of the ongoing improvisations that may inhibit the force of desire. T. S. Eliot's Prufrock speaks out of this clogged sense of time:

> In a minute there is time
> For decisions and revisions which a minute will reverse.

And again:

> That is not what I meant at all.
> That is not it, at all.[27]

The provisional self is always open to questions. Unacknowledged ghosts speak through one; one may find oneself speaking beyond one's means. Understanding oneself becomes an aspiration at best; at worst, an illusion.

Eliot writes of poetic inspiration:

> If the word "inspiration" is to have any meaning, it must mean just this, that the speaker or writer is uttering something which he does not wholly understand—or which he may even misinterpret when the inspiration has departed from him. This is certainly true of poetic inspiration.[28]

At the upper reaches, the unstable self opens to poetic inspiration or to prophecy; at the lower, there is babble and perplexity. Something enigmatic speaks through one, if one can suspend the desire for explanation. As Adam Phillips points out, Eliot's description of poetic inspiration might also be an account of what Freud was to call free association and might even, "from a certain psychoanalytic point of view be simply an account of what happens when we speak and write. We never wholly understand our words. . . . And we are never in a position to authoritatively interpret them."[29]

The *da'at*, the knowledge that begins with taking in the fruit of the Tree, is a kind of force field in which unconscious dynamics constantly create turmoil. Does eating the fruit of such knowledge constitute a "Fall," as the Christian tradition largely views it? While the Rabbinic tradition in general avoids the vertical idiom, it does sometimes occur in midrashic sources.[30] In the biblical narrative, however, the vertical imagery of falling is entirely absent. Instead, an *outward* movement expels Adam and Eve from the Garden: "And the Lord God *banished* him from the Garden of Eden. . . . He *drove* the man *out*" (Gen. 3:23–24). This is not a fall but, in a sense, a birth. Paradise is lost, but a larger, if more agitated life looms.

A NEW INCOHERENCE

Ambivalence haunts such moments of birth. Describing a childhood lie, Joseph Brodsky cryptically comments, "A real history of consciousness starts with one's first lie."[31] A new incoherence signals a new awareness of complexity.

Even before he is physically expelled from the Garden, Adam enters for the first time into dialogue with God. Previously, a classic midrash had him name himself, simply and effectively ("I should be called Adam for I was created from *adamah*, the earth").[32] At this moment of the "first lie," however, he moves into very different language. For the first time, he speaks to God. And his first words to God are, if not quite a lie, at least an evasion: "The woman You put at my side—she gave me of the Tree, and I ate" (Gen. 3:12).

This is the moment of birth into human language. In the most obvious sense, he is denying responsibility for his act: he blames the woman and he blames God. One might say that this is the point at which he becomes embarrassingly recognizable to us as human. However, Ha'amek Davar points to a less obvious aspect of his speech: he does, in effect, confess to his act ("and I ate"), while at the same time attempting to evade responsibility. He is equivocating, saying two things at the same time.

He is, in a sense, *babbling*. He has lost his original command of language. Walter Benjamin uses the word *Geschwatz*, the common German term for chitchat, to designate the empty speech after the Fall, speech that has lost Adam's power of naming.[33] Paul Celan uses the same word for the "babbling" of the Jews who, after the cataclysm, are unable to find the pure "speech that counts."[34] Klein, Celan's Jewish "babbler," goes up into the mountains to confront the *Leerstelle*, the vacant space, the inhuman silence that has them babbling into the void; and just here unfurling a new language, part babble, part poetry:

> This means going beyond what is human, stepping into a realm that is turned toward the human, but uncanny—the realm where the monkey, the automatons and with them . . . oh, art too, seem to be at home.[35]

This is the new mode that, I suggest, will constitute the richness as well as the indignity of human language. In the course of speaking a sentence, Adam is opened to the turbulence of, at best, a partially known self. Progenitor of those who will find themselves saying at least two things at the same time, Adam replies to God in mixed genres: confession and rationalization. This equivocation may become, in nobler evolutions, poetic language.

In all its forms, however, it will require interpretation: Which element is to be emphasized? How is the complexity to be read? Is Adam perhaps not as embarrassingly evasive as we had thought? Could one say, for instance, as Hizkuni does, that he spoke the simple truth about the woman as the instigator of his sin, and that the death penalty is mitigated in recognition of this?[36] Or even that his plea has some validity: he had regarded the woman given him by God as a reliable guide?[37] Whatever the merits of such interpretations, the very possibility of interpretation arises when language holds more than one possible meaning.

This equivocal language is Adam's response to God's opening question: *Ayekah*—"Where are you?" (Gen. 3:9). Apparently simple and factual, the question is itself questioned by Rashi: "God knew where he was. . . . But He asked this in order to *enter into language with him*. If He had suddenly punished him, he would have been too agitated to respond." Rashi emphasizes that God's question is not a request for information; rather, it is intended simply to get Adam talking, in dialogue with God. One might almost say that God's main wish is not for a particular content or truth to be spoken, but for a world of language to be broached in which, for the first time, man can express some of his meanings to God. *Ayekah* is a conversation opener. This one seductive word will unlock the new language that, after the unequivocal competence of Adam's naming of all things, will liberate conflicting voices within him.

This, paradoxically, is the discourse that God desires. From now on, the incisive, imperious wisdom of naming will be compromised by the free associations of a self newly uncanny to itself. I am not, of course, claiming that Adam's response is in any obvious sense satisfactory; it is simply an entry point into the kind of language that may evolve toward the poetic or the prophetic, or toward the authentic rigorous confessions of a soul aroused to its own endless challenges.

There is one particular feature of Adam's speech that betrays this new ambiguity. He uses the peculiar Hebrew tense form known as the conversive *vav:* this standard mode of biblical narrative prefixes the *vav*—"and"—to the future tense, thus converting it into the past tense. (*Va-yomer*—"And he said"—for instance, is written, "He will say," with a *vav*—"and"—as a prefix.) Less standard, however, is the use of the first person in this mode. Adam inserts three verbs, of this converted, complexly tensed kind, into his speech to God: "And I [will be] was afraid . . . and I [will hide] hid . . . and I [will eat] ate" (Gen. 3:10,12).

The effect of this purely grammatical feature is that the time worlds of past and future drift out of their clear places. The past will not stay securely in the past; it generates a present and future that, in turn, reinvent each other and the past.

This elaborate temporal weave, in which desire is everywhere palpable, is powerfully addressed in the midrash, which comments on *Va-okhel*—"and I ate": "I have eaten, *and I shall eat.*"[38] Playing on the double tense, the midrash reads as though the Torah had written, "I shall eat." An astonishing acknowledgment is detected in Adam's words: "I will always be one who has eaten." Is this a brazen defiance of God?[39] Or is it perhaps a not entirely conscious acknowledgment of the ways in which past, present, and future will permeate one another in consciousness, requiring such verbs of ambiguously tensed desire?

In "A Difficulty in the Path of Psychoanalysis," Freud described his discovery of the unconscious as the psychoanalytic equivalent to Copernicus's astronomical discovery: in both, man receives a painful narcissistic wound. Freud writes,

> Man feels himself to be supreme within his own mind . . . [but] the ego is not master in its own house. . . . In certain diseases . . . thoughts emerge suddenly without one knowing where they come from. . . . These alien guests even seem to be more powerful than those that are at the ego's command . . . the ego says to itself: "This is an illness, a foreign invasion."[40]

In entering into dialogue with God, I suggest, Adam first engages with unconscious crosscurrents, alien guests that complicate his sense of self and time. There is no return to the language of pure naming: no longer master in his own house, Adam[41] must learn to use a flexibly tensed speech in which meaning is continuously transformed.[42]

Ironically, then, the chronology of Adam's narrative seems regressive. He moves "backward," from an adult, competent use of language to name his world, to the early language of the inarticulate child. In a sense, his language—and his wisdom—breaks down, as he responds to God's question.

BAFFLED INTENSITIES

But there is no sign of God's being displeased with his answer. Could it be that his very perplexity expresses a significant development in his emerging humanity? In that case, the development would run counter to the movement from chaos to order that marked the creation of the world. Here, an original and impressive command of language collapses into inarticulate disorder, as though man were not, after all, master in his own house. Language brushes against its own limits. For Freud, this is a catastrophe; in the biblical narrative, it may constitute the very development God was provoking by His question.

It is striking, for instance, that God does not attempt to "enter into language" with the serpent. An unexpected explanation is offered in *Bereshit Rabbah* (20:3): God refrains from addressing the serpent because he is a *ba'al teshuvot*—a master of answers! Precisely because he has such impressive command of the resources of language, his answers will be pointless. His spurious sovereignty over the plausible answer will open up no new depths; it will serve only to allay his own anxiety. It is Adam's response, it seems, in all its baffled intensity, that is courted by God.

The value of Adam's sudden linguistic incompetence, indeed, may be hinted at in the play on words in this midrash. A *ba'al teshuvot* is different from a *ba'al teshuvah* (master of repentance), although the former is merely the plural form of the latter. Perhaps surprisingly, God is not interested in the glib word-manipulator, with an answer to every charge; it is the response to events that is called *teshuvah*—repentance—that He desires: the painful confrontation with confusing truths. In such a situation, words may fail one, simply because one is confounded by the newly perceived relationship with the Other. At this point, there is no way back—no simple return *(teshuvah),* either to the Garden or to that original sense of things that Freud called oceanic. Adam no longer experiences himself as part and parcel of God; Eve is no longer part and parcel of Adam. Both are aware of being strangers not only to each other, but to themselves. The sphere of creation no longer revolves around them. An otherness speaks out of their mouths.

To return, in some sense, to each other, or to God, a process of *arousal* must take place. Indeed, *hit'orerut* (arousal) is the term used by Shem Mi-Shmuel, a nineteenth-century Hasidic master, to describe the dynamic that may lead to repentance. Strikingly, he understands God's apprehension—"And now, what if he should stretch out his hand and take also from the Tree of Life and eat, and live forever!" (Gen. 3:23)—as concern that man may evade the true imperative of his situation by seeking an instant cure. In his anxiety at the travails of consciousness, he may snatch compulsively[43] at the Tree of Life. God wishes, instead, that he work through his new condition, coming to repentance[44] by way of *arousal.* God banishes Adam and Eve from the Garden, not as a punishment, but to bar them from specious remedies. Their way must be forward and outward; each must struggle with a new map of desire, a new self-knowledge and isolation, if they are ever to bridge the chasms that now divide them.

Indeed, Shem Mi-Shmuel quotes the midrashic reading[45] of "He banished *[va-yigaresh]* them" (Gen. 3:24) as "He *divorced* them." A primal connection has been sundered; a primal ease of communication will now be rare. The confusions of feeling that Adam and Eve now experience require recognition, not sedation. A sense of shame[46] is born, as self-consciousness both impedes and impassions the simple movement to union.

In a sense, they are thrown back into the condition of the *infant* (lit. nonspeaker), who first enters the world of language—a condition that, biologically, they have never known. The stormy feelings of the preverbal child, "cradled by tempests" (Shelley), now struggle for awkward expression. Adam Phillips writes of this movement into language as one in which a sacrifice is involved of the prearticulate self, in all its baffled intensity. "Pre-reflective lived experience," as Seamus Heaney calls it, may be tamed as the child grows into verbal competence.

Phillips reminds us of how evocative the linguistic incompetence of small children can be. Wordsworth notes the "consciousness of the inadequateness of our own powers, or the deficiencies of language," that arises in any attempt to "communicate impassioned feelings." Psychoanalysis, Phillips claims, "is one way of speaking up for our formative linguistic incompetence. . . . [It] can show us . . . the conflict and collaboration inside each person between . . . a part of the self that can, and sometimes wants to, speak, and part of the self that is verbally confounded." One would not give up those moments when words fail. Language as a total "cure for infancy" might be a mixed blessing. In this area, but not only in this area, "if you know too well how to do something, you will be less likely to fall into originality."[47]

The moment when Adam most startlingly displays this breakdown in his command of language is when he finally names his wife. We remember how his facility with naming abandoned him when God "brought" him his helpmate, in the same manner as He had "brought" him the animals for naming. The word fails him. He speaks a diffuse language, celebrating the uniqueness of this relationship: never again will there be such oceanic totality—wife, daughter. And he merely intimates a future naming that will record these mysterious primal mergings: "This one *shall be called* Woman *[ishah],* for from man *[ish]* was she taken" (Gen. 2:23). Obliquely, he is acknowledging that he, now, *cannot name her.* The impact of her presence floods him, striking him dumb. Here, in fact, we can notice his first use of the conversive *vav:* "and he shall cling [lit., has clung] to his wife."[48] As he speaks of her, a premonition of future complexities breaks out and confounds the time frames of his language.

But when he does finally name her, he seems to abandon, or be abandoned by, any cogent meaning: "And Adam named his wife Eve *[Chavah],* for she had become mother of all life *[Chai]*" (Gen. 3:20).

God has just declared sentence of death upon him: "By the sweat of your brow shall you eat bread, until you return to the earth, for from there you were taken. For dust you are and to dust you shall return" (3:19). And Adam immediately names his wife, who, by his own testimony, is the cause of his downfall, *mother of all life*. Even on the level of common sense, his explanation falls short: she is mother, not of *all* life, but only of human life. Significantly, Adam speaks of her *having become* mother of all life—become, that is, for him. In naming her in this way, he marks a passionate and ambiguous knowledge that he can express only with the baffled intensity of one who has stepped into a transformed world.

Beit Ya'akov[49] engages with this name. Eve, Chavah, has brought Adam into a world of uncertainty and agitation, of process and risk—"beyond the grasp of his intellect." His sovereign relation to his world and its meanings yields to her enigmatic vitality: "The essence of life flows to him from her." She has proven irreducibly other, an otherness he experiences as intense life. The way he now uses language to name her contains the irony, the doubleness, the revelation of poetry. She takes him beyond himself, and he strains to communicate this transcendence.

ENIGMATIC IMPACT

In a word, Eve has seduced Adam. One effect of seduction is to move the other to speechlessness, and then into a new, dazzled language. The sheer impact that Eve has on Adam ultimately banishes them both from the Garden. By the same token, Eve is seduced by the serpent—by an enigmatic impact that his recorded words only partly convey.

Eve stands, then, at the hub of the narrative of seduction; she is both object and subject of this treacherous activity. She has gone down in cultural memory as both feeble and slyly powerful; incapable of resisting seduction, she is nevertheless irresistibly seductive. The weak link between the serpent and Adam, she has borne the brunt of responsibility for events read, quite simply, as a Fall.

I would like to revisit the notion of seduction, bearing in mind our unresolved questions about God as the first "seducer": taking, captivating Adam into the Garden. The word for seduction in Hebrew—*pittah*—derives from the root meaning "to be open wide, accessible to influence, credulous, compliant; so, to entice, tame, persuade, open the heart, deceive." Many, but not all, of these translations are negative; the overtone of sexual seduction or exploitation is rarely far off.

But in this dubious semantic field we must make room for biblical usages like that in Hosea 2:16: "Therefore, behold, I will seduce her, and bring into the wilderness, and speak tenderly [lit., upon her heart] to her." Here, God speaks with longing of His people, through the experience of Hosea's tormented love for his faithless wife. Seduction, one might have thought, is the province of the adulterous lovers. Yet, in this text of poignant desire, there is, ultimately, no other way for God/Husband to win back his errant wife; reunion is imaginable only through a process of "speaking upon her heart"— tender messages addressed once again, in the original site of courtship, to the estranged beloved. "Upon her heart" conveys something of the taming power of such seduction: this is not direct address, nor rational language arguing a case. It acts obliquely, overpowering by the sweetness of its promises.[50]

In quite another register, Jeremiah cries out against his God: "You have seduced me, and I let myself be seduced. You overpowered me and You prevailed. I have become a constant laughingstock" (Jer. 20:7). Here, seduction carries the overtone of betrayal. Against his better judgment, Jeremiah allowed God to move him into accepting the prophetic mission. Now, though he may regret opening himself to God's power, there is no going back:

> I thought, "I will not mention Him,
> no more will I speak in His name."
> But He was like a raging fire in my heart,
> caged in my bones.
>
> (Jer. 20:9)

Once he has opened to God's seduction, Jeremiah is, as it were, impregnated with God's word. This word is now both intimate and alien, and it threatens to collapse the boundaries that separate inner and outer worlds. He is no longer master in his own house. And, most strangely, he himself is complicit in this invasion: "I let myself be seduced."

Here, Jeremiah makes disturbingly erotic use of the seduction motif: first, he is overwhelmed, an inner ambivalence exploited by God's efforts to move him; then, he is inundated, possessed, the receptacle of a force that will come to tragic birth through him. What does this imagery communicate with such uncanny power? Clearly, God can compel the human being, Jeremiah or Adam, to His will; He can command, or He can ignore human agency altogether. What is it that He can achieve only by use of seductive language?

THE SEDUCTIVE CHAIN

A brief glance at some midrashic passages will suggest a direction for thought. Here is Rashi on the hostility that will prevail between woman and serpent:

> "And I will put enmity between you and the woman": Your sole intention was that Adam should die by eating it first and that you should then take Eve for yourself. You came to speak first to Eve only because women are easily seduced and they know how to seduce their husbands; therefore, "I shall put enmity between you and the woman. (Gen. 3:15)

The woman will eternally resent the serpent's just evaluation of her: both gullible and manipulative, she will perfectly serve his ends. This sinister, serpentine portrait of Eve, and through her of all women, is implicitly validated by the narrator: the serpent knows his victim, or, at least, he knows what he can make of her. His desire for her is perversely transformative: he will select that facet of her that is still unknown to her and make it central to her fate.

One of Rashi's midrashic sources, *Pirkei de-Rabbi Eliezer*, 13, articulates the seductive gender issue in more ambiguous terms:

> The serpent argued with himself, saying: If I go and speak to Adam, I know that he will not listen to me, for a man is always

hard to persuade [lit., to move out of his *da'at*]. As it is said, "For the man was a hard man and evil in his doings" (1 Sam. 25:3); but behold I will speak to the woman, who is easily influenced [lit., whose *da'at* is light upon her], for I know that she will listen to me; for women listen to all creatures, as it is said, "They are simple *[petti'ot]* and know nothing" (Prov. 9:13).

The serpent chooses to address Eve, because of the different natures of men and women: "a man is always hard to move out of his *da'at* [mind, opinion]"; "women have light *da'at*." At first sight, the judgments are unequivocal: women are easy game, wide open to all comers, while men are stable, consistent. However, the proof text for male stability inverts our expectation: it refers to Nabal, whose stubborn defiance almost precipitates a massacre. The balance of the midrash shifts: intransigence, totally closing one's mind, is a potentially deadly quality, just as its contrary, listening to everyone, may be.

In a later passage, the midrash[51] returns to the question of persuasion "out of one's *da'at*," between men and women. At Mount Sinai, the people prepare to receive the Torah:

God said to Moses: Go, speak to the daughters of Israel [and ask them] whether they wish to receive the Torah. Why were the women asked [first]? Because the way of men is to follow the opinion *[da'at]* of women, as it is said, "Thus you shall say to the *house of Jacob*" (Exod. 19:3); these are the women. "And tell the children of Israel"; these are the men.

Here, too, women are addressed first, because they have a unique ability to sway their husbands' minds. It seems that the only hope a man has of transcending his own mind lies in his relation with his wife. She will use words to take her husband beyond himself. The impact of her being and her words is so evocative that, mysteriously, he is moved.

At Sinai, therefore, women are addressed first: she is asked if she wishes to receive the Torah. Not commanded, but asked: an offer is made, a suggestion. In a sense, God is described as having Moses seduce, arouse desire, move the women by evoking a possibility of delight. That is, the seduction chain of the Eden narrative is redemptively reenacted, with God/Moses in place of the serpent, arousing woman, who will arouse man. The issue is one of changing, transforming minds.

Women are at the heart of this process, because, say the Sages, they are "light-minded." This uncomplimentary characterization refers not to intellectual power but to an emotionally volatile nature, a lack of steadfastness. However, I would like to suggest an alternative understanding.[52] To be light-minded means to be focused on the immediate, on the resonant impact of the other who is before one. It is to be receptive to this particular person, sensitive to the currents of communication and feeling circulating between self and other. It is to be fully present to experience, to see heaven in a grain of sand. To be heavy-minded, on the other hand, is to give weight to general principles, overarching narratives, the larger picture, where the particular may seem negligible. Each mode has its dangers and its strengths.

Midrashic sources extol the virtues of being open to seduction—provided, of course, that the seducer is God, or the human being persuading God to compassion, or human beings moving one another to a larger desire. To move someone "out of his mind" means, on one level, to drive him mad. But, on another level, it means to open the other to different forms of existence, to affect the current of his desire.[53] Everyone, it seems, wants to be moved; there is a longing to be free from choice, to surrender to the other. Seductions can arouse a force toward growth. Perhaps this is the reason that the imagery of seduction is adopted, even in contexts where it resonates strangely.

THE DESIRE FOR DESIRE

In biblical and midrashic texts, God must seduce, because God desires. What He desires cannot ultimately be gained by force. For instance, in one midrash, He delays the full growth of the grass, compromising His own sovereign command ("Let the earth sprout vegetation" [Gen. 1:11]). Growth is arrested just below the surface of the earth, till after man's creation, till man comes to recognize his own desire, his need for rain and fruitful earth; only then, in the words of the midrash, he "asks for compassion for the grass." All this, because "God desires the prayers of the righteous."[54]

Here, God surrenders to the force of a desire, suspending the full realization of His command for three days. The processes of nature stall, even as they are set in place: no grass, because no rain, because no human prayer to word human desire. *"Ve-adam ayin*—There was no man" (Gen. 2:5); the human is absent; and human desire is what God must wait for. To this end, there must be an absence, a gap, a time lag; and there must be a human being, who will *ask for compassion* for the stalled world. Only when Adam recognizes his desire for God to act lovingly toward His creation, will he achieve full being, and will God achieve His desire.

So God, in many midrashic sources, must wait in longing. For His desire, like human desire, is for that which cannot be forced. With a strange modesty, He takes His place among those who desire. He enters into the force field of human language, with its intensities and its perplexities—His habitation in the lower worlds. Here, compassion is needed; without the prayer for compassion, nothing will grow.

Addressing the woman, God speaks of desire: "Your desire shall be for your husband and he shall rule over you" (Gen. 3:16). Poignantly, desire is associated with loss of sovereignty. Rashi quotes a midrash that delineates the enigmatic silence to which female desire is destined. And another midrash creates a set of references to desire, with God's desire as simply one among several points on a map of longing:

> "Your desire shall be for your husband": There are four desires. The desire of a woman is for none but her husband: "Your desire shall be for your husband." The desire of the evil inclination is for none but Cain and his friends: "Sin crouches at the door, and for you is its desire" (Gen. 4:7). The desire of rain is for nothing but the earth: "You have remembered the earth and those [the rains] that desire her" (Ps. 45:10). And the desire of God is for none but Israel: "His desire is for me" (Songs 7:11).[55]

Like the rain, like the evil inclination, like the woman, God is the subject of an exclusive desire.[56] In each of the four biblical cases where the word *teshukah*—desire—is used, however, the midrash emphasizes an inversion. Should it not be Cain who desires the evil inclination? Is it not the earth that desires the rain? Does man not desire woman? Does the human being (Israel) not desire God? In a less obvious sense, however, rain desires that the earth will desire and enjoy it, as a woman wishes to be desired by her husband, and sin is imagined as wanting nothing so much as human desire. In all cases, it is the spontaneous desire of the other that is desired. God, too, though manifestly powerful, must wait on the unpredictable rhythms of the other.

This position places the woman in a dependent role. Yet just here, in spite of the evident indignity of this position, the midrash makes its complex move, including God among those who desire the desire of the other. What opens up for the one who desires in this way? Clearly, to force the desire of the other would defeat one's purpose. In many biblical contexts, God will act with power to compel human beings to His will. But this midrash touches on the heart of God's relation to the world. Where force fails, seduction may prevail.

Between God and the human being, seduction may mean many things. What differentiates it from more forceful, argumentative, or unequivocal forms of speech, I suggest, is its enigmatic character. A verbal seduction is fraught with ambiguity: it is a message to the other that the other will not wholly understand. God forbids the fruit of the Tree of Knowledge, but He places it at the center of the Garden and seduces Adam into the Garden. *What does He really want of me?* The "beautiful words" with which God tempts Adam into Eden hold depths of meaning that Adam may dimly sense but cannot plumb. Such a message captivates, implants itself in the heart of the listener, who must strive to translate it into imaginable terms.

In the complex theory of Jean Laplanche, every infant begins life in this way. The mother transmits messages that are beyond the infant's comprehension. The mother herself is not aware of these unconscious messages, which lodge like foreign bodies in the mind of the infant. "The unconscious," he writes, ". . . is an other thing *[das*

Andere] in me, the repressed residue of the other person *[der Andere]*. It *affects me* as the other person affected me long ago."[57]

Bearing such an unconscious, the human being is decentered from the outset. There is an otherness within, which is the residue of the enigmatic transmissions of the original other. This is the Copernican vision of the infant caught up in the solar glory of the mother. Open to her radiance, the infant also senses her world of other desires. This traumatic excess of meaning inundates the infant, who must translate unconscious communications into a comprehensible language. What cannot yet be translated is implanted within, awaiting future retranslations.

From the outset, Adam is seduced by God. By using this expression, the midrash suggests an area of communication that holds enormous power. Beyond the two classic notions of the other—the objective, that he is "speaking from the neighboring room," and the subjective, that he exists mainly in one's perception, or fantasy—seduction evokes the lasting alienness of a message that has yet to be fully understood. The traumatic reality of the message, ranking alongside material and psychological reality, moves Adam to a desire that he cannot fathom.

We might say that God's desire that human beings desire Him is most profoundly realized when He can move them, when He can captivate them beyond their conscious comprehension. The enigma in how God reveals Himself, whether in words or in visions, lodges as an otherness in the depth of human experience. The lives of Adam's children will become the attempt to translate and retranslate these enigmatic messages. They will oscillate between openness to the mystery, the humbling and decentering acknowledgment that one is not master in one's own house, and a recurrent effort to retranslate the old translations, recentering, domesticating the enigma.

THE FLOW OF LIFE

Adam is, in fact, twice seduced—by God and by the woman/serpent. He is flooded by their messages, each more complex than either transmitter or receiver can grasp. The impact of the other can never be fully translated; it evokes questions about what the other *really wants of me*. This flooding provokes to a life beyond conscious comprehension: the *flow* of life itself that inspires Adam's naming of Eve.

Eve, we remember, was provoked in this way by the serpent, who, in turn, was provoked by the vision of the naked couple. In this force field of seduction and desire, however, God, too, takes His place. The notion of God *unconsciously* transmitting messages to Adam may at first seem theologically incorrect, if not absurd. And yet, if God is to enter into human language, into a conversation with human beings at their most human, He must find for Himself a "habitation in the lower worlds," a humanly imaginable place in the dynamic of desire.

The God who inhabits the lower worlds is perhaps also the site of an internal otherness. He is imaged as angry and forgiving father, lover, and husband; as warrior and scholar; as one who desires human desire. *Within these roles,* He cannot totally know about Himself: that would invalidate the dramatic force of the imagery. If He is to be intimately connected to human beings, His messages cannot be transparent to Himself, even as their meanings transcend the comprehension of those for whom they are intended.

The enigmatic depth of divine desire resonates in words that only seem to accommodate human meanings. These messages—fraught, excessive—are heard in such a way as to compel the recipient, *who knows he is being addressed,* to translate and retranslate. This is the position of Job; God and Satan form an enigmatic partnership whose messages Job's "comforters" attempt to master by reduction. God's final translation, however, is resonant with mystery, and sets in motion generations of retranslation.

So God first seduces Adam, and then commands him— *Va-yikach . . . Va-yitzav . . .* (Gen. 2:15,16). He sets an enigmatic distance between man and Himself, to intensify desire. Within the seduction, implicitly, there is a promise. And man trusts in the truth of the One who promises. The demands that God makes of the human being depend, then, on this foundational experience—the captivating moment to which man surrenders in faith.[58]

· · ·

AROUSALS

We return to the question of resemblance. "God created man in His image." A classic midrash raises a provocative possibility: perhaps the human resemblance to God does not come into full play with Adam at all but only with his children, who more clearly resemble ourselves? In a meditation on this double resemblance, Mei Ha-Shilo'ach develops midrashic themes we have touched on, in order to arrive at an enigmatic translation for "the image of God."

> "R. Samlai said: In the past, man was created from the earth, Eve from Adam. From now on, 'in our image and after our form': no man without woman, or woman without man, and neither without the Shekhinah."[59] Also, in Avot de-Rabbi Natan 4:3, we find: " 'This one, this time, is bone of my bones': This one time, God became Adam's matchmaker; from now on, a man finds a matchmaker for himself. This one time Eve was taken from Adam; from now on a man marries his friend's daughter."
>
> God created man and instituted the order of procreation, so that one human being would generate another. Even though He wanted to create many people and could have begun with several prototypes, directly created by God, He did not do this, since His intention was that people should be born of one another, like cause and effect. . . . Therefore, He established human procreation through father and mother. And He implanted compassion in the heart of parents, so that even though the child defies the will of his parents, with full intention to anger them, nevertheless they respond in compassion, in spite of everything, begging God not to punish the child. It is natural to have compassion on what one has brought into the world, and compassion covers over all sin.[60] This arousal to compassion in the human parent will then compel God, by the same token, to have compassion on Israel, even though they defy His will.

Mei Ha-Shilo'ach grounds his daring reading in traditional midrashic texts. Already in these ancient texts, it is not Adam but his children, born in the normal way to human parents, who are to be in the image of God. In this familiar model of the family, the child is to arrive in a world in which others precede him—father, mother, and Shekhinah. This is to be a world of passionate and intricate relationships, where he is decentered from the outset.

The paradox is that the only human being to be created directly by God, to have God's breath fill his nostrils, is disqualified from realizing the potential of God's image. At one with God, and with his mate, all-of-a-piece with himself and with them, Adam's state is too literally "part and parcel of God." It is within the force field of the family, with parents whose own internal otherness transmits enigmatic messages, that the image of God is to be developed. The child grows to thwart and anger those to whom he owes his being. The foreign words of defiance that speak from the child provoke a natural anger in the parents. Strangely, though, they discover in themselves resources of compassion, praying to God to discover His own compassion.

This is a drama of natural but uncanny voices speaking from within human beings. Anger provoking anger: according to the Talmud, this is the "strange god within you." But compassion (rachmanut), welling up from the womb (rechem), interior place of containment, unexpectedly prevails. The parents release a divine potential that is both intimate and alien ("implanted" by God); it is experienced as hit'orerut, arousal from a traumatic condition of anger and separation. Precisely this separation, the gap created by self-assertion, evokes longing for a transcendent reunion. And, most strangely, this arousal process models to God a similar, necessary arousal within Him of the latent voice of compassion for His children.

In the end, Mei Ha-Shilo'ach has taken us to a place beyond any original imagining. It seems that he is translating God's intent in creating man in His image as His desire for the complexity of the human family—father, mother, Shekhinah, and child—which will produce a model for God. What can suggest to God how to conduct His inner economy in relation to His children? Only the dynamic system of the family, with its interference patterns of conscious and unconscious forces, its longing for intimacy straining against, even aroused by, the experience of conflict and alienation. The victory of compassion would not be possible without the dialectic of identity and anger.

And so God, in the daring imagination of the Hasidic master, desires the complex desire of human beings for God and the godly in their tents. More than that, He waits for them to create the model of compassion that will inspire Him—and that will, in effect, create an imaginable God with whom they can engage.[61] Thus He enters into a conversation that is human in its very uncanniness. "Deep calls unto deep, in the roar of Your cataracts" (Ps. 42:8). Unconscious desires inform family relationships, constructing an intimate universe of knowledge and mystery, language and silence. And God allows Himself to be mirrored in this universe, enigmatic, seductive, evoking transcendence.

TWO

Despondent Intoxication

The Flood

THE DARK RESIDUE

Ten generations after creating the world, God destroys it. The narrative that connects creation and destruction tells how one generation succeeds the other, how each generates its replacement. It is a tenfold narrative of birth, procreation, and death. "This is the record of the *toledot,* the generations begotten by Adam" (Gen. 5:1). Unlike the first man, these men are *toledot:* they are born into a human world, they bear human memories, effects, stains from the past.

Indeed, as we read this overview of the generations from Adam to Noach, a murder has already taken place; one brother has killed another. But neither brother is named in the list. Instead, a third brother, Seth, born after murder, is recorded to represent that generation:

> When Adam had lived 130 years, he begot a son in his likeness after his image, and he named him Seth. After the birth of Seth, Adam lived 800 years and begot sons and daughters. All the days that Adam lived came to 930 years; and he died. (Gen. 5:3–5)

The birth of Seth has, in fact, already been narrated. He belongs to that first generation, born of woman, and named by woman; Eve names him as a replacement for her murdered son, Abel: "God has provided me [*shat* = Seth] with another offspring in place of Abel" (Gen. 4:25). His name records his mother's relationship with God, and condenses a narrative of loss and restitution. In telling the story this way, the Torah harks back to the birth of Cain, similarly born to and named by his mother: he was the first fruit of the human partnership with God in procreation (4:1).[1] With the birth of Seth, however, Eve marks a complex new experience: one child may, in some sense, substitute for another, who has been killed by a third. The name Seth, then, records a poignant history, makes it unforgettable.

By the time this name enters the list of generations (Gen. 5:3), however, it has become a sign whose meanings are obscured. The substitute child with two dead brothers is now born to a father, rather than a mother, and serves a purely functional role in the chronicle of generations. In the way of the world, he replaces his father rather than his brother. Who, now, remembers the repressed history of murder and bloodguilt, of the murderer's strangely blurred death by archery?[2] It is, in a sense, forgotten, as the march of life continues. In another sense, however, it can never be forgotten, since Seth bears the mark of the past in his name, more surely than Cain did on his brow. Seth, after all, unlike Cain, fathers the essential line leading from Adam to Noach. What dark residue does this repressed memory bequeath to the future?

THE DANCE OF DEATH

A repeated formula conveys the march of life:

> When Seth had lived 105 years, he begot Enosh. After the birth of Enosh, Seth lived 807 years and begot sons and daughters. All the days of Seth came to 912 years; and he died. (Gen. 5:6–8)

The essential framework of a life is clear: the birth of the (named) son who will continue the line, the number of years before that birth and after it, the birth of other (unnamed) sons and daughters, the total numbers of years lived, and death. In this account, each life centers on a particular act of "generation," although it contains other nameless births, lost to the future; and each life ends in death. The two focuses, then, are procreation and death. The relentless narrative of "those dying generations"[3] becomes a dance of death; each life has its brief hour in the sun, produces a substitute for itself, and departs. One child achieves a name, only to bury his father. Even the act of birth is subsumed into the melancholy of the account: neither the intimacy of the parents nor a relationship with God finds expression here. This account evokes, rather, Franz Rosenzweig's somber words about the human condition: "All that is mortal lives in the fear of death; every new birth augments the fear by one new reason, for it augments what is mortal."[4]

The fear of death opens Rosenzweig's great work, *The Star of Redemption*. This fear provokes philosophy to provide a palliative that, Rosenzweig roundly asserts, palliates nothing. "Only the singular can die and everything mortal is solitary." Like the replaceable heroes of the line of generations from Adam to Noach, the solitary mortal gives birth: thinking to escape mortality, he only extends its domain.

The death knell haunts this passage. Strangely, however, the formula changes in the next chronicle of generations; after Noach, there is no mention of death.[5] Ten more generations lead to Abraham; biological death must play its natural role, but it is no longer the haunting focus of consciousness. A subtle change is intimated; the early generations, which at first, in Heidegger's phrase, live unto death, later yield to another mode of structuring history.

The doleful litany of these earliest generations suggests a possible understanding of God's original warning to Adam: "As for the Tree of Knowledge of good and evil, you must not eat of it, for on the day you eat of it, you shall surely die" (Gen. 2:17). In fact, Adam lives many years after eating that fruit; God's words seem strangely unfulfilled. One response to this problem is articulated by Hizkuni: eating the fruit will make man mortal, will cloud human consciousness with the prospect of inevitable death. The fear of which Rosenzweig writes will begin on that day: children will be fathered as a function of mortality, rather than as its consolation. Ramban (Nahmanides), likewise, speaks of the awareness of death that is more than a simple knowledge; it is the total vulnerability, at every moment, of one who, in John Donne's phrase, "owes God a death."[6]

When, however, God does declare His sentence, death is barely mentioned: it does not appear at all in Eve's fate, while in Adam's, it appears only at the end of the principal sentence, to "hard labor," which spans three verses: "Cursed be the earth because of you. . . . In the sweat of your brow you shall eat bread, until you return to the earth from which you were taken; for you are dust, and to dust you shall return" (Gen. 3:17–19).

The return to the earth is clearly subsidiary to the graphic description of the cursed earth.[7] And the biblical narrative so mutes the death theme that it seems to ratify the serpent's provocation: " 'You shall definitely not die!' " Not only do Adam and Eve indeed "become like God, knowing good and evil" (Gen. 3:5), as God later confirms (3:25), but God never, apparently, fulfills His own death warning.[8]

THE *ITZAVON* DIMENSION

However, a closer look at the sentences imposed on both Adam and Eve reveals a significant deathly dimension. Adam is told:

"Because you listened to your wife's voice and ate of the tree about which I commanded you, 'You shall not eat of it,' cursed be the earth because of you; by toil shall you eat of it all the days of your life: thorns and thistles shall it sprout for you. And your food shall be the grasses of the field. . . ." (Gen. 3:17–18)

Rashi comments:

"Thorns and thistles shall it sprout for you": the earth—when you sow it with various kinds of grain, it will sprout thorns and thistles, artichokes and cardoon, which are fit for consumption only after special preparation.

"And your food shall be the grasses of the field": What curse is involved here? Was it not a blessing when he was told, "Behold, I have given you every seed-bearing plant . . ." (Gen. 1:29)? But what is said here at the beginning of God's words?— "Cursed be the earth because of you; by toil [*itzavon*] you shall eat of it" and after your *itzavon*, "thorns and thistles shall it sprout for you." This means that when you sow it with cereals and vegetables it shall sprout thorns and thistles and other weeds, and you will have to eat them, in spite of yourself.

At the heart of his scenario, Rashi places the experience of *itzavon*. Eating of the fruit of the Tree leads to eating thorns and thistles:

the curse lies not in the vegetarian diet (that is characterized as a blessing), but in God's first words: "by *itzavon* you shall eat of it." The peculiar anguish of *itzavon* will shape the eating experience: *itzavon* is the discrepancy between sowing grains and vegetables, and reaping thorns and thistles. These can be made edible, thanks to human ingenuity; but they will never lose the taste of failure, of the gap between intention and reality. "In spite of yourself, you will eat them": it is the bruising of will and desire that Rashi understands by *itzavon*. The word is a variation of *etzev*—pain, sadness—that occurs only in this primal narrative of punishment. In Rashi's reading, Adam is condemned to know frustration in his basic dealings with the world, a frustration imagined as a madness: the effect of speaking one language to the earth only to have it respond, brutally, in a kind of gibberish. The curse undermines his confidence in a rational dialogue with the world; *itzavon* brands a new consciousness of internal and external divisions.

Itzavon, then, is the consequence of eating of the Tree: even the two Hebrew words, *etz* (Tree) and *itzavon,* resonate with each other ("since you have eaten of the *etz* . . . in *itzavon* you shall eat"). But the taste of this anguish has already been intimated in God's words to Eve: "And to the woman He said: 'I will greatly intensify your *itzavon* and your pregnancy; in pain *[etzev]* shall you bear children'" (Gen. 3:16). Here, both *etzev* and *itzavon* appear. *Etzev* is the objective pain of childbirth: the concrete level of punishment, parallel to the unappetizing thorns and thistles in Adam's curse. What, then, is *itzavon*? Rashi translates, rather mysteriously: "This is the sadness of child rearing." What is the sadness, the sorrow, that is now inscribed as a universal human experience?

An interesting wordplay is suggested by Torah Temimah: *itzavon* is related to the root *atzev*—to fashion, form[9]—and refers to the human wish to shape reality after one's design. Even the newborn baby, in Talmudic idiom, can be physically manipulated into proper shape.[10] Now Eve is initiated into a world in which this creative will meets inevitable frustration: parents raise children as projections of their own desires, only to discover that children develop desires of their own. Here, the planting may come to bear very little resemblance to the yield.

In both love and work, then, *itzavon* is the strange fruit of intentionality, of "sowing seed" toward an imagined future. For Eve, this will mean a radical suspense, throughout pregnancy[11] and child rearing, about outcomes. The experience of "generation," of bearing and rearing children, becomes the very type of *itzavon*—maternal desire confronting the otherness of what had been part of one's being.[12]

For Adam, a similar discontinuity will haunt his relations with the earth. The gap, the arbitrary response of the earth to his desire, expresses a radical irrationality in human experience. Creative aspiration acquires an ironic edge.

Here, perhaps, is the fulfillment of God's original threat: "You shall surely die." Before the fact of death, at the very heart of life, death lurks in the form of this dissonance. Both Adam and Eve experience alienation—from the earth and its produce, which mocks his plantings, from the child who elaborates or parodies or ignores the mother of whom (s)he was a part. They can no longer command the meanings of the world: uncanny languages answer theirs. In this sense, God's original description of the deathly effects of the Tree is profoundly validated.

NOACH—THE PROMISE OF RELIEF?

Against this background of discontinuity that is *itzavon,* there arises a strange hope for relief. This is Noach, whose birth is heralded by a name that promises consolation; ending ten generations in which death haunted the record of life and its bearings, a child is born who disrupts the pattern:

> When Lamekh had lived 182 years, he begot a son. And he named him Noach, saying, "This one will provide us relief from our work and from the toil *[itzavon]* of our hands, from the earth that God has cursed." (Gen. 5:28–29)

The formula, we see, has changed: his father produces "a son," who is then ceremoniously named as consolation for "the *itzavon* of our hands." Noach is, in effect, the second child to be born as "a son," nameless until consciously named; the first was Seth, also heralding a new beginning. In Noach's case, the father, and not the mother, names him; unlike Eve, who acknowledges God's gift after murder and accidental death have visited the family, Lamekh mentions God only as the author of the evils of the past, while it is the child Noach who is to restore the world from its anguished state. Rashi comments:

> "He begot a son *[ben]*": for from him the world was rebuilt *[nivneh]*.
>
> "This one will provide us relief": He will relieve us of the toil of our hands: before Noach, they had no ploughing implements and he developed them. The earth had brought forth thorns and thistles when they sowed wheat in consequence of the curse imposed upon Adam: in the days of Noach, however, this ceased. That is what is meant by *y'nachamenu*—he will comfort us: *yani'ach mimenu*—he will relieve us. If, however, you do not explain it in this way, but from the root *nachem*, to comfort, then it will have no connection with the name Noach; you would have to call him Menachem.

Since Noach's name translates as "ease, relief," Rashi interprets the word *y'nachamenu* also as *yani'ach mimenu*—"he will bring us ease," rather than "he will comfort us." Otherwise, as he notes, the explanation would be unrelated to the name—he should have been called Menachem!

The dissonance between Noach's name and its explanation, however, has a more than formal significance. Noach is to bring humanity an easing off, a relief, from the alienated condition of *itzavon*: sowing wheat and reaping thistles. On the technical level, he is to be an inventor of agricultural labor-saving devices: the plough will replace the frustrating limitations of manual labor. This, however, will constitute a far-ranging transformation: his father expects an existential restoration of primal harmony. And, indeed, according to some midrashic sources, such a healing does take place. Noach is responsible for the relaxing of a radical contortion in human experience. In terms of language, too, the contortion in which words gap apart from meaning (*lo ha-shem hu ha-midrash, v'lo ha-midrash hu ha-*

shem[13]) is healed by playing with meanings, easing words together to cover gaps. At some point, "easing off" and "comfort" begin to meld.

The curse of *itzavon,* then, is to be neutralized by Noach: that is the grand conviction of his father. One midrash offers a specific scenario:

> When God created Adam, He gave him total dominion: both the cow and the furrow would obey the ploughman. When Adam sinned, they all rebelled: neither the cow nor the plough would obey the ploughman. When Noach arrived, they all eased off from their rebellion.[14]

Noach will bring about a return to responsive relations between man and nature; this *ben* will rebuild the world. This, at least, is Lamekh's conviction. If one asks simply, "How did he know?" one finds that midrashic and later commentaries conclude that he must have been either a prophet or a sage.[15] Other possible answers are that the curse on the earth was to apply only for the period of Adam's lifetime ("Cursed be the earth . . . *all the days of your life*" [Gen. 3:17])—Noach's birth coinciding with Adam's death;[16] or that Noach was born circumcised, thus fulfilling a sign given to Adam for the end of the curse.[17] Behind all these interpretations is the assumption that Lamekh was right in his reading of Noach's name.[18] In general, this would be a safe assumption about biblical namings: the name and its explanation prove to foretell the life accurately. Why else record them?

The Zohar, however, subverts such an assumption: "When Noach was born, he was named for consolation, that God would give them consolation. *But God did not do so.*"[19] God does not necessarily acquiesce in human scenarios. Here, tragically, instead of relief, Noach's life brings apocalypse. The effect of his naming, then, is ironic, a comment on human narcissistic assumptions. Instead of easing the condition of *itzavon,* God intensifies it. And Noach's name becomes an index, not to prophecy or wisdom, but merely to desire. The parent, who represents mastery and competence—the one who is supposed to know—has his limitations satirically exposed. At best, he can name his son in the mode of blessing or prayer—in this case, tragically unfulfilled.

DIVINE ANGUISH—CREATION AND DESTRUCTION

On this reading, Noach's life becomes the purest expression of the gap between human design and reality. *Mann tracht, Gott lacht,* says an old Yiddish proverb ("Man plans, God laughs.") But God, at this juncture, does not laugh. In a final resonant use of the word *itzavon,* the Torah describes God's inner world:

> God saw how great was man's evil on earth and how every thought devised in his heart was sheer evil all day long. And God regretted that He had made man on earth, and He was saddened [*va-yit'atzev*] to His heart. (Gen. 6:5–6)

God contemplates the evil formations of the human heart and experiences profound anguish in His own heart. This acute anthropomorphism reveals God's heart responding in regret and in pain to the evil promptings of the human heart. Theological correctness is swept aside as the Torah twice tells of a God who now regrets His earlier decision: He has changed His mind about the creation of man. Moreover, He is credited with that peculiar anguish of which human beings alone are capable—the sense of disillusion, at a profound emotional investment proved sterile. "He was saddened to His heart": Rashi translates, He mourned the loss of the work of His hands. God mourns *before* the world is destroyed: the work of His hands is a project that has failed to come to life, a world that has already slipped back into chaos.

This is a pure moment of divine *itzavon,* introduced without apology or palliation. It is as though, from God's perspective, the essential loss of a desired world *precedes* His decision to destroy it. God brings home to His heart[20] a state of passionate loss, which only then becomes a determination to destroy. Like the human being in Rashi's profound midrashic parable, who fathers a child and knows that the child must eventually die, God created in joy, even though He must have known of the future failure of His creation: "In the time of joy, rejoice; in the time of mourning, mourn." The skeptic questions the meaning of God's disappointment, in view of the doctrine of God's omniscience. He uses the idiomatic term for foreknowledge: "Does not God see the future, the *nolad,* that which is about to be born, already present to His gaze?" R. Yehoshua wonderfully catches up the word *nolad* and focuses on its concrete meaning: "Did you ever have a *nolad,* a newborn child?" The switch in register is breathtaking: from metaphysics to the beloved child who will die. This is the register that serves as the model for God's relations to the world. Like the human father, He enters into the contingencies and risks of passionate creation, experiencing joy and mourning, each in its season.

This version of God is, of course, highly improper from a theological perspective. The skeptic's question is not answered; by a change of metaphor, it is evaded. Rashi gives his readers the most intimate and paradoxical perspective on God's inner life. Perhaps the most striking aspect of this is a kind of inner splitting: omniscience is set aside, in the joy in the moment of creation, which gives way to the wrecking of high hopes. As though suspending His divine prerogative of omniscience, of a superordinate narrative, this God applies to His own heart the full human experience of foreshortened time, the hopeful beginning lived totally in the moment.

Such a humanized portrayal is writ large in the midrashic tradition that holds that God "created worlds and destroyed them—He said, This one pleases Me—those others did not please Me."[21] Serially, as though each successive world descends from unconscious regions of the divine mind, God performs the action that is creation-destruction. If the Flood narrative is read against this backdrop, only the survival of Noach suggests that God's habitual practice is this time modified. That is, the midrash creates the expectation of yet another discarded world—as though worlds, by their nature, sooner or later slip back into the *tohu va-vohu,* the primal chaos from which they emerged. What had seemed extraordinary, inexplicable—God's sadness, His disappointment, His readiness to destroy—suddenly seems to arise from a deep necessity in the divine mind.

Seeking a world that will gratify Him, He is filled with regret and sadness at the failure of his work. This description of divine affect then moves into a soliloquy in which He consciously crystallizes His destructive intention: "And God said, 'I will blot out from the earth the men whom I created—men together with beasts, creeping things, and birds of the sky; for I regret that I made them'" (Gen. 6:7). God's decree is absolute and total—one more in the series of world obliterations. But the narrator speaks again, ending the *parashah* with the tantalizing sense of a cryptic exception: "But Noach found favor in the eyes of God." Against God's undifferentiated decree, the narrator notes a personal liking, as it were: Noach gives God pleasure. The narrator who presumes to know the unexpressed mind of God is, of course, from the traditional point of view, none other than God Himself.

I am suggesting that the portrayal of God here plays out in almost scandalous manner the *plural* expressiveness with which He originally declared: "Let *Us* create man in our Image." The complexity of God's inner world as narrated in these early chapters of the Torah finely matches human complexity. God sees human evil, penetrates to the very heart of darkness, takes it to His own heart, where it becomes regret and mourning. From that emotional depth emerges a decree, unequivocal in its scope, of destruction. Against this, the narrator immediately equivocates, noting that, gratuitously, Noach brings out something in God's eye that is called *chen*, grace. That is, God's conscious intent to annihilate the world is qualified by the truly omniscient narrator. Destruction has become almost a divine reflex. It is Noach's survival that is the inexplicable element in the narrative. Through him, this world is, after all, to survive, and we are not sure why. Nor, it seems, is God the narrator. It is not He who at this point can explain the decision that is uncannily forming.

But God's *itzavon* does not, after all, find resolution through Noach's birth. Rather, it intensifies to the point where it becomes unbearable: the disappointing world project is obliterated. Noach, it seems, might have constituted a force for transformation, reducing the pressure of frustration for God and man alike. But, in the event, God looks again at the earth and sees that it has already been wrecked: "And God saw how corrupt [*nish'chata*] the earth was, for all flesh had corrupted [*hish'chit*] its ways on earth" (Gen. 6:12). Decomposition has already, in a sense, set in. Nothing is left but for God to address Noach: "The end of all flesh has appeared before Me, for the earth is filled with violence because of them: I am about to destroy *[mash'chitam]* them with the earth" (6:13). All flesh, human and animal, has corrupted its way upon the earth, it has degenerated to a point where the end both of flesh and of earth rises up before God, a reality that God has only to ratify.

GOD'S ROLE IN THE FLOOD?

Powerfully, the Torah suggests that a world of violence and anarchy has disintegrated of its own accord. In the Zohar, God declares: "You wish to repudiate the work of My hands: I shall fulfill your wish."[22] Again, God, as a character in the narrative, merely acquiesces in the (unconscious) human wish to destroy the world. The purpose of His address to Noach is to alert him to this state of affairs and instruct him to build his escape vehicle. The covenant between God and Noach will save his immediate family, as well as specimens of all animal life from which to breed a new world.

God's active role in the Flood is thus reduced in the narrative. Even the apparently forceful expression *"And I, behold I am about to bring the Flood upon the earth"* (Gen. 6:17) is translated by Rashi, following the midrash: "I am now ready to agree with those who urged me long since, What is man that you should remember him?" Destroying the world is, after all, a long-term consultative process: those angels who originally disputed God's intention to create man have now convinced God of their case. The complexity of God's mind is thus intimated: sometimes divided, sometimes at one with itself.

Here, the consensus is sinister: there is no dissenting voice to plead for mercy. Even His name is transformed, from the Tetragrammaton *(Adonai)* to *Elohim*, the name of strict justice.[23] At the moment of reversal, strikingly, the merciful name is used, together with a decree of doom: "And *Adonai* regretted that He had made man on earth . . . *Adonai* said, I will blot out from the earth the men whom I created" (Gen. 6:6–7), as though a habit of mercy is being undermined from within. And, conversely, when God remembers Noach and ends the Flood, His name of justice, *Elohim*, is still used, even as the tide turns toward mercy (8:1). This yields the effect of movement within the divine ecology, from one modality of relation with the world to another.

A sense of processes under way arises also from the midrashic notion that before the Flood, one third of the world was engulfed by the ocean, a kind of early-warning signal.[24] The world of human beings has initiated a sinister collaboration with God, drawing from Him a habitual response. Creation and destruction are, in a sense, a natural pair; if the Creator seeks perfection, a world that yields Him pleasure, each attempt becomes an experiment, built on the experience of past failures. In any creative project, one might say, the creator knows when he has got it right; the footage that ends up on the cutting floor can give greater force to later work. A ruthless judgment is at work that has little connection with external standards: God is looking for a world that, simply, pleases Him.[25] One might wonder whether changing His unspoken criteria for such a world might soften the judicial voice and allow the new creation to develop.

But now, this world is clearly slated to go the way of previous discarded worlds. Human evil and violence have already wrecked the structures that God has designed. Specifically, this disintegration is understood to be sexual: human beings and animals are engaged in indiscriminate sexual relation, without regard for species:

> R. Yochanan said, "All flesh": Cattle and wild beast fornicated together, as did all animal life with man.[26]

If sexuality is a kind of language, then the sound that arises from the world is a babble, submitting to no rules of grammar or syntax, signifying nothing. This babble sweeps away meaning and connection. The Flood, the *Mabul*, describes a catastrophic human movement that informs language and sexuality. Rashi comments: *"Mabul:* which *demolished [bala]* everything, and *confused [bilbel]* everything and *thrust [hovel]* everything downward to *Babylon [Bavel]"* (Gen. 6:17). A destructive anarchy surges through the world, a downward cataclysm that ends in the place called *Bavel*. The wordplays suggest a field of meanings, where the Flood and human degeneracy reflect, replicate, and elaborate upon one another.

As we have seen, God's role, apparently omnipotent, is qualified. Even as He issues His death sentence, His words contain undertones: He is merely consummating a human death wish; He concedes the justice of the angels' critique; in effect, a process is under way that leaves no room for maneuver. "The end of all flesh has come before Me": apocalypse is *now*, even before God can judge the matter.[27] And, in the event, as the Flood is narrated, God is barely active:

> Noach was six hundred years old when the Flood came, waters upon the earth . . . on that day all the fountains of the great deep burst apart and the floodgates of the sky broke open. . . . The Flood continued forty days on the earth, and the waters increased and raised the ark so that it rose above the earth. The waters swelled and increased greatly upon the earth, and the ark drifted upon the waters. . . . All existence on earth was blotted out—man, cattle, creeping things, and birds of the sky; they were blotted out from the earth. Only Noach was left, and those with him in the ark. (Gen. 7:6–23)

Impersonal processes inundate the world and destroy all life. God reappears only at the end, to "remember Noach" and initiate an end to the Flood. But even in the process of recuperation, God's only gesture is to send the healing wind; all else happens impersonally—the waters subside, the rain stops, the mountaintops appear, the earth dries up.

Where is God active, then, in this narrative of destruction? When He addresses Noach, the large part of His words is devoted to instructions to build the Ark and prepare for boarding. Later, there is the promise of a future covenant, and there is the emotional intensity of "God remembered Noach . . . and God caused a wind to blow across the earth." But the overwhelming influx simply happens; and is attributed to human violence, natural forces, or, in the midrash, angelic misanthropy and a habitual divine perfectionism.

· · ·

"THE WATERS OF NOACH"

If God's role is unclear, what are we to say of Noach? At first, he is the almost whimsical exception to God's sentence of total destruction: "And Noach found favor in the eyes of God." It is as though God in the narrative is moved by the *chen*, the beauty or grace of Noach. The unfinished sentence dangles at the end of the *parashah;* only in the next sentence is the observation of God-the-narrator vindicated: "Noach was a perfectly righteous man in his generations" (Gen. 6:9). However, even here, we notice that the unparalleled[28] description of Noach's righteousness forms a kind of anxious parenthesis: the real burden of the verse is to tell of Noach's family. Apparently, the narrator must justify God's choice of Noach. This narrative voice—which, we remember, is traditionally read as God's voice—adds a hasty, principled clause to explain a choice that otherwise might seem whimsical. And yet, God-in-the-narrative clearly sees Noach as the source of *chen:* even the words *no'ach* and *chen* are mirror images of each other. Love is at work. God's eyes invert Noach into beauty, and God's eyes see Noach as righteous: "You *I have seen* as righteous before Me" (7:1).

From this uneasiness about Noach's claim to survival—and about the quality of God's love for him, as the Torah narrates it—arises a midrashic tradition that consistently questions the justice of Noach's selection: "Noach had a death sentence sealed against him. But he found favor in the eyes of God."[29] Without any substantial reason, God favors Noach: mercy delivers him from the death to which all others are condemned.

At the heart of this tradition lies a specific critique of Noach. He is not accused of the crimes of his contemporaries. Instead, the charge against him is of *silence.* If they express themselves in *babble*, he is totally silent. In response to God's speeches, he speaks not a word. Impassively, twice, the text records, "And Noach did just as God had commanded him."[30] Perfect obedience is a virtue, undoubtedly. But he might, for example, have prayed for his doomed generation; or he might have tried to alert his contemporaries and avert disaster.

A classic midrash does describe him as building the Ark over 120 years, a protracted process intended to provoke discussion among his contemporaries.[31] In this he is clearly unsuccessful. The Ark was meant to be nothing more than a conversation piece, its effectiveness measured in its power to move the world to radical change. Instead, it becomes a literal necessity, since Noach does not find the words to save even one soul. Prayer, too, is absent from his lips: the world is under sentence of death but he maintains his silence.

Only after he emerges from the Ark into the devastated world does he offer a sacrifice; the Zohar remarks acerbically that he might have done better to offer a sacrifice *before* the Flood to appease God's anger. And, even more sharply, the Zohar compares Moses's reaction to God's sentence against his people in the Golden Calf narrative with Noach's impassive reaction in a similar situation. Moses refuses God's offer to found a new nation upon himself, as sole survivor of the debacle:

> When God said to Moses, "And now, just let Me be that My anger may blaze forth against them and that I may destroy them, and make of you a great nation" (Exod. 32:10), immediately Moses replied, "Should I abandon Israel to their fate and not ask for mercy? Everyone will say that *I killed Israel as Noach did!*"[32]

The Zohar indicates a moral consensus about Noach's passivity, his silence that is judged as complicitous. Indeed, the Zohar continues to read most provocatively Isaiah's expression for the Flood— "the waters of Noach" (54:6): Noach is responsible for the Flood.[33] It is eternally to be known as Noach's flood, since his silence brought it about.

In contemplating the hazards of silence, I would like to bring into play two testimonies. Shem Mi-Shmuel, the nineteenth-century Hasidic author of teachings on the Torah, comments on the word *chamas*—violence. It is used twice: when God judges the world before the Flood (Gen. 6:11,13), and when Sarah reproaches Abraham for not protecting her against Hagar's insults: "My *chamas* is your responsibility," (16:5), she cries; and Rashi comments: "You deprive me of your words, since you listen in silence as I am vilified." *Chamas*, thus, can refer to withholding words where speech is necessary, just as it can refer to the violence of inappropriate language. Both are forms of violation of the space between people.

Kierkegaard, too, compares the two forms of violence or, as he terms it, despair: infinitude's despair and finitude's despair. Of these, he judges the latter the worse:

> Whereas one kind of despair plunges wildly into the infinite and loses itself, another kind of despair seems to permit itself to be tricked out of its self by "the others." . . . For example, we say that one regrets ten times for having spoken to once for having kept silent—and why? Because the external fact of having spoken can involve one in difficulties, since it is an actuality. But to have kept silent! And yet this is the most dangerous of all. . . . Not to venture is prudent. And yet, precisely by not venturing it is so terribly easy to lose what would be hard to lose, however much one lost by risking, and in any case never this way, so easily, so completely, as if it were nothing at all—namely, oneself.[34]

The attraction—and the danger—of silence is its safety. Noach avoids participating in a world of transgression and violence by withdrawing from exchanges with it. Here, however, is the danger of silence that deprives one of the risks of confrontation. What is lost in such a silence is oneself: "To venture in the highest sense is precisely to become aware of oneself." Fear for himself silences Noach, and deprives God, his contemporaries, but perhaps mostly himself of the encounter with language.

When the Zohar reads the narrative in this way, it clearly reads against the grain. Noach, after all, simply obeys God's commands. Elsewhere, the Torah will present such obedience as exemplary, and its failure as sinister.[35] Moreover, as we have seen, God presents the issue of destruction as closed: "The end of all flesh has come before Me . . ." (Gen. 6:13). It would be difficult to read this as an invitation to Noach to intercede. Unlike the similar situations when God tells Moses that He is about to destroy the Israelites, or when He tells Abraham that He is about to destroy Sodom, there are no openings in God's words to provoke Noach to act as God's "loyal opposition." In this situation, uniquely, the obvious reason for God to inform

Noach of the coming cataclysm is to prepare him to escape. Indeed, Or Ha-Chaim goes as far as to declare unequivocally, "God gave Noach no space for prayer. . . . *He blocked his prayer.*"[36] If that is the case, Noach is clearly not culpable when he does not, in fact, pray.

And yet, in spite of these difficulties, the Zohar's reading haunts us. Perhaps both God and Noach express the reality of a closed world, the space of potentiality blocked off, language occluded. Just as the Flood reflects and elaborates an existing state of disintegration in the human world, so Noach's silence plays back a metaphysical condition of stasis.

A FANTASY OF OMNIPOTENCE

This God and this Noach are characters within a narrative constructed by God, who tells the story: this is the traditional reading premise. The God who corroborates the wrecking of the world and the skepticism of the angels is the God who blocks the flow of language in a Noach whose voice has never developed. Even his obedience is a function of his fear rather than of his faith. He is finally driven into the Ark "from before the waters of the Flood" (Gen. 7:7). Rashi comments: "Noach too was of little faith—he believed and did not believe that the flood would come. So he did not enter the Ark until the water drove him inside." Rashi describes an ambivalence that would certainly have diminished his rhetorical power, whether in praying to God or in exhorting his contemporaries. Essentially, he has nothing to say, no personal conviction in the face of received opinion. In this sense, the failure of language betrays a spirit unaware of its deepest self.

The Ark, though it was meant to generate words and transformations, thus becomes Noach's kingdom for a year. It is, of course, not a ship, but a box *(teivah)*. Noach is boxed up in the symbol of a failed conversation. The midrash spells out the conditions of life in that box. Most significantly, no sexual relations take place there. This is intimated in the order in which his family enter the Ark: "And Noach entered the Ark, *with his sons,* and his wife *with his sons' wives,* from before the flood waters." Rashi comments: "Men and women separately, for they were forbidden to have sexual relations at a time when the world was suffering." A neutral account becomes loaded with sexual meaning; it represents Noach's obedience to the similarly encrypted message in God's instructions: "I shall keep My covenant with you—and you shall enter the Ark, you *with your sons,* your wife *with your sons' wives*" (Gen. 6:18).

Sexual abstinence is the rule of this floating box, extending even to the animals.[37] Noach's life is also characterized by a hectic devotion to feeding the animals, meeting their different feeding schedules. One effect is that "he never had a taste of sleep."[38] He is the sustainer and feeder of the floating world—like Joseph, who saves the world from famine. Both deserve the title *tzaddik,* righteous one.[39]

However, if we contemplate these three features of life in the Ark—sexual abstinence, sleeplessness, and role of world sustainer—we cannot avoid the sense that Noach is playing a godlike role. God is, of course, classically described as the one who "neither sleeps nor slumbers," as He holds vigil over His people; as the Sustainer and Feeder *(zan u-mefarnes);* and as One—unpartnered, without the erotic life of the pagan gods.

Noach's austere and selfless existence is subtly opened to question. Strangely, the midrashic reading of his abstinence shows him as clinging to his "box identity" even after leaving the Ark. After the Flood abates, God tells Noach to leave the Ark; and, again, the midrash intuits an intimate meaning: " 'Leave the Ark—*you and your wife':* man and wife together; here they were again permitted to have sexual relations."[40] Surprisingly, Noach refuses: "And Noach came out, *together with his sons,* his wife, and his sons' wives" (Gen. 8:18). He leaves the Ark, but carries with him its sexual abstinence. Why this reluctance to resume the conversation of man and woman?

Rashi intimates that Noach is afraid to bear children after the trauma of destruction; he asks God to promise never to send such a cataclysm again upon the world.[41] Noach's anxiety is understandable, since procreative life has acquired a menacing edge. However, one senses that with all its austerity the world of the Ark may offer Noach a role that he is reluctant to relinquish. The Ark is a silent place, where no sexual meanings are expressed, where an intimate constriction mirrors the constrictions of the floating box. It is the reverse image of the babbling world that has succumbed to the roar of the mighty waters. At the end, Noach refuses God's command to open conversation again with his wife. The Ark-world, it seems, has offered him a kind of autistic security. Sexuality and childbearing are risky; a sustainer is not required to create anything new; and sleep brings dreams—"Perchance to dream," says Hamlet, "Ay, there's the rub."[42] Dreams create worlds of desire and fear, teeming with *itzavon*. A dreamless year, feeding animals, separated from the female—has perhaps generated a fantasy of omnipotence that makes Noach reluctant to resume the strains of the world beyond the Ark.

A classic midrash explains Noach's refusal to resume sexual life:

> "To everything there is a season, and a time to every purpose" (Eccles. 3:1): there was a time for Noach to enter the ark, as it is written, "Go into the ark, you with all your household" (Gen. 7:1), and a time for him to leave it: "Come out of the ark" (8:15). He may be compared to an administrator *[parnas]* who leaves his post, putting someone in his place. On his return, he said to the other, "Leave your place." But he was reluctant to go out, saying, "Am I to go out and beget children for a curse?" Until God swore to him that He would not bring another Flood upon the world, as it says, "For this to Me is like the waters of Noach: as I swore that the waters of Noach would never again flood the earth" (Isa. 54:9): you will indeed be fruitful and multiply.[43]

This is Rashi's source, emphasizing Noach's anxiety after the Flood trauma and God's promise never again to destroy the world. However, the theme of the *parnas,* the administrator, the sustainer-feeder who appoints a substitute while he is away, invites speculation. The "place" mentioned five times in the midrash is the Ark that Noach feels is now "his" place; even the *parnas* says, "Leave *your* place." Noach, playing God in the microcosm of the Ark, finds it difficult to surrender his temporary omnipotence; God has "left the place," mysteriously departed, and Noach has fulfilled the demands of the time in substituting for Him. However, in refusing to relinquish the place when a different time demands it, Noach focuses on the issue of celibacy and procreation. It is in silencing his sexuality that Noach has most intimately filled the place of God; boxed off from sexuality and procreation, without sleep and dreams, maintaining rather than initiating life, Noach holds mastery over his world.

THE EXILE OF THE WORD

As sexual silence, and as a figure for the failed conversation that might have preempted the Flood, the Ark comes to represent both survival and erotic closure. This is the place to which Noach clings, without desire for life, sustaining the surfaces of existence. Here, nothing can move. As an antidote to the chaos of the corrupted world, as a temporary workshop in the rigors of finitude, it has its place and time. But Noach will not leave. The sterile environment that is the residue of a world destroyed holds for him the relish of finitude. Anna Freud writes of the psychotic delusion of the destruction of the world as "a reflection in consciousness of the withdrawal of libido from the object world."[44] The loveless quality of Noach's life is represented by a devastation, which he in some way authors; it is *Noach's* flood, his subjective experience.

In this midrashic tradition, withdrawing from woman is Noach's only act of disobedience. God invites him to reengage with the feminine, but for him the terrors of exchange are too great. Indeed, Noach's wife is strangely absent from the narrative; not even a hint of dialogue modifies the solipsism of his existence.

This silence crystallizes the condition known in the Zohar as the exile of the word *(galut ha-dibbur)*. Between husband and wife, this condition begins with Adam and Eve, who never, in fact, speak to each other. According to one midrash, Eve originates not only in Adam's body but, perhaps even more significantly, in his mind, his fantasy: he dreams of her and she appears.[45] As a figment of his imagination, she moves him to speak about her, not to her: "This one shall be called woman" (Gen. 2:23). She is part of himself, and then, surprisingly, awesomely, she is other. But dialogue never develops between them.

Instead, God diagnoses his failure: *"Because you listened to your wife's voice* and ate of the tree that I commanded you not to eat" (Gen. 3:17). In this literal translation, Adam is faulted for listening to his wife's voice, for being in some way too fused with her, incapable of contesting her view.

André Neher, in his classic study, *The Exile of the Word,* describes the relationship that is a duet, rather than a dialogue. Its nature is harmonious ("The soprano and the bass are literally made for agreement"[46]), unlike the dialogue that depends on the "need for contestation." Here, silence has an independent and essential function, enabling a true hearing and response. "Every dialogue, then, implies an aggression, a renunciation, a death to oneself, and an absolute silence, which are attitudes preliminary to opening up, to communication, to dialogue, to life-within-dialogue, and to love."[47] Drawing on the thought of Maharal, Martin Buber, and Raymond Carpentier, a French psychologist, Neher describes the desire to admit the universe of the other that requires a "double renunciation": "it would be the sacrifice of two partners ready to throw themselves open to the creation" (Carpentier).[48] It requires also improvisation: it takes place in the context of the unforeseen. "The world is wide open, nothing is fixed."

In this sense, Adam hiding from God, or God pretending to have lost sight of Adam ("Where are you?"), is the first, critical theological moment of the "missed encounter."[49] Between Adam and Eve, however, the missed encounter happens earlier, I suggest, when Adam listens to his wife's voice. In his fantasy, she is still part of him; her voice intimately compels him. The truth, however, is that she has separated from him, she has had an encounter with the serpent, and when she returns to her husband, she knows herself in ways unimaginable to him. As she eats the fruit, she sees the Angel of Death approach her;[50] she senses her first menstrual blood-flow; she feels death within her.[51] When he "listens to her voice," the midrash offers three readings:

> "She took of the fruit and ate": R. Aibu said: She squeezed grapes and gave him.
>
> R. Simlai said: She came upon him with her answers all ready, saying to him, "What do you think? That I will die and another Eve will be created for you? 'There is nothing new under the sun' (Eccles. 1:9). Or do you think that I will die while

you remain alone? 'He created it not a waste, He formed it to be inhabited' " (Isa. 45:18).

The Rabbis said: She began wailing with her voice over him.[52]

On the first view, she deceives him by offering him a liquid to drink (the squeezed grapes). On the second view, she argues him into agreement, on the grounds that the fruit cannot be fatal, since she has eaten and his future is unthinkable if she were to die. Overwhelmed by her sophistry, he eats. And, thirdly, "she began wailing [*meyalelet*] with her voice over him." This is the *yelala*, the ululation, the howl of Nothing, that expresses the death she feels within her—a quality of female voice that no man can withstand.

This midrash scans some classic modes of feminine power: deception, sophistical argumentation, and—mysteriously—the wailing cry. This cry is induced by the fruit of the tree, which is identified, in one tradition, with the vine:

> It has been taught: R. Meir holds that the tree of which Adam ate was the vine, since the thing that most brings wailing upon a man is wine, as it says, "And he drank of the wine and became drunk."[53]

Wine makes one wail. Graphically, the Talmud invites us to *hear* the wail in the text as it records Noach's encounter with the same poignant fruit: *Vai . . . vai . . . vai . . .* thirteen times, the wail is heard in the series of narrative verbs: *Va-yachel, Va-yitta, Va-yesht, Va-yishkar* ("And he began, and he planted, and he drank, and he became drunk").[54] The connectives acquire a keening sound, relentless, uncanny.

Another Talmudic passage makes the connection between Noach's plantings and Adam's Tree of Knowledge:

> God said to Noach: Noach, should you not have learned from Adam, whose transgression was caused by wine? This agrees with the view that the forbidden tree from which Adam ate was a vine.[55]

Apparently, the lesson of the Tree of Knowledge is not well learned. Eve wailed the unearthly wail of the being who has lost and is lost. Mysteriously, Noach, too, is said to have wailed the same intoxicated, desolate wail. Eve thus compels Adam to join her in her loss. Her voice overwhelms him, so that, together, they hide from the voice of the Lord God in the Garden. One missed encounter generates another.

And so the Exile of the Word gathers momentum through the generations, until Noach responds in silence to the destruction of the world, clings to the omnipotent illusion of his role in the Ark, and, finally, seeks refuge in intoxication. The *itzavon* that began with the Tree has gathered volume till it culminates in the isolation of Noach, who ventures toward neither God nor man, whose faith is compromised, and whose life seems far from vindicating his father's hopes in naming him.

DESPONDENT INTOXICATION

In *Black Sun,* Julia Kristeva offers an analysis of depression that elaborates on themes that we have noticed in this midrashic narrative. She describes a "noncommunicable grief" that makes one "lose all interest in words, actions, and even life itself."[56] An immediate loss or disaster awakens echoes of an old grief, a wound that has never healed. This despair is audible in the breakdown of speech: "Faced with the impossibility of concatenating, [the depressed] utter sentences that are interrupted, exhausted, come to a standstill."[57] In their total immersion in the archaic and indispensable object, they repudiate the symbolic dimension. Dialogue, language itself, depends upon undergoing a mourning for the primal object—the mother—and upon a willingness to accept a translation in the realm of representations. The depressed "give up signifying and submerge in the silence of pain or the spasm of tears that celebrates reunion with the Thing. . . . If I did not agree to lose mother, I could neither imagine nor name her."[58] "Melancholia then ends up in asymbolia, in loss of meaning: if I am no longer capable of translating or metaphorizing, I become silent and I die."[59] And again, "My depression points to my not knowing how to lose—I have perhaps been unable to find a valid compensation for the loss? . . . The depressed person is a radical, sullen atheist."[60]

Kristeva maintains that it is only through desire, expressed in language, that reconnection between people, and a sense of meaning, can be secured. The depressed person refuses to acknowledge his loss and embark on the translation process of representation, desire, imagination. An unwillingness to mourn leads one to abdicate from language and from the pain it represents. As Adam Phillips succinctly phrases it, "Depression is a self-cure for the terrors of aliveness, of being alive to one's losses and therefore to one's desires."[61] Denial mechanisms are "forms of anaesthetic, unconsciously sustained poverties of language that pre-empt a knowledge of feeling."[62] Kristeva speaks of the "despondent intoxication"[63] that greets idealized new versions of the old love.

One achieves one's loss through mourning, through a commitment to language. Depression, on the other hand, is "the negation of loss: it works to deny the possibility of meaning." "The speech of the depressed," Kristeva writes, "is to them like an alien skin; melancholy persons are foreigners in their maternal tongue. They have lost the meaning—the value—of their mother-tongue for want of losing the mother."[64]

In this psychoanalytic account of melancholy, an original unspeakable grief is never acknowledged but remains sullenly alive, poisoning language, meaning, and desire. The depressed disavow loss and "nostalgically fall back on the real object [the Thing] of their loss, which is just what they do not manage to lose, to which they remain painfully riveted." Speechless, or speaking an "artificial, unbelievable language," the depressed have learned the omnipotence of apathy.[65]

Kristeva's "Black Sun" of melancholia can, I suggest, be identified in the *itzavon* of these first human generations out of Eden. A primal loss has never been fully achieved, mourned, translated. No erotic or even expressive connection has developed between people, or between the self and God. And with the Flood a new devastation awakens echoes of the old loss. But Noach, like all before him, is still painfully riveted to the gates of Eden. Skeptical about language, dialogue, meaning, he reigns supreme in the microcosm of the Ark. Significantly, his first planting in the new, death-razed world is a vineyard. That is, he has prepared ahead of time a form of anesthetic to dull the terror of being alive. At this point, the midrash detects within the narrative the ground bass of despair:

> There are thirteen *Vai's* in the story of wine: *Va-yichal, Va-yitta, Va-yesht* . . . [He began, he planted, he drank . . .].[66]

One one level, this is a sermon against intoxication: *"Vai!*—Woe to those who lose themselves in drink!" But we remember the *yelala* of Eve, and the Tree of Knowledge, which may also have been a vine and brought *yelala* upon humanity; and God's reprimand to Noach for not learning from Adam's mistake. For Noach, the anesthetic is necessary because of the cumulative despair of the disenchanted world. Haunted by a double loss, he takes refuge in a fragile euphoria. Clinging still to the gates of Eden, with some consciousness of his inevitable despair, he prepares the vine shoots ahead of the Flood; they will ease his passage into the new world. Where do these vine shoots come from?—"They were banished from Eden."[67] A vestige of Eden, they promise primal bliss but issue in the howl of Nothingness with which Eve greeted the Angel of Death.

Noach becomes a man of the earth (Gen. 9:20), cultivating the seeds of bliss. The condition that Kristeva calls "despondent intoxication" well describes him. Paul Valery writes: "God made everything out of nothing. But the nothing shows through." Banished from Eden, human beings confront the nothing that shows through. Through dialogue, meanings may be articulated, a world of feeling and thought created and kept fluid, alive. But Noach drinks, becomes drunk, and (literally) unspeakable things happen to him. Ham sees his father's nakedness and "told his two brothers outside": a repressed narrative lurks here. What does Cham tell his brothers? And what does Noach realize on waking from his wine, about "what his youngest son had done to him?"[68] Some violent act against the father—a castration, a homosexual rape . . . These things cannot be put into words, but they contribute a haunting and sinister coda to Noach's story.

FORBIDDEN TO PRAY

"Despondent intoxication" is the subject of a powerful Hasidic meditation by the Beit Ya'akov. Citing a Talmudic passage, in which "an
intoxicated person is forbidden to pray,"[69] he suggests that prayer is
at root an acknowledgment of a void, a gap in one's being, that
brings one to God; intoxication, on the other hand, is a state of com-
pleteness, euphoria. Riding high, the intoxicated person "regards the
whole world as a plain":[70] that is, he feels sublimely masterful, lord of
all he surveys. Prayer in such a condition is impossible. Beit Ya'akov
reads the Talmudic passage metaphorically, to indicate a state of
euphoric self-possession; to pray in this state is to "utter falsehoods
in the presence of God."

A technical prohibition has become an existential claim: a sense
of incompleteness constitutes the posture of prayer. This creaturely
consciousness recognizes God as the source of all that is good; the
awareness of need constantly brings one back to the illumined face
of the Giver. Intoxication blinds one to limits, distances, gaps; but it
is precisely these painful experiences that generate self-awareness,
desire, and language. The oceanic sense delights but deceives; real
power is developed in the conscious struggle to overcome the void.
Shocked into awareness of the "nothing that shows through," Noach
and those who follow him are to develop the capacity to pray. As
Kristeva puts it, "If I did not agree to lose mother, I could neither
imagine nor name her." Agreeing to lose Eden, they may begin to
imagine and name their loss in the presence of God.

This new and necessary power will "strengthen the collapsing
foundations of the world." In mystical tradition, a primal and perilous instability, a labile condition in which chaos is always coming
again, is intimated in Job's words: "The pillars of heaven tremble,
astounded at His blast" (Job 26:11). The "blast," the harsh cry that
makes the cosmos shudder, recalls human beings to responsibility
and self-knowledge. A euphoric dream is shattered, but Creation is,
paradoxically, only placed on a firmer footing. The brush with Nothing concentrates the mind wonderfully, as Dr. Samuel Johnson said
in a similar context.

R. Yitzhak Hutner[71] writes of the generations of pure *chesed*, the undemanding shower of divine goodness that marked God's early dealings with the human world, and of its evolution toward a humanly more mature condition that he terms *chesed shel mishpat*— divine goodness commensurate with human worth. In a simple analogy, he speaks of enabling a person to earn his own living: this is clearly preferable to outright acts of charity, since it encourages the development of autonomy. In rearing children, too, a more mature form of parental love restrains its effusiveness so that the child may acquire a responsible sense of self. In kabbalistic sources, similarly, this modulation of *chesed* constitutes one dimension of God's *tzimtzum,* His withdrawal of full presence, in order to leave space for a human world.

In a similar vein, Emmanuel Levinas inscribes a midrashic ban on intoxication as epigraph to the first section of *Difficult Freedom:* "Let them not enter the Sanctuary drunk." Drawn from Rashi's comment on the deaths of Aaron's sons—possibly because they transgressed in just this way[72]—the words come to express the stern demands of an adult spirituality. (One chapter is headed: "A Religion for Adults.")

Marguerite Duras testifies to her experience of intoxication. In words of passion and despair, she writes of her own history with alcoholism:

Alcohol makes people talk. It's spirituality carried to the point where logic becomes lunacy: it's reason going mad trying to understand why this kind of society, this Reign of Injustice, exists. And it always ends in despair. . . . The void you discover one day in your teens—nothing can ever undo that discovery. But alcohol was invented to help us bear the void in the universe—the motion of the planets, their imperturbable wheeling through space, their silent indifference to the place of our pain. A man who drinks is interplanetary. He moves through interstellar space. It's from there he looks down. Alcohol doesn't console, it doesn't fill up anyone's psychological gaps, all it replaces is the lack of God. It doesn't comfort man. On the contrary, it encourages him in his folly, it transports him to the supreme regions where he is master of his own destiny. No other human being, no woman, no poem or music, book or

painting can replace alcohol in its power to give man the illusion of real creation. Alcohol's job is to replace creation. And
that's what it does do for a lot of people who ought to have
believed in God and don't any more.[73]

The "illusion of real creation" is the barren gift of alcohol to those
whose minds cannot bear the void. Noach prepares his vine shoots
of intoxication for the day after the Flood, after the Ark has expelled
him from another form of intoxication: the godlike silence without
sexuality or dreams ("I could be bounded in a nutshell, and count
myself a king of infinite space," cries Hamlet, "were it not that I have
bad dreams."[74]) Drunk, he is "interplanetary," or, as the Talmud puts
it, "he looks down on the whole world as a plain." Sublimely isolated
from any actual dialogue—with man, woman, poem, or music—
whose resistance might lead him to knowledge, he ultimately lacks a
God—the God who is accessible to those who acknowledge their
lack. The intellectual pain of which Duras writes seeks instant relief,
which is no relief. Kristeva's depressed person, in his "despondent
intoxication," is a "radical, sullen atheist."

RADICAL, SULLEN ATHEIST?

Yet this same Noach offers burnt-offerings to God:

> And God smelled the sweet savor, and God said to His heart:
> "Never again will I doom the earth because of man, since the
> devisings of man's heart are evil from his youth; never again
> will I destroy every living being, as I have done." (Gen. 8:21)

Clearly Noach's sacrifice has affected God, moved Him to the
essential oath[75] of "Never again." Noach has *sacrificed* to God; he has
opened up a space for divine love. This, surely, is a form of prayer,
arising out of the gratitude and anguish of the survivor. Hizkuni
comments: "He offered burnt-offerings: in the manner of those who
go down to the sea in ships, and sacrifice thanks-offerings (Ps.
107:22)—also of one who has suffered great anguish, when the whole
world is destroyed and he alone survives."[76] The prototype for such a

sacrifice is the sailor who has survived the routine rigors of life at sea. But Psalm 107 tells of many sufferers who escape extinction; whether they are lost in the wilderness, or fettered in darkness, they cry to God in their suffering, and offer thanksgiving offerings when He saves them. In each case, this peril transports them into a world of prayer: "And they cried to God in their adversity." And, in each case, the new world is a world of destruction, where illusions of omnipotence break down. Here, a kind of madness reigns: they melt, they stagger like a drunken man, they are at their wits' end. Here, intoxication becomes a figure for radical instability, which they live fully and which moves them to prayer.

What is Noach's position in this constellation? Unlike the grateful souls in the psalm, he does not pray to God in his anguish; and if his sacrifice on survival is a thanks-offering, it should be named *she-lamim,* or *zivchei todah,* as in the psalm. Instead, it is a burnt-offering, which is traditionally understood to expiate the impulses of the heart.[77] Some new inwardness is intimated here, as his heart, closed to dialogue, begins to be aware of itself. Unlike the rescued sufferers in the psalm, he has never asked for rescue. And yet his sacrifice expresses a shift, a prayerful recognition of some kind.

PRAYING TO PRAY

Even in the Ark itself, where the Torah records no prayer, the midrash blurs our certainty. A strong midrashic tradition[78] has it that he does pray during his year in the Ark. What is the prayer of one who both wants and does not want to leave the Ark? "Release me from prison, that I may praise Your name" (Ps. 142:8). He prays for release from the constriction that makes prayer impossible. He prays, then, to pray. Divided within himself, he commits himself to language.

The power of language is all but closed to him; language is still in exile. But there is one glimmer of light. God, who has never *spoken*[79] to Noach, in the full sense of a dialogic speech that demands response, speaks to him just once: "And God spoke *[Va-yidabber]* to Noach: 'Leave the Ark, you and your wife . . .' " (Gen. 8:15). This is a moment of challenge that, as we have seen, he resists. But the midrash yields a sense of evolving processes. The logic behind the midrash suggests that if God engages Noach with the full rigor of "Leave the Ark . . ." this must be a response to a real speech by Noach: "Release me from prison, that I may praise Your name" (*Tzei*—"Leave the Ark . . ." is God's answer to a prayer beginning "*Hotzia*—Release me"). Noach blocks himself off against exchanges that may obliterate him. Yet, at the same time, he prays for release from all the prisons of his own making. And he offers sacrifices of thanksgiving once he is released.

Sefat Emet[80] addresses the psychology of inward blocking as an issue of times and seasons. The light of the soul is in general occluded, but "there are seasons when the gates of heaven open. And then, here below, too, the human heart opens." Noach beseeches God to "release me to give praise," to release him to a moment of expressive praise, in a world where continuous praise is impossible. Only at special times, the gates of the heart are opened to praise: Shabbat, Festivals, the New Moon, when *Hallel*—a paean of praise—is uttered, which includes the words "The dead shall not praise God, nor those who go down into silence." This indicates that "anyone *who has death in him*" cannot properly praise the God who transcends all praise. Only on Shabbat and Festivals, when one is visited by a transcendent soul *(neshamah yeteirah)*, which *has no death,* does praise flow freely.

Noach becomes Everyman, unable to bear the exposure to divine light that might obliterate him. The problem is death-within-him, which awakens echoes of *itzavon*—the knowledge of failure in every exchange with the world. It is this death-within that brings a wail to Eve's lips, and then to Noach's. Language is in exile; and Noach, who was named for restoration and relief, lives through the despair of his time, playing out its despondent intoxication. But for Sefat Emet, Noach, this Everyman, lives through cycles and seasons: there are moments when his heart opens, and the presence of death is balanced by the "transcendent soul" that knows nothing of death. He may lose these moments as soon as Shabbat is over. But he develops a yearning for the seasons of full presence, and he may pray for their return.

Noach's prayer for release becomes in this version an allegorical account of the human condition. But the commentary works both ways. Brought into contact with our own oscillations, we can turn again to Noach with greater generosity. This Hasidic text gives the initiative to God: the gates of heaven open and the human heart responds.

SYMBIOTIC MOVEMENT

This notion of times and seasons, a periodicity in the cosmos, on which the human being must wait, restores us to the core dilemma of the Flood narrative. A question haunts the narrative, about the relationship between the human world of freedom and the rhythms of God's inner world. We remember the shifting personae of God-in-the-narrative—mourning, disappointed, decisively condemning the world, revealed by the narrator as indescribably affected by Noach. This God warned Noach of the imminent Flood, in terms that "blocked his prayer":[81] "the end of all flesh has come before Me." Where does Noach's responsibility begin, in a situation where he is blocked by God? How are we to conceive of the relationships, limned in the text, between God and the world, God and Noach? Do they inform, elaborate, play off one another recursively? Like a hologram, is the "closed" condition of the world replicated in each of its parts, and within God as well?

It seems that God is staged by the divine narrator in such a way as to provoke the human protagonists to their own energy of being. He responds anthropomorphically to human situations as they arise. He moves between *middot,* between postures and responses.[82] Like a human being, He regrets the failed projects of the past, as new thoughts supersede the old ones. He seeks the gratification of a world that will respond musically to His note. He moves and can be moved—by memory, by the gratuitous beauty *(chen)* of Noach that is the mirror image of his apparent identity *(no'ach).* As a protagonist in the narrative, His omniscience is occluded; but He evolves toward greater self-knowledge and acceptance of human beings who are in His image. In doing so, He withdraws still further in an act of *tzimtzum*[83] that allows for the existence, not only of the world, but of the personal world of each human being.

I suggest that we read God in the Torah as a character created by

God the Narrator. The two are not identical. Extending the point, I suggest also that God the Author of the Torah cannot be naively identified with the Narrator. The metaphor of authorship has conventions of its own: the Author writes, creates a narrative persona, which tells a story in which a character appears in changing moods. All are God. But at each level, God comes closer to human reality, and each level represents a construction by the previous persona. Indeed, the God who is the Author, too, may be playing a role, in which human language is essential: He too represents an act of *tzimtzum*, a focusing and narrowing of the full divine presence. In this way, the reader can engage with the limited projections of that full Being.

Another metaphor might be the psychoanalytic relationship, in which the analyst remains essentially hidden, unknown to the analysand. He presents challenging or comforting pieces of himself to the analysand, responding to the latter's movement, and activating new movement. The key is movement, fluidity, the need for improvisation, on both sides. These versatile roles are part of the repertoire or reality of the analyst—separated out, known more fully by him in all their fragmentariness. Behind all these masks, there is a core of unknowable presence, which contains all contraries.

It is the final movement of God in the narrative of Noach that most urgently invites the reader to the use of such narrative or psychoanalytic metaphors. Noach builds an altar and offers sacrifices. I have suggested the complexity of these sacrifices, the way they intimate that his occluded, frozen state is in process of thawing. But it is God's response that engages us now:

> God smelled the sweet savor, and God said to Himself: "Never again will I doom the earth because of man, since the devisings of man's heart are evil from his youth; never again will I destroy every living being, as I have done." (Gen. 8:21)

God seems to be so delighted by the fragrance of the burning meat that He vows never again to destroy mankind and his world. Moreover, He speaks to His heart, evoking the process that initiated the Flood: "He was saddened to His heart." The separation of God from His heart seems unhealed. But Hizkuni suggests that the later phrase represents a real advance over the earlier: God is now in dialogue with His own heart.[84] However mysteriously, some metaphysical alienation does find healing. Language is no longer totally in exile. Mourning and destruction have unexpectedly led God to dialogue and renewed desire. He responds to Noach's sacrifices, with their sweet smell, in a tone modulated to indulgence: "The human heart is evil *because of its youth:* I no longer need to avenge Myself of him as I have done." We remember how God originally saw that same human heart filled with evil thoughts, in a mode of frustration and mourning that undermined the entire creation. Now, implicitly, God is more at peace with His own heart and with the human heart, so that youth can become a pretext for tolerance.

This is a moment of greatest divine inwardness: Who can know what God said to His heart? Clearly, Noach is not aware of God's change of heart.[85] But this most intimate moment has now been communicated—to Moses, when, at God's dictation, he writes the Torah. So that God's inwardness is enacted in the process of unfolding toward the reader.

The agent of change in God's inner world is called the "sweet savor" of Noach's sacrifice. In a striking passage, Beit Ya'akov describes a symbiotic movement between God and the human world: something shifts in God's relation to the world, so that Noach understands that its survival is from now, in some sense, assured, and he responds by opening himself to receive the new divine beneficence. His sacrifices are sparked by an intuition about the metaphysical movement toward a nurturing restraint. God has withdrawn, creating an illusion of absence. The sweet savor of Noach's sacrifice represents his mirroring movement as he shifts from his "despondent intoxication" and gives himself back to God.

SEDUCED BY HIS OWN WINE

The Talmud comments:

> One who allows himself to be seduced by his own wine, has something of his Creator's mentality, as it is said, "And God

smelled the sweet savor; and God said to Himself: Never again will I doom the earth."[86]

The gracious host—like God—allows himself to feel gratified when his guest toasts him with his own wine; he makes no further demands. Here, God is satisfied with the sweet savor of the sacrificial animals that He Himself has saved from the Flood.

Beit Ya'akov,[87] however, amplifies the concept: God accepts human ways of worship, which place individuality and free will at the center. But from a mystical viewpoint, this is an illusion, or a concept tailored to human thinking: there is only God and the divine energy that moves all things. And yet God chooses to be satisfied, *seduced,* by the illusion of human consciousness and free will. He thus models for man a similar humility, accepting the restricted roles of conscious life.

The human being may be in the image of God, but paradoxically he comes to achieve that identity only by fragmentary and limited enactments. Even the omniscient God can come to know His own heart as well as the hearts of volatile human beings by improvising roles of restricted knowledge. Both analyst and analysand must relinquish a masterful knowledge if meaningful knowledge is to emerge. The analyst may understand the problem of his analysand from the beginning. But he finds a place of not-knowing, from which to work together with his analysand and in resistance to him, so that vital knowledge may be born.

The imagery of wine and pleasure has undergone transformation. Here, it is no longer a figure for escapism, for the illusion of real creation, in Duras's phrase. It has become the choice to be pleased by the partial, the less-than-adequate, for the sake of what may emerge from such discipline. The effect of this wine is not a *yelala* but a self-effacing enjoyment of the other. The motive of this conscious gratification is *rachamim,* compassion, and its purpose is creation. Now, there emerges a vulnerable willingness to be "seduced by one's own wine," to enter into the dialogue with the other that involves both official and unofficial exchanges. For God, this means taking pleasure in the "misconception" of human freedom, which allows man to earn what can properly only be given; the sweet savor of Noach's sacrifice seduces a God whose subjectivity spans conscious and unconscious projects. This is *tzimtzum* in a psychoanalytic sense: God withdraws from the presumption of total power and knowledge[88] to leave a play area in which human worlds can be created. Gaps open up, absences, where God, apparently, is not.

In one of his most important teachings,[89] R. Nahman speaks of the *challal panui*, the vacated space, the void, in which the human world can form without danger of being inundated by God. This cosmological narrative, derived from Lurianic kabbalah, becomes a psychological narrative of civilization and its discontents. R. Nahman tells of the irresoluble paradox of a space where God is absent and present at once: absent necessarily, if there is to be anything finite and knowable apart from the Infinite (the *Ein Sof*); but present, with equal necessity, since nothing exists apart from Him. Perhaps He is never more powerfully present than when He is apparently absent, forgotten, exerting an unconscious pressure.

Within that potential space, however, as worlds crystallize, they harden, become occluded, self-possessed. *Klipot* form, crusty accretions, husks, lifeless surface phenomena, dense and empty at once.[90] If one's world becomes constricted in this way, a kind of sorcery blocks access to other selves, within and without. Having a defined self is sanity; too densely packed, it becomes madness—without self-division, or motive for change.[91] This congealed world, empty of God, is dense with what R. Nahman calls *kushiyot*—questions: frozen, insoluble fragments that block movement.

And yet it is only in this void that dialogue, in the radical form that R. Nahman calls *machloket* (contestation), can define the distance and difference between two who speak to each other. This dialogue creates a world in the space between them. An essential dimension of the dialogue is *silence:* an intuitive knowledge of the dialectic of presence and absence, consciousness and unconsciousness, the notes and the pauses that constitute a musical interchange. It is through music, indeed, that R. Nahman proposes to traverse the essential but perilous void. The tzaddik, the righteous person who can move freely into and out of the void, expresses this dialectical movement in a *niggun,* a melody. So God becomes present in absence. The tzaddik sings himself into an awareness of his full being; and sings God, too, into greater presence.

Noach, too, like God, may be seduced by his own wine. By making space for others both within and without, he may know pleasure in exchange, allowing the irrational, the unknown elements of selfhood freer play. This is a form of sacrifice, replicating a new divine dynamic of incompleteness, of vacated voids.

NEVER AGAIN . . .

The paradox of yielding mastery in this way is that the void does indeed produce worlds that give pleasure—that are no longer automatically slated for destruction. As we have seen, God's fundamental pattern is to "create worlds and destroy them": a plausible pattern, given the encrusted and bewitched nature of such worlds. What makes it possible for God to say, "Never again will I doom the earth . . . never again will I destroy every living being"? In effect, Rashi says, the double utterance constitutes an oath.[92] A serious commitment is made here by a God who has destroyed worlds in His quest for the one that will be pleasing to Him. What is the force of this commitment? And what has changed to elicit it from Him?

Human nature, apparently, has not changed. We have noticed Hizkuni's suggestion that God now speaks of human evil as a function of youth, so that He can be more tolerant in face of a hopeful developmental process. Even on such an optimistic reading, however, the change is in the mind of God: He evaluates the human situation more charitably. So that, again, we can ask: What moves God to this oath of unequivocal commitment?

God's repeated words—"Never again"—contain a clue to a paradoxical development. Originally, God created the world in language: He said and it was. That original utterance, performative in essence, bears compelling authority; its effect is an action that exceeds mere statement. It carries implicit promises, which nevertheless God found reason, as the world changed, to regret. Now, God says, twice, "Never again," promising the world immunity from further destruction. But this promise, too, constitutes a performative utterance, no stronger than the original creative word.

The philosopher J. L. Austin, who initiated speech-act research and introduced the notion of the performative utterance, offers the example of the linguistic act by which a marriage is performed. When the bride answers in the affirmative to the clergyman's "Do you take this man . . . ?"[93] she is not *describing* what she is doing, she is *acting;* she is accomplishing the marriage. Saying "I promise," likewise, produces the event that is designated. According to Austin, such utterances, which produce acts, cannot be either true or false, only successful or unsuccessful, "felicitous" or "unfelicitous."

The performative can fail; indeed, as Shoshana Felman argues, "the capacity for misfire is an inherent capacity of the performative": as an act, it is defined by the capacity "to *miss its goal* and to *fail to be achieved,* to remain *unconsummated,* to *fall short* of its own accomplishment."[94] As in the Freudian slip, she claims, the act of failing reveals that language is not everything. Consciousness extends only so far; and beyond that limit, there are failed operations, misfirings, which yield unforeseen possibilities.[95] Among these possibilities is humor, the humor of the fall, which, too, is an act, a *lapsus,* a slip. Slides and slips are not sheer disaster. Even Kierkegaard wrote: "Vainly I strive against it. My foot slips. My life is still a poet's existence." And Felman comments: "The seduction of slipping is thus the seduction of poetry, of the *poetic* functioning of language. 'Stumbling over words like cobblestones' is, in one of Baudelaire's definitions, the nature of the poetic act."[96]

Poetry and humor achieve an unsettling effect with respect to knowledge; they lead to an explosion, a "cracking up" of portentous certainties. Since promises contain their own capacity to fail, to slip, man as the promising animal[97] is involved in a fundamental contradiction.

This dilemma, I suggest, informs the rhetoric of God's promises. Man has to renounce playing God. More pointedly, God renounces playing God. At the end of the Flood narrative, when God utters a repeated promise, the possibility of failure, change, slippage, as context and circumstance change, is specifically evoked. In this sense, this oath is not any more impregnable than the performative utterances of creation. And God is aware of the fact, speaks with a self-consciousness that belongs to a moment when falling, slipping, failing are fully acknowledged. If He speaks human language, He exposes Himself to the casualties implicit in the use of language.

Paradoxically, as theological correctness relaxes, as the promise, especially if spoken in soliloquy, undermines its own seriousness, destruction becomes a less probable outcome. In a world in which God has acquired a larger repertoire than is suggested by the stock character of God, *itzavon* becomes less inevitable. God allows Himself to be seduced by His own wine; human beings, bearing a trace of divinity, allow more room for the other, within and without. Acknowledging voids, lacks, failures may leave space for worlds to be created.

Before, the earth was full of violence, as the deathly litany of generations left its residue of grief and drunken bravado. After Noach, strikingly, the litany changes: over the ten ensuing generations, the original formula of life, procreation, and death omits the reference to death. Clearly, no biological change is implied: the generations lived, procreated, and died, as before. But the chronicle of generations is no longer punctuated by the closing word *va-yamat* (and he died). The curse of *itzavon* has perhaps loosened its grip: Noach has taken the despondent intoxication of the world through its crisis.

Falling, slipping, stumbling is endemic to the nature of the world. According to the midrash, the next slip, the Tower of Babel narrative, begins with a calculation about the next cosmic disaster: "Every 1,656 years, the heavens will collapse as they did at the Flood. Come let us make supports for them!"[98] The collapse of the heavens has become—after one occurrence—a predictable phenomenon, which people absurdly try to preempt. This narrative, moreover, takes its place in a field of midrashic imagery that is haunted by the mythic terror of slipping and falling. In one sinister metaphor, grasshoppers in a jar try in turn to climb out, only to fall back into the jar.[99] In this way the early generations are figured as failing to learn from previous experience: the Flood was preceded by more limited disasters, and followed by the Tower of Babel narrative. The sense of doomed sequences of attempts to transform the trapped condition of mankind conveys an obtuseness or an emotional resistance.

However, falling, stumbling, can sometimes, paradoxically, prove fortunate. "One never gets the true sense of the words of Torah except after mistakes."[100] Literally, this reads, "One never comes to stand upon the words of Torah unless one *stumbles over them*." Stumbling, slipping becomes the condition for stability. It is by way of errors, misconceptions, inadequacies that one moves beyond the banality of first assumptions.

A richer, more imaginative experience opens up as prejudices are abandoned and one dares to stumble in unknown territory. Proust speaks of "that perpetual error that is known, precisely, as 'life.' "[101] And Austin refers to the tension in such moves: "I must explain again that we are floundering here. To feel the firm ground of prejudice slipping away is exhilarating, but brings its revenges."[102] To act is to risk slipping, which can be both painful and exhilarating. More than that, whether they make one laugh or cry, such failures constitute the royal road to a different mastery. To stumble over the words of Torah is to be struck down by some abrasive contact; one knows one's finitude, one's clumsiness. Paradoxically, one may rise up with a truer grace.

EXTRAORDINARY LOVE . . .

The Flood narrative, then, is God's last exercise in cataclysm. He commits Himself to the growth and invigoration of the wrecked world. He moves from soliloquy ("And God said to His heart") to enunciating to Noach the terms of His covenant and showing him the rainbow that will forever remind Him of it. Between soliloquy and covenant, however, God blesses Noach and his children: "Be fruitful and multiply, and fill the earth . . ." (Gen. 9:1). A virtual repetition of His blessing to Adam immediately after Creation, these words declare that the empty world needs to be filled. But this emptiness is different from that primal void. Now, in the devastated world after the Flood, God's blessing resounds with a new poignancy.

Particularly resonant now is God's insistence that man is created in the image of God: "Whoever sheds the blood of man, by man shall his blood be shed; for in His image did God make man" (Gen. 9:6). Forbidding murder, God for the first time *tells* a human being that he is made in God's image. Only now, as the *itzavon,* the despondent intoxication of the human being in an already-failed world, gathers to a head, and as Noach prepares to plant his vineyard, God affirms directly to him that he bears the royal seal. In the words of the Mishnah:

> Beloved is the human being, since he was created in God's image. Extraordinary is this love when it is made known to him that he was created in God's image, as it is said: "In the image of God did God make man." (Gen. 9:6)[103]

Two possibilities are compared, one more valuable (precious, beloved) than the other. They are represented by Adam and Noach: Adam, created by the hand of God, is, in some sense, created also in the image of God; Noach, who has witnessed the collapse of that creation, has *become conscious* that he is created in God's image. Just when flesh and blood have become valueless, as apocalypse has ruined the beauty and significance of the human face, God for the first time tells a human being of the divinity marking that face. God's message challenges Noach's imagination with a counterintuitive sense of value. What "extraordinary love" can emerge from so much death? And yet Noach, at this moment, *knows,* as no one has before him, that he is made in the divine image. Heir to the stumbling generations, he becomes conscious of a mystery within himself. Uncannily, he becomes conscious of being beloved, and commits himself to releasing the secret meanings of his state.

THREE

Jonah

A Fantasy of Flight

FLIGHT FROM GOD

The book of Jonah is the most enigmatic of biblical narratives. Its central mystery—Jonah's flight from God—haunts the narrative till the end. Classical interpretations have offered to resolve this enigma and its satellites, proposing straightforward meanings for the text. But the text will not yield to such solutions; its meaning both invites and eludes interpretation.

> The word of God came to Jonah son of Amittai: "Rise up and go to Nineveh, the great city, and cry out against it; for their evil has come up before Me." But Jonah rose up to flee to Tarshish from God's presence. (Jon. 1:1–3)

Jonah, a man with no credentials other than his father's name, responds to God's call by fleeing to Tarshish, at the other end of the known world.[1] His destination is mentioned three times, suggesting that his project is to travel as far away as possible from Nineveh. But what does he mean by his flight? What does Jonah imagine he is doing in evading the omnipresent, omniscient God?

It is striking that the theological absurdity of such an attempt never arises in the text. The sailors on his ship may question him: "What have you done?" But their "great fear" derives from the terror of the storm and the sense of a powerful pursuing God who is angered by the flight of His subject, not from a sense that such a notion is in itself absurd. "When the men *learned that he was fleeing from God's presence—for so he told them*—they said to him, 'What must we do to you to make the sea calm around us?' " (Jon. 1:10–11); for them, his flight is a provocative but comprehensible act.

When is his flight brought to an end? Is it after his prayer from the belly of the great fish, when he is forcibly ejected and proceeds to obey God's call? This seems plausible, in view of the shift in language:

> The word of God came to Jonah a second time: "Rise up and go to Nineveh and cry out . . ." And Jonah rose up and went to Nineveh in accordance with God's command. . . . And he cried out . . . (Jon. 3:1–4)

Instead of flight, there is the movement of obedience, instead of silence, the cry. And indeed, his cry of doom provokes an instant change of heart in the sinful city. If the book ended at this point (the end of chapter 3), we would understand that its subject is the power of repentance in the narrative of the city and of Jonah himself.

But chapter 4 undoes this glimpse of closure. Jonah prays for a second time and, astonishingly, justifies his flight:

> "Oh God! Isn't this just what I said when I was still in my own country? That is why I fled beforehand to Tarshish. For I knew that You are a compassionate and gracious God, slow to anger, abounding in loving-kindness, renouncing evil." (Jon. 4:2)

In a tone of aggrieved rationality, he explains why he fled—and how right he was to flee. Essentially, then, he is *still fleeing*.

Moreover, his flight issues in a final prayer: for death. (" 'Therefore now, O God, take, I beseech you, my life from me, for my death is better than my life!' " [Jon. 4:3].) Apparently, death has been his true destination all along. The sea journey that was to take him to Tarshish has another covert function, which emerges in his request to the sailors to throw him overboard: death is his heroic choice, his sacrifice to save the sailors, but it is also his profound desire.

The Mechilta brings this obscure death wish to the surface: "Jonah went to sea in order to lose himself in the sea." There is a suicidal desire in Jonah's flight that is intimated in the insistent verbs of *descent* that carry him downward into a posture of regressed stupor: "And he went down [va-yered] to Jaffa . . . and he went down [va-yered] into the ship . . . and he went down [yarad] into the ship's hold where he lay down and fell deep asleep *[va-yeradam]*"[2] (Jon. 1:3–5). The wordplay subtly involves him in a project of withdrawal from consciousness, as his trajectory carries him down into the ship's hold— a womblike enclosure—from which he is roused only to ask to be surrendered to the sea. Now, restored to life, he has apparently submitted to God's call. But, in his own depths, he is still fleeing. Nothing is resolved.

MOTIVATED IRRATIONALITY

This final chapter is dense with enigmas from beginning to end. The evil of Nineveh, which was the starting point of the narrative, has been neutralized by the repentance of its inhabitants; and God, in response, has suspended His evil decree. But evil has returned in intensified form within Jonah himself:

> God saw what they did, how they were turning back from their *evil* ways. And God renounced the *evil* He had planned to bring upon them, and did not carry it out. And Jonah was filled with anguish [lit., it was *evil* to Jonah a great *evil*], and he was angry. (Jon. 3:10–4:1)

This is the critical moment that leads Jonah to vindicate his flight to the God from whom he is still fleeing. The word *ra'ah* connects Nineveh, God, and Jonah: the external evils—of moral and social violence, of divine vengeance—are resolved; and it is this, precisely, that "is evil to Jonah a great evil," that plunges him into unaccountable despair and rage.[3] The mystery of his flight condenses into the specific absurdity of his reaction to the disappearance of evil.

A kind of malaise inhabits him, a dis-ease that is manifested as anger.[4] Anger and depression are frequent bedfellows, both in modern psychological thinking and in biblical discourse.[5] In this state, he expresses the full toxicity of his flight: "And now, oh God, please take my life, for my death is better than my life." The core of his prayer constitutes an inversion of the public norms of prayer: death is his desire and it is associated with goodness *(tov)*.

He has already inverted the consensual uses of the Thirteen Divine

Attributes, which classically celebrate God's mercy. Moses first articulated them in pleading for the lives of his people; in different forms
and condensations, they occur repeatedly in Scripture; and they
have become a consecrated liturgical recitative in the prayer lives of
the Jewish people. Indeed, on Yom Kippur, they play a central role in
every service of the day, not simply as descriptions of God's loving
ways, but as invocations, invitations, performative pleas that allow
the loving face of God to emerge. But on Yom Kippur, the narrative
of Jonah is also read—where Jonah inverts the hopeful meanings of
the Attributes.[6] Jonah alone speaks them in a tone of aggrieved
despair. Even before his flight, he *already knew* God's nature, its
deplorable compassion. The survival of the repentant city proves
how right he was in his expectations of the God whose ways he
knows so thoroughly. The God who is classically celebrated as
"renouncing evil" has acted true to form; and Jonah is mortally sick
because of it.

Who, then, is this Jonah, who unsettles the associations of words,
demonically repudiating love while desiring death and calling it
good?[7] The text allows us no insight into a rational world of shared
meanings that might resolve the enigmas of this narrative.[8] A kind of
"motivated irrationality"[9] inhabits his words. It is as though he is
speaking a darkly private language, an *idiolect*,[10] giving voice to an
inscrutable inner world. But this language serves as a vehicle by
which he attacks prayer itself.

Indeed, it is striking that, in this last chapter, the phenomena of
the external world that are so often—fourteen times—called *great
(gadol)* yield place to the climate of Jonah's inner world, where there
is, now, "great evil," and, later, "great joy." His world up to now has
been inhabited by a great city, a great wind, a great storm, a great
fish, the great fear of the sailors. He has been a small figure, overwhelmed by gigantic forces, a child who shrinks to fetal size as he
withdraws into his stupor in the ship's hold. Now, for the first time,
he experiences great forces *within* him—great evil and great joy.

At this point he can, for the first time, speak to God of his flight,
as a condition of his present life. He can articulate, however
absurdly, the sense that his death is better than his life. This is his
truth, in this place and at this time, in the presence of God, whom he

is still fleeing. Unlike the philosopher-king, Kohelet, who arrives at a similar repudiation of the value of life ("Better is the day of death than the day of birth" [Eccles. 7:1]), Jonah speaks without the larger context of theological argument that makes Kohelet intelligible if provocative. Jonah speaks of his own life, destroying meaning as he speaks. But he speaks, for the first time, in dialogue with God—like a child who begins to be conscious of dark forces within him; like a patient who cries his true pain and rage, in a language that none but the doctor can understand.

THE QUINTESSENTIAL STORY

Who, again, is Jonah? He appears without historical background or personal affiliations, other than his father's name. Significantly, he is nowhere called a prophet. The only historical clue is the existence of Nineveh, the great evil city. He is possibly to be identified with the prophet Jonah son of Amittai, whose short narrative appears in 2 Kings, 14:25–26. On this view, he is a historical figure and his book can appropriately be interpreted in a public historical framework. However, although it is unlikely that there existed two prophets by the name of Jonah son of Amittai, the absence of any other historical links weakens the impact of such an identification.

The unique nature of this narrative and of its hero has always been recognized. As Uriel Simon points out, the book of Jonah is difficult to classify among either the historical or the prophetic writings, although it has some characteristics of both.[11] Essentially, it stands alone. If this text tells of a largely unidentified figure who inhabits a world of great forces, who flees from God and who ultimately speaks only to choose death over life, then perhaps it belongs to the world of mythic, or symbolic, rather than historical narrative. Perhaps its resonances include a sense that his name, Yonah, a dove, communicates something essential about him: elusive, always in flight—*pore'ach, bore'ach*—evading the reader's desire for clear understandings. And perhaps his story, in all its enigmatic force, is never to be finally decoded, its mystery resolved; but is to evoke the elusive nature of narrative meaning, the internal silence at the heart of all stories. To the Greeks who coined the word *enigma,* it meant simply a *tale*, a *story*—as though they understood how meaning moves constantly in a story, how it is inhabited by conflict, how it resists literal translation and rejoices in the larger resonances that are silenced by conclusive readings.

In this sense, Jonah is the quintessential story, enigmatic to the end. The reader who hopefully notes that God has the last word in the narrative is then tantalized by those last words:

> "You pitied the gourd, which you did not work for, and which you did not grow, which appeared overnight and perished overnight. And should I not pity Nineveh, the great city, in which there are more than a hundred and twenty thousand human beings who do not know their right hand from their left, and many cattle?" (Jon. 4:10–11)

God speaks with an all-embracing logic, which covers Jonah's feeling and His own: the reader hopes for godlike resolution of the enigmas of the story, only to remain with a question and with the questioning resonances of *many cattle?* . . . At the fraught moment when Jonah is read on Yom Kippur, as the day turns toward evening, the time of closure, of decision, these resonances tease us out of thought.

For there is no last word. There is a *question*, framed by God in His dialogue with Jonah. The question remains suspended, resonant. It touches on God's pity for those who, in the most important sense, know nothing; who are themselves like cattle. Rashi reads the first expression ("who do not know their right hand from their left") to refer to the children, who do not *yet* know their right hand from their left; while "many cattle" refers to the adults, whose religious understanding is like that of cattle, "since they do not know who created them." But the cattle have a literal presence in the narrative: like the inhabitants of Nineveh, they fast and are clothed in sackcloth and cry out to God: a surrealistic vision that levels human and animal in a common anguish. And as the last words of the narrative, *many cattle* unsettles conclusive understandings of God's concern for the created world.

God's rhetorical question clearly invites Jonah's assent. But ambiguity hangs over this ending. Is this assent simply assumed, and therefore not narrated? Or is there a real question that remains? Is Jonah's response obscured because it is unknown, open to interpretation? Enigmas, stories never reach full closure, the place of no further interpretation. In this sense, the book of Jonah invites interpretation from the first verse to the last; but its elusive meanings are never fully netted. There is no conclusive answer to its questions.

God's final question is, moreover, couched in a language that, like Jonah's, is inscrutable, attuned to Jonah's private world of meanings. The mystifying analogy between the gourd and the city, between Jonah's pity and God's, eludes understanding. Does Jonah pity the gourd? Surely it is himself that he pities! How does God engage with Jonah's death wish? And if God asserts His loving concern for the city, why does He shift from the public, theological meanings of chapter 3, where He spared Nineveh because its people—even the cattle—repented of their evil ways, publicly, theatrically, clothed in the costume of repentance? Why, then, does God leave all this out of the count, and withdraw into a mysterious language, which focuses on the sheer numbers of the people, their ignorance, their cattle?

THE HUMAN CRY

God initiates His relationship with Jonah by telling him to *cry out*. Instead, he flees, moves down and away, into the depths, curled in silence. This is his response to God's call, and to the great wind and the great storm that God sends after him. The ship's captain gives voice to a natural protest: "How can you be sleeping? Rise up and cry out to your god!" Like God, he urges Jonah to *cry out*—as his sailors have already done. Jonah's stupor begins, then, as an escape from the common human fear; he alone sleeps instead of *crying out*, as God and common sense require him to do. His flight takes on an aspect of withdrawal from himself, from his own voice, his own depths.

If his flight is downward, into the depths of the ship, the depths of the sea, these fail to achieve metaphorical resonance. Unlike the Psalmist, who uses the depths of the sea as a metaphor for his spiritual anguish,[12] Jonah plumbs literal depths without touching any chord of mystery in his soul. Even after the captain's reproach, he is unable to find his voice, his personal expression of fear. In a sense, he sleepwalks his way through the adventures of his life.

The captain's words are amplified in *Pirkei de-Rabbi Eliezer*, 10:

> They cried out each to his god to no avail. Jonah, in the anguish of his soul, sank into a sound sleep. The captain of the ship came to him and said, "Behold, we are standing between death and life, and you are sound asleep!"

The captain expresses the existential plight of those who *stand between death and life*. Uneasily straddling death and life, the sailors *stand* and *cry*. Jonah escapes into a stupefied sleep.

Here, the midrash registers the core of Jonah's flight. To flee from God is to refuse to stand between death and life; it is to refuse to cry out from that standing place. The opposite of the flight from God is, in a word, prayer. Or, to stand one's ground in the human place between death and life is, in itself, to cry out. Standing—*amidah*—is the essential posture of prayer. Standing in the king's presence sustains an intimate attentiveness that is not exhausted by the formal words of prayer. This posture is, for Jonah, untenable, perhaps unbearable, so that he sinks into unconsciousness, suppressing the human cry.

The sailors cry out of fear (Jon. 1:5), which intensifies into a *great fear* (1:10), when they realize that he is fleeing from God, whom, as he himself acknowledges, he fears: the God "who made the sea and the dry land" (1:9). In other words, the sailors fear the consequences of his flight: it is not absurd but disastrous. The God whose power extends even into the sea—the place of inhuman mystery where all human perspectives fail—will not allow Jonah to evade Him. Jonah becomes the object of their appalled wonder. Dissociated from his own fear, he refuses to stand in that place and cry out. Sleep and silence are his flight response, his immediate refuge from his fear. In a sense, God's call to him to cry out represents a terror that he must immediately evade.

To flee, then, is the opposite of *to stand*. Cain, who "leaves the presence of God" after killing his brother, Abel, protests against God's punishment: "You have banished me this day from the land, and I must be hidden from Your presence and become a fugitive and a wanderer on earth" (Gen. 4:14). Ramban comments: "Since I will be a fugitive and a wanderer and unable to *stand in one place,* behold I am banished from the land: there is no place where I can find rest. 'And I must be hidden from Your presence,' since I will not be able to *stand before You to pray*" (4:13). Here, Cain's greatest fear is of losing the possibility of prayer, which depends on being able to stand in one place.

Elijah's first words describe his relationship to God: "As the Lord God of Israel lives, *before whom I stand*" (1 Kings 17:1). An attitude of alert responsiveness marks this stance: "Man in his wholeness wholly attending" (D. H. Lawrence). For Cain, to be unable to find a stable place on earth from which to pray to God is, essentially, to be cast out, denied the pivotal spot between death and life: "Anyone who finds me will kill me." For Jonah, to evade that place is to deny his vulnerability, to prefer death—the foregone conclusion—to the anguish of the human place *between.* "The heart of standing," writes William Empsom, "is you cannot fly." But Jonah, the "dove," flies, he flees; he is *pore'ach, bore'ach.* Fear leads him to deny his own fear.

He chooses death. When he turns to the sea, he turns toward death. In the words of the Mechilta: "Jonah went to sea only so as to perish [lit., *lose himself*] at sea." The sea is the place where human beings can find no earthly foundation for their perspectives:

> it is human nature to stand in the middle of a thing,
> but you cannot stand in the middle of this;
> the sea has nothing to give but a well excavated grave.
> . . .
> [it] advances as usual, looking as if it were not that ocean in
>   which dropped things are bound to sink—
> in which if they turn and twist, it is neither with volition
>   nor consciousness.
>
> Marianne Moore, "A Grave"[13]

In the sea, human beings act "as if there were no such thing as death," as if they were "in some sense dead to the mortality that defines their condition."[14] Jonah urges the sailors to throw him into the sea, into that condition of unconsciousness. On one level, he displays courage and willingness to die in order to save others. But, on another level, his real desire emerges here—to die, to sleep a dreamless sleep.

WHERE SHALL I FLEE FROM YOUR FACE?

"You cannot stand in the middle of this": Jonah's flight from God represents an evasion of standing. *"The heart of standing is you cannot fly."* But fear and desire are often linked. Adam Phillips describes a state in which "we are pursuing something by running away from it. . . . Once every fear is a wish . . . our fears become the clue to our desires; aversiveness always conceals a lure."[15] Jonah fleeing God is, in some sense, Jonah pursuing God. His fear of the human *standing* is also a fascination.

The Psalmist describes this ambivalence most poignantly:

> You hedge me before and behind;
> You lay Your hand upon me.
> It is beyond my knowledge;
>> it is a mystery; I cannot fathom it.
> Where can I escape from Your spirit?
> Where can I flee from Your presence?
> If I ascend to heaven, You are there;
>> If I descend to Sheol, You are there too.
> If I take wing with the dawn
>> To come to rest on the western horizon,
>>> even there Your hand will be guiding me,
>> Your right hand will be holding me fast.
> If I say, "Surely darkness will conceal me,
>> night will provide me with cover,"
>>> darkness is not dark for You;
>> night is as light as day;
>> darkness and light are the same.
> It was You who created my kidneys;
>> You fashioned me in my mother's womb.
> I praise You,

For I am fearfully, wondrously made;
Your work is wonderful;
I know it very well.

(Ps. 139:5–14)

This psalm is cited by the Mechilta, among many other proof texts, as evidence of the absurdity of the very notion of fleeing from God. "Could he possibly have intended to flee from God? Has it not been said, 'Where shall I escape from Your spirit . . . ?' "[16] The biblical culture in which Jonah lives makes such a notion nonsensical. So impregnable is this theological premise that the Mechilta feels compelled to narrow its focus: it is specifically the prophetic role that Jonah is escaping. Whether or not one finds this solution plausible, the problem that the Mechilta stages is certainly compelling: in a culture in which every schoolchild learns texts preaching that God is omnipresent, how can Jonah even think of escaping Him?

Yet Psalm 139 presents the Psalmist himself—and not some benighted pagan—as attempting to do just that. The energy of his desire to escape is palpable, even as it is thwarted at every turn. He tries every direction of evasion, heaven and hell, sea and land. Mythic opposites draw him, in experience or in imagination, to elude the God who, mysteriously, turns out to be holding his hand, leading him in his very evasion. Ultimately, the primal imagery of flight through space yields to the imagery of interiority: darkness fails to hide him from God's eyes; God knew him before he knew himself; God's consciousness filled his mother's womb, shaping his protoplasm into himself.

Such a God is inescapable: the Psalmist knows this precisely because he desires and attempts to escape. This is the knowledge of one who has allowed himself the full range of his imagination. And his response to finding God precisely where he thought to elude Him is fraught with ambivalence. He feels hedged, besieged; as fast as he moves, God, like a shadow, moves with him. If the theological conclusion is impeccable—one cannot flee from God—its power derives from the fact that he does flee, that something human, which is not alien to the Psalmist, compels him to flee. Ultimately, the mystery that baffles him—"It is beyond my knowledge; it is a mystery; I cannot fathom it"—relates to God's incursion into his very being: his privacy, his consciousness of self, his claims to knowledge of himself, are infiltrated by the God he flees.

Emmanuel Levinas reads the psalm as the context for the Talmudic statement: "Two faces did God create in the first man, for is it not written (Ps. 139:5): 'You hedge me before and behind; You lay Your hand upon me.' "[17] Levinas discusses the meaning of "two faces":

> With only a single face, I have a place in the rear of my head, the occiput, in which my hidden thoughts and my mental reservations accumulate. Refuge which can hold my entire thought. But here, instead of the occiput, a second face! Everything is exposed; everything in me confronts [fait face] and must answer. . . . But in this spirited psalm you are discovered with joy; it is the exaltation of divine proximity that this psalm sings: a being exposed without the least hint of shadow.[18]

For Levinas, the emotion of the human being who finds himself exposed, obsessed, totally responsible, is joy, exaltation: this is an "obsession which is experienced as a chosenness." But in celebrating "the end of interiority, the end of the subject," the Psalmist seems to acknowledge his ambivalence. To have two faces is to surrender an important illusion: that one possesses a private self. Repeatedly, he declares, "You know"; "I fail to grasp, to comprehend." The mystery of human origins represents a limit on human self-knowledge: "For God, I was an object, even before I began to think of myself as a subject. And yet *I think of myself as very knowing.*[19] But in relation to myself, my understanding fails." The mystery that obsesses the Psalmist is the mystery of the soul that desires to flee, to be hidden from God's eyes, to be unfound, even as it rejoices in being touched, seen, found.

A similar ambivalence haunts D. W. Winnicott's description of the dilemma of the artist: "the urgent need to communicate and still more urgent need not to be found."[20] In general, Winnicott claims:

> Although healthy persons communicate and enjoy communicating, the other fact is equally true, that *each individual is an isolate, permanently non-communicating, permanently unknown, in*

fact unfound. . . . At the center of each person is an incommunicado element, and this is sacred and most worthy of preserva-
tion.[21]

Winnicott's discussion presents the two dimensions of being
human—the desire to communicate and the "incommunicado
element"—as needs to be equally respected. For Levinas, being found
by God, being totally exposed to His eyes, is a matter for joy, exaltation. But for the Psalmist, a real ambivalence persists. His cry,
"Where shall I flee from Your face?" intimates an inexpressible and
profoundly human dilemma.

ALWAYS ALREADY KNOWING

In his allegorical commentary to Jonah, the Gaon of Vilna recounts
the history of the soul in the world. He sets Jonah's flight in a context
where "everyone flees from God's presence, and is reluctant to *stand
before Him*." Jonah as Everyman is attuned to flight; the human soul
is averse to standing before God. If this is a pathological refusal, it is
a universal pathology. And if it leads to a death that is not conscious
of itself, this, too, is familiar territory.

To flee, to refuse to stand before God, means, then, to evade an
essential uncertainty. From this unbearable place, Jonah flees into a
compulsive *knowingness*. He always *already knows:* there is nothing,
therefore, that can surprise him, throw him back into that uncertainty from which he flees. Even as Jonah asks the sailors to kill him,
he speaks of his *knowledge: ". . .* for I *know* that because of me *[b'sheli]*
this great storm has come upon you" (Jon. 1:12). His knowledge is
accurate—the storm is entirely about him: *b'sheli*, it is his storm. But
this knowledge leads him unequivocally to death, as though that
were the only possible conclusion. This is knowledge to die by, not
to live by. That the storm may abate if he does what God has commanded—if he stops fleeing, if he stands, and cries—this has no
place within his idiom of knowledge. We remember, too, how he
later professes his knowledge of God's ways: "I *knew* that You are a
compassionate and gracious God." Jonah wears his knowledge with
bitterness and cryptic rage, to justify his flight and his death.

In such a condition, knowingness acts as camouflage for fear. A dangerous world between death and life makes him cling to his certainties. The sailors, strikingly, act as a foil for Jonah. They pray to their gods, and urge him to pray to his—but without certainty: *"Perhaps* God will be kind to us and we will not perish" (Jon. 1:6). The future hangs in the balance, and the sailors know they do not know. Similarly, the people of Nineveh repent of their evil ways, demonstratively acting out their contrition. But the king promises them nothing stronger than a *"Who knows?"*: "Who knows but that God may turn and relent? He may turn back from His wrath, so that we do not perish" (3:9). To be or not to be . . . The king knows that he does not know. A sense of mystery, of standing in a Presence, shapes the responses of all the characters in the narrative—of whom God in the end testifies that they *"do not know* the difference between their right hand and their left" (4:11). The only exception is Jonah, whose knowledge remains unshadowed by wonder.

Perhaps is a peculiarly Jewish response to the mystery of God's ways. When Moses strives to atone for his people, he says: *"Perhaps* I will win forgiveness for your sin" (Exod. 32:30). *Who knows?* is also the idiom of the prophet Joel: "Who knows but He may turn and relent?" (Joel 2:14). *Who knows?* speaks of humility and hope, and a sense of the incalculable element in the relation of God and human beings. In the end, forgiveness and survival are a matter of God's *chesed,* a gratuitous gesture that cannot be already known.

Such "dangerous Perhapses," as Nietzsche called them, gather around the standing place from which Jonah flees. They even inform the relations between human beings, who cannot claim to *know* one another. The midrash grounds the sailors' reluctance to throw Jonah overboard in an awareness of this kind: "They took Jonah and they stood on the side of the ship, saying, 'God of the world! Do not lay upon us innocent blood, for *we do not know* the nature of this man.' "[22] Not knowing Jonah, finding him uncanny—strange and familiar at the same time—how can they jump to conclusions about him?

Ultimately, "dangerous Perhapses" inform not only human relations with God and with others but also the relationship with oneself. The enigma of oneself, the "motivated irrationality"[23] with which one may feel and act—this awareness is hard to evade. But

Jonah allows no qualms to trouble his certainties. He seems to find nothing to puzzle him in his own behavior. He already knows the salient facts that endow his acts with sufficient meaning. His flight, his death wish, his anger—none of these rouse him to curiosity about his own soul, its deep currents and crosscurrents.

MYTHS OF KNOWINGNESS

In ignoring unconscious meaning, Jonah resembles Oedipus, whose tragedy, Jonathan Lear suggests, should be read as the "fundamental myth of knowingness." Oedipus's mistake "lies in his assumption that meaning is transparent to human reason."[24] We remember the plot. In horrified response to the Delphic oracle, which dooms him to kill his father and sleep with his mother, Oedipus flees the couple he mistakenly takes to be his parents—even though he has already been sufficiently dubious about their identity to consult the oracle in the first place. Immediately, he kills a man who is old enough to be his father, and whom he resembles; and proceeds to Thebes—a city from which the king has mysteriously disappeared—and marries the possibly widowed queen, a woman old enough to be his mother, a woman who does not know what happened to her husband, and who cannot give a full account of what happened to all of her children. In this way, Oedipus fulfills his fate in the very act of trying to escape it.[25]

Ignoring the inconsistencies and ironies of his own behavior, Oedipus, in Lear's account, "attacks the very idea of unconscious meaning." He prides himself on his conscious reasoning, which saved the city from the Sphinx, and angrily repudiates the prophet Tiresias, who tries to hint at unavowed, obscure meanings. Relying on his mind—"I hit the mark by native wit, not by what I learned from birds"—he achieves worldly success. But the pressure to answer questions, to arrive at a conclusion, ironically prevents him from grasping the full meaning of his own behavior.

The notion of another realm of meaning would require an attitude of wonder, the quality with which, according to Aristotle, philosophy begins. But Oedipus cannot risk the terror of such a response to his reality. Instead, he thinks in terms of riddle-solving, ignoring the problems that cannot be solved in this way. His reason acts as a defense against the nakedness of wonder or awe. "What he doesn't know is that he doesn't know."[26]

Jonah, similarly, does not know the phenomenon of "motivated irrationality" in his own behavior: in his flight from God, in his desire for death that dissolves into joy in the shade of the gourd, in his avoidance of the standing place *between*. . . . Not understanding himself, he yet obeys an internal logic that allows him to persist, without apparent curiosity or conflict. He already knows that the storm is for him, that God is a God of love and forgiveness; but the sinister meanings he gives these perceptions seem to him transparent, inciting him to no further interpretation.

Kierkegaard writes of those "whose misfortune is that they know too much":

> This being the case, the art of *communication* at last becomes the art of *taking away*, of luring something away from someone. . . .
> When a man has his mouth so full that he is prevented from eating, does giving him food consist in stuffing still more of it into his mouth, or does it consist in taking some of it away so that he can begin to eat?[27]

Too much knowledge becomes trivial knowledge, no longer dynamic or transformative. In taking some of it away, the aim is to enable one to eat: to taste, digest, metabolize knowledge. In the end, the self is to return to vigor and to the possibility of transforming itself. In terms of the language of *return*, or *repentance*, which is central to this narrative, Jonah will need to lose some of his knowledge so as to rouse himself to his own distance from God, to his own desire to return.

"Fear," says Adam Phillips, "makes us too clever."[28] Jonah is transfixed by what he already knows; he assumes that the future will be like the past. "In fear the wish for prediction is immediately gratified; *it is as though the certainty—the future—has already happened*"[29] (my emphasis). The nature of Jonah's fear relates, we have suggested, to the perilous standing place in God's presence. He refuses to straddle the conflict of death and life. "The cost of wanting," writes Phillips, "is the terror of losing . . . what you have received. This is what we know in fear."[30] Where trust has failed, knowing becomes essential.

THE FLIGHT FROM PRAYER

The moment when this dynamic becomes most vivid is, paradoxically, when Jonah prays from the belly of the great fish. The paradox, of course, is that Jonah, whom we have described as fleeing the posture of *prayer,* is said to pray *twice* in the course of the narrative. The second time, as we have seen, he prays for death and justifies his flight. The first time, in the belly of the great fish, however, his prayer seems beyond reproach. His language is the classic language of the psalms, speaking of disaster and salvation, of terror and gratitude. He powerfully describes the experience of drowning, of the downward plunge to the depths of the sea, and he thanks God for restoring him to life.

And yet, precisely here lies the bizarre quality of his prayer. As has often been noticed, he prays in the *past tense.* Essentially, this is a psalm of gratitude for past salvations—a strange prayer for one who needs salvation *now.* What is missing is any religious or moral awareness of his situation: he confesses no sin, nor does he pray for forgiveness.[31] The existential terror of his condition remains quite unexpressed in this formulaic prayer of gratitude for past salvation.

In fact, the dissonance has led some scholars to regard this chapter as a later interpolation into the text. Ibn Ezra, on the other hand, regards it as a prophetic prayer, divinely inspired, in which Jonah uses the "prophetic past tense," to express his vision of salvation. This reading seems strained; as Uriel Simon points out, Ibn Ezra himself, in writing a liturgical *piyyut* for Yom Kippur, based on this prayer, adopts the future tense as the natural vehicle for prayer. Similarly, Midrash Yonah inflects Jonah's prayer in the future tense.

I suggest that the dissonance between Jonah's perilous situation and his prayer of gratitude sheds a stark light on the character of Jonah and of his flight. One who stands between death and life, cry-

ing out to God, will confess, entreat forgiveness, pray for salvation
from the terror of now and here. But this standing place is closed to
Jonah. Instead, he flees to the past moment of salvation, to a gratitude already experienced, as though the future were already secured.
What he cannot encompass is the transitional moment of danger
and desire, when one is lost, the future obscure. The experience
of *not knowing,* of being *at sea, at one's wits' end* is too terrible to
bear.[32] Inevitably, his flight generates a spurious confidence and
gratitude.

Essentially, Jonah's prayer is not a prayer at all. The core of prayer
is wishing, asking for the fulfillment of one's needs.[33] This is beyond
Jonah's capacity. In this sense, he utters a kind of anti-prayer, knowing, derivative, emotionally plagiarist. Albert Hutter's remark seems
apposite:

> Every time we face a blank page . . . the page mirrors our own
> blankness, our emptiness. There is nothing left to say. Filling up
> that page requires a certain kind of courage . . . because beyond
> any immediate criticism there is always, I believe, a more fun-
> damental fear that if the criticism goes far enough or deep
> enough it will uncover a vacuum. One way to protect ourselves
> from such a revelation is to hide behind someone else's words.

The emotional plagiarist is thus one who assumes a false identity,
substituting what is felt to be someone else's more authentic experience for one's own fragmented sense of self.[34] In this sense, Jonah
uses borrowed words to express a classic stance of gratitude, instead
of speaking, or crying, out of his own unresolved situation of terror.
The fear of his own blankness aborts his voice.

It is ironic, then, that in both cases where the text describes Jonah
as praying, his words constitute a kind of attack on the possibility of
prayer. One midrash gives a poignant, even a humorous account of
Jonah's struggle to pray. In the belly of the great fish, Jonah is taken
on a tour of the seabed:

> He showed him the Foundation Stone *[Even Shetiyah]* of the
> Temple, fixed in the depths under God's temple. He saw there

the sons of Korah standing and praying over it. The fish said to him, "Jonah, here you are standing beneath God's temple—pray, and you will be answered!" Jonah answered, "Stand in your standing place, for I wish to pray!" The fish stood still, and Jonah began to pray in the presence of God: "Sovereign of the Universe! You are called 'The One who casts down and raises up': I am cast down—raise me up! You are called, 'The One who deals death and gives life': my soul has reached death—restore me to life!" But he was not answered, until this phrase issued from his mouth: "What I have vowed I will fulfill!"[35]

The scene is tailored to his needs: here are the *depths* that run beneath the Temple, populated by those who *stand and pray*. The fish suggests that this might be an appropriate place and time to pray— that is, to cry out from his depths. Jonah requires the fish to *stand still*, so as to position him for prayer. But his prayer does not arise from his own depths, it depends on the initiative of the fish—and it emerges hidden in the words of others, framed in theological terms ("You are called the one who casts down and raises up").

These words are from Hannah's song of gratitude when her prayer for a child is answered.[36] This song is called a prayer, but Hannah's true prayer was her original anguished cry, so unknowing that the High Priest accused her of being drunk. She defended herself by describing the passion of prayer: "I have been pouring out my heart to God. . . . I have only been speaking all this time out of my great anguish and distress" (1 Sam. 1:15–16). The true prayer, the cry from the depths of pain and perplexity, unnerves even the High Priest. It is, then, ironic that when Jonah quotes Hannah, it is not her unguarded plea that he quotes but her later song of triumph. Essentially, he is exploiting her resolved situation to give him borrowed assurance in his unresolved one. His prayer becomes an act of emotional plagiarism, covering an emptiness.

Only when he utters a vow, at the end of his prayer, is he answered: here, he speaks out of his own being, committing himself to the future—"What I have vowed I will fulfill." This is the one authentic moment in which his voice can be heard. Perhaps, the midrash suggests, it is this moment alone that justifies the claim that

Jonah *prayed:* here, he returns to the earlier moment of Hannah's passionate prayer, when she, too, made a vow.

To take the risk of a vow is to confront the uncertainties of the future. A powerful midrash listens closely to Hannah's vow:

> "And she vowed a vow and she said, O Lord of Hosts *[Tz'vaot]*" (1 Sam. 1:11). R. Eleazar said: From the day that God created His world, there was no one who called Him *Tz'vaot* [Hosts], until Hannah came and called Him *Tz'vaot*. Hannah said to God: Sovereign of the Universe, of all the hosts and hosts that You have created in Your world, does it seem so hard for You to give me one son? A parable: What is this like? A king who made a feast for his servants and a poor man came and stood by the door and said, Give me a bite! But no one took any notice of him. So he forced his way into the presence of the king and said, Your Majesty, out of this whole feast that you have made, does it seem to you so hard to give me one bite?[37]

The midrash celebrates Hannah's unprecedented courage in calling God the God of Hosts. Her anguished need does not impoverish her imagination: she can still vividly imagine God's plenitude. In this sense, she straddles her own poverty and God's wealth and finds a place to stand and cry out. Her prayer creates a completely personal standing place, original, as she is original.

Jonah's vow, however, has none of this urgent quality. Where she offers her unborn son to God's service, his vow remains unspecified. Even when he vows, he is not original, since the sailors have already set a precedent for this as a conventional religious response to trouble. And the main body of his prayer is in the past tense, in flight from his situation between death and life. His fear jolts him into a premature future, so that a narrative of gratitude camouflages the anguish of the present moment.

THE TRAUMA OF SURVIVAL

The history of his fear becomes more intelligible in the light of a haunting midrashic suggestion about Jonah's identity. He is identified with the child whom Elijah saved, revived from the dead in 1 Kings 17. This is another story about a mother, a child, and prayer. It is a time of famine, and the child's mother, a widow in Zarefat, has nothing but one jar of flour and one flask of oil, when Elijah arrives. He demands that she "fear not," but provide him with a meal. Having demonstrated her faith in this way, she is rewarded when the flour and oil feed her household for many days. Later, her son dies, and Elijah prays for him to return to life. This child, claims the midrashic tradition, is Jonah, for whom biographical details are so lacking.

This claim appears in several midrashic sources,[38] and, strikingly, in Don Isaac Abarbanel's commentary on Jonah's prayer. Here, it is used to justify Jonah's past-tense prayer of gratitude: when he says, "From the belly of Sheol I cried out, and You heard my voice," (Jon. 2:3), Jonah is speaking of his own death and resurrection. He is one who has survived his own death. Indeed, the Zohar refers to Jonah's double experience of resurrection in the more immediate past: thrown into the sea, his soul left him—that is, he died—and he was restored to life when the fish swallowed him. Inside the fish, too, he dies again, is carried to the seabed, prays, and is restored to life.[39] In these midrashic narratives, serial experiences of death and resurrection constitute Jonah's history. If Jonah is, in some sense, Everyman, radical human questions about death and life are intimated in these narratives.

What does it mean to survive? What does this tradition intimate in identifying Jonah with that nameless child? And in repeating the theme of resurrection in his present experience?

Elijah's miracle with the flour and the oil is related to an act of *chesed,* of faith and gratuitous generosity by the widow. Her last cake before she and her son die is shared with Elijah. The child dies and his mother bitterly implies that Elijah's presence has caused his death. In a general context of drought and death—first proclaimed by Elijah himself, to express God's displeasure with Ahab, the sinful king of Israel—the possibility of a miracle is engulfed in the reality of mass starvation. But the miracle happens, twice—once to the food and once to the child, once after the widow's act of *chesed,* and once when bitterness has largely eroded, for both the widow and Elijah, the sense of possibility.

To be the child saved from death in such a dire context is to know resurrection as trauma. When God restores the child to life, the pure *chesed* of this gesture runs counter to the fatality of the time. Like the miraculous abundance of flour and oil, the child's resurrection depends on a gratuitous, apparently arbitrary intervention. This child knows himself to be, in some sense, like flour and oil: without any way of comprehending the violent intrusion into the continuity of his life.

The relation between survival and trauma is illuminatingly discussed by Cathy Caruth:

> What Freud encounters in the traumatic neurosis is not the reaction to any horrible event but, rather, the peculiar and perplexing experience of survival. . . . What causes trauma, then, is a shock that appears to work very much like a bodily threat, but is in fact a break in the mind's experience of time. . . . The shock of the mind's relation to the threat of death is thus not the direct experience of the threat, but precisely the *missing* of this experience, the fact that, not being experienced *in time,* it has not yet been fully known. . . . It is because the mind cannot confront the possibility of its death directly that survival becomes for the human being, paradoxically, an endless testimony to the impossibility of living.
>
> From this perspective the survival of trauma is more than the fortunate passage past a violent event . . . but rather the endless *inherent necessity* of repetition. . . . What is enigmatically suggested, that is, is that the trauma consists not only in having confronted death, but in *having survived precisely, without knowing it.*[40]

In terms of Caruth's model, Jonah's fear is the consequence of having missed, not only his own death, but his survival, his return to life. The midrashic history of his origins yields a Jonah who is an object of God's *chesed,* who experiences himself as repeatedly attempting to reclaim his own survival. The gap in his consciousness leaves him allergic to reminders of his human vulnerability, allergic, we may say, to fear. His flight from fear may read like a reflex response to God's command, but it represents an elaborate and obscure history. At the core, there is a desire to stand in God's presence, to bear the enigma of his own death and resurrection: in other words, to trust sufficiently to *be* in the space between death and life.

The enigma of his own survival continually returns. "Not having been fully integrated, the event cannot become . . . a 'narrative memory' that is integrated into a completed story of the past."[41] It is thus traumatically reenacted because it has eluded comprehension. Jonah protects himself against the place where understanding breaks down. The "platitudes of knowledge,"[42] in Caruth's phrase, defend him from the terrifying space where he might speak what cannot yet be understood.

I suggest that Jonah's identity as the child restored to life in a time of drought allows us access to one of the paradoxes of *chesed* (grace). From the viewpoint of the child, both death, the arbitrary withdrawal of life, and survival, its arbitrary gift, are equally traumatic. Both inflict the shock of incomprehensibility; both testify to the impossibility of living.[43] An anger, which expresses itself as an engulfing sadness, makes the child flee—and desire—the reenactment of the original shock. It returns, in dreams, flashbacks, in a great storm at sea, and in the belly of a great fish.[44]

The midrashic narrative of origins lends a psychoanalytic dimension to the portrait of Jonah. Everyman as infant has experienced repeated endings of consciousness. Engendered in his mother's womb, he stirred unknowingly into life. "For every illumination in an infant's life," writes Christopher Bollas, "there are long periods of sleep and darkness . . . we are forever fated to live in recurring darkness, our livings ended for a moment." Even the Psalmist is troubled by the darkness in which he is seen by God's eye alone. Some can engage in "generative interplay between life and death, between origins and endings, between absolute dark and enlightenment."[45] Others are engulfed in terror at the loss of self; they cannot tolerate the incomprehensible fact of "being chosen for a future that remains . . . yet to be understood."[46]

· · ·

THE THERAPEUTIC QUESTION

Finally, Jonah confronts God in all his inward "great evil." He is angry; vindicating his flight from God and his sterile deathly knowledge of His *chesed*, he prays his anti-prayer—"Please take my life from me, for my death is better than my life." It is not of life and death that he speaks, but of *his* life, *his* death. Unlike the philosopher in Ecclesiastes 7:1, who declares: "Better is a good name than good oil, and better is the day of death than the day of birth," Jonah is not meditating on the paradoxes of origins and endings, on the newborn's unknown future as compared to the achieved narrative of the dead.[47] He speaks out of an intimate despair about *his* life.

In a similar vein, Elijah, Jonah's spiritual father, asked to die. ("He prayed that he might die: 'It is enough; now, O God, take my life, for I am not better than my father'" [1 Kings 19:4].) But Elijah's anguish rises from his failure to reform the people, while Jonah's rises enigmatically from the *success* of his mission. Both find the world unintelligible—the dynamics of reward and punishment arbitrary; both are distressed by the failure of reality to meet their own sense of *emet*, of truth, of rational meaning.

In fact, Jonah is introduced as the son of Amittai, which immediately indicates his concern with the issue of *emet*, with truth. And it is significant that when he lists God's attributes, he *omits* the attribute of truth. In the original version of the Thirteen Attributes revealed by God to Moses after the sin of the Golden Calf, *emet* (truth) immediately follows *chesed* (loving-kindness, grace). But Jonah omits truth and emphasizes loving-kindness, in order to protest against what he perceives as God's unwarranted compassion.[48] To him, the survival of Nineveh represents God's arbitrary *chesed*: how can He allow three days of theatrical repentance to outweigh a long and evil history? Acts of *chesed*, unaccountable dispensations, even benign ones, have a traumatic aspect. Significantly, Jonah still hopes for God to revert to the mode of destruction; he leaves the city, and waits under his sukkah "to see what will happen in the city" (Jon. 4:5). Unlike Elijah's despair, his has a personal edge: he hates his own life; from its beginning, it has baffled his comprehension.[49]

God responds to his prayer. For the first time, a dialogue occurs between God and Jonah. In fact, this is a rare phenomenon in the entire biblical narrative: that a human being prays to God, under the rubric of the Hebrew word *va-yitpalel,* and God responds by inviting further dialogue. More typically, prayers do not draw an immediate divine response; they hardly ever open up a dialogue with God. But now, with an astonishing naturalness, God replies to His angry prophet, precisely as he reaffirms his refusal to pray: *"Are you thoroughly angry?"*[50]

God's reply is a question, which goes unanswered. The dialogue breaks off. What answer could God expect to such a question? What kind of question is it? I hear in it a *therapeutic* question, palpating the emotional reality of the human being who is still in flight. Apparently, it is important that Jonah acknowledge his own anger. Unlike the reader, who has been informed by the narrator ("And he was angry" [Jon. 4:1]), Jonah is unconscious of the nature of the "great evil" that possesses him.

In order that he may claim his own experience, God stages a drama of life and death. Gratuitously, the gourd appears—and disappears. It both gives him shade *(tzel)* for his head and *saves (lehatzil)* him from *his evil,* from the malaise, the dejection that engulfs him *(lehatzil lo me-ra'ato).* Subtly, something shifts in Jonah's consciousness. The story manifests itself to him in terms of felt experience: *his* storm, *his* death and *his* life, *his* evil. For the first time, they are incorporated in him, he has received their force, they have altered his structure of feeling. Suddenly, unaccountably, the "great evil" is transformed into "great joy." And, equally unaccountably, the worm and the east wind wither the gourd—and his joy—and he reverts to his death wish: "He begged that he might die, saying, 'Better for me to die than to live.' " Strikingly, he addresses his own soul *(et nafsho),* his life, rather than God. He wishes, rather than prays.

In this intimate drama, God stages the life and death of a nondescript plant in such a way that Jonah becomes aware of the quick succession of intense feelings. His great joy, his physical relief, which is also metaphysical release, comes as a surprise; unbidden, it comes, and goes. And, like a psychoanalyst, God repeats His question. This time, the narrator assumes a more formal, grave tone: "And God said *to Jonah,* 'Are you thoroughly angry *about the gourd?*' "

(Jon. 4:9). Jonah's voice had fallen inward, into soliloquy. Now, God re-calls him to dialogue, shaping His question so as to focus on the gourd that was and is not. This time, he will answer and he will speak his truth to God: "I am angry to death!"

CRYING FROM THE DEPTHS

Something has been put on display between Jonah and God: a deathly anger that belongs to the space between them. Unawares, Jonah has been caught oscillating between intense joy and a dejection that is anger. A gust of his own experience, its conflicting desires, moves him to the depths of his being. Now, for the first time, he can be said to *have* depths to his being. His body knows the intensity of human need; his mind makes no attempt to make sense of the enigma. God asks cryptic questions that turn Jonah's attention to himself—and so to God.

> "Are you thoroughly angry about the gourd?" . . . "You pitied the gourd, which you did not work for and which you did not grow, which appeared overnight and perished overnight. And should I not pity Nineveh, the great city, in which there are more than a hundred thousand human beings who do not know their right hand from their left, and many cattle?" (Jon. 4:9–11)

God's last word is a question, which leaves the enigmas of the narrative—the enigma of Jonah—unresolved. Outside the frame of the narrative, Jonah must answer. But the suspended question lodges in the reader. To call it a rhetorical question is to beg the question. What is the force of God's final words that seem to offer resolution, even as they withhold it?

Seemingly ignoring Jonah's desire to die, his intensely felt anger, God speaks instead of *pity*: "You *pitied* the gourd . . . should I not *pity* Nineveh. . . ." But the Hebrew word translated as pity—*chasta*—more accurately means concern, appreciation for an object that might otherwise be overlooked. This is the feeling that links God and Jonah, as God reflects on the objects of their concern—Nineveh and the gourd. Jonah valued the gourd and deplored its extinction; its life in the world had laid its claim on him—even though it came and went like a mirage, without his effort. On the basis of Jonah's experience, God stages His reluctance to destroy Nineveh. He leaves unsaid the obvious grounds of analogy and difference: He created the city, and therefore He values it; and it has existed from the beginning of history, unlike the volatile gourd. Instead, God specifies the large population of the city, "who do not know the difference between their right hand and their left, and many cattle."

In other words, there is a dimension of God's relation to the world that, like Jonah's affirmation of the gourd, is a matter of feeling, of value for life, whether human or animal. While at first it seems that God forgives the population of the wicked city because of their repentance, now God tells a more intimate story, of generous compassion for their vulnerability, of a strange appreciation for their very ignorance, for their animal entreaty for life. All this cannot be rationalized into a system. God's feeling, like all feeling, is mysterious.

And all this is not a declaration, a divine manifesto. It is framed as a question, directed at Jonah. Almost as if He were pleading with Jonah to accept an imaginative possibility that transcends his understanding, God presses the claims of those who require *chesed* in order to survive. The slender basis on which Jonah may lend himself to God's feeling is his own fleeting intensity of need. Knowing himself suddenly in the mode of creaturely dependence, he finds himself standing in God's presence, even as he speaks of anger and death. Fully present to his own lack, he cries out. Perhaps, for a moment, he trusts his experience in God's presence enough not to need to already know its meaning.

The posture of standing-before-God that is prayer, writes R. Yitzhak Hutner,[51] is a state that remains unbroken even after the words have ceased. It is a posture of intimacy with God that ends only when one moves one's feet and withdraws[52]—"like a student who separates from his teacher."[53] For this reason, one who travels far to reach a synagogue, even though there is another closer at hand, receives reward:[54] the journey is not simply a means to fulfilling the mitzvah of prayer, it is itself part of the process of growing intimacy, of approaching God.

The traveler is *drawn* toward God, writes Maharal (R. Judah Loew ben Bezalel).[55] The force that draws one is the very heart of prayer: need, wish, desire, the human emptiness that yearns to be filled. The Talmud calls prayer *chayei sha'ah*[56]—the expression of human life in time, with all its contingencies of need. Whether one prays for sustenance, health, family, or forgiveness, it is precisely the experience of *chisaron*—of lack—that draws one into the vulnerable place of standing and asking. Although formal prayer begins with praise and ends with thanks, the essence of prayer is asking for the fulfillment of one's needs.[57] So much so, writes R. Hutner, that one who lacks nothing is by that fact barred from prayer. "The heart of standing is you cannot fly." The power of need, poverty, lack, is to create a space of dynamic intimacy with God. The emptiness is transformed into a vessel for receiving what still transcends one's grasp.

In this sense, Jonah does in the end stand before God. His flight had been an act of dislocation, repudiating his human vulnerability. But precisely in his most withdrawn moment, speaking to himself of death, he encounters God. Like the Psalmist who, in baffled joy, finds God at the poles of the world, holding his hand, leading him, finding him, Jonah is claimed by God in the open wound of anger, grief, and death. All knowing fails, as he names his deepest, most hollow place.

"From the depths, I have called you, O God!" (Ps. 130:1). These are the inner depths that God desires: hard to reach, obscure, alive with currents and crosscurrents. Crying from this place of reality, man transforms pain into intimacy with God. From the depths of his heart, Jonah cries to God of his dis-ease. God answers him with a question, which gives Jonah back the last word. Can he allow God to value life, to act in *chesed*? Can he lend himself to the glimmer of imaginative meaning that God offers him? Can he, standing between death and life, sustain the depth of need and entreaty that opens within him?

God's question, rhetorical as it may be, penetrates and disturbs. He is, in a sense, asking Jonah to be the artist who, in Keats's words, "is capable of being in uncertainties, mysteries, doubts, without any irritable reaching after fact and reason."[58] This "Negative Capability" is not a passive stance, but an exquisitely attentive one. The enigmas that enrage and sadden Jonah are not riddles to be solved. They remain; God invites Jonah to bear them, even to deepen them, and to allow new perceptions to emerge unbidden. In a word, to stand and pray.

Who is the one who must ask? It is man, for he alone is capable of asking. Man asks—and it is for this reason that his lips have been unsealed. . . .

To ask, to pray, is the most human of acts. Even man's silence may entreat; and mute nature acquires speech when it supplicates—as in the case of the silent eyes of an animal. Prayer awakens the man in man. A child demands with his first word. And the first word from him who awakens from the slumber of childhood is also a request, a prayer. . . .

In his prayers he is alone, a solitary human. "Help me, O Lord, for the waters have risen to my throat." "My God, my God, why hast Thou forsaken me?" But as he offers thanks, he goes forward to the whole world. The world must acquire the power of speech to include him. "Let everything that breathes, praise the Lord." "To Thee silence is praise." The silent world praises and thanks God; man mingles his praises with its. *As he gives thanks he becomes part of the world. But if man only thanked, he would be swallowed up by the world; he would cease to be man. His voice would be barely audible in the chorus of praise sung by the world. But man is not swallowed up; he is confronted by his need again and again* [emphasis added].[59]

FOUR

Esther

"Mere Anarchy Is Loosed upon the World"

Turning and turning in the widening gyre
The falcon cannot hear the falconer;
Things fall apart; the centre cannot hold;
Mere anarchy is loosed upon the world
                W. B. Yeats, "The Second Coming"

IN AN ESSAY *written to accompany the prayer book,* Machzor Wolfsberg, *published by Yad Vashem, David Weiss Halivni remembers the prayer service in the Wolfsberg labor camp Rosh Hashanah, 1944. The service was led by the Satmar chazan Naftali Stern; he prepared for it by transcribing the prayers from memory onto "paper torn from cement bags that I purchased . . . in exchange for bread."¹ This was the only time that the inmates were ever permitted to pray in public. Halivni, then a young man of sixteen, heard one prayer as unique to the incomparable conditions of the time and place. "There is no time," he writes, "without someone who prays." Which particular prayer expressed most profoundly the longing of the inmates to overcome the forces arrayed against them? "They found such a prayer in the prayer . . . 'Our God and God of our ancestors, reign over all the world in your full glory. . . .' In this prayer, which belongs to the Amidah for Rosh Hashanah, we ask God to reign alone, to take the reins in his hands and not allow these satanic forces to prevail."²*

AFTER A SCHOLARLY and passionate discussion of the Jewish theology of evil, Halivni concludes that through this prayer, "Reign over all the world," the prisoners perceived the "incomprehensible evil that happened as the consequence of the Holy One's abdicating His rule, transferring the reins of government into the cruel hands of bloodsuckers, and of His own decision not to intervene against them but to grant them unlimited authority. Against them, they prayed, 'Rule over all the world in Your full glory. . . .' And they said: . . . Remove this power from them and punish them according to their deeds, and then, 'Every soul will say "The Lord God of Israel is King and His dominion" '—the right and true one—' "rules over all." ' "

Halivni poignantly ends with a personal memory. On the point of being beaten by an enraged SS trooper, the terrified young prisoner pleaded in German, " 'Herr Ubersturmfuhrer, Merciful One' *[ha-rachamim]. And I escaped by the skin of my teeth.*" Now, he grieves daily for having used this holy word—which applies only to God—to pray for mercy from this villain: "I simply knew no other words of entreaty. I drew them from the prayer book and translated them directly into German. Perhaps, subconsciously, I thought of the SS, as it were, as a God. They ruled over the camp with absolute authority; life and death—literally—remained in their hands, and I unconsciously used an expression appropriate to God."[3]

THE HIDDEN FACE OF GOD

In Halivni's account, Rosh Hashanah in Wolfsberg becomes a cry of protest at God's withdrawal from the world. The tragedy of the individual and the nation is set in the context of a cosmic drama. The theology of *tzimtzum*[4] expresses the idea that there are times when God withdraws His power from the world, allowing human beings complete autonomy. In order that the conflicting values of divine presence and human free will maintain equilibrium, cosmic adjustments have to be made. Therefore, a certain "vacuum" *(chillel rek)* is continually regenerated, creating space for free will. In the Nazi period, God withdrew in this way, and the reins of government were seized by totalitarian forces. The experience of the victims was of a world given over to powers of unprecedented evil. Their essential prayer, then, was for God to reassume the reins: "Rule over all the world, in your full glory."

Halivni prefers the concept of God's withdrawal to the more usual concept of His "hiding His face" *(hester panim)*, since the latter expression is associated with the notion of sin and punishment,[5] which it has been the purpose of his essay to reject.

While appreciating Halivni's sensitivity to this expression, I would like to suggest that "hiding His face" sometimes describes precisely the condition that Halivni is discussing. In Psalms 44:25, for example, we read: 'Why do You hide Your face, ignoring our affliction and distress?" Here, the Psalmist cries out to God in protest for hiding His face, for ignoring (forgetting) the atrocious sufferings of His people. Here, there is no sin, only bewildered loss of relationship.

"Why . . . ?" cries the Psalmist, unanswered, and expecting no answer. A time has come when human sin is no longer the justification for God's apparent abandonment. Without such an explanatory framework, the Psalmist addresses God in baffled longing.

As total destruction threatens her people, Esther prepares her strategy. Is prayer part of her preparations? Scanning the surface of the text, we find not one prayer. Is her time, then, that exceptional time in which no one prays?[6] Against the evidence of the text, however, the midrash affirms that Esther did cry out to God, like the Jews at Wolfsberg, in protest at the mere anarchy that had been loosed upon her world. As she stands in the presence of the king, with her fate and that of her people hanging in the balance, she prays the words of Psalm 22: "My God, My God, Why have You abandoned me?" Again, the "Why . . . ?" that is unanswered, and expects no answer: not a prayer for immediate salvation, but a longing that God reassume the government of an unruly world.

In other words, apparently Esther does not pray. Only in the depths of her being does she cry out to God. It is the midrash that gives voice to this voice of Esther, barely audible even to herself. Who, then, is Esther, in the midrashic perception? What does such a secret prayer represent?

A different but related question is asked in *Hullin* 139b: "Where is Esther indicated in the Torah? R. Matan replied: 'Then I will indeed hide My face [*haster astir*] on that day. . . .' "[7] The word-play (*haster astir*/Esther) defines Esther and her world as embodying the terror foreshadowed in the biblical verse: in her time, God hides His face. God is absent, occluded from her world, as His name is, in fact, absent from her text. This salient feature of the book of Esther holds dark implications; without God's name, both text and world lose meaning, legibility. Chaos is come again. What Nietzsche described as the death of God is intimated in this Rabbinic reading of the Scroll of Esther. To add force to their observation, the Rabbis ground it in a biblical verse that predicts just such a historical moment: "Then, I will indeed hide My face."

MERE ANARCHY IS LOOSED UPON THE WORLD

In marrying Ahasuerus, Esther comes to be queen of a world empire, encompassing 127 states, ranging from India to Ethiopia. This means a position of dazzling and effective power. For Persia commands enormous wealth as well as the technical means to promulgate the king's decrees to the furthest reaches of the empire. Its information and communication systems feature prominently in the narrative, which speaks, in exotically Persian or pseudo-Persian terms, of couriers and "runners" who publish the king's decrees throughout the realm. Written edicts, texts in which the royal will is inscribed, are a central feature of this culture: in this way, both the destruction of the Jews and the later edicts that give license to these same Jews to defend themselves are effectively promulgated. Carried posthaste by riders and runners, these texts—books, scripts, edicts—are disseminated to their many destinations.

The actual workings of this elaborate textual system, however, are shown, at significant moments, to be almost comically ineffective. The plot against the king's life, for example, is foiled only because Mordecai overhears the plotters' conversation.[8] By such makeshift means, the king is saved, where his elaborate intelligence system fails to protect him. Ironically, however, the event is written down in the royal chronicles—and promptly buried in the archives. The written text secures the event, stores it for the future—but, at least in the short term, condemns it to oblivion. The result is that when, immediately after this, the king needs a new grand vizier, the obvious candidate for promotion, Mordecai, is overlooked and Haman, for no apparent reason, is appointed. The advanced technological systems of this empire come to seem a facade for an essential anarchy.

The king's first edict exposes to mockery his use of written texts to promulgate his will. He rules that "all wives will treat their husbands with respect, high and low alike . . . and each man shall wield authority in his home and speak the language of his own people" (Esther 1:20, 22). Vashti's exemplary punishment for disobeying the king—the act that opens the narrative and sets its tone—allows him to flex his royal muscles, activate his couriers, and evacuate his anger. Its totalitarian pomposity broadcasts the king's insecurity and the absurdity of his conception of what law can accomplish.

Like Kafka's couriers, indeed, Ahasuerus's carry messages that become meaningless, sometimes even before they leave their point of origin:

> They were offered the choice between becoming kings or the couriers of kings. The way children would, they all wanted to be couriers. Therefore there are only couriers who hurry about the world, shouting to each other—since there are no kings— messages that have become meaningless.[9]

Here, too, there is, effectively, no king. Subject to whims, to spasms of anger and desire, Ahasuerus never issues an edict that has not been directly suggested to him by an adviser, whether Memuchan, or Haman, or Esther. Variously described in the midrash as a "foolish king" and as a "volatile king,"[10] he is a lord of misrule, tricked out in the panoply of majesty. Essentially, no king at all. His ostentatious banquets, grotesquely extended through time (180 days), are "to show" a splendor and glory that lacks substance. Visual beauty is to indicate royal prestige, in the same way as the written text indicates a royal power that proves to be meaningless. From his original summons of Vashti, calculated to impress his subjects with the beauty of a trophy queen, to the lavish show of robes and vessels, all is designed to make a symbolic claim to royal stature. According to one midrashic tradition, indeed, he has usurped the throne, on which he sits rather tentatively: a throne that is a replica of the throne of King Solomon, which he coveted during the sack of Jerusalem.[11]

Weak, volatile, invested in the structures and technologies of power, Ahasuerus stands at the center of a world in which God's face is hidden and His name is absent. The Jewish exile in such a world has been foreshadowed in the biblical text and in its midrashic reading. Instead of God there are the meaningless maniacal gestures of a fool. To pander to him, his ministers wield a totalitarian language: "Not only against the king did Vashti sin but also against *all* the officials and against *all* the peoples in *all* the provinces of King Ahasuerus. For the queen's behavior will make *all* wives despise their husbands" (Esther 1:16–17). The pseudolegal language, free of exceptions, is then transferred to the king's love of Esther "more than *all* the other women, and she won his grace and favor more than *all* the virgins" (2:17); and to Haman's inability to limit his anger to Mordecai alone: "He disdained to lay hands on Mordecai alone . . . but he plotted to do away with *all* the Jews" (3:6). The infantile totality of this destructive frenzy—"to destroy, to kill, to annihilate *all* the Jews, young and old, children and women, in one day" (3:13)—comes to its climax when he boasts to his family about "*all* his wealth and power": "But *all* this means nothing to me every time I see that Jew Mordecai sitting at the palace gate" (5:13).

Bombastic rhetoric and passive verbs replace the measured, effective, and responsible exercise of power that, in a traditional symbolic universe, makes the king a representative of order, of God Himself, in the social and political world. A Jewish custom inscribes the words "the King" at the head of every column of the scroll on which this narrative is traditionally written. In other words, the writing of the scroll is designed so that the reader is constantly reminded of kingship, of order and meaning. But the effect is largely satirical since the vapid reality of this king mocks the visual claim of the text.

AN ILLEGIBLE WORLD

The narrative itself is also infected by the eclipse of meaning. Toward the end of the book, the institution of Purim is legislated by Mordecai, together with a summary of the story:

Therefore, these days were named Purim, after pur—lots. In view, then, of all the instructions in this letter and of what they had experienced in that matter and what had befallen them, the

Jews undertook and irrevocably obligated themselves and their descendants, and all who might join them, to observe these two days in the manner prescribed and at the proper time each year. (Esther 9:26–27)

These rather convoluted verses are interpreted by Rashi:

"What they had experienced" [lit., "what they had seen"]: What were the motives of the characters in the narrative for the things they did? What was Ahasuerus's motive in making use of the Holy Vessels, and what had befallen them when Satan danced among them, and he killed Vashti? What was Haman's motive for being jealous of Mordecai; and what had befallen him that he and sons were hanged? What was Mordecai's motive for refusing to bow to Haman? What was Esther's motive for inviting Haman to her banquet?

The four main characters act out of motives that are fully explicated in the text: this is the claim of this verse, according to Rashi. However, Rashi's comments point at precisely the areas where motive is enigmatic. In the case of Ahasuerus's use of the Holy Vessels, indeed, the narrative recounts nothing of this "fact": Rashi assumes that the reader is familiar with the body of midrashic material about Ahasuerus's plundering the Holy Temple in Jerusalem.[12] To claim that this is written in the text is, in fact, to draw attention to an elaborate reading practice that aims to fill the gaps in the text. In fact, those highly detailed accounts in the book of Esther of the "vessels" of the royal banquet seem rather meaningless; it is midrashic fictions that attach Ahasuerus to a moment of historical crisis in Jewish memory, lending it intense and private meaning for the Jewish reader. And it is only in such midrashic readings that Ahasuerus's motives in plundering the Temple are indicated.

Similarly, Haman's motive for jealousy is nowhere explained. Indeed, even the idea that he was jealous does not emerge obviously from the narrative; he seems simply to be piqued by Mordecai's lack of respect. And Mordecai's motive for refusing to bow to Haman is likewise withheld; as is Esther's in inviting Haman to her feast. All these gaps in the text are highlighted by Rashi, precisely because he refers to midrashic material that offers to fill them. Without these midrashic narratives, the written narrative stands exposed with all its bald patches, its failure of causality, of plausible motivation.

Even in terms of plot, the book of Esther represents a world of realistic surface effects, but no grammar of causality. This world is, effectively, illegible. Frank Kermode discusses the "sense of an ending"—the sense of time that allows us to perceive meaningful duration in history and in narrative. He cites an experiment showing that subjects listening to rhythmic structures such as a repeated *tick-tock* "can reproduce the intervals within the structure accurately, but they cannot grasp spontaneously the interval between the rhythmic groups," that is, between *tock* and *tick*.[13] This human fiction (the naming of the beginning as *tick* and the ending as *tock,* even when the interval between the ticks of the clock remains constant) enables us to give the middle a special significance.

By the end of Esther, we can retroactively trace the threads of plot that ultimately—over a nine-year period—feed into the reversal of tragic expectation. But in the course of reading—from beginning to end—no such providential expectation, no sense of an ending, is inscribed in the narrative, so as to charge it with meaning. On the contrary, events are narrated with a sterile facticity, lacking any significant relation with past and future. A lavish banquet, the destruction of one queen and her replacement by another, the discovery of an assassination plot, the annihilation decree against the Jewish population—loosely strung beads, these promise little in the way of meaningful pattern. The protagonists act in unintelligible ways: Esther refuses to speak of her origins, Haman's fury knows no bounds, Mordecai endangers his people by refusing to pay proper respect to a representative of royal authority, Ahasuerus refuses Haman's bribe in his unqualified enthusiasm for the plot against the Jews. Human nature seems bizarre and human action arbitrary.

THE PURIM MIRACLE

It is striking that the authors of this narrative ignore even the historically plausible indications of providential purpose. For the strange

fact is that a significant ending was available to the writers: the
return to Jerusalem and the rebuilding of the Temple. As Rashi points
out in his opening comment, these events in Shushan transpired at
the end of the seventy-year Babylonian exile. Instead of closing on
the prosaic note of Ahasuerus's new taxation laws and Mordecai's
rise to fame and popularity with most of his brothers, Esther might
have moved toward a climax of national redemption. The plot, running between the poles of national exile and national redemption,
would then have been charged with historical significance.

As it is, the miracle of Purim and the sense of meaning in the text
are both obscured. The Jewish people survive; but it would be hard
to claim this as, in the normal sense, a miracle. No natural laws are
set aside, no seas split, no barren wombs give birth. No prophets
speak in the name of God, inspiring their suffering brothers with
hope. No "biblical glow," to borrow James Kugel's expression, invests
the plot or language of this text.

Kugel describes this moment in Jewish history as a moment of
transformation. The world of the Bible, where God directly inter-
venes in history, has come to an end; even the restoration of Israel
and the rebuilding of the Temple follow no clear pattern of fulfillment; years of struggle and disappointment follow Cyrus's edict,
with the work on the Temple suspended for nine years. The age of
Scripture, however, maintains its impress on the present:

> The Bible's time was other time, discontinuous with later events
> and yet, because of its special character, one which was con-
> stantly about to impose its mark on the present. Bible-time was
> forever looming. The reading of the Torah's history itself
> became cyclical, indeed, eventually an annual event: Creation,
> Exodus, Sinai, and Moses' death were regular occurrences,
> and at the end the accumulated roll of scroll was unwound from
> one spindle and rolled back onto the other as it was in the
> beginning.[14]

No longer one simple, consequential story, history divides into
the age of Scripture, of the sacred texts, on the one hand, and present
time, when Rabbinic Judaism arises to interpret those texts and

detect the ways in which they may be seen to intersect with this quite different time. If the scroll has become the symbol for a new cyclical awareness, then Esther is, significantly, like the Bible itself, to be written on a parchment scroll and read once a year. Will the events of this narrative, too, become regular occurrences, acquiring a mythic character? But how can this be, if God's meanings here can only be traced retroactively? This provides little comfort to those who are living "forward," in successive time. What is lacking now is precisely the biblical confidence that *tock* is certain to follow *tick:* the conviction, as we read, or as we live, that we are housed within a "plot" that humanizes time. For this, a fiction is needed, like the fiction that makes *tick* different from *tock.*

Significantly, one of the laws governing the reading of the Megillah (The Scroll of Esther) states that it may not be read *l'mafrei'a*—out of order, or backward.[15] That is, if one changes the "meaningless" order of events, so as to construct a more "meaningful" plot, one has not fulfilled the mitzvah, the obligation of reading the Megillah on Purim. Time cannot be reversed; the text is read *kikhtavam u-kizmanam,* in sequential order, in all its frustrating disorganization.

Again, this text, with its hollow center where God is absent, is to be read before the rejoicing and feasting of Purim begin—as though this reading is necessary to evoke the singular sense of miracle that belongs to Purim. Reading Esther on Purim reawakens the "hidden miracle," says Sefat Emet.[16] An awareness that was dormant needs to be awakened. Within the account of God's absence, some subtle presence can be evoked; only then can we rejoice and feast. In order to achieve this, however, we must remain true to the text, we must *read* it—the disorganization of the plot, the opaque motivations of the protagonists, the mere successiveness of time.

The paradox of the Esther story—and of the Purim festival—emerges in the classical formulation of Rambam:

All Prophetic Books and the Sacred Writings will cease [to be recited in public] during the messianic era except the Book of Esther. It will continue to exist just like the Five Books of the Torah and the laws of the Oral Torah that will never cease.

Although ancient troubles will be remembered no longer, as it is written: "The troubles of the past are forgotten and hidden from my eyes" (Isa. 65:16), the days of Purim will not be abolished, as it is written: "These days of Purim shall never be repealed among the Jews, and the memory of them shall never cease from their descendants" (Esther 9:28).[17]

Here, Rambam makes a statement about messianic times. Basing himself on B. Sanhedrin, he singles out Esther as the only text to survive, along with the Five Books of Moses (the Torah itself). When all the texts of prophecy and Scripture have, in some sense, fallen into oblivion, when all the epic narratives of miraculous redemption will be forgotten,[18] this scroll and this festival will, according to its own internal testimony, "never be repealed among the Jews, and the memory of them shall never cease from their descendants." Rambam's statement, in fact, articulates the paradoxical stature of Esther and of Purim. The only text where God's face is hidden, where His absence comes to signify that "mere anarchy is loosed upon the world," is selected for eternity. Why should this disorganized narrative of oriental intrigue and misrule be granted a staying power that exceeds that of all the records of prophecy, where God's presence and will are conveyed to the world?

THE SENSE OF AN ENDING

The sense of an ending does, however, paradoxically mark the way in which some of the characters in Esther experience their reality. Ahasuerus and Haman are quite noticeably concerned with the issue of significant endings. The king, for example, celebrates the triumphant closure of his seven-day feast by summoning Vashti. His display of royal grandeur is brought to a climax by this gesture of power. The repetition of the number seven and the submission of an authentic queen to his will lends quasi-mystical authority to this moment. On the seventh day of the feast, he instructs his seven servants to bring "Vashti the queen before the king in her royal crown, to display to the nations and the princes" (Esther 1:11). Always named

Vashti the queen when she is considered part of the king's narcissistic project, she is to bring her authentic royal ancestry to support the king's hollow claims to the throne. A sense of theatrical closure invests the king's summons. When she refuses to collaborate, it is as Queen Vashti—queen first, woman after—that she is judged (1:15). But when she is condemned to exile (or death), she is, simply and vulnerably, Vashti. The king's anger is more than personal: she has disrupted a seven-day fantasy of meaningful time, designed to celebrate his reign and to culminate in the queen's appearance. His pageant of pretension has failed to achieve closure.

A similar sensitivity to the closure that will lend transcendent meaning to time is displayed by Haman, when he casts lots to decide on the day of destruction of the Jewish people. The act of casting lots, a rather marginal element in the plot, which gives the Purim festival its name, seems to indicate a reckless dependence on chance, on the fall of the dice. On the contrary, claims the midrash:

> When the lot fell on the month of Adar, Haman rejoiced greatly: "The lot has fallen for me on the month when Moses died!" However, he did not know that on 7 Adar, Moses both died and was born.[19]

Haman rejoices at his vindication by the gods; it is of great significance to him that the omens are auspicious. Since Adar is an ominous month for the Jews (which Moses's death seems to indicate), Haman feels certain of the triumphant conclusion of his plot. Casting lots expresses an anxious desire for foreordained closure; an auspicious fall of the dice will preserve him from the terrors of contingency. Essentially, Haman is attempting to make his life immune from luck. The ending of the midrash emphasizes the irony: insistent on knowing the future, Haman does not know that the same month marks both Moses's birth and his death—that is, that there is no particular security to be drawn from such fictions about time.

Haman and Ahasuerus, then, are concerned with significant endings that will grant retrospective meaning to merely successive time.

In other words, they seek clear indications as to how things will turn out. In order to plot their course, they need to know the end. For this, they require an ordered world of numbers and patterns that can be read and used to advantage.

TAKING A HINT

Mordecai, on the other hand, is said to "know all that had been done" (Esther 4:1). This stands in stark contrast with the panicked disarray with which the city of Shushan reacts to the ambiguity of the edict of destruction. Rapidly copied and disseminated with all the sophisticated communication resources of the empire, its message is yet strangely ambiguous: "to be ready for the future [atidim], for that day" (3:14). Ready to kill, or to be killed?[20] The city of Shushan is confused, baffled.

What—and how—does Mordecai know? Rashi comments:

> The Master of Dreams told him that God had consented to this destruction because the Jews had worshipped idols in Nebuchadnezzar's time, and had participated in Ahasuerus' feast.

What Mordecai knows is the reason for the impending catastrophe: the people's spiritual failure. But perhaps equally important is the means by which he knows: God communicates with him through a dream. This kind of communication leaves him essentially in the dark about the end of the story. He knows only what has happened and why. His only possible response to his dream is to tear his clothes, put on sackcloth and ashes, and cry loudly and bitterly in the city square. A dream as a source of meaning conveys no certainty about the future. In his very uncertainty, Mordecai enacts mourning for an inevitable catastrophe: a provocative mourning that aims to affect the course of history.

Mordecai enters the narrative as the cousin and foster parent of Esther. He is her mentor who, when she is taken to the palace, instructs her not to reveal her people of origin. And his first action is recorded in these words: "Every single day, Mordecai would walk about in front of the court of the women's house, to know Esther's welfare and what was to be done with her" (Esther 2:11). The midrash comments:

> Mordecai was one of four righteous men who were given a hint: and one of two who responded sensitively. He said: "Is it possible that this righteous woman should be married to an uncircumcised man unless some great salvation were about to happen to Israel by her means?"[21]

Mordecai is characterized as being capable of responding to hints, of taking note that the hint exists. In this case, the hint is enigmatic in the extreme. How could the righteous Esther have been doomed to such a grotesque mismatch? Just because it defies understanding, it must intimate some purpose yet to be revealed.

A hint, according to OED, is "an occasion, an opportunity. A slight indication: a suggestion or implication conveyed covertly but intelligibly." In hinting, one hopes that no one but the target will notice, and that the target will not only notice but interpret correctly. The hint, then, is precisely not obvious or explicit. Only Mordecai can sense in Esther's marriage to the king a kind of communication, an opportunity for salvation. But Mordecai is alert to hints, to the almost imperceptible intimations of possibility.

The delicate status of the hint as communication becomes clearer if we compare the verse about Mordecai with a similar verse about Miriam: she stands at a distance to observe her baby brother, Moses, who has been put into the river in a basket—"to know what would be done to him" (Exod.2:4). Miriam is a prophetess, clearly named as such in the Torah itself: "Miriam the prophetess, Aaron's sister" (15:20). The Talmud defines her moment of prophecy: when she was Aaron's sister, but not yet Moses's sister, she foretold that her mother would give birth to Israel's savior. She knew with absolute clarity that Moses would grow to deliver his people from Egypt. Her knowledge gave her the force to reunite her parents, who had separated in despair over the genocidal decree of Pharaoh. When Moses was born, says the Talmud, the house was filled with light:

Her father rose up and kissed her on her head, saying, "My daughter, your prophecy has been fulfilled." But when they put him into the river, her father rose and smacked her on her head, saying, "Where, now, is your prophecy!" That is what is written, "And his sister stood afar off to know what would be done to him"—what would be the fate of her prophecy.[22]

In the dark waiting time, Miriam has no doubt that Moses will be saved, in order to save his people; she waits on knowledge *(l'de'ah)* only of the next stage of the narrative—the specific turn of the plot. Unlike her, however, Mordecai has no prophecy to reassure him. He has only a hint, a tenuous response to an opaque reality. And— later—a dream.

Miriam's prophecy sets into sharp relief Mordecai's condition, at a period when prophecy is coming to an end. Although the last prophets—Haggai, Zechariah, Malachi—are almost his contemporaries, they make no reference to his situation. With Mordecai begins the period of the Sages (the *chakhamim*), of the midrash, of those who comb texts for hints and deploy wisdom to interpret anomalies for meaning. *Dai l'chakima b'remiza,* say the Sages of their own kind of consciousness: a hint is sufficient for the wise. A word is sometimes sufficient basis for a castle in the air. A hint is something one can use, transform: one experiences it as an intimate call, its very subtlety inspiring imagination.

In his responsiveness to hints, the Sage's mind resembles the imaginative sensibility of the artist, which Henry James describes as

> a kind of huge spider web of the finest silken threads suspended in the chamber of consciousness, and catching every air-borne particle in its tissue . . . it takes to itself the *faintest hints of life,* it converts the very pulses of the air into revelations [emphasis added].[23]

Taking the hint, then, is Mordecai's mode of inspiration. One midrash calls him a *balshan*—a "linguist," since he knew seventy languages.[24] The root *balash* indicates one who hacks at stony clods of earth, in order to plant a vine, or who searches for concealed goods. Searching, examining possibilities in inhospitable territory, the "linguist" is a detective,[25] working in rough ground where truth is well hidden, to be accessed by creative acts of discovery. "Back to the rough ground! Look and see!" Wittgenstein wrote about the language game. Moved by desire for meaning, inhabiting the world of *hester*, where God's face is hidden, Mordecai never ceases to search for intimations: "Might this be the hidden meaning, the promised end?"

ESTHER SPRUNG FREE

Like Mordecai, Esther has no privileged communication from God. However, although prophecy is fast fading at this period, it is striking that Esther is listed in the Talmud as the last of the seven prophetesses.[26] Not even the Talmud, however, suggests that she receives messages from God. On the contrary, when Mordecai persuades her to intercede for her people, their conversation displays with painful clarity how a human being responds to a situation in which God's face is averted from her—a situation in which, that is, He withholds communication from her. In what sense, then, can she be perceived as a prophetess?

In this crucial scene, Mordecai plays a strangely oblique role. Wearing sackcloth, he approaches the palace gate, knowing that the law forbids him to enter. He simply waits by the gate, making no attempt to send Esther a message. Esther's servants report the silent appearance of Mordecai; she sends a change of clothing, so that he may enter, but he refuses to accept it. In other words, he claims her attention by the report of his costume, but refuses to speak directly to her, since that would mean divesting himself of his mourning. She then takes the initiative, summoning a messenger—"to know why and wherefore" (Esther 4:5).

From this point on, the dialogue is conducted solely through a third party; they do not see each other; the messenger carries their words. Mordecai tells her of "all that has befallen him": of the edict of destruction against the Jews. He instructs her to beseech the king for her people's lives. The midrash picks up on the expression

"all that had befallen him," hearing in it a reference to Mordecai's dream—his source of knowledge. "Befallen" suggests a chance
event—unpredictably, in a dream, knowledge has "happened" to him.

Esther responds unequivocally, on the basis of her own knowledge: "All the king's servants and the people of the king's provinces
know that if any person, man or woman, enters the king's presence
in the inner court without having been summoned, there is but one
law for him—that he be put to death" (Esther 4:11). The end is clear
for anyone who approaches the king unsummoned; everyone knows
that her fate will be death. The alternative is almost purely hypothetical—"unless the king extends his golden scepter to him"—particularly in view of the fact that the king has shown no interest in her for
thirty days.

This last observation comes as a shock to the reader. If the king
has lost interest in Esther, the possibility of a providential purpose
to this marriage vanishes. Even if, on the most sanguine reading of
the text, the threads of divine intentionality have been prepared
over the course of many years, their convergence at this moment of
need has been foiled by the whim of the king's fancy. A month earlier, Esther might have responded differently to Mordecai's plea,
confident that she could use the king's love to save her people. Now,
a bitterly dysprovidential tone haunts her words. Now, if she
attempts to approach the king, she will surely die.

Mordecai's answer is heard after a verse that starkly reports: "And
they told Mordecai Esther's words" (Esther 4:12). An entire verse suspends the course of the dialogue, creating space for speculation.
Strikingly, such verses are interspersed throughout the long-distance
dialogue—verses whose sole content is the fact that a message is
delivered.[27] The effect is not only to arouse suspense but to draw
attention to the process of transmission. In fact, in Esther 4:9–10,
this process is extended through two verses, emphasizing the two-
way transmission. This is not a face-to-face dialogue; three parties,
rather than two, are involved. Mordecai and Esther do not respond
to each other's presence, but precisely to the other's absence, as represented by the mediation of the messenger. There is coming and
going, the messenger is told to tell; but the other is invisible, represented in language.

In this context, Mordecai's answer is almost aggressive in its directness. Where his previous message had been cast in indirect speech, here he assaults Esther with harsh rhetoric:

> Do not imagine that you, of all the Jews, will escape with your life by being in the king's palace. If you keep silent at this moment, relief and deliverance will come to the Jews from another quarter, while you and your father's house will perish. And who knows, perhaps you achieved royal status for just such a moment. (Esther 4:13–14)

This is a demoralizing, even a convoluted message: if the people are destroyed, she will die as well; but they will be saved by some other means, and she will perish; and who knows?—perhaps she was positioned in the palace for just such an opportunity? Mordecai offers her nothing in the way of encouragement or security. She will die if she refuses to help, while her people will survive in one way or another. And if she does take up the challenge, who knows? He withdraws the support of any privileged knowledge. It is no more than a possibility, a hypothesis, that she was placed in this position precisely for this moment of crisis: if the king does indeed extend his scepter to her, the providential possibility will have demonstrated its truth. But at this moment, what is to impel her to risk her life? No providential knowledge, no prophecy, not even an intuition—merely a *Who knows?*—a fiction that may retrospectively make sense of the whole narrative.

Moreover, while Mordecai does have faith that the people will be saved in one way or another, he cannot cover Esther with that mantle of confidence. All he can tell her is, "If you keep silent at this moment . . ." In the words of the midrash, "If you are silent now, and do not defend your people, you will have nothing to say in the world to come."[28] Throughout her marriage, Esther has remained silent about her origins (Esther 2:20). Now Mordecai, who commanded that silence, urges her to break it. That silence was for the sake of this moment. Now she must speak, take up a position, or else lose her voice forever. This moment is all she has, her chance to make herself heard. But who knows? . . .

In her crisis, she is alone. Mordecai will not blur the stark nature of her situation. At this moment, he is no longer her touchstone—her tutor, nurturer, father, mother. Even his visual presence is withheld from her. She had opened the dialogue with a wish to know. When he replies, *Who knows?*, he cuts the traces of her dependency and springs her free.

ESTHER'S PRAYER

This lonely freedom begins in her body, in the physical intensity of her reaction to Mordecai's spectral appearance at the palace gate. *Va-tit'chalchal*—"She was greatly agitated" (Esther 4:4). Midrashic translations evoke the notion of extreme fear or associate the expression with *challul*, referring to the cavities of the body: "Her menstrual blood began to flow" or "She suffered a miscarriage."[29] The doubled root intensifies meaning. In these extreme readings, the body apertures gape wide in terror, as the implications of Mordecai's sackcloth assail her. She cannot contain herself. Nothing contains her. If the king has not summoned her, the fiction of a meaningful personal narrative has just become untenable. Even Mordecai hides his face from her. In this crisis, Esther launches herself toward an austere freedom.

By accepting Mordecai's challenge, Esther fully enters, for the first time, Ahasuerus's world.[30] This is the world of arbitrary sequences, where nothing can be predicted, where the happy ending that will justify the whole plot cannot be ascertained in advance. From one viewpoint, this is a world of pure contingency, of *Who knows?* Without guarantees of any kind, Esther will act, speak, enter into her freedom.

For three days, Esther will fast. With a voice of new authority, she charges Mordecai with assembling the people and having them fast for her. With this, she will go to the king. Fasting may seem a dubious preparation for the fateful encounter on which her life depends: her beauty will suffer.[31] But perhaps she is removing her last and most basic source of worldly confidence, as though to acknowledge that even the king's favor is, in the end, in God's hands. By making a public issue of this, she discourages the people, too, from relying on comforting fictions. As the midrash puts it, "Let Israel not say: We have a sister in the king's palace; and distract themselves from praying for mercy."[32]

At this critical moment, Esther works to shift herself and her people clear of the usual providential view of the story. If she, or they, might have hoped that the meaning of so many arbitrary events is now revealed in the fortunate presence of Esther, "our sister," in the palace, she now strips herself of any such consolation. If Mordecai's slim possibility of a meaningful history *(Who knows?. . .)* is to be vindicated, it will not take the form of such a conventional fiction.

On the third day, she "clothes herself in majesty": "in the Holy Spirit," says the Talmud.[33] A prophetic spirit invests her. But as she stands in the king's presence, in the eye of the storm, without father or mother, without tutor or husband, "God's presence abandoned her."[34] At this moment, she prays inaudibly, "My God! My God! Why have You abandoned me?" (Ps. 22:2).

This is the prayer that most truly expresses Esther's experience in the world of anarchy, where God's face is hidden. Like the Jewish prisoners on Rosh Hashanah, Esther cries out in pain and yearning to her hidden God. This is the prayer of the broken heart.[35]

The existential quality of this "abandonment" is amplified in the midrash:

The first day [of her fast] she cried, "My God!" The second day she cried, "My God!" The third day she burst into a passionate cry, "My God! My God! Why have You abandoned me?"[36]

Maharal explains:

When God did not answer her prayer on the first day, this did not mean that He had abandoned her. Similarly, on the second day, she still did not cry, "Why have You abandoned me?" But, since God does not abandon the righteous in their distress for longer than three days, when the third day came, she cried out, "Why have You abandoned me?"[37]

The three-day fast delivers Esther to the fraying edge of meaningful time. If her prayer is still not answered, then God's promises to
the righteous no longer apply. Caught in alien time, she reflects on
her own historic moment:

> "Why have You abandoned me?" The order of the world has
> changed in my time. The world order of the matriarchs has
> changed in my time. Sarah was held by Pharaoh for one night,
> and he and his whole household were punished with plagues
> (impotence); while I have been subjected to this wicked man all
> these years, and You do no miracles for me!"[38]

All the biblical archetypes fail her. The first prophetess, Sarah, the
paradigm figure for such narratives of royal rape, was saved by miracle. Without undue modesty, Esther knows that she, too, has
prophetic stature ("She clothed herself in majesty . . ."[39]); but the time
is out of joint, no miracle saves her, mere anarchy is loosed upon the
world.

In their comments on this moment of Esther's narrative, the
Sages reflect on their own situation. Cut adrift from the biblical
world of miracle, from the fictions of closure that redeem and organ-
ize time, Esther, as the last prophetess, must discover new meaning
for prophecy. After her, the world of prophecy and miracles yields
place to the world of *chokhmah,* of wisdom, of hints and interpretations. Instead of the overwhelming revelations of Sinai—with its
visual, perhaps blinding[40] manifestations of God's presence—there
is the world in which God and the human are separated and linked
by a third force—by the text, the messenger, the transmission.

But this new symbolic order, which offers fragmented perspectives, also yields larger play for human will and desire. In this triadic
order, the direct presence of God—or of the beloved human other,
whose presence has given coherence to life—is replaced by "triangu-
lated" structures: here are Esther, Mordecai, and the messenger;
Esther, Ahasuerus, and Haman; even, at the close, Esther, Mordecai,
and Ahasuerus. Here, Esther falls back into her own mind, into her
own way of encountering God's hidden face. A prophetess without
revelation, she finds a dark light within herself.

THE WHOLE/BROKEN HEART

These midrashic narratives have Esther situate herself at the cusp of changing time. José Ortega writes:

> And this is the simple truth—that to live is to feel oneself lost—he who accepts it has already begun to find himself, to be on firm ground. Instinctively, as do the shipwrecked, he will look round for something to which to cling, and that tragic, ruthless glance, absolutely sincere, because it is a question of his salvation, will cause him to bring order into the chaos of his life. These are the only genuine ideas; the ideas of the shipwrecked.[41]

The ideas of the shipwrecked: in different language, Maharal articulates the wisdom of Esther as the realization that the human being is, in himself, lacking, incomplete; the fatal illusion is to ignore finitude, to imagine the self omnipotent.[42] The genuine ideas of the shipwrecked bring one to recognize one's creaturely vulnerability, and to the possibility of self-transcendence.

For Kierkegaard, this process is fraught with an inescapable anxiety that schools one in faith:

> Now the dread of possibility holds him as its prey, until it can deliver him saved into the hands of faith. In no other place does he find repose . . . he who went through the curriculum of misfortune offered by possibility lost everything, absolutely everything, in a way that no one has lost it in reality. If in this situation he did not behave falsely towards possibility, if he did not attempt to talk around the dread which would save him, then he received everything back again, as in reality no one ever did even if he received everything tenfold, for the pupil of possibility received infinity.[43]

In this spiritual process, writes William James, "something must give way, a native hardness must break down and liquefy."[44]

This critical point in experience is lived by Esther, as she dissolves into a prayer that acknowledges truth and yearning at once: "My

God! My God! Why have You abandoned me?" A Hasidic proverb has it that "There is nothing so whole as a broken heart" (R. Mendel of Kotsk). Esther's heart breaks as her fictional supports fall away; God cannot withstand the prayer from a broken heart, say the Sages.[45] When she reaches that moment of breakdown, she touches the place from which prayer rises with greatest force. She knows the freedom of one who knows nothing, and is nobody.

BLINKS OF AN EYELID

The world where God's face is hidden is experienced by human beings as a world of chance. In this world, Esther chooses to act on the strength of a *"Who knows?"*—a possible scenario of meaningful time, within which her orphanhood, her exiled condition, her bizarre marriage to the king, all will become accidents that were meant to happen. But there is no way she can know, at the moment of entering the presence of the king of Misrule, whether his scepter will move toward her. All the odds against her, she—unlike Haman—casts no lots to assert control over time. She lives her contingency, at the same time as she protests: "My God! My God! Why have You abandoned me?"

From a different perspective, J. M. Coetzee describes such a way of living time:

> In a world of chance is there a better and a worse? We yield to a stranger's embrace or give ourselves to the waves; for the blink of an eyelid our vigilance relaxes; we are asleep; and when we awake we have lost the direction of our lives. What are these blinks of an eyelid, against which the only defence is an eternal and inhuman wakefulness? Might they not be the cracks and chinks through which another voice, other voices, speak in our lives?[46]

The "other voices" of which Coetzee speaks can be heard only through the "cracks and chinks" of an unknowable world. In the "blinks of an eyelid," when the eye loses its vigilance, those other voices become audible. The midrash uses a similar expression to describe the moment, the crack in time, "like the blink of an eyelid," that transfigures destiny. In sleep, in dream, when consciousness fails, uncanny messages seep through.

Marcel Proust describes the chance event that led him to write his great novel:

> There is a large element of chance in these matters. . . . The past is hidden somewhere outside the realm, beyond the reach of intellect, in some material object (in the sensation which that material object will give us) of which we have no inkling. And it depends on chance whether or not we come upon this object before we ourselves must die. . . . One day in winter, on my return home, my mother, seeing that I was cold, offered me some tea, a thing I did not ordinarily take. I declined at first, and then, for no particular reason, changed my mind. She sent for one of those squat, plump little cakes called "petites madeleines" . . . No sooner had the warm liquid mixed with crumbs touched my palate than a shudder ran through me and I stopped, intent upon the extraordinary thing that was happening to me.[47]

For Proust, the past is revealed through a coincidence, a moment of happy encounter with a taste, or a smell, that transfigures his life. The "happiness" of such moments, as the word itself suggests, is a matter of chance; predicting or planning them is out of the question. They are, in Adam Phillips's expression, a "secular epiphany."[48]

But such unbidden moments are also at the core of the paradoxical religious notion of *nes nistar,* the hidden miracle, the event that no chronicler or journalist would record, and whose meaning remains a matter of private sensibility. The world where God hides His face is a world of chinks and cracks, of intimations, evocations. Esther responds to a hint—*"Who knows?"*—that is invisible to the naked eye. Her soul is entirely her own at this point. Her act is the true miracle of Purim.

André Neher describes the experience of being "entirely exposed to the radiations of the future." These radiations, he writes, are totally silent:

The future is ambiguous like silence. It can offer all, and surrender itself in successive waves, each one of which, following the one before, leads a little further on the path of eternity. But it can also rise to the surface of life like a bubble of soap, bursting at the very instant when the sun's rays cross it with their sparkling fires.[49]

The hazard offered by the future is a function of God's withdrawal, face hidden, into silence. Esther says "yes" to the future, to its silence. Her act is prophetic in a paradoxical sense suited to its moment. Without foreknowledge, she assumes the hazard of a certain hour, the hour for which she may—*Who knows?*—have come to the throne. Buber calls the prophetic moment the one when "the customary soul enlarges and transfigures itself into the surprise soul."[50] In the face of "mere anarchy" ("sheer anarchy," in modern English), Esther enacts the prophetic faith that "the unique being, man, is created to be a center of surprise in the universe."[51]

THE LAST PROPHETESS

This heroine, and this narrative, says Rambam, will retain their vitality even into messianic times, even when "the books of the prophets and the other sacred writings" have been, in some sense, suspended. The Scroll of Esther and the Purim festival will survive, after the rest have been forgotten.

R. Yitzhak Hutner offers a parable:

Two people are charged with the task of recognizing a face in the darkness. One lights a candle and examines the face to identify it. The other, without a candle, trains himself to identify people by the sound of their voices alone. The first person achieves a clearer recognition, by sight, than the other can, merely by sound. However, the second person has taught himself a new talent, of listening to the voice of the other. And when dawn breaks, the first person will extinguish his candle but will be none the wiser as a result of his nocturnal experience; while the other will emerge from it with a newly developed capacity for listening as a channel of recognition.

Similarly, R. Hutner writes, Purim and Pesach, always just a month apart,[52] represent alternative modes by which Israel may recognize God, who stages Himself in two different modes of *anokhi*: "*Anokhi*— I shall indeed hide My face on that day," on the one hand; and "*Anokhi*—I am the Lord your God who brought you out of the land of Egypt," on the other. The God of the book of Exodus is recognized by the "candlelight" of miracles and prophecies; while the God of hiddenness, of *hester*, of Esther, is recognized by means of a new sensibility attuned to the voice of that hidden *I* of God. In the messianic era, when God will be revealed by light seven times the brilliance of the sun, the candles that were so necessary in the dark will be extinguished: all the festivals that are linked with the Exodus will be subsumed into the light of ultimate redemption. But the Purim redemption story, in which Israel has taught itself to recognize the *anokhi* of God even in darkness—this, surely, will remain as eternal spiritual gift even after sunrise.[53]

In the world where God hides His face, human life seems to be of no concern to Him. He neither communicates through prophecy nor responds to human distress by miraculous action. What remains is a highly brocaded surface reality, a hallucinatory focus on materials, modalities, laws, techniques, advisers, texts, time consumed in banal successiveness.

> Turning and turning in the widening gyre
> The falcon cannot hear the falconer;
> Things fall apart; the centre cannot hold;
> Mere anarchy is loosed upon the world.

The law of women is—six months in oil of myrrh, and six months in perfume and cosmetics. In her transit from the harem to the king's palace, the woman is given whatever she desires. In this brief season, her will is law. After her night with the king, she is returned to a second harem and passes the rest of her life subject to the king's desire.

In this world, God is heard, not seen; He hints, His voice resonates with the attunement of his listener. For Mordecai, it is
through dreams, through the suggestive strangeness of events, that
meaning is evoked. He takes to himself the faintest hints of life, converting disorder into intimations of redemption. "I will indeed hide
My face on that day." One talmudic sage (Rava) demonstrates this
new kind of listening in his reading of the biblical verse: " 'Then I
will indeed hide My face on that day'—Even though I hide My face
from them—I will communicate in dreams."[54] "On that *day* I will
hide My face, but not at night, not in dreams" (Rashi). Mordecai's
knowledge is a dream knowledge, obscured, not directly communicable. What he can do is demonstratively clothe himself in sackcloth
and cry out in the city square.

Esther has a different role. The book that bears her name is hiddenness itself. She is its author, inscribed into the text (Esther 9:29).
The world in which she is called—*Who knows?*—to play a part is "an
abyss in which the eye is lost" (Cézanne). In the waking world, she is
abandoned—by father and mother, cousin, mentor, by God's presence. She has lost her place in time, as well as in space. God inhabits
the navel of her dream, where it plunges into the unknown.[55] In this
dark dream, she cries to the God who has abandoned her, invoking
Him[56] as the terror of unknowing possesses her.[57] Eyes closed, she
yields to another reality, another voice, to the nonsilence that André
Neher describes as "a shaft hollowed out beneath silence which leads
to its most vertiginous depths."[58] In the blink of an eyelid, silence
draws her into the kingdom of nothingness.

In the twilight of prophecy, she is named as the last prophetess.
But, unlike prophets before her, she has no way of knowing if she is
dreaming or awake. Perhaps, as mere anarchy is loosed upon the
world, her dream will make her fall back inside herself, lead her into
the unknowable future. Here, perhaps, is the chink through which
another voice may be heard.

PART TWO

Stranger Within

FIVE

In the Vale of Soul-Making

Abraham's Journey

DESTINATION UNKNOWN

God said to Abram, "Go forth from your land, from your birth place, and from your father's house to the land that I will show you." (Gen. 12:1)

Without preamble, God commands Abraham[1] to leave all the places of his past and to travel to a destination not yet revealed. In one sense, of course, he is simply consummating a journey begun by his father, Terach, who had taken his family from Ur of the Chaldeans "and set out for the land of Canaan; but when they had come as far as Haran, they settled there" (Gen. 11:31). Terach had ended his life without completing the journey. But why, then, does God enter the narrative with the historic *Lekh lekha* command, as though this signifies a new project?

And if in fact God has a distinct project in mind, why is Abraham chosen to implement it? Unlike Noach, who is described as "a perfectly righteous man" (Gen. 6:9), Abraham appears without the slightest personal recommendation.

A further question arises about the expression *lekha: Lekh lekha*— Go forth. . . . What is the force of *lekha*? Is it merely—as Ramban declares—a stylistic grace note, fairly common in biblical Hebrew? Remarkably, the same expression is used again in God's final call to Abraham. In the *Akedah* narrative (the "Binding of Isaac"), God tells Abraham to take his beloved son Isaac and *"lekh lekha*—go forth to the land of Moriah, and offer him there as a burnt offering on one of the mountains that I will indicate to you" (Gen. 22:2). It is only on this first appearance, however, that *lekh lekha* is deliberately translated by Rashi: "*lekha*—for your benefit and for your good." Clearly, Rashi is not content to regard the word as a stylistic ornament. Condensed

within *lekha* is a promise—this journey will benefit Abraham—
which Rashi then spells out:

> 1) . . . and *there* I will make you into a great nation, while *here*
> you will never merit to have children. Moreover, I will make
> your character known throughout the world
> 2) "And I will make you into a great nation": since traveling
> generally has three effects—it decreases fertility, wealth, and
> renown—he therefore needed these three blessings that God
> promised him: children, wealth, and renown. (That is the
> meaning of "I shall make your name great": I will add a letter
> to your name. Till now, your name was Abram, from now
> it will be Abraham. The numerical value of the letters of
> "Abraham" is 248, equivalent to the number of limbs in the
> human body.)
>   "And I shall bless you": with wealth . . .

Abraham will be blessed with children—but only *there,* in
Canaan, not *here,* in Haran. Rashi pointedly adds the words *here* and
there to define the condition of blessing. Only once he has arrived at
his destination will he meet his destiny of blessing: it inheres in the
land of Canaan. In undertaking this journey, moreover, he will not
suffer the usual consequences of travel—infertility, poverty, and
loss of reputation. He will not be the loser: on the contrary, he will
be blessed in just these three areas. This paradox of his journey he
will discover *there,* on arrival.

The issue of *shem,* renown, is particularly striking. In order to
make the point about Abraham's *name* becoming great, Rashi
deploys a midrashic pun: his name will change to *Abraham*—literally
amplifying his name by adding the letter *heh,* thus arriving at the
numerological equivalent of the limbs in the body—248. Abraham's
body image suddenly becomes essential, consummating God's
promise: he will achieve a full human body. By implication, before
the journey, his body lacks five organs (identified in many sources[2]
as eyes, ears, and sex). In the more general sense, however, Abraham
is simply promised *fame:* one wonders about such an inducement,
and about its relevance to Abraham's later history. In any event, he is

invited to a journey whose obvious hazards will be neutralized: far from being the loser in this transaction, he will profit from it.

In his last comment on the verse, however, Rashi seems to shift his emphasis away from Abraham's destination:

> "To the land that I will show you": He did not reveal which land immediately, in order to make it precious in his eyes, and to give him reward for each word spoken. Similarly, "Take your son, your only son, whom you love, Isaac . . ." (Gen. 22:2); and also, "Proclaim against it the proclamation that I shall tell you . . ." (Jon. 3:2).

Here, Rashi emphasizes the process of journeying to a destination unspecified. The effect of deferring essential information is—strangely—to make his destination more precious. He will travel without the support of prior knowledge, in a sense without solid ground under his feet. The land that God will show him will first live in his imagination. Off balance, in suspense, his condition is compared with the later *lekh lekha* moment, in the *Akedah* narrative. There, too, crucial information is withheld, yielded in slow increments: "your son, your only one, whom you love, Isaac"; and "on one of the mountains that I will indicate to you." In all these moments, then, Abraham is invited to an inner journey as well as a physical one; into his own depths as well as over the landscape of the ancient Near East.

Strangely, suspense is said to intensify the *preciousness* of the object. One might have thought, rather, at least in the last two cases, of a painfully *tantalizing* process, in which delay only increases the horror of realization. Apparently, the effect of suspended naming is to achieve an intimacy, in which reverie makes the object one's own. In imagination, one apprehends an infinitude where the eventual disclosure can lodge. When God, therefore, launches Abraham on a journey "to the land that I will show you," He both tantalizes him and endows him with an experience of mystery.

Here is Ramban's evocative account of Abraham's journey:

> He wandered about from nation to nation, from kingdom to kingdom, till he arrived at the land of Canaan, when He said, "To

your seed I have given this land" (Gen. 12:7). Then the promise, "to the land that I will show you" was fulfilled and Abraham stayed there. As for the verse that says, "And they went forth to go to the land of Canaan" (12:5), that does not mean that they headed there to settle there, for he did not yet know that that was the land God had meant. Rather, the righteous man set his goal in that direction, since that had been his intention, as well as that of his father, when they originally set out from Ur of the Chaldeans. This is the reason that Abraham later said, "And it was when God caused me to wander from my father's house. . ." (20:13): he was indeed wandering like a lost lamb (Ps. 119:176).

This journey, he suggests, may have traversed many countries without any clear sense of destination. "He did not yet know": Even though, by way of completing his family's original project, he sets his course toward Canaan, his situation is that of one who does not yet know. He travels, then, with a certain provisional intentionality; but, on some deeper level, he is off balance, he is *nodded v'holekh,* a wanderer to whom Ramban applies the tragic expression of Cain's doom: *"Na va-nad*—a fugitive and wanderer you shall be on earth" (Gen. 4:12). Abraham has committed no crime; nothing is to be expiated. And yet, Ramban hints in his allusive text at some similarity with Cain's fate. In his final comment he describes Abraham as "wandering like a lost lamb," this time responding to Abraham's own resonant language: "When God made me wander *[hit'u oti elohim]* from the house of my father." In these poignant words, Abraham covers this early period of his life. Ramban associates the word *to'eh,* to wander, with another proof text that he embeds in his own text: the Psalmist cries, "I have been wandering like a lost sheep—Seek out Your servant." The sense of *lostness* on Abraham's lips is associated with a larger human predicament: God is invoked as the One who can retrieve the sheep straying in unmapped territory. The Psalmist cries out of his sense of imperiled contingency: only the absent Shepherd can find what has been lost.

Ramban's complex evocation of Abraham's early life, then, yields a kind of vagrancy: traveling as a travail[3] of spirit and body. This experience of *lostness* provides a depth of experience that is the very purpose of God's invitation. The journey is not, after all, merely a necessary evil. It becomes a constitutive ordeal of consciousness.

What is the freight gained in such travails? Othello woos Desdemona with his "traveller's history," with its terrors and hardships.[4] The travel narrative, in general, is at minimum a record of survival. Indeed, all narratives can, in a sense, be considered travel narratives, taking the reader on a journey. As Gillian Beer writes, they are "organized to move through time, to transport the reader, and to bring us home again, augmented by the experience and by the knowledge we have acquired."[5] To what knowledge and what experience, beyond sheer survival, is Abraham invited, so that, implicitly, we, too, are asked to participate?

We remember Rashi's decoding of *lekha*: "to your benefit and for your good." In general, as Rashi points out, disruptions of stable existence are detrimental—to one's family life, one's financial standing, or one's renown. As he moves aimlessly through the world, Abraham is starkly characterized in the midrash as a *madman*: "Look at this old man! Traveling through the country, looking like a madman!"[6] "Is there a man who travels without knowing to what destination he travels?"[7]

Such a condition is *meshuga*, haunted by an *elsewhereness*, never here, always drawn to a horizon. To be *meshuga*, or *shogeh*, is to be unbalanced, off target, to reel away. The world perceives and pities Abraham as passionately absent, restlessly alert to the intimations of possible relationship.[8] What freight does this traveler gather? And, by extension, what do we gather through our participation in his journey?

Given the general view of journeys, the only benefit is the blessing of *arrival* in the Holy Land, which cancels all deficits. From this rational viewpoint, journeys deplete one of resources of all kinds: a rolling stone gathers no moss. In what sense, then, do journeys enrich, fertilize, amplify one's name? Or is the romance of travel simply a sophisticated and perhaps compensatory idea?

The Zohar brings us back to the *lekha*, offering an alternative translation: "Travel in order to *transform yourself, create yourself anew*." At its simplest, *lekh lekha* translates: "Travel—*to yourself*." Not to the present, resident self—but to the self of aspiration, the perhaps unimagined self. On one level, it is Abraham's difference from others that God invokes and provokes; but mostly, it is his *difference from himself*.[9] God mobilizes an aversion in Abraham to the conformities of his world, which, at this initial stage, is his own conformity. An uncanny process is under way; drawn beyond himself, he is to transfigure that self.

TOWARD A NEW BODY

As a result of that process, Abraham will evolve a different way of seeing. When God provokes him toward "the land that I will show you," He tempts him with a future vision. "Lift up your eyes and see," he is told later, "from the place where you are" (Gen. 13:14). Or Ha-Chaim comments that it is only after the final separation from Lot that Abraham enters into his visual kingdom, seeing from his own place, north-south-east-west, without turning. He sees the whole field, holding together disparate objects. This moment is the fulfillment of God's original invitation "to the land that I will show you": a transfigured power of vision will belong to that future self, to the future body transfigured by the journey.

Even more strikingly, Or Ha-Chaim adds: "I will show it to you, and you to it." A mutual interplay of self and world will make the land visible to Abraham and Abraham visible to the land.

Maurice Merleau-Ponty, the French phenomenologist, writes:

> He who looks must not himself be foreign to the world that he looks at. . . . He who sees cannot possess the visible unless he is possessed by it.[10]

As Elizabeth Grosz, the feminist theorist, notes, "Seeing entails having a body that is itself capable of being seen, that is visible." This "fundamental reversibility" is like that of touch, which Merleau-Ponty calls the "double sensation": "My right hand is capable of touching my left hand, as if the latter was an object. But in this case, unlike an object, my left hand feels the right hand touching it. My left hand has the double sensation of being both the object and the subject of the touch." The toucher is always touched; likewise, Merleau-Ponty argues, the seer's visibility conditions vision itself. This claim runs counter to the classical conception of vision, in which "the seer, in seeing at a distance, is unimplicated in what is seen." Here, though, reversibility is asymmetrical. "It is in this sense that the trees can be said to 'see' the painter. . . . The trees are a mirror of my visibility, as is anything I see."[11]

If Abraham, then, comes to see the land of Canaan, it is because he is made of the same "flesh" as it is: embodied to the fullest extent. Such embodiment, implicating him in the holiness of the Holy Land, is, according to Rashi, what God has promised him: by adding a *heh* to his name, his body is completed. Significantly, the midrash points out, he acquires eyes, ears, and sexuality (five organs)—equivalent to the numerical value of the letter *heh*. Some fullness of vision, hearing, and touch will allow him to communicate with the world at a different level of intimacy. Individual senses become part of an organic body image. As Grosz notes, "It is through the mediation of the body image that the information provided by the different bodily senses can be integrated, unified, coordinated, or even put into comparison or conflict."[12]

This new body is, apparently, part of the freight that Abraham is to gain from his journey. In other words, the traveling itself, the travail, the labor, the birth pangs will transfigure him; create him anew, as the Zohar claims. This is the promised freight of *lekha*—a matter not of arriving at a destination but of the process itself that engenders that future, unknown self.

This process is, essentially, a private one: *lekha* emphasizes a personal transfiguration. Strikingly, even though Abraham's journey is clearly no solitary one—he is accompanied by family and others, cryptically referred to as "the souls they had made in Haran" (Gen. 12:5)[13]—the repeated thrust of God's invitation is toward a privacy of experience. Opening our ears to the repeated sound, *kha*, "you," in the text—*lekha, artzkha, moladtkha, beit avikha, e'es-kha, va'avarkha mevorkhekha, vekha*—we are drawn into an almost hypnotically intimate address to a past and future self.

.   .   .

REDUCING THE HABITUAL SELF

Accessing this unknown self, however, requires relinquishing much of the habitual vision of the past. Abraham is to leave his land, his birthplace, his father's house. It is as though he is to remove all biases, in order to achieve a pure, unclouded vision. This would approximate Husserl's rule, the "phenomenological reduction": to perceive intuitively, without thinking about perceiving. Picasso is reputed to have said that it took him just a few years to draw like Raphael, but the rest of his life to paint like a child. But both Picasso and Husserl clearly recognized the difficulty of such a process: many years of work go into learning to see what stands before our eyes.

Freud developed a method, free association, for reducing the cloud of conscious assumptions. By suspending judgment about the contents of his mind, the analysand is asked to speak without censorship, in effect, to reduce himself. "One suspends what one knows so that one might discover what one could not see before." The analyst, too, is asked to maintain a state of "evenly hovering attention," in which one "proceeds, as it were, without any purpose in view, allows oneself to be taken by surprise by any new turn in [one's cases], and always meets them with an open mind, free from any presuppositions."[14] As Paul Ricoeur puts it, "Corresponding to the 'total communication' on the part of the patient is the 'total listening' on the part of the analyst."[15]

Out of this analytic relationship, new possibilities emerge. What is discovered is the offspring of constant transformations, an endless dialogue. The element of surprise in such a journey is emphasized by Freud. In Abraham's journey, this element is continually released by the unknown-ness of his destination: it *will* be shown him, he *will* become visible. In a sense, he will never arrive: "the land that I will show you" is the name of his destination, that place of infinite desire.[16]

THE NEW SELF—RADICAL ANXIETY

But the other significant dimension of such a journey in which one suspends what one knows is, simply, anxiety. Most concrete in God's invocation are the worlds to be relinquished. How to imagine Abraham's situation? In a famous but startling analogy, the midrash compares him to a young woman who is urged to forget her past and embrace her future:

> "God said to Abraham, Go forth from your land . . ." R. Isaac commenced with, "Listen, daughter, and see, and incline your ear; forget your own people, and your father's house" (Ps. 45:11).
>
> Said R. Isaac, This may be compared to a man who was traveling from place to place when he saw a castle on fire. He said, "Would you say that the castle is without a lord?" The lord of the castle glanced out at him and said, "I am the lord of the castle." Similarly, because Abraham our father said, "Would you say that the world is without a master," God glanced out at him and said, "I am the master of the world."
>
> "So shall the king desire your beauty" (Ps. 45:12): to make you beautiful in the world. "For he is your lord, so do homage to him" (Ps. 45:12) So, "God said to Abraham, Go forth . . ."[17]

With this passage, *Bereshit Rabbah* opens its section on *Lekh lekha*. God's invocation to Abraham is juxtaposed with the text from Psalms: a young woman is invited to see, and to hear; and to forget. Like Abraham, she is to forget her people and her father's house. She becomes an iconic figure, clarifying something essential about Abraham's position. She is Everybride: leaving her father's house involves a *forgetting*, an inner suppression, the need to turn away from a powerful attachment. The purpose of this forgetting is spelled out at the end of the verse—and at the end of the midrash—"so shall the king desire your beauty": if she is to enter into a barely imaginable erotic relationship with her husband, she must abandon an ancient love with its secret erotic freight. This most commonplace journey, outer and inner, of young women in all times and places becomes the emblematic Abraham situation, signified by the words *Lekh lekha*. Playing strangely across gender lines, the midrash configures Abraham as a young woman poised between identities. In order even to entertain this notion, (s)he must listen, see intently, beyond habitual perceptions.

This demand, however, the ordinary demand made of any young woman who leaves home to marry, is radically threatening. Abraham is cast into a condition of anxiety—not simply as an uncomfortable feeling, but as a structural conception. Herbert Fingarette summarizes a number of perspectives on anxiety: he uses the term to describe a process of ego disintegration, in which he defines the ego as the autonomous drive toward meaning, and anxiety as meaninglessness.[18] In the movement toward a "new self," a radical gap opens between old self and new; a genuinely new organization of ego has to be, at least partially, created or invented. The breakdown of one's past inner integrity is a breakdown in meaning, with its inevitable concomitant of anxiety:

> The encounter with anxiety is at least temporarily a de-moralizing blow, and the response, except in the most degenerated psychoses, is one of attempting to re-moralize the self, to re-establish the foundations of one's autonomy, of personal integrity. . . . The religious ordeal is a crisis in which man seeks autonomy, an autonomy which in its concrete reality is inherently unknown because as yet unexperienced or at most dimly glimpsed by him. Though unknown in its content, it must be sought. One must be open to it, ready to receive it. Indeed, one must accept it *before* fully and concretely knowing what one has achieved. . . . It is, in this sense, arbitrary.[19]

The structure underlying such processes is, Fingarette claims, the same, whether one uses religious, psychoanalytic, or existential language: a quality of primal chaos accompanies the intuition of a future order. This anxiety must be encountered openly and without defenses: ego disorganization is in itself neither neurotic nor creative. The ego's response to stress may either assume compulsive postures of avoidance or surrender itself to a new, unknown form of integrity. The ego in the process of dissolution may then give birth to a new self that is *inherently unknown* and, in a sense, arbitrary.

God's call—*Lekh lekha*—evokes in Abraham just such an anxiety. The midrash brings him into a framework of commonplace experience: the experience of young women throughout the ages. But, of course, the language in which the psalm couches this experience is not at all commonplace. Rather, it emphasizes the poignancy of anxiety and desire released in the bride. And it lends Abraham's situation something of that same anxiety and desire, caught between old meaning and new meaning, desiring he knows not what. *Lekh lekha*, the Zohar translates—"Go *create yourself anew*." And Midrash Tanchuma reads God's promise: " 'I shall make you into a great nation'—You I shall make as *a new creation*."[20] Abraham's very being is to dissolve, while some new mutation emerges.

THE FEMININE METAPHOR

The spiritual freight of his journey, then, is an emergent self. The character of this new self is, in the language of the midrash, *beauty:* " 'So the king shall desire your beauty'—to make you beautiful in the world." Why are these the terms—feminine, erotic—that are chosen to delineate Abraham's journey? There is a dissonance between the erotic intimation of the bride's future and Abraham's destiny: in what sense is his relation with "the world" to be colored by beauty and desire? Might wisdom not have constituted a more dignified attraction in Abraham, gracing him in the eyes of God and man? And why, precisely, does the midrash focus on his relation with "the world" rather than on his relation with God, where the erotic theme might have been easier to assimilate? It is almost as though Abraham's essential "marriage" is with the world rather than with God. Furthermore, why does the midrash interpose the parable of the burning castle into the midst of its discussion of the bride's anxiety?

THE FIERY FURNACE: VINDICATING GOD'S CHOICE

With these questions in suspension, we return to the more concrete level of God's invocation. What, in fact, is the value of this journey? Ramban cogently argues that the information given in the Torah is insufficient:

Now this passage of Torah is not completely elucidated. What reason was there that God should say to Abraham, "Leave your country, and I grant you goodness beyond all precedent," without first explaining that Abraham worshipped God or that he was a perfectly righteous man? Or it should explain that Abraham's journey to another land constituted a quest for God. The custom in the Torah is to call for spiritual growth: "Walk before me; and listen to My voice, and I will do good to you," as with David and Solomon, as well as throughout the Torah: "If you walk in My statutes; And it will be, if you listen intently to the voice of your God." And in the case of Isaac, it says, "For my servant's Abraham's sake." But simply leaving his country is no reason for God to offer Abraham reward.

However, the reason for God's promise is that the people of Ur of the Chaldeans persecuted him on account of his belief in God, and he fled from them to go to the land of Canaan, staying for a while at Haran, till God told him to leave these places as well and to fulfill his original intention to worship God alone and to call upon people to worship God in the chosen land. There he would make his name great, and these nations would bless themselves by him, not as they treated him in Ur of the Chaldeans, where they abused and cursed him, put him in prison or in the fiery furnace. He further told Abraham that He would bless those who bless him, and if some individual would curse him, he would in turn be cursed.[21]

In this compelling passage, Ramban raises fundamental questions. His most general problem is about the gaps that undermine the cogency of the narrative. Why is Abraham chosen for a destiny of blessing? No clue to justify God's selection can be detected. Moreover, what is the spiritual valency of the journey? There is no overt expression of an inner quest: surely a merely physical journey would not carry such blessing in its wake? Both questions have to do with what is absent from the text.

In order to provide an answer to his questions, Ramban has recourse to a classic midrash, according to which Abraham is condemned to death, by fiery furnace, for refusing to worship the idols of his homeland—indeed, in some versions, for smashing his father's idols and defying Nimrod, the king. This midrash, which justifies the choice of Abraham as a would-be martyr for the One God, is de-mythicized by Ramban. The fiery furnace becomes merely one possible form of persecution: his contemporaries abuse and curse him, cast him in prison, *or in the fiery furnace*. This general atmosphere of persecution inspires Abraham to flee—first from Ur of the Chaldeans, then, urged by God, from Haran. The *Lekh lekha* command, therefore, comes to ratify Abraham's desire to serve Him alone and to promise him a more receptive audience in the land of Canaan.

It is striking that Ramban treats the fiery furnace midrash as not only historically true but essential for the meaning of Abraham's narrative. Without a persecution story, representing Abraham as a martyr figure, God's choice of him becomes arbitrary. Another striking feature is that God's command merely confirms Abraham's own determination to flee persecution. The blessings are to compensate for the abuse he has suffered. His journey is not a spiritual quest initiated by God's command, but rather a move to a more hospitable climate for his message. In this way, Ramban fills in the prehistory of *Lekh lekha* with a pragmatic version of the fiery furnace midrash. Only later will the journey become metaphorical or spiritual—when God invokes him to "walk before Me and become whole" (Gen. 17:1) in precisely the terms that Ramban fails to find here.

One final comment closes Ramban's discussion: the question of the omission of the fiery furnace narrative from the Torah text. If, indeed, some version of this midrash is essential for a coherent reading, why is it not included in the Torah itself? Ramban's answer raises the issue of the politics of faith: the Torah avoids dwelling on theological debate over idolatry. In order to avoid such discussions, the whole martyrdom narrative is omitted; an essential narrative of the past is repressed.

Like other commentators—Rambam and Abarbanel, for instance—Ramban gives the fiery furnace midrash historical status and, by that move, aims to reduce the mystery of God's invocation. But the mystery—or mysteries—that he himself so powerfully indicated are constitutive of the Torah text as we have it. The repressed persecution story leaves us with a significant gap. After all the explanations are exhausted, we are struck anew by the irreducibly enig-

matic quality of God's call: *Lekh lekha*—*Who? Why? When? Where?*
Ramban's historical hypothesis cannot tame the baffling starkness
of the words.

Later, God will reintroduce Himself to Abraham—"*I am God who
brought you out* of Ur of the Chaldeans to give you this land as inheritance" (Gen. 15:7). Echoing within the words is God's opening statement in the Ten Commandments: "*I am the Lord your God who brought
you out* of the land of Egypt" (Exod. 20:2). The histories of both fore-
father and nation begin when God releases them from a perilous
place of origin. In both narratives, God plays a role, His presence
manifest in miracles and plagues in the national history, more
cryptic in Abraham's story. If God's command merely confirms
Abraham's own decision to flee persecution, little remains of its
transfigurative power.

LEKH LEKHA: THE PEDAGOGICAL VOYAGE

Rambam, also basing himself on the fiery furnace midrash, provides
an alternative prehistory for Abraham:

> After this mighty man was weaned, he began to explore and
> think. Though he was a child, he began to think incessantly, by
> day and by night, wondering: How is it possible for the sphere
> to continue to revolve without anyone controlling it? Who is
> causing it to revolve? Surely, it does not revolve by itself?
>
> He had no teacher, nor was there anyone to inform him.
> Rather, he was mired in Ur of the Chaldeans among the foolish
> idolaters. His father, mother, and all the people around him
> were idol worshippers, and he would worship with them. How-
> ever, his heart was exploring and gaining understanding.
>
> Ultimately, he achieved the way of truth and understood the
> path of righteousness through his accurate comprehension. He
> realized that there is one God who controls the sphere, that He
> created everything, and that there is no other God among all the
> other entities. He knew that the entire world was in error. What
> caused them to err was their worship of the stars and images,
> which made them lose awareness of the truth.

Abraham was forty years old when he became aware of his Creator. When he recognized and knew Him, he began to formulate replies to the inhabitants of Ur of the Chaldeans and debate with them, telling them that they were not following a proper path.

He broke their idols and began to teach the people that it is fitting to serve only the God of the Universe. To Him alone is it fitting to bow down, sacrifice, and offer libations, so that the people of future generations will recognize Him. Conversely, it is fitting to destroy and break all the images, lest everyone err in relation to them, like those people who thought that there are no other gods besides these images.

When he overcame them through the strength of his arguments, the king wanted to kill him. He was saved through a miracle and left for Haran. There, he began to call in a loud voice to all, informing them that there is one God in the entire world and that it is proper to worship Him. He would go out and call to the people, gathering them in city after city and country after country, until he came to the land of Canaan—proclaiming God's existence, as it says: "And He called there in the name of the Lord, the eternal God" (Gen. 21:33).

When the people would gather around him and ask him about his claims, he would explain them to each one individually, according to his understanding, until they turned to the path of truth. Ultimately, thousands and myriads gathered around him. These are the men of the house of Abraham.

He planted in their hearts this great fundamental principle, composed texts about it, and taught it to Isaac, his son.[22]

In this narrative, Abraham's inner world explorations are matched against his life in the social and physical world: from his early years as a thinker to his later years as a teacher. From early childhood, his wanderings begin as intellectual forays. His questions are inspired by wonder, which is according to Aristotle the motive-force behind philosophy: his wonder about the cosmos and its movements leads him inexorably to the notion of a Prime Mover. Strikingly, Abraham's thought is conducted in isolation from his physical and social context: he continues worshipping the idols of his "stupid" family and contemporaries. The contemptuous epithet could be read as the editorial comment of the writer, but seems also to express the split in Abraham's consciousness, evoking Abraham's inner dissociation from the world in which he, to all appearances, participates.

This thinking process, which, according to Rambam, lasts from age three to age forty,[23] brings him to full enlightenment about the One God. Then he enters with full and antagonistic force into the world of his society—smashing idols, both literally and metaphorically. His intellectual iconoclasticism takes the form of debates in which he is so successful that he becomes a threat to the reigning pieties. The king's intention to execute him is foiled by a miracle, so that he escapes to Haran, where he continues to teach the truth of the One God to masses of students who accompany him on his long journey to Canaan. His teaching consists most significantly of one-on-one dialogues; myriads of students attach themselves to him.

LEARNING AND TEACHING

In Rambam's narrative, Abraham's life is constituted of stark contrasts. Thinker and teacher, he first seeks for truth and later disseminates it: secrecy marks his early life and publicity his later life. Rambam emphasizes the intellectual conquest of truth and its propagation by debate; he also, significantly, separates the two stages—the quest for knowledge of God and the teaching of that knowledge. Strikingly, the fiery furnace disappears into a generalized death threat from the king. *Lekh lekha* is also absorbed into Abraham's pursuit of the widest audience for his message: persecution and enforced exile evolve into a pedagogical voyage of a myriad encounters.

Here, the mythic terror of the furnace midrash has been entirely effaced. Abraham is the pure philosopher, his true life hidden from the vulgar view until he has achieved his own closure. Then begins the other life, in which he teaches and travels, unprompted by divine voices, to Canaan. The truth that Rambam is concerned with is the Aristotelian truth that is first acquired and then propagated.

This clear distinction between learning and teaching delineates, of course, a particular view of the learning process. The radical American thinker and educator John Holt, attacking views of this kind, writes about "learning to play the cello" and "about the strange idea" that there exist two very different processes: learning to play, and playing. "Of course, this is nonsense. There are not two processes, but one. We learn to do something by doing it. There is no other way."[24] This performative dimension of learning can be applied to a wide range of projects, beyond the literally performance arts. For Rambam, however, the kind of learning that Abraham is engaged in is clearly of a different order: it can be achieved once and for all, to be followed by the quite different activity of teaching. His narrative does not embrace the idea of an endless learning process, in which the teacher continues to learn in and through the act of teaching.[25]

SOCRATIC ABRAHAM

Another significant aspect of Rambam's account is his version of Abraham as Socrates. In emphasizing both Abraham's solitary work toward truth and the tutorial, dialogic nature of his teaching, Rambam is rather clearly modeling his Abraham on the great Athenian philosopher. Abraham's strategy to overcome the "stupidity" of idolaters is to stage "therapeutic" debates, which ultimately engage with the nature of the good life. In these dialogues, which are initiated by the questions of others, his purpose is iconoclasm, the breaking of idols. Plato describes Socrates in similar terms. Socrates is accosted by questioners who find that he has seized the reins of the dialogue and led them, inexorably, to undermine their own assumptions. In both cases, success in debate makes the philosopher a threat to the state: Socrates is charged with corrupting the young and repudiates all attempts to save his life, whereas Abraham is saved from execution "by a miracle."

I suggest that Rambam's account of Abraham's ultimate success as a teacher-philosopher deliberately evokes Socrates' unhappy end. Among his last words, Socrates famously said, "The unexamined life is not worth living," suggesting that thinking may transform, even heal a life. But the fact that he was sentenced to death and executed can be regarded as an indictment of his therapeutic method. This is Jonathan Lear's claim: "His cross-examination was meant to make people better, but it provoked the demos to act out its murderous impulses."[26] Abraham, on the other hand, uses a similar dialogic method and lives to affect myriads. We will return later to the question of Socrates' failure.

BURNING CASTLE

This alternative prehistory creates a Socratic Abraham who, mysteriously, evades Socrates' fate. In constructing the early Abraham in this way, Rambam is, I suggest, consciously countering the central midrashic tradition that we have already begun to explore. Nothing could be further from Rambam's triumphant philosopher than the young woman who is provoked by some unnamed voice to see, to hear, to forget, and to be desired for her beauty by her lord. How far Rambam has moved from the midrashic configuration can be seen from the middle section of the midrash, which we have not yet discussed:

> Said R. Isaac, This may be compared to a man who was traveling from place to place when he saw a castle on fire. He said, "Would you say that the castle is without a lord?" The lord of the castle glanced out at him and said, "I am the lord of the castle." Similarly, because Abraham our father said, "Would you say that the world is without a master?" God glanced out at him and said, "I am the master of the world."

Breaking away from the young woman caught between father and future husband—in fact, in the midst of discussing the proof text from Psalms—the midrash configures Abraham as a traveler "from place to place," who is transfixed by the enigma of the burning castle. He asks, ambiguously, "Would you say that the castle is without a lord?" Does he assume that the owner must be absent, since the castle is ablaze and no one cares to extinguish the flames? Or—on the contrary—is he incredulous: "Could you possibly say that the castle is ownerless?" In line with this would be a different reading of the expression *doleket:* the castle is not burning, it is alight, illumined. Someone, clearly, is in residence.

What, then, is the traveler's question? What does he expect by way of an answer? Is there a way of knowing if the lord of the world is in fact in residence—other than by the evidence of the conflagration—or illumination—that the traveler witnesses? The scandal of a world afire—with injustice, sin, violence—torments our traveler, whose journey leads him without clear destination from one place to another. Or, alternatively, he is dazzled by the beauty and order of the world—the castle is fully lit—so that his question becomes a celebration, and a critique of skepticism. The ambiguity engenders two contrary expressions—of despair and of hope, of skepticism and of intimacy—within the same question. Does Abraham know what is before his eyes? Desire and dread emerge from the interplay of meanings.

To this question there is no unambiguous answer. The owner "glances out at him and declares, I am master of the castle." This is the transformative moment: a flash of eyes meeting, something suggested. It seems that the vehemence of the traveler's question provokes the lord of the castle to reveal Himself, with no more than the barest identification.

MUTUAL SEEING

What is Abraham to do with this revelation? Abraham Joshua Heschel writes: "Religion, the end of isolation, begins with a consciousness that something is asked of us. . . . Wonder is not a state of esthetic enjoyment. Endless wonder unlocks an innate sense of indebtedness."[27] The master of the castle meets Abraham's gaze with His own: What is the enigmatic message of this fraught moment?

In the reading of Mei Ha-Shilo'ach,[28] this *hatzatzah*, the glance of the Master, is an intimation, a glimmer produced by the courage of the traveler's question. Ultimately, the intimation reveals the traveler to himself: it is a moment of self-awareness, in which he takes the measure of his own protest and his terror/wonder at the Masterless world. In this flash of knowledge, the question becomes the answer; in the midst of his torment, the traveler finds an avenue to consciousness. The emphasis here is on Abraham's quest for *himself,* for the "root of his own life." This is the literal rendition of *Lekh lekha*—"Go *to yourself."*

On this reading, there is a moment of mutual seeing, as Abraham becomes suddenly and shockingly aware of God's glance. "He who sees cannot possess the visible unless he is possessed by it, unless he is of it."[29] What possesses Abraham is God's vision of his own passionate questioning. Suddenly, God inhabits Abraham's own hope and despair, the doubleness of his outcry. "Would you say there is no master to the world?"

Knowing himself seen by God in all his desire and dread, his question becomes suffused with the force of Isaiah's question, with which the Zohar opens: *"Who created these?"* Skepticism and intimacy animate the question. As Adam Phillips puts it, "Questions are . . . the grammatical form we give to our desire."[30]

On this reading, then, Abraham's turbulent questioning engenders a new consciousness: the quest for God is a quest for a yet-unknown self. In Heschel's words, "something is asked" of him. In its context, however, the traveler theme is embedded in the frame narrative of the young woman urged to see-hear-forget her father's house—so that her beauty may be desired by her husband. The moment of *Lekh lekha* is the moment when a God-voice urges the bride to a fuller, ineffable self, which can be realized only by "forgetting" her familiar identity. This is also the moment when God's glance transfigures the traveler's knowledge of the world and of himself. In both parables, Abraham knows himself seen and is urged to act on that sense of being seen. *Lekh lekha* becomes a provocation to endless unfoldings of self under the glance of God. *Lekh lekha* offers an exposure to God as "the subject of all, as the life of our life, as the mind of our mind." "In thinking of Him, we realize that it is through Him that we think of Him."[31]

In this sense, the Zohar's translation of *Lekh lekha,* in all its simplicity, offers a larger revelation: "Go about the remaking, the transfiguration of you." In their historical narratives of Abraham's journey, Rambam and Ramban clarify the good, the benefit of his move from the persecution of Ur of the Chaldeans to the pedagogical triumphs of his life in Canaan. But in doing so, they suppress the mystery of his movement toward an always unknown future self. The midrash, on the other hand, emphasizes the erotic nature of this quest: the future holds beauty and desire, as well as anxiety.

THE PUBLIC GAZE

As we have noticed, however, the midrash translates the bride's beauty in her husband's eyes into a dialect of *general* desirability: "The king shall desire your beauty: to make you *beautiful in the world.*" A beauty is to unfold in Abraham that will affect all who see him. That is God's desire: that Abraham should be experienced as beautiful by the whole world.

At this point, the gap between the midrash and Rambam's version of Abraham's prehistory becomes most striking. For Rambam, Abraham affects the world powerfully, by debate, by dialogue, Socratic in nature, whose aim is to expose contradictions in the worldview of his protagonist, thus inexorably leading him to a lucid vision of truth. In this classic midrash, however, he is to be desired for his beauty. His effect on the world will be of an erotic rather than an intellectual order. His *Lekh lekha* journey will create a deepening subjective awareness of himself as seen by God; and this will constitute his beauty in the eyes of others.

The emphasis on beauty, desire, and especially the public gaze, is arresting. In order to think further about this, I suggest that we turn now to another midrash, in fact the next passage in *Bereshit Rabbah*. These two passages evoke an Abraham who eludes prosaic description:

R. Berachiah began: "Your ointments yield a sweet fragrance, your name is decanted oil" (Songs 1:3). What did Abraham resemble? A vial of myrrh sealed with a tight lid and lying in a corner, so that its fragrance was not diffused; as soon as it was moved, however, its fragrance was diffused. Similarly, God said to Abraham: "Travel from place to place, and your name will become great in the world!"—So—"Go forth. . . ."[32]

Abraham has become a vial of myrrh—a bottle of perfume. God addresses the perfume—*Lekh lekha*—Travel from place to place so that your fragrance may waft far and wide. This is Abraham, whose name is to be made great. The subject, then, is fame, the spreading of Abraham's renown in the world. And the strategy is to unseal, to agitate *(tiltul)*—a turbulent motion that will disseminate the fragrance through the world.

The perfume image evokes many associations—sealed off in a bottle, wadded in a corner, the perfume is, essentially, not acting like perfume: its power and beauty are, at best, potential. Once unsealed and in motion, it affects in intimate and unpredictable ways the desire/life of human beings. Barely belonging to the world of matter, a drop seduces to incalculable effect. At one limit, it brings new life into the world. Precious, a drop fills endless space, haunts endless time; it evokes idiosyncratic histories; although it is usually worn by women, it has a masculine, generative power. Abraham is urged to unseal himself and to set himself in a kind of blind motion—in order to create love connections in the world.

Here, the *Lekh lekha* command provokes Abraham to relinquish a certain constraint: he is to lend himself to a more dynamic selfhood. Traveling from place to place, he becomes a medium for agitated questions; he discovers the world as a "vale of Soul-making."[33] Spontaneously, the perfume disseminates, and evokes, and creates other souls. This is the literal meaning of the expression used at the beginning of Abraham's journey to describe his travel companions—"the souls they had made in Haran" (Gen. 12:5).[34]

Abraham's erotic impact finds a precise expression in the proof text from Song of Songs: "Your ointments yield a sweet fragrance, your name is decanted oil." The verse ends: "Therefore young girls love you." Another midrash elaborates:

> R. Yochanan decoded this to refer to Abraham. God said to Abraham, "Abraham, Many good deeds are yours, set yourself in motion in the world, and your name will be made great in My world"—as it is said, "Go forth. . . ." What is written directly after this? "And I will make you into a great nation." "Therefore young girls *[alamot]* love you" (Songs 1:3). God said, "You have

many *olamot,* many worlds"—as it is written. "And Abraham took . . . the souls they had made in Haran" (Gen. 12:5). If one were to mobilize the whole world to create one mosquito, one could not do it . . . ! [How did they create souls?] These are the proselytes that Abraham and Sarah made. . . . This teaches that anyone who brings one creature under the wings of the Shekhina is described as though he had created him.[35]

Abraham has become the prototype of *tiltul:* the restless movement that releases a personal perfume. Here, *mitzvot u-ma'asim tovim,* Abraham's ethical and religious being, becomes, without any effort of representation on his part, perceptible in the world. The young girls who are drawn to this essence of self are a figure for proselytes, attracted by the fine diffusions of Abraham's inwardness. Here, the midrash plays with the word *alamot* (young girls): he will be loved by many *olamot,* many worlds, many souls roused to fuller being. The erotic energy of the young girls mingles with the complex associations of the world that is a human soul.[36]

Like perfume, too, Abraham's effect diffuses over large distances. Its initial exposure, however, is a simple act of *decanting,* pouring from one flask to another. This is the moment of transaction, when Abraham goes out in spirit toward the worlds of others, and when what had been only potentially fragrant is released.

The power of the perfume image lies, ultimately, in its absurdity. Sealed in a vial, perfume is, effectively, nothing at all. Diffused, penetrating fantasy worlds, it evokes infinite longings, it may create new souls and, indeed, new life. *Lekh lekha*—perhaps the midrash reads the two words as identical—*lekh lekh* ("Go! Go!")—a restless enactment of the *tiltul* God provokes in Abraham. In his generative diffusion, without knowing his trajectory ahead of time, he will transfigure the worlds of others.

THE SYMPOSIUM: EROS UNDONE

It is striking to compare this midrash with Plato's work on the same subject, the *Symposium.* Here Plato describes Eros as bridging the gap between the transcendent and the immanent realms, between humans and gods. Tragically, however, the narrative demonstrates that Eros cannot perform this function: Socrates cannot influence the all-too-human Alcibiades with his own divine version of Eros. Alcibiades, drunk and unruly, not only disrupts the philosophical salon that is the Symposium but, in Jonathan Lear's powerful reading, he also undoes the Symposium's account of love. The very idea of Eros as a developmental force is undermined by the spectacle of Socrates' failure to reach Alcibiades, who is trapped in the human erotic condition: "As any contemporary reader would have known, Alcibiades will go on to betray his polis with tragic consequences for Athenian civilization."[37] Socrates' dialogues examine the question "How shall I live?" in ways that are reminiscent of the psychoanalytic project; but in that case, Lear claims, his therapeutic method is signally unsuccessful. Far from making people better, it provokes them to murder him. It is a "psychotherapeutic disaster."[38]

Socrates' main mistake, Lear claims, was to ignore the psychological dynamic of transference. Only the conscious beliefs of his interlocutor are elicited. He pays no attention to the web of private meanings and fantasies, of wishes and fears, in which conscious ideas are embedded. This network of unconscious associations creates a meaningful world for the analysand—Lear calls this an *idiopolis,* an idiosyncratic polis. In a psychoanalytic relationship, the analyst is drawn into this private world, with all its conflicts and fantasies. The transference, the patient's relationship with the analyst, becomes a "playground," with the analyst now inside the game and able to analyze the psyche's conflicts. The aim is to take apart a private world that held the analysand captive.

The paradox at the core of the psychoanalytic enterprise, as Freud himself noted, is that transference regularly manifests itself as a *resistance* to analysis: it is an expression of erotic longing that makes the world over to an image of what would gratify one's most basic wishes. A case in point is Alcibiades, who resists Socrates' modeling of divine love, avoids any form of reflection that might lead to development, and uses his erotic attachment to Socrates to stay just where he is. Socrates, for his part, shows no real interest in Alcibiades; he is indifferent to those trapped in the human realm, since he himself has left behind all particularity: "he has become as divine as humanly possible."[39]

Socrates' failure, Lear argues, is catastrophic in its implications: "Nothing less is at stake than the future of one of the world's great civilizations." In contrast with the Socratic approach to the human-erotic, the psychoanalytic approach places individuation, particularity, subjectivity at the center. Idiosyncratic experience, phantasies, drives are explored, not jettisoned. "Phantasy takes up the body and the bodily to express itself, and may enliven the body in so doing."[40] Eros comes to provide a gradient against which development can occur. The analyst is seen as beautiful, and archaic love demands function as a resistance to the process of analysis. The resistance itself, however, the erotic distraction, is worked through. "Transference which seems ordained to become the greatest obstacle to psychoanalysis becomes its most powerful ally."[41] Only in this way can the human being, in all his/her concrete reality, become freer to "give birth in beauty."

TRANSFERENTIAL LOVE

On this view, wish, desire, and fantasy can be mobilized toward a more creative and meaningful life. It is here, at the point of keenest difference between the Socratic and the psychoanalytic approach, that the midrashic imagery of Abraham as perfume gathers life. For Rambam, we have suggested, Abraham may be a redeemed version of Socrates: he is saved by a miracle from the fate of those who accost others, challenging them to change their world. But Rambam's account of Abraham's teaching by dialogue pays no more attention to transference, it seems, than does Socrates. Abraham's debates engage only with the conscious beliefs of his "analysands." If he is more successful than Socrates, the reason is not psychologically evident.

In the midrash, however, perfume represents precisely that allusive world that Abraham evokes in others. Transferential love is aroused for the beauty that becomes, in those who open themselves to it, a *subjective* experience. Erotic yearning is released but, strangely, is not fixated on Abraham as charismatic object. Young girls may love him, but this love generates in them new worlds. He suggests, rather than teaches. Perfume, after all, is not adored; what is adored is what it evokes.

Heschel writes of the experience of wonder: "What we encounter in our perception of the sublime, in our radical amazement, is a spiritual suggestiveness of reality, an *allusiveness* to transcendent meaning."[42] Inexpressible, allusive, Abraham is experienced by others in the same way as he himself senses the ineffable in his own life.

We remember Rashi's comment on God's provocation: " 'Go forth . . . to the land that I will show you': He did not immediately reveal to him which land . . . to make it *precious* in his eyes." Abraham's journey, open, allusive, inexpressible in conscious terms (Where is he going? What good will it do him?) is sensed as precious, as creating an intimacy with God. Those who encounter him may think him mad. But as he moves, a new fragrance permeates the world.

The perfume metaphor, then, suggests a third possibility, between the Socratic and the psychoanalytic. Transferential love may be released in a mode that remains relatively free of the person of the beautiful object. Redemptive rather than therapeutic, something is sparked around which unconscious associations gather.

Wittgenstein, in discussing ethics with the philosopher Bouwsma, spoke of reading Kierkegaard:

He [Wittgenstein] had read some. Kierkegaard is very serious. But he could not read him much. He got hints. He did not want another man's thought all chewed. A word or two was sometimes enough. . . . The most important things just happen to you.[43]

"He got hints." The slightness of the input makes it volatile, dynamic. Hints penetrate in a mysterious way. Adam Phillips notes: "We are unconscious of where our affinities—our psychic affiliations—might come from, and where they may lead us."[44]

Abraham as perfume, then, suggests the unconscious pathways

by which his teaching affects others. The effect is that they think their own thoughts. In this sense, he brings the glance of God into their worlds.

THE BREATH OF THE QUESTION

Perfume, of course, can be disturbing, invasive. It may engage with areas of experience that are, in a real sense, *not there*. It raises questions, lowers barriers, evokes the unthinkable, transfigures the known. Words can be like perfume; hints can implicate people with one another. In the end, however, these microprocesses of the inner life declare themselves in explicit ways. Abram's name is changed to Abraham. His body is changed, as he circumcises himself. Five organs become in the fullest sense his own—eyes, ears, and sexual organ; so that his name gains the letter *heh* (connoting five) and signifies the 248 organs of the human body.

Human body and psyche are completed only by the existence of the letter *heh*, which also signifies the *question*.[45] As Abraham arrives—in Canaan, in a complete body image, in an enlarged name—a particular subjectivity comes into being. That this process of emergent being might be a religious process is the suggestion of, among others, R. Yitzhak Hutner.[46] He addresses the *Braita* that outlines the course of Jewish history: "At first, our ancestors were idolaters; but now, God has brought us close to His service."[47] The process of growing intimacy with God, he notes, was initiated by God's command, *Lekh lekha*. The open-ended command brings Abraham into the field of questioning: he will find his destination only after prolonged not-finding; he will question every place he encounters; and only by way of the urgency of his questions will he come at knowledge at all.

Moreover, as we have noticed, in his autobiographical account of his departure from his father's house and his growing intimacy with God, Abraham emphasizes the pathos, the uncanny nature of his journey: "When God *made me wander* from my father's house. . . ." Made me wander, lost me, charged me with questions . . . All redemptive processes, R. Hutner implies, are informed with this dynamic:

real questions, real perplexities create the hunger that makes knowledge vital. Knowledge ingested without hunger starts nothing, sparks nothing. "Often, a solution has much greater need of a problem than a problem has of a solution." The question, the desire, is the vital energy of knowledge.

This is the energy that moves Abraham from idolatry to intimacy with God. The *heh*, the breath of questioning, releases a particular fragrance: "Would you say that the castle is without a lord?" *"Who created these?"* Like Socrates' question—"What is involved in being truly human?"—such questions can be answered in more or less facile ways. The puzzle behind the words can be resolved easily and simply, but it releases new depths with every resolution.

VALE OF SOUL-MAKING

R. Hutner cites the Rabbinic aphorism "One never gets the true sense of [lit., stands upon] the words of Torah until one has mistaken them [lit., stumbled over them]."[48] Only when stability is lost, when given answers no longer offer support, can one reach for a different kind of stability. Stumbling and falling are the means by which standing is achieved; once one's nerves and muscles have lurched out of control, one can know what it is to hold one's position. The prophet Micah says: "Do not rejoice over me, my enemy! Though I have fallen, I will rise again; though I sit in darkness, God is my light" (Micah 7:8). The midrash adds: "If I had not fallen, I should not have risen up; if I had not sat in darkness, God would not be my light."[49] The dialectic transcends a simple notion of, for example, appreciating the light best after the dark. Light has *no meaning* unless darkness has preceded it; answers are vapid unless they respond to deeply felt questions.

John Keats poignantly celebrates this world as a "World of Pains and troubles" and as a "vale of Soul-making":

There may be intelligences or sparks of the divinity in millions—but they are not Souls till they acquire identities, till each one is personally itself. . . . How then are Souls to be made? . . . How, but by the medium of a world like this? . . . Do you not see how necessary a World of Pains and troubles is to school an Intelligence and make it a Soul?[50]

In an earlier letter, he writes of the effect of such a world in

sharpening one's vision into the heart and nature of Man—of convincing one's nerves that the world is full of Misery and Heartbreak, Pain, Sickness and oppression . . . . We see not the balance of good and evil. We are in a Mist. *We* are now in that state—We feel the "burden of the Mystery."[51]

Uninhibited by the seriousness of his subject, Keats plays with "mist" and "mystery": the darkness of the inner chamber is a cloud of unknowing. But here and only here, he later realizes, can Souls be made, here the God-given Intelligence becomes individual, idiosyncratic. "How, but by the medium of a world like this?" To school the intelligence, a heart must feel and suffer. Identity can be suckled, in Keats's precise metaphor, only by a heart and nerves sharpened to a vision of the world of Misery and Heartbreak. So are souls made: in darkness, by stumbling and falling. The paradox is relentless. "Until we are sick, we understand not."[52] A vital knowledge emerges from suffering—even, he maintains, a kind of beauty.

Keats's personal myth of the mind's creativity—how the soul emerges, "each one personally itself," from a world of "Pains and troubles"—carries us back to Abraham emerging into the world as perfume. *Tiltul*—the restless movement of the perfume flask—draws others, through their passionate associations, to a beauty both strange and familiar. In this way, he "makes souls"; or, more precisely, he becomes the catalyst for those who are affected by his own Soul-making.

TAKING THE HINT

It is to Abraham's inner world that we ultimately return. An essential dimension of his identity, it seems, is his *shem*, his ever-growing name: his fuller body image, his ability to affect others. And yet, one last midrash on *Lekh lekha* takes us into the intimacy of his own history. Here, apparently, there are stumblings, there is darkness:

> "Yours is the dew of your youth": (Ps. 110:3) because Abraham was anxious and said to himself, "Perhaps [lit., Would you say that] I bear guilt for having worshipped idols all these years," God reassured him: " 'Yours is the dew of your youth': even as dew evaporates [lit. flies away], so have your sins evaporated; as dew is a sign of blessing to the world, so are you a sign of blessing to the world."[53]

Abraham is concerned about his past. "Would you say," he asks, in the same form of question with which he mused over the burning castle, "Would you say . . . ?" A question resonant with fear and desire compels him: Can the dark past be forgotten? Or is it still, literally, "in my hand" *(b'yadi)*—part of me? Can the past be turned into something that does not need forgetting? God's answer seems evasive. How does dew, evaporating in the morning, relate to Abraham's sins? If the point is that they are to *fly away*, would a bird image not be more expressive? Should the expression, in any case, not be "they will fly away *from you*"?

Shem Mi-Shmuel, a nineteenth-century Hasidic master, reads the image of dew dynamically:[54] dew rests for a moment on the grass and vanishes, evaporates. In that moment, however, it "arouses the inner moisture of the grass"—unlike rain, for instance, which moistens the earth and remains absorbed by it. The contrast between dew and rain he finds in the Talmud:

> R. Berachiah said: The congregation of Israel also made an inappropriate request, yet God granted that request, as it is said, "And let us know, eagerly strive to know God. His going forth is sure as the morning; and He shall come to us *as the rain*" (Hosea 6:3). God said to Israel: My daughter, you ask for something which at times is desirable and at other times is not desirable, but I will be to you something which is desirable at all times, as it is said, "*I will be as dew* to Israel" (14:6).[55]

One verse in Hosea gives the human request for God-as-rain; another gives God's offer of God-as-dew. God models a different sensibility of relationship. In the reading of Shem Mi-Shmuel, rain penetrates, implants itself; if God relates to Israel in this way, nothing will emerge *machamat atzmam*—from them, spontaneously. Dew, on the other hand, delicately touches, awakens inner vitality, and disappears. To know God as dew is to respond to a hint, like perfume; a word or two is sometimes enough. It is to respond unconsciously.

So God reassures Abraham: "Yours is the dew of your youth: your youthful sins acted like dew—they roused you to search for God. They spoke to you through promise and frustration, they suggested love and beauty. Having done this work, they vanished."

In this evocative reading, Shem Mi-Shmuel reads the vanishing dew as the delicately effective stimulus. The idea is deeply paradoxical: Abraham's sins set processes in motion within him. That is their imprint: they led him to God. In this way, souls are made, converting impressions into personal experience. In the end, nothing needs to be forgotten, since all has been transfigured.

> This
> Is the process whereby pain of the past in its pastness
> May be converted into the future tense
> Of joy.[56]

Henry James meditates on what it means to write from experience:

> Experience is never limited and it is never complete; it is an immense sensibility, a kind of huge spider web of the finest silken threads suspended in the chamber of consciousness, and catching every air-borne particle in its tissue. It is the very atmosphere of the mind; and when the mind is imaginative— much more when it happens to be that of a man of genius—it takes to itself the faintest hints of life, it converts the very pulses of the air into revelations.[57]

Unconscious experience as a spiderweb, exquisitely receptive to the merest particles, responsive to hints, transfigures the banal into the work of art. "It takes *to itself* the faintest hints of life": there is a self that, unawares, metabolizes random events. A lightness is required.

In the midrash, the word *lekha* conveys just this paradox of lightness and significance: "*To you* is the dew of your youth": your imaginative capacity to take a hint allows the dew to do its work before vanishing. There could not be a lighter word than *lekha*, unless it were *tal*, dew. And, of course, this is the heart of the midrashic suggestion: *Lekh lekha* is God's provocation to Abraham's *lekha*, his ability to allow transfiguration.

Here, finally, is Keats again:

> Now it appears to me that almost any Man may like the Spider spin from his own inwards his own airy Citadel—the points of leaves and twigs on which the Spider begins her work are few and she fills the Air with a beautiful circuiting. . . . Let us not therefore go hurrying about and collecting honey-bee like, buzzing here and there impatiently from a knowledge of what is to be arrived at: but let us open our leaves like a flower and be passive and receptive—budding patiently under the eye of Apollo and taking hints from every noble insect that favors us with a visit.[58]

The web is spun from the spider's "own inwards," making use of growth points—or, in the later letter, "teats"—to nurture itself. "Almost any man may spin his own airy Citadel," if he has the gift of receptivity. Points, germs, whisperings, hints—such modes of air, like dew, or perfume, may precipitate creation. The requisite posture Keats calls "diligent indolence." So, unconsciously, the Citadel rises into the air; the question transfigures the world; the dew wakens vital moisture.

Tal (dew), like *tiltul*, invokes, provokes, evokes. All the midrashic passages—the young woman inspired to leave home for an unknown world of beauty and desire; God's glance at Abraham that answers his question by acknowledging it; the vial of myrrh—Abraham as perfume—disseminating and generating beauty; the dew that evokes inwardness and vanishes—all perform what they describe. They hint at a process that resists description.

BECOMING A BLESSING

Indeed, the most uncanny of these images, Abraham as perfume, may have its origin in the mysterious expression found among God's blessings: *ve-heyeih berakhah*—"Become a blessing!" (Gen. 12:2). If, as Rashi claims, the three main areas of blessing—children, wealth, and fame—have already been promised him in the first part of God's speech, what is the force of "Become a blessing!"? Seforno beautifully suggests that Abraham is to bless God. God, it seems, needs human blessing.

God commands—not promises—"Become a blessing to me!" Seforno elaborates this to refer to Abraham's attaining spiritual perfection and educating others in the ways of God; to realize the godly in the world is to bless God. "The blessing of God is that *God should rejoice in His work.*" Abraham is to open himself, his world, and God to blessing. Such a notion almost defies expression. Perhaps only by way of a metaphor could the Rabbis convey the elusive and allusive impact of a human being on the world and on its God. Perfume gives pleasure, yields God the joy He seeks in the life of His creation.

In a haunting Talmudic passage, God urges the High Priest, "Ishmael, my son, bless Me!" And the High Priest replies, "May it be Your will that your compassion prevail over Your other attributes!" The story ends: "He bowed His head in assent."[59] God, it seems, needs human blessing. To be a source of blessing to God comes to mean to help God achieve His compassionate self. Daringly, the Talmud models God's states of mind on human emotional dynamics. To bless is, at base, to integrate complex elements. The bride will, if she undertakes the journey, become a link between the world of the past and that of the future, between her father and her husband. Abraham, more successful in his erotic project than Socrates, will help others—God, too—to integrate heaven and earth, the godly and the human.

Overcoming anger, God attains His compassionate self, that "womb" mode[60] in which all is contained so that new life may be born in beauty.

We return to our original question: Why, indeed, did God choose Abraham? Sefat Emet answers simply, quoting the Zohar: Abraham deserved to be addressed by God because he was capable of *hearing* the *Lekh lekha*, which God utters to all human beings, at all times.[61] His ears are open to register an invitation that others repress. A form of circular reasoning triumphs: Abraham was the right choice for God's provocation because he did, in fact, respond to it. "Visions come to prepared spirits."[62]

Abraham's relation to others is not that of a teacher, uniquely privileged to know, who implants his knowledge in others. Like Emerson's genius, he rather arouses others to *listen* to their own thoughts: "In every work of genius, we recognize our own rejected thoughts; they come back to us with a certain alienated majesty."[63] Unexceptional, the work of genius is exceptional only in the capacity to take seriously, not to reject, or repress, one's own thoughts.

When God calls Abraham—*Lekh lekha*—is this Abraham's own thought? Why, then, does God speak it to him? Or is it not his own thought? How then can it benefit him? But—Sefat Emet implicitly suggests—it is neither exactly his nor not his. It represents his "further, next, unattained but attainable self."[64] God speaks, Abraham listens; he rejects the rejecting mechanism so well developed in others—perhaps in himself till now. *Lekh lekha* evokes his difference from himself. A new majesty is born, a citadel rises into the air, perfume generates new life.

SIX

Abraham Bound and Unbound
The Akedah

HOW MANY DID IT RENDER SLEEPLESS?

God's last word to Abraham is His command to sacrifice his son, Isaac. Never again will God address Abraham. When the command to sacrifice is annulled at the last moment, it is not God but an angel who calls Halt! from the heavens. God's final words will forever resonate in Abraham's mind: "Take your son, your only one, whom you love, Isaac, and offer him as a burnt offering on one of the mountains that I will show you."

The terror of the narrative is the plainest thing about it and the most mysterious. It permeates its every detail and its total structure. How has Abraham's beloved God changed His tone! For Kierkegaard, sensitivity to this terror and mystery is the essential qualification for approaching the narrative: "There were countless generations who knew the story of Abraham by heart, word for word, but *how many did it render sleepless?*" (my emphasis). Implicitly, he dismisses those who have not lain awake at night, gripped by the enigmas of this last moment in Abraham's life of conversation with God. Insomnia becomes the criterion for a true reading of Abraham's experience. *Knowing* the story blocks the heart; only in the sleepless dark can one engage with its paradoxes.

Nothing, it seems, has prepared Abraham—or the reader—for this turn. The shock of God's words comes at a moment when all tensions, within the family and with the surrounding culture, seem resolved, so that Abraham can finally live the fatherhood that God has promised him. The long-desired son is born, nursed, weaned. Hagar and Ishmael—alternative, provisional solutions to Abraham's childlessness—are sent away. Abraham makes peace with his Philistine neighbors. At this point, out of the blue, God demands a sacrifice. Abraham's response is a silence that contrasts

169

strikingly with his expressive reactions in previous encounters with God.[1]

THE UNTHOUGHT KNOWN

But perhaps God's demand does not, after all, come out of the blue? Perhaps the *Akedah* has its own history, linking it in profound ways to the current of Abraham's innermost life? Perhaps the expression "After these things," which introduces the *Akedah*, refers to the secret archive of Abraham's past, to meanings that make the *Akedah* its almost inevitable consummation? His silence would then be an acknowledgment of something known though never before fully thought.

Such an idea, integrating the *Akedah* into the trajectory of Abraham's history, lies at the heart of the traditional midrashic claim that this was the last of ten tests that Abraham had to undergo.[2] Only here, at the culmination of a process and a relationship, we read explicitly, "God *tested* Abraham." But this final and decisive test is the tip of a midrashic iceberg: extending back through Abraham's history, there is a recurrent theme of *testing*.

What are we to make of such a quality of relationship between Abraham and God? In a classic comment, Ramban treats the test as an expression of human freedom—"if he wishes, he will act, if he does not, he will not act."[3] God tests in order to bring this freedom to its fullest expression, so that a potential may flower into reality. The test, therefore, is always for the good of the human subject undergoing it: it helps him/her to act out intuitive convictions, to make real what might otherwise remain hypothetical. The aim would be, then, to take the subject through an experience that will remap a world of self-knowledge with transformative clarity.[4]

Ten times, then, God takes Abraham through an experience that extends and deepens his self-awareness. We will return later to this notion of the test. Here, we may notice simply that the *Akedah* is traditionally viewed as the culminating moment in a lifetime preoccupation with *realizing* the quality and meaning of a relationship with God. For the first time, however, the *test* is explicit in the text: its physical reality makes indisputable, it defines forever something about Abraham and his way of loving God.

BECOMING WHOLE

There is an earlier moment when God makes a sacrificial demand that Abraham receives in fraught silence. In Genesis, chapter 17, God tells him to circumcise himself and his sons after him, to mark an everlasting covenant. This covenant of blood is introduced with the weighty words "I am Almighty God; walk before Me, and become whole" (Gen. 17:1). We notice the theme of *walking* that permeates God's addresses to Abraham: from the first *Lekh lekha,* through this clearly metaphorical injunction, to the final *Lekh lekha* of the *Akedah.* Here, however, God is manifestly speaking of a spiritual movement, connected with *becoming whole.*

How is this wholeness to be achieved? By entering into a covenant that involves circumcision, the removal of the foreskin. The confluence of high spiritual demand and intimately physical act, of the aspiration to wholeness and a violent procedure of reduction, removal, constitutes a paradox that the midrash articulates: "Great is circumcision, for with all the commandments that Abraham fulfilled, he was called whole only when he circumcised himself."[5] In Rashi's version, we find: " 'Walk before Me': in the commandment of circumcision; and in this way, you will become whole. For as long as the foreskin is on you, you are blemished in relation to Me."[6] In yet another midrash, Abraham responds with astonishment to the paradox: "He said, 'Till now, I have been whole! If I am circumcised, I will become defective [in losing a body part]!' God replied, 'What do you think? That you are so whole? You lack five organs.' " Only by an act of apparent diminishment can Abraham acquire a complete body image.

Abraham's response to the tension raised by God's paradoxical demand is a silent act of submission: "And Abram fell upon his face" (Gen. 17:3). Rashi comments: " 'He fell': in dread before the presence of God. For until he circumcised himself, he had no strength to stand upright while God stood over him." In this reading, he falls, not in submission, but in a more primal gesture of collapse: the weight of his blemished body brings him to his knees, shame undermines him, and the place of circumcision, which is the mark of *unwholeness,* is hidden.

Why is it only now that standing erect in God's presence has become impossible? Inhabiting the same uncircumcised body, he has repeatedly spoken, even argued, with God, without collapse. In a brilliant discussion of this midrash,[7] Meshekh Hokhmah focuses on the status of a newborn before and after the eighth day of life: there is no stigma attached to the foreskin of the newborn until the time when the commandment of circumcision comes into effect eight days after birth. In Abraham's situation, similarly, before the concept of *circumcision as wholeness* is framed, the foreskin is a natural and unproblematic part of the body. He can therefore stand with perfect assurance in God's presence. However, as soon as God says, "Become whole," the foreskin[8] becomes *orlah,* problematic, disturbing—and destabilizing: "And Abraham fell upon his face."

The body, it seems, is constructed by language: the same body becomes a subject of self-consciousness when God declares, implicitly, that it is not yet whole. "Become whole" problematizes a sense of established reality: now the body has to be thought about. By opening up a vista of wholeness, God hints at a future never before conceivable. A moment of ripeness—the eighth day of the newborn life—radically reconstructs reality. And a new context is established for future responses to the events of the past. Past integrations break down; new meanings appear.

This transformation affects also the hopes and desires of the past. Freud quotes a witticism to this effect, in *Jokes and Their Relation to the Unconscious:* of a would-be political leader it is remarked that "he has a great future behind him."[9] Once, that man had a great future before him; he has it no longer. In fact, that futural condition is now behind him. The present is, in large part, informed by a particular sense of the future, which can be lost as the present becomes past. Malcolm Bowie writes: "The history of an impassioned individual life carries with it . . . a history of the wished-for states by which that life was impelled."[10] The history of desire is encrypted within: the victim of the witticism carries his great future *behind* him. It is in language that these past futures appear, lost and found at once.

Abraham has come to a watershed moment in which language creates his body anew. This is a moment of aspiration—charged with the words, "Become whole"—and shame. Physically, nothing has changed; his psychic reality is decisive. A moment in time anticipates a more stable and complete reality; but the immediate effect is an embarrassed review of the past, with its "wished-for states."

THE MOMENT OF AFTERTHOUGHT

This reading of a transformative moment in Abraham's life offers us a preamble and prefiguration of the *Akedah*. Here, too, I suggest, the past, with its established ways of integrating experience, becomes subject to question. *"After these things,* God tested Abraham." The test is the effect of past things, of afterthoughts about those things. Here, a motif in Abraham's inner life, an emotional habit, reaches a critical moment. Repeatedly, the midrash describes him as reflecting about the facts of his experience. But these reflections have an anxious quality; he suffers from *hirhurim:* qualms, misgivings. Constantly questioning and redefining the meaning of his past, he inhabits a double history: outwardly, he flourishes; but inwardly, he is troubled by possible interpretations of his life.

Before we address the *Akedah*, a few examples of this midrashic theme will establish a sense of its prevalence. For instance, after Abraham wins the battle against the four kings led by Kedarlaomer, God, rather mysteriously, has to reassure him: "Do not fear, Abram" (Gen. 15:1). What is Abram's fear? In the text, the question is never answered. But the midrash[11] listens for Abram's qualms:

R. Levi explained this in two ways, the Rabbis in one. R. Levi said: Abraham was filled with misgivings saying to himself, "Would you say that there was one righteous man among those troops that I slew?" This may be compared to a straw-merchant who was passing the king's orchards, and seeing some bundles of thorns, descended from his wagon and took them. The king caught sight of him, and he tried to hide himself. "Why do you hide?" he asked him. "I needed laborers to gather them; now that you have gathered them, come and receive your reward." So God said to Abraham: "Those troops that you slew were thorns already cut down"; as it is written, "And the peoples shall be as the burnings of lime; as thorns cut down, that are burned in the fire."[12]

R. Levi gave another explanation: Abraham was filled with misgivings, saying to himself, "Would you say that the sons of the kings that I slew will collect troops and come and wage war with me?" So God said to him: " 'Do not fear, Abram, I am your shield': just as a shield receives all spears and withstands them, so will I stand by you."

The Rabbis explained in this way: Abraham was filled with misgivings, saying to himself, "I descended into the fiery furnace and I was saved; I descended into the perils of war, and I was saved: would you say that I have already received my reward in this world and I have nothing reserved for the future world?" So God said to him: " 'Do not fear, Abram, I am your shield [magen],' meaning a gift of grace [maggan] to you: all that I have done for you in this world was an act of grace; but in the future world, 'your reward will be very great.' "—just as we read, "Oh how abundant is Your goodness, which You have reserved for those who fear You."[13]

Abraham is anxious (mitpached is the reflexive form of the word for fear): he expresses his anxiety with the interrogative tomar: "Would you say . . . ?" In each of his three speculations, a nightmare possibility retrospectively ruins his military success: Did he perhaps kill one innocent man in battle? Will there be unforeseen consequences to the apparently conclusive battle? Both the moral qualm and the pragmatic one are countered by God's reassurance. But the third qualm is harder to counter: Does a charmed life, marked by miraculous escapes, deplete some essential reserve of identity? Twice, he has been saved from death: in the early (midrashic) story of the fiery furnace, and now in battle. In both cases, the expression is yaradti v'nitzalti: "I was already in the jaws of death ('I descended . . .')

and I was saved. *Would you say* that I have received my reward in this world, so that I have no reserves for the world to come?" In the grip of his misgiving, his triumph becomes a liability. He has won the battle, but lost his intimate claim on the future. Miraculous interventions diminish one's substance, one's autonomy.

In this scenario, too, God reassures him. But it is the misgiving rather than the reassurance that now claims our attention. In several such midrashic passages, a habit of hypothetical reconstructions of the past characterizes Abraham. He is said to be anxious *(mitpached)*, worried *(do'eg)*, or full of qualms *(meharher)*. These often demoralizing afterthoughts are introduced in the biblical text with the words "After these things." Even in the famous midrash about his encounter with the burning castle, he begins his question: *"Tomar. . . .* Would you say that this castle is without a lord?" A fearful possibility is entertained which jeopardizes both past and future. On each occasion, his speculation wins a comforting response from God, as though it is only after a qualm is articulated and confronted that it can be resolved.

Another example of this emotional structure immediately follows the *Akedah* narrative (Gen. 22:20):

> "After these things . . .": When he returned from Mount Moriah, Abraham had qualms: "If my son had really been slain, he would have died without children! I must marry him to one of the daughters of Aner or Eshkol or Mamre." God therefore had the news sent him that Rebecca, Isaac's destined bride, had been born. This is what is meant by "After these things [or words]": after the words that were evoked in him by the *Akedah*.[14]

Here, the word *hirhur* indicates a compulsive thought; the classic form is *hirhur averah,* sexual fantasies. These are thoughts with a life of their own, speculations that blur the clear boundaries of time and perspective. Abraham's failure to arrange for Isaac's marriage to a local bride was, *at the time,* a reasonable decision. It is only by benefit of hindsight that it seems delinquent: he almost lost his whole future. He has an untroubled future behind him; as a result of the *Akedah* retrospective guilt now possesses him. Again, God allays his anxiety, without dealing with the radical question of this kind of thinking.

THE SACRIFICIAL WISH

With these examples in mind, we can approach the *Akedah* as an event haunted by misgivings:

> "After these things": after the misgivings of that moment. Who then had misgivings? Abraham did. He said, "I have rejoiced and made everyone joyful, but I have never set aside a singe bullock or ram for God." God replied, "In the end you will be told to sacrifice your only son to Me, and you will not refuse." According to R. Leazar, who maintained that *ve-ha-Elohim* means God *and His court,* it was the ministering angels who said this: "This Abraham rejoiced and made all others rejoice, yet did not set aside for God a single bullock or ram." God replied, "Even if we tell him to offer his own son, he will not refuse."
>
> Isaac and Ishmael were engaged in a controversy. The latter argued, "I am more beloved than you, because I was circumcised at the age of thirteen," while Isaac replied, "I am more beloved, because I was circumcised at eight days." Ishmael said, "I am more beloved, because I could have protested, yet did not." At that moment, Isaac declared, "Oh that God would appear to me and bid me cut off one of my limbs! I would not refuse." [Another version: Ishmael said, "I am more beloved, since I was circumcised at the age of thirteen, but you were circumcised as a baby and could not refuse." Isaac replied, "All that you lent to God was three drops of blood. But I am now thirty-seven years old, yet if God desired of me that I be slaughtered, I would not refuse." God responded, "This is the moment!" Immediately, "God tested Abraham."[15]]

Again, the familiar *hirhurim,* the qualms that, on this occasion, lead directly into the *Akedah* command. In this case, Abraham's misgivings interrogate the authenticity of his entire life. "I have rejoiced and made everyone joyful . . ." refers to the midrashic tradition about his open-door hospitality, his feasts shared with all comers, the blessings with which he contagiously celebrates God's bounty. Now, he notices the absence, in all the celebration, of any sacrifice. At first, it seems that his self-criticism is unjustified: he is, after all, described as having built altars.[16] However, reading closely, we notice that nowhere is he described as *sacrificing* to God: instead, "he called out the name of God." He taught the world about God; but the altar remains a symbolic presence in the text, rather than a place where real animals are sacrificed.

This is the critical moment when the idiom of a lifetime comes under harsh scrutiny. If there was no sacrifice, in the fullest sense, could all that celebration have been mere self-gratification? In the absence of sacrifice, the question of authenticity becomes an obsessive thought, which God defuses by declaring His confidence in him: "If I were to ask you to sacrifice your only son, you would not refuse." There is a double-edged sharpness to God's words: they are reassurance and shocking demand.

In the second reading, the same suspicion is cast on Abraham's sincerity—this time by the angels, who are similarly answered by God. Here are two histories of the *Akedah* command: "After these things" refers either to Abraham's own self-recriminations, or to the criticisms of the angels. In either case, almost inevitably, the doubt leads to the literal demand for ultimate sacrifice, as the only reality test for thoughts of this kind. The more radical of the two versions is undoubtedly the first: here, it is an internal event, a purely psychic crisis within Abraham, that precipitates the terror of the *Akedah*.

In the next section, the midrash presents two versions of a similar episode, this time about Isaac. In his debate with Ishmael—"Who is more beloved?"—Ishmael seems to hold the high ground: he was of the age of consent when he allowed himself to be circumcised. Isaac, who was a mere baby, incapable of conscious assent, is left without rational answer. He can only cry out a sacrificial wish: "*I wish* God would ask me. . . ." Only so will his good faith be demonstrated—by sacrificing his limbs, or his very life, if God desires it. God's response is immediate—"*miyad*—instantly—God tested Abraham." In the second version, God responds, "This is the moment!" In both versions, the drama of immediacy makes it clear that Isaac, by his words of desperate readiness, even of sacrificial desire, has precipitated God's demand.

In this subversive midrash, the *Akedah* becomes the fruit of a human psychic crisis. There are situations, apparently, when a human being desires self-sacrifice. If we focus on Abraham rather than Isaac, we are confronted, in the less radical version, by angelic criticism of God's favorite. Continuing the midrashic tradition in which angels carp at God's interest in human beings, they here express suspicion about Abraham's sincerity; they constitute an objective voice that is also a projection of Abraham's inner misgivings. In the first, more radical version, however, the claim is unequivocal: Abraham's *hirhurim* generate the *Akedah*. A habit of retroactive suspicion of his own motives and actions produces the reality test of literal and ultimate sacrifice. How else are such qualms to be allayed? The *immediacy* of God's response (emphasized in the second half of the passage) focuses the causal connection: Abraham's words, once spoken, can be answered in no other way. All along, God's faith in Abraham's total commitment was awaiting vindication; the reality check was always impending.

Through the prism of this midrashic account, a theory of sacrifice emerges. The subject is the human desire for sacrifice—as a clarification, as a simplification, a showing-forth, in a world of moral ambiguity. At the heart of all symbolic and hypothetical rhetoric about commitment waits the possibility, even the necessity, of literal enactment.

At the moment of the *Akedah,* then, Abraham's fear and desire make him ripe for the sacrificial act. "After these things": such moments hold a potential violence that threatens past integrations of reality. But this violence breaks out within the soul; it is not simply a matter of God's word descending like lightning at noon. It expresses a discontinuity with the past, but also a hidden continuity. All of Abraham's *hirhurim* undermine the past, as they all contain a desire for violent enactments. A suspicion of the apparent and the manifest, an agitated wish for unequivocal knowledge, informs them all.

If the *hirhur* is the repressed theme and tone of Abraham's inner discourse, a startling dissonance is suggested. A life of *chesed,* of loving and active involvement in reality and in the lives of others, a *charmed* life, in all its meanings, has, it appears, its shadowy underside. A habit of skepticism develops into a questioning of the essential idiom of that life. A doubt about authenticity leads directly to the demand that Abraham sacrifice the dearest thing in life. His doubt, God's demand. . . . In these midrashic sources, the *Akedah* is fathered by Abraham.

SACRIFICE AND INTIMACY

Such a view of the complexity of Abraham's inner world invites a psychoanalytic reading of his narrative. Before we turn to such a reading, however, I would like to meditate briefly on one possible meaning of sacrifice: the violent act that offers to establish a new intimacy with the transcendent, to "lose everything to gain everything" (Gaston Bachelard).

In his evocative study *The Psychoanalysis of Fire,* Bachelard begins by exploring the "reverie before the fire." "If fire . . . was taken to be a constituent element of the Universe, is it not because it is an element of human thought, the prime element of reverie?"[17] Fire warms and cooks, it gives comfort, but more immediately it calls forth a special kind of attention, a *reverie* on a specific object.

> [Fire] suggests the desire to change, to speed up the passage of time, to bring all of life to its conclusion, to its hereafter . . . it links the small to the great, the hearth to the volcano, the life of a log to the life of a world. The fascinated individual hears *the call of the funeral pyre.* For him destruction is more than a change, it is a renewal.[18]

Bachelard gives the name "Empedocles complex" to the union of love and respect for fire, "the instinct for living and the instinct for dying" that are born of this reverie. Empedocles was a fifth-century philosopher who threw himself into the volcano at Mount Etna, so that he would be believed to be a god. Bachelard cites German Romantics who construct Empedocles' act as the "total death which leaves no trace. . . . To lose everything to gain everything." "Through its sacrifice in the heart of the flames, the mayfly gives us a lesson in eternity." He quotes George Sand: "With what transports of blind joy and of love's frenzy these swarms of little white moths come to hurl themselves into [the fire]! For them this is the volcano in all its majesty."[19] For the dreamer, the life of the ant and the firefly configure the "death in the flame" that is "the least lonely of deaths,"[20] an act that fuses one with the whole universe.

The fundamental poetic theme here is the "call of the funeral pyre," which, Bachelard suggests, remains "profoundly real and active for unconscious reveries."[21] The fire reverie, then, represents a passion for love, death, and fire, in which sentimentality and ambivalence are in an instant transcended, all qualms and misgivings consumed in a single sacrificial moment. In this fire, loneliness is healed. Opposites meet, paradox reigns: destruction and renewal are one. Making no judgment, Bachelard conveys the content of this prime element of reverie, with its roots in the unconscious.

In another essay on fire, written in 1970, "The Sinister Ease of Dying," Marguerite Yourcenar expresses both her empathy and her horror for the young suicides of the Commune, who threw themselves into the flames a century earlier. With this voluntary immolation, she suggests, they protested against the violence and greed of the world. She titles her essay after lines from a poem by Victor Hugo:

> . . . And we must tremble so long as
> we have not learned to heal
> The sinister ease of dying.

In her own time, too, other young idealists similarly died in protest against the destructiveness, materialism, and hypocrisy of French society. Yourcenar raises a moral question about suicides of this kind. On the one hand, there is the necessity of uncompromising commitment: she quotes a Buddhist sutra, "The world is on fire, the fire of ignorance, the fire of lust, the fire of aggression is devouring it."[22] It is purity of heart that motivates those who refuse to live in such a world. But, she asks, in the face of "this Buddhist-monk type of sacrifice," what reasons can we give for living?

Those who have departed were surely of the best: we have need of them. Perhaps we might have saved them if we had persuaded them that their refusal, their indignation, their very despair were necessary; if we had known how to urge against the sinister ease of dying the heroic of difficulty of living . . . in such a way as to make the world a little less scandalous than it is.[23]

The fire of sacrificial death draws the pure of heart, but its "sinister ease" expresses a radical despair of the world. Ultimately, Yourcenar's judgment goes against the fire; life itself must be invested with a more fiery heroism.

In his major philosophical work, *The Theory of Religion*, Georges Bataille analyzes the nature of sacrifice. In his conceptual scheme, "death actually discloses the imposture of reality." Reality, the real order, reduces animals and human beings to the condition of *things*, valued largely for their *duration*, their capacity to endure through time. What has no place in the world of reality is the affirmation of intimate life that is fully realized only in death. Sacrifice, Bataille claims,

> is the antithesis of production, which is accomplished with a view to the future; it is consumption that is concerned only with the moment. . . .
> This is the meaning of "sacrificing to the deity," whose sacred essence is comparable to a fire. To sacrifice is to give as one gives coal to the furnace.[24]

Sacrifice restores objects to "the vague sphere of lost intimacy," which is "not compatible with the positing of the separate individual." The individual participating in sacrifice is filled with anguish because he is an individual, and part of a world of things that requires duration. "Man is afraid of the intimate order that is not reconcilable with the order of things. . . . Because man is not squarely within that order . . . intimacy, in the trembling of the individual, is holy, sacred, and suffused with anguish."[25]

In Bataille's scheme, sacrifice and the sacred constitute a moment of glorious consumption in which a hidden, spiritual reality—intimacy—flares up, even as it destroys the order of "things." The values he stages are those of life in the moment, fusion (intimacy) with the universe, a violent outbreak against the world of work, duration, and fear of death. The sacrificial reveals a truth of intimacy that eliminates the contours of the individual. Although Bataille's sympathy with the sacrificial order is evident, he acknowledges the real danger of this order, the "unlimited fire," that "inflames and blinds in turn." Human life requires a balance between the extremes of surrender to immanence, which would return man to the "unconscious intimacy of animals,"[26] and the neutrality of individual and productive life.

The experience of anguish constitutes the pivotal moment when the individual moves toward an intimacy that threatens his individuality. Bataille's use of the term *intimacy* reminds us that the Hebrew term for sacrifice—*korban*—means "coming close" to God. At the heart of the biblical concept of sacrifice is the concern for intimacy, and the readiness to shed all that stands as a barrier between the self and God—even that very self.

Death by fire is the fate, we remember, of Aaron's sons—who *"came close* into God's presence"[27]—and *"brought close* a strange fire that He had not commanded."[28] On this enigmatic episode, the midrash comments: "They added love to love."[29] Here, too, apparently, we witness a human passion that is sacrificial in its nature, and can find its apotheosis only in fire. In the biblical text, a ritual act of gratuitous intimacy is mysteriously punished by fire; in the midrashic narrative, while guilt and punishment are clearly involved, one detects a real admiration for the fiery spirit of those who, in their fervor for a lost intimacy, transgress the order of the real.

Gathering the sparks of these fires, we can approach the passionate heart of the Talmudic figure of R. Eleazar ben Dordia:

> It was said of R. Eleazar b. Dordia that there was no harlot in the world that he had not visited. Once, he heard that there was a certain harlot in one of the seaboard towns who took a purse full of *denarii* for her hire. He filled his purse and he crossed

seven rivers for her sake. While he was with her, she emitted wind, and said, "As this wind will never return, so will Eleazar never have his repentance [return] accepted."

At that, he went and sat between two hills and mountains and cried out, "Hills and mountains, plead for mercy for me!" They replied, "How shall we plead for you, when we must first plead for ourselves?—as it is said, 'For the mountains shall depart and the hills be removed . . .' " (Isa. 54:10).

He then cried: "Heaven and earth, plead for mercy for me!" And they replied, "How shall we plead for you, when we must first plead for ourselves?—as it is said, 'For the heavens shall vanish away like smoke, and the earth shall wax old like a garment' " (Isa. 51:6). He then cried: "Sun and moon, plead for mercy for me!" And they also replied, "How shall we plead for you, when we must first plead for ourselves?—as it is said, 'Then the moon shall be confounded and the sun ashamed' " (24:23). He cried, "Stars and constellations, plead for mercy for me!" And they too replied, "How shall we plead for you, when we must first plead for ourselves?—as it is said, 'And all the hosts of heaven shall molder away' " (34:4).

Then, he cried, "The thing depends on me alone!" And he placed his head between his knees and bellowed in weeping until his soul departed. Then, a heavenly voice was heard proclaiming, "Rabbi Eleazar b. Dordai is welcomed into the life of the world to come!" . . . Rabbi heard of this and wept and said, "One person may acquire eternal life over many years, another in one hour!" Rabbi also said, "Is it not sufficient for penitents that they are accepted, but they are even called Rabbi!"[30]

The penitent libertine dies in an ecstasy of contrition; thus, he "acquires his world"—that is, eternal life—in one instant. Within the natural world, the world of objective things—sun, moon, mountains, hills—he cannot be helped: like them, he is a thing threatened by death. He places his head between his knees and bellows aloud, till his soul departs: like an animal, he bellows in anguish as he relinquishes his hold on life.

The reaction of Rabbi, on hearing the story, is profoundly

ambivalent. To achieve eternal life in one hour is to threaten the values of the Rabbinic world that Rabbi represents: the rigorous and unceasing culture of spiritual work. For, in essence, it is to choose death, the moment of anguish and glorious consumption: to lose all to gain all. Rabbi is committed to life and its anxieties, its qualms and misgivings, and its danger of attrition. And yet, he acknowledges the authenticity of eternal life gained in an instant. Even the title "Rabbi," the very title that he himself has earned through a lifetime of discipline, has been bestowed peremptorily on the penitent sinner. Rabbi, we are told, weeps when he hears the story of R. Eleazar b. Dordai. His tears belie the apparent equanimity of his words. For in order to achieve his eternal life, he has over many years been crafting a disciplined inner world. R. Eleazar, on the other hand, dies full of primal impulses; his sexual extravagance is simply transfigured in an instant into a death wish. Both men weep; one dies of it, while the other remains to contemplate the outrageous efficacy of the sacrificial moment. Mysteriously, R. Eleazar's desire for intimacy with God brings him to the same place as Rabbi's productive life.

These different versions of the notion of sacrifice intimate one dimension, at least, of that complex subject. All address the human need for intensified experience, in which time is sped up, polarities of life and death are fused in an instant, and the cloudy ambiguities of life in time are violently charged with apocalyptic clarity. Marguerite Yourcenar, while recognizing the idealism of this sacrificial radicalism, is clearly invested in restoring the value of the heroic difficulty of living. For Bachelard, the "call of the funeral pyre" remains a potent source of unconscious reveries. Bataille focuses on the moment of *intimacy,* which is created by an act of violence that consumes the individual: the moment of sacred anguish. And in the Talmudic passage, R. Eleazar clarifies in one incandescent instant the nature of his true world: he subverts time and natural process to achieve his intimacy with God.

QUALMS OF THE HEART AND BURNT OFFERINGS

With these sources in mind, we return now to Abraham's sacrifice of Isaac. We recall the daring midrashic suggestion that it is Abraham's *hirhurim,* his retroactive anxiety about the authenticity of his life, that directly generates God's demand for sacrifice. In a real sense, it is Abraham's inward reality, his thoughts, that make the sacrifice necessary. Once he has been assailed by those thoughts, God—*immediately*—articulates their irreducible meaning. Abraham's voice, in its unconscious register, is intuited and amplified in God's command. Can we call this a *wish* for this sacrifice? If so, what is the quality and the root of that wish? What do Abraham's fears and misgivings suggest about a desire for clarification? And how does his particular kind of fear engender this particular unthinkable thought?

Before we approach this question of the particular idiom of Abraham's sacrificial desire, it is striking that a classic midrashic tradition connects the *olah*—the burnt offering, which involves the total consumption of the sacrifice in fire, and which constitutes God's *Akedah* demand—with the problem of *hirhurei ha-lev*—"qualms of the heart," mental misgivings. In another version of the midrashic material we have already explored, we find this connection compellingly affirmed in the double context of Abraham and Job:

> "After these things [words], the word of God came to Abram in a vision, saying, 'Do not fear, Abram . . .'" (Gen. 15:1). Our Rabbis teach us: for what reason would the burnt offering, the *olah,* be brought? R. Ishmael taught that the *olah* would be brought for positive and negative precepts [to atone for acts of commission and omission]. R. Shimon bar Yochai said: an *olah* would be brought to atone for qualms of the heart, *hirhurei ha-lev,* as it is said: "When a cycle of feast days was over, Job would send word to them to sanctify themselves, and, rising early in the morning, he would bring burnt offerings, one for each of them; for Job thought, 'Perhaps my children have sinned and blasphemed God *in their thoughts.*' This is what Job always used to do" (Job 1:5). You find that Abraham would have misgivings about the workings of divine justice *[hayah meharher achar midat ha-din],* and what would he say? "God helped me against those kings in the war and saved me from the furnace. Have I perhaps already received all my reward in this world? Does no reward remain for me in the world to come?" God said to him, "Because you

have misgivings about My ways, you owe Me an *olah,* a burnt offering." So He said, "Take your son, your only one, whom you love, Isaac, and go to the land of Moriah and offer him there as a burnt offering. . . ." (22:2).[31]

Qualms of the heart require a burnt offering: this is the view of R. Shimon bar Yochai. His proof text is the enigmatic practice of Job, who offered burnt offerings, individually, for each of his children, in case they had sinned against God *in their thoughts.* It is striking that Job's thought about his children also bears some of the character of a "qualm of the heart." Perhaps the death of his children is the *olah,* the terrible debt payable by one whose mind is haunted by misgivings? When his children die, one report frames the catastrophic news as a burnt offering: "God's fire fell from heaven, took half of the sheep and the boys, and burned them up" (Job 1:16).[32]

In any case, it is a purely mental event that requires atonement by the *olah.* In this way, R. Shimon bar Yochai relates Abraham's qualms about God's dealings with him to the demand for Isaac's sacrifice as an *olah.* Abraham's fear, in itself, precipitates the *Akedah.* Of course, the immediate context is not the *Akedah* (Genesis, chapter 22) but the Covenant between the Pieces (chapter 15). The association is probably the preamble to both narratives: "And it was after these things [words]." In both cases, the Rabbis attribute *hirhurim,* subversive afterthoughts, to Abraham.

In this midrash, unlike the previous version, God does not simply reassure Abraham. Instead, He forces his secret fears to the surface and declares that they *need* a burnt offering. Some toxic uncertainty about God's justice may, it seems, be allayed only by an absolute and literal enactment, a total death, leaving no trace.

Here, all is mystery. The midrash is not speaking of punishment but of a psychic requirement: that obsessional thoughts be resolved by unequivocal act. What is the meaning of the burnt offering—the *holocaust,* as it was once called: wholly consumed—in Abraham's inner world?

. . .

IDIOMS FOR THE UNTHINKABLE

I want to propose a psychoanalytic reading of Abraham's life, a reading that attempts to articulate his specific and personal connection with the fire reverie, with the complex desire to lose all in order to gain all. In this case, of course, to lose all means to sacrifice his beloved and long-awaited son. Sacrificing one's son was a well-documented practice in the ancient world, signifying the most total imaginable gift. But while such a sacrifice is undoubtedly more radical, to him, than losing his own life, it nevertheless remains a departure from the examples of *self*-sacrifice that we have looked at. Our question, therefore, is about the meaning this bears *for Abraham,* in the particularity of his experience, as we find it narrated in biblical and midrashic texts.

The traces of this history are to be found, first, in the Torah text itself: images of fire of a peculiar and hallucinatory intensity that intimate suppressed experience. Freud argues that in a text, as in a murder, it is hard to eliminate all traces of the "crime": metaphors, signs, symptoms betray the traumatic event for which there is no overt evidence. Although the surface retains no explicit record—the text may sometimes "displace" the unbearable narrative, put it elsewhere—an early experience has left its deep impression.[33]

Such a trace of Abraham's early history is the unusual simile that he applies to the scene of the destruction of Sodom: "And he looked down over Sodom and Gemorrah and the whole land of the plain, and he saw, behold, the smoke rose up from the land like *the smoke of the furnace*" (Gen. 19:28). The catastrophic scene is mediated by Abraham's imagination. The simile of the smoking furnace is striking, if only because similes and metaphors are not common in the biblical text. The landscape burns with a strange fire.

Moving backward in time, we find Abraham's attempted plea to save Sodom. Here, he declares himself unworthy to speak to God so aggressively: " 'Here I venture to speak to my Lord, I who am but *dust and ashes*' " (Gen. 18:27)—again, a metaphor: for the modern reader, perhaps, a dead metaphor, but for Abraham who invents it, most live.

Ashes? Rashi comments: "I should already have been dust, at the hands of the kings, *and ashes, at the hands of Nimrod*—if Your compassion had not supported me!" Abraham's metaphor is unpacked: he speaks—perhaps unaware of his own full meaning—of the two narrowest escapes of his life, when death had him by the throat.[34] He means, quite literally, "I was almost ashes." Or, more exactly, *"I am ashes."* In this sense, the idiom, dust and ashes, is not merely a modest disclaimer, but a radical acknowledgment of a truth normally veiled: he has survived death, which means that he is alive, but barely. To the naked eye, he seems alive, but in some other vision, he is dust, he is ashes. Some unconscious truth speaks from his mouth.

Earlier, in the vision that precedes the Covenant between the Pieces, we read: "As the sun was about to set, a deep sleep fell upon Abram, and a terror of great darkness fell upon him. . . . When the sun set and all light was eclipsed, there appeared *a smoking oven and a flaming torch* which passed between those pieces" (Gen. 15:12, 17). His hallucination[35] of dark horror focuses on a smoking oven. Rashi briefly notes that this is an intimation of the anguish of Jewish history that visits Abraham in dream or reverie. But if the moment refers to the future, it arises authentically out of the past. For in the past, forgotten, repressed, absent from the biblical text, is the story of the fiery furnace, into which the child Abraham was thrown, to test his faith in the invisible God.

The fact that this story appears only in the midrash, that it is absent from the Torah, testifies, I suggest, to its unthinkable nature. It leaves its record in Abraham's mind and manifests obliquely in the imagery of fire and furnace that repeatedly marks his perception. This story, known to every schoolchild, is regarded by Ramban as essential to the simplest "plot" understanding of Abraham's history. Since it portrays an Abraham who is willing to be martyred for his belief in God, it serves to rationalize God's original choice of him. It appears in several midrashic sources, as well as in nonmidrashic contexts, like Rambam's *Laws of Idolatry*. In the collective consciousness of the Jewish people, that is, it holds a privileged position. Its total absence from the written biblical text suggests that it is an unthinkable, even an unbearable narrative, banished from Abraham's memory.

Perhaps its most fraught version is to be found in Rashi's comment on the mysterious death of Abraham's brother, Haran: "And
Haran died in the presence of his father Terach, in the land of his
birth, Ur of the Chaldeans" (Gen. 11:28):

> "In the presence of Terach": in his father's lifetime. But the
> midrash says: Some say that he died *at the hands of his father*—
> since Terach brought charges in the court of Nimrod against his
> son Abraham, for smashing his idols. The king threw him into a
> fiery furnace. Haran sat and thought, "If Abraham wins, I will be
> on his side, but if Nimrod wins, I will be on his side." When
> Abraham was saved, Haran was asked, "On whose side are you?"
> and he answered, "On Abraham's side." So they threw him into
> the fiery furnace and he was burned. That is the meaning of *Ur*
> (fire) of the Chaldeans. However, according to Menahem ben
> Saruk, Ur means a valley or gorge. . . . Any cave or deep cleft is
> called Ur.

In this stark retelling of the midrash,[36] the essential fact is that
Abraham's brother was killed *by his father*, who had originally
intended Abraham's own death. By handing him over for execution,
Terach is, virtually, killing him. And when he is saved, his brother's
actual death is directly attributable to Terach. This tale is listed in
several midrash collections as one of Abraham's ten tests, and, in at
least one, as the first test.[37] If the point of the story is to demonstrate
Abraham's staunchness in the face of martyrdom, then the notion of
a *test* is clear. But if the theme of filicide is set in high relief, as Rashi
sets it here, what does *testing* mean? What does emerge from Rashi's
pared-down version of the midrash—and, quite plausibly, from his
reading of the Torah text—is that the event that lays the foundation
for Abraham's recorded life is an act of filicide, in which his father
(virtually) kills him and (in fact, if not in intention) kills his brother.
This memory of horror is not recorded in the written biblical text.

The fire of Ur of the Chaldeans is encrypted in oblivion. But at
certain moments it flares and licks the surface of memory. Rashi
even suggests, citing a midrash, that that fire is inscribed in the

name of that place: Ur means fire. Some such moments occur in the Torah itself, as we have seen. Others appear, obliquely, in midrashic sources:

> "God said to Abram, Get you out of your land . . ." (Gen. 12:2). What precedes this passage? "And Terach died in Haran" (11:32), which is followed by, "God said to Abram, Get you out of your land. . . ." R. Isaac said: Chronologically, Terach still had sixty-five years to live. But first you may learn that the wicked, even in their lifetime, are called dead. For Abraham was anxious, saying, "Shall I leave my father and bring dishonor upon the Divine Name, for people will say, 'He left his father in his old age and went off'?" So God reassured him, "I exempt you *(lekha)* from the duty of honoring your parents, though I exempt no one else from this duty. Moreover, I will record this death before your departure." Hence, "And Terach died in Haran" is stated first, and then, "God said to Abram, Get you out. . . ."[38]

This earliest biographical appearance of Abraham's habitual anxiety is his response to God's original *lekh lekha* call: he resists, on the grounds that if he abandons his aged father in order to obey God's call, he will appear, at the very outset of the history of monotheism, to betray universal ethical standards. The ethical issue is strangely addressed in God's answer: *"You* I exempt from the duty of honoring your parents." Why is Abraham to be the sole exception to this imperative of a civilized society? And how, in fact, does this answer his anxiety? On the face of it, it simply rehearses the paradox of founding a higher religion on the violation of a civilized norm.

I suggest that since the fiery furnace motif is so prevalent, our midrash can rely on the vitality of this narrative to explain Abraham's exceptional relation to the duty of honoring his father. Since, in terms of intention, his father has killed him, he no longer owes him obedience. He acquires the mythical status of an unfathered child.

So powerful is this counterfactual truth that the midrash represents it by revising the chronological biblical account. Even though he lives sixty-five years after Abraham's departure, Terach's death is recorded *before* Abraham leaves home. In this way, Abraham is protected against criticism: his father was already dead when he obeyed God's call. What may at first appear a cavalier approach to historical truth takes on a different cast in the larger context: Terach is "killed" in the text, since his fatherhood of Abraham has been long dead. Abraham is exempted of duty since, in the realm of psychic reality, the normal relations of father and son have been radically undermined. Daringly, the midrash even attaches this unique exemption from filial duty to the word *lekha* in God's command: in leaving his place of origin, he reenacts a traumatic cut that has long alienated him from family and society.

A sinister and unconscious meaning is thus read into a biographical anomaly in the narrative. Abraham's anxiety at the violation of God's honor screens a deeper violation that implicates his whole culture. At the basis of his relation to God lies a trauma, which strains the very concept of fatherhood.

Abraham's life with God is, on the one hand, a charmed life, for it is God's grace that has delivered him from the fire, as it will later deliver him from the warring kings. In kabbalistic thought, he represents *chesed,* the loving relation with others displayed in energetic acts of benevolence and empathic imagination. And yet, on the other hand, in the midrashic portrait, this sunlit Abraham is haunted by *hirhurim:* by his own testimony, only his ashes remain. "I am dust . . . I am ashes . . ."—God's grace on the one hand, his unfathered soul on the other.

THE HEART OF DARKNESS

The fiery furnace motif indicates more than a purely private trauma. Such practices—the sacrifice of sons—mark the beginnings of human society and, specifically, of the history of religions.[39] An extraordinary midrash[40] links the fiery furnace with the furnace in which the builders of the tower of Babel fired their bricks (Gen. 11:3). Abraham's unconscious place of origin is at the foundation of a civilization.

This place is described, strangely, as a valley (Gen. 11:2). Why does this community build their tower, whose top is to touch heaven, *in a valley?* And this valley is named *Shinar,* a name that reveals a sinister history. A Talmudic passage puns on *Shinar:* to this place all the corpses of the flood were precipitated (*she-ninaru*—lit., shaken).[41]

Mei Ha-Shilo'ach[42] offers a provocative reading of this material. After the Flood, society constructs its civilization, its values of unity and solidarity, which, it is hoped, will preserve it from a recurrence of catastrophe, in a valley of death. The Flood generation had been characterized by violence and rapine; this new generation will aspire high by cultivating social harmony. ("Everyone on earth had the same language and the same words" [Gen. 11:1].) The basis of this civilization, however, is *fear*—the fear of death, as symbolized by the corpses that lie at the foundation of the city and tower. This repressed fear will compulsively shape religious and social life; the terror and denial of death will motivate all its achievements.

In contrast to this structure, the Holy Temple is to be built on a lofty base and to generate a different kind of solidarity. What God wants, insists our Hasidic master, is not a compulsive fear, but *avodah*—which refers, on one level, to the ritual service of the Temple, but on another to *work*—the slow, gradual work on human nature that moves beyond visceral fear as the basis of the religious life.

This evocative reading of the Tower of Babel provides Abraham with a spiritual history. Later, God will say to him: "I am God who brought you out of Ur of the Chaldeans" (Gen. 15:7). This was the foundational moment of Abraham's life, as God's almost identical declaration at Mount Sinai ("I am the Lord your God who brought you out of the land of Egypt") is to be the foundational moment of Israelite history. The encounter with God makes Ur uninhabitable for Abraham—as later it makes Egypt uninhabitable for his children. If Ur is a religious civilization based on fear—the reflexive fear of death, of all the ills that flesh is heir to—Abraham must be moved to leave this civilization. In the world where he originates, the primal religious impulse is terror, and the gods are sought for their protection. But however tall the tower that is built here, it can achieve no more than a fantasy of intimacy with God, since it involves no *work:* its base is in those smoky caverns where children are slaughtered to appease the gods. Built in a low place, its aspirations are largely pretenses.

Implicitly, Mei Ha-Shilo'ach is offering a critique of the violent intimacies of the sacrificial about which Bataille writes so compellingly. As against the anguish of fear and the ecstasy of desire, there is the requirement of *work,* of working through primal instincts, so that religious experience can be founded on higher ground: not the annihilation of the individual in the sacrificial moment but the clearer delineation of the human face.

Abraham's history begins here. He survives the fire of Ur where his father killed him. But his journey contains its own heart of darkness, a memory that is not a memory. In a sense, therefore, the *Akedah* was always destined to happen. Wherever Abraham travels, his destination is Mount Moriah:

> "And Abram journeyed, moving on toward the south": he drew a course and journeyed toward the future site of the Temple.[43]

In all his apparently random wanderings, he is fated to reach that place. For what has been implanted in him—the father who kills his son—will have to undergo a *test:* something implicit in his past, an "unthought known," will have to be unfolded, lived through in the present, so that it can finally assume its proper place in the past.

DIVINE INTIMATIONS

In the following midrash, Mount Moriah is not only his destination but the symbolic projection of his journey:

> "He saw the place from afar": How did it look from afar? This teaches that at first this was a low place. But when God decided to have His presence [the Shekhinah] reside there and to make there a holy place, He said, It is not a king's way to reside in a valley, but in a lofty, exalted place, that has become beautiful, visible to all. Immediately, God hinted to the region round the valley that all the mountains should gather together to form a site for His presence [the Shekhinah]. That is why it was called Mount Moriah, since out of fear [*yirah*] of God it became a mountain.[44]

A geological drama—the sudden shifting of tectonic plates to create a mountaintop—becomes a spiritual drama. God, it seems, is fastidious about dwelling in low places. He is to be found in the stark light of the mountaintop, not in the smoky caverns of the religious mysteries. His transactions with human beings are founded on the highest achievements of human thought; His mysteries are to be translated into terms that the conscious mind can grasp.

The catalyst for movement from low to high is no more than a *hint;* God's power may be expressed in thunderous commands on Mount Sinai, but if God is to dwell in the world, the low ground that has been the residence of the pagan gods must be transformed by different means. In the imagination of the midrashic writer, *fear of God* is the force that turns a chasm into a mountain; but it is aroused by a *hint.* Hints are elusive, allusive, often ambiguous: the work that they initiate is to be done by one who *takes the hint.* What can be made of such intimations? They exist in a world apart from the instinctual *fear* that compels acts of terror and anguish.

PRIMITIVE AGONY

The trajectory that lies between Ur and Mount Moriah can be viewed through the prism of D. W. Winnicott's psychoanalytic thought. He addresses a clinical phenomenon that he terms "the fear of breakdown":[45] the patient is preoccupied with a sense of impending doom that Winnicott understands as referring to a breakdown that *has already happened* in early childhood, before the ego was sufficiently developed to encompass it. Never fully experienced, and therefore in a sense unthinkable, this original experience of primitive agony haunts the individual; the future must provide a way of accessing, for the first time, the unthinkable catastrophe of the past:

> It must be asked here: why does the patient go on being worried by this that belongs to the past? The answer must be that the original experience of primitive agony cannot get into the past tense unless the ego can first gather it into its own present time experience and into omnipotent control now. . . . In other words the patient must go on looking for the past detail which

is *not yet experienced*. This search takes the form of a looking for this detail in the future.[46]

Becoming aware of this paradoxical possibility, the analyst can help the patient *reach to the madness:*

> The patient needs to "remember" this but it is not possible to remember something that has not yet happened, and this thing of the past has not happened yet because the patient was not there for it to happen to. The only way to "remember" in this case is for the patient to experience this past thing in the present, that is to say, in the transference. This past and future thing then becomes a matter of here and now, and becomes experienced by the patient for the first time.[47]

An experience of "madness" has long potentially been a fact. The paradoxical status of *potential experience* becomes the subject of a strangely lyrical analogy:

> I saw a hyacinth bulb being planted in a bowl. I thought, there is a wonderful smell locked up in that bulb; I knew of course that there is no place in the bulb a smell is locked up. . . . Nevertheless there is in the bulb a potential which eventually will become the characteristic smell as the flower opens.[48]

The developing self constantly reaches toward a realization of the original unthinkable moment. The patient lives more and more of the particular form of madness that belongs to him individually.

.

REACHING TO THE MADNESS

I suggest that Winnicott's "queer kind of truth" sheds light on the hidden logic of Abraham's life. The sense of impending doom that takes the form of *hirhurim*—qualms, misgivings—is an expression of a past agony. The story of the fiery furnace functions, on one level, as proof of Abraham's commitment to the God that he has come to know. But the heart of the story—disowned even within the midrashic tradition, which is itself disowned by the biblical text—is the father's murder of his son, of both sons—one virtually and one in fact.

In Abraham there is thus a need to find that which has not been experienced. He circles around the trauma, coming closer with each *test*. Furnaces, smoke, ashes unaccountably haunt his imagination. Just before the *Akedah* narrative, he resists Sarah's pressure to send his son Ishmael into the desert to probable death: "And the thing was very evil in Abraham's eyes, for it concerned his son" (Gen. 21:11). Only on God's prompting and reassurance does he accede to her will. His intense sense of evil is about fathers and sons and the destruction that may flare between them.

With the *Akedah,* the primitive agony of his life comes to full flower. Now, God offers no palliative, no reassurance, and Abraham makes no objection. He rises early, travels three days, expresses no reluctance. The angel, who at the last moment prevents the slaughter, has to call out twice: "Abraham! Abraham!" before he desists. To his first cry, "Do not raise your hand against the boy!" the angel adds, "Do not do anything to him!" Some strange eagerness is at work in Abraham to consummate the sacrifice, at least with a symbolic scratch.[49] To stem this, the angel calls, "Do not do anything *[me'umah]* to him!—Do not make a blemish *[moom]* upon him!" Abraham wants to make the sacrifice real in some physical way; the angel tells him that such an act would irreparably *blemish* the sacrifice.

The narrative yields an uncanny sense of Abraham as impelled toward Mount Moriah. What has been locked within him is now released. The *Akedah* moment is the moment of fullest *testing,* in precisely the traditional sense of *living through an experience* so that its potential is realized. Perhaps because he has accumulated strength over a lifetime of *testings,* he is now able to bear the full brunt of the primitive agony.

Most significantly, however, it is God whose relation with Abraham creates the conditions under which his past experience may be lived through in the present moment. If God can be figured in biblical and midrashic imagery as lover, betrayed husband, brother, man of war, artist, then, I suggest, He may sometimes act as psychoanalyst. It is through this dimension of Abraham's relation with God that his *hirhurim* are forced to the surface.

God never fully relieves Abraham of his qualms, since these pressure points of his inmost life are, it seems, precisely what he needs, in some intimate sense, to *know*. God, therefore, plays enigmatic roles, so that Abraham can encompass what, originally, was unthinkable. God makes demands that cast Abraham now in the father role. Now, he will confront what was locked within him; an original breakdown will be relived with a difference.

In this narrative, the issue of the *Akedah* is not simply one of obedience; the test is not a *pass/fail* question. Rather, he is given an opportunity to reexperience from the vantage point of maturity what he has never truly experienced, to respond with full freedom to an inquiry that will probe the depths of his being.

THROUGH A DIM GLASS

Mei Ha-Shilo'ach[50] presents Abraham's dilemma in the complex light of this kind of exposure. God's demand is enigmatic and absolute, making no gesture to reconcile this horror with past promises. God the Father bears the lineaments of an inexorable paternity. The greatness of Abraham lies in his ability to hold fast to his belief in the past promises of destiny and life, and in the Father who made them. Even as God precipitates him into the deepest currents of his life, His presence remains with him, benign and enigmatic at the same time.

The Zohar points out that the God who tests Abraham is called *Elohim*, which indicates that He communicated "through a dim glass." The exact meaning of His command is unclear: its ambiguity is of the essence of the test. For Isaac, the test is slighter, since he fully believes in his father's account: if it is God who has commanded the sacrifice, a lesser heroism is involved in obeying. Only from Abraham's perspective is this radically a *test*, since the command comes to him clouded with possible meanings. His uncertainty about God's meaning makes the test more difficult, since it invites Abraham to respond with his whole being. *How* he responds—the authenticity with which he struggles with the ambiguity of the situation—will be more significant than *what* he does.

Rashi cites a classic and disturbing midrash, which addresses the ambiguity in God's words:

> Said R. Abba: Abraham addressed God, Let me spread before You my complaint. Yesterday, You told me, "In Isaac, your seed shall be named." Then, You said, "Take your son . . . and offer him as a burnt offering . . ." And now, You tell me, "Do not raise your hand against the boy!" God answered him: I shall not profane My covenant and the utterance of My lips I shall not change. When I said to you, "Take your son . . ." the utterance of My lips I shall not change: I did not say, "Slaughter him," but "Bring him up." You have brought him up, now bring him down.[51]

All the obvious contradictions in God's communications to Abraham are resolved in one radical rereading: "I never told you to *slaughter* him." God's consistency is preserved, He has not changed course. The cost of this rhetorical move, however, is high. Abraham has, all along, misunderstood the nature of God's demand. All God ever desired was that Abraham *raise Isaac up* (the literal translation of *ha'aleyhu*).

On the face of it, the midrash seems to trivialize Abraham's agony. God has put him through a meaningless test, which bears no relation to His real intent. In addition, since Abraham's understanding of *ha'aleyhu* as a command to *sacrifice* is the idiomatic and consensual understanding, the literal reading of the word emerges as a sophistry.

Clearly, there is no room for ambiguity at the time of God's demand. Particularly in view of Abraham's history, the stark nature of the command could only mean sacrificing his son. For Abraham alone, this is a real test, an experience through which unconscious conflicts will be staged; for him, there is the unspeakable desire to do as was done to him. The cathartic wish drives him to the mountaintop. Will this compulsion to act out the past deceive him into slaughter?

Here is Abraham's dilemma: on the one hand, the compulsive

wish to exorcise the past; on the other, the horror of a sacrifice that would deprive him not only of his beloved son, but of his moral and spiritual standing in the world. As Beit Ya'akov puts it,[52] he had spent his life teaching the world "the glory of heaven"—God's desire for the ethical human life. If he had killed his son, he would have looked simply like a murderer, a filicide. "All would have been lost in one instant."

In this situation, Beit Ya'akov remarks, Abraham might have found sophistical ways to reinterpret God's command so as to evade its obvious meaning. He might, for instance, have realized that God had not, in fact, commanded him to *slaughter* Isaac but simply to *raise him up*. In this way, he would have desisted from the sacrifice, thus confirming "the glory of heaven." Such a course of action, however, would have been self-serving and evasive, since it was clear that *ha'aleyhu* quite unequivocally meant, "Slaughter him!"

He is given three days, a time of doubt, ambiguity, confusion,[53] to work through his conflict. His doubt is not only about the meaning of God's command but even about the identity of the speaker, the source of the command. Is this obscure, dimly lit speaker indeed God, the God whom Abraham knows and loves? Or is it, perhaps, a satanic force, created by his own dark needs?

One daring midrash[54] imagines Satan accosting Abraham on his journey and making just this maddening suggestion: "The one who told you to commit murder—for which you will be found guilty—*he was Satan!*" Abraham staunchly rebuffs this satanic notion. But, for the reader, the damage has been done. Ambiguity has insinuated itself into the narrative. How is Abraham to know for sure which is God's voice, which Satan's?

When the angel of God (this time God is YHWH—the lucid light prevails) calls out twice, "Abraham! Abraham!" the Zohar comments: "The first 'Abraham!' is not the same as the second." In the short time, a heartbeat, between calls, Abraham has become different. Something confused in him sharpens into focus. Initially deaf to the angel's cry, he becomes present and capable of hearing the second "Abraham!"

A Hasidic reading amplifies the midrashic tradition: the double call, "Abraham! Abraham!" is an expression of divine love[55] that Abraham is granted only at the point when he fully registers—responding *Hineni*—the command *not to slaughter* his son.[56]

Another Hasidic reading: "He did not hear the angel, for he was preoccupied with his intent to complete the act. Or, alternatively, he realized that he was being signaled to stop; therefore, he acted as one in a trance, in order to complete the act" (Kli Yakar). Abraham is in a trance, unconsciously—or perhaps willfully—deaf to the angel's call. The lure of the funeral pyre is informed by an individual history in which primal fears have become personal.

The angel's second call, however, is heard by Abraham. Only someone who has worked, worked through the complex layerings of his relation to God, can hear the call that will interrupt his trance. In Beit Ya'akov's powerful reading, it is only at this moment, when the angel cries, "Do not raise your hand against the boy!" that he becomes capable of hearing the hidden meaning of the original command: *ha'aleyhu* is now—always ambiguous; it can now be understood to mean, simply, "Raise him up!"

THE POSSIBILITY OF SUBLIMATION

Abraham's work is to fathom the compulsions that lead to filicide; to know in the present the full force of an experience of terror that lies enfolded in his past; to wake from his trance at the angel's call. This is the work that is to shift the tectonic plates, so as to create a site where God may dwell: exalted, beautiful, visible to all.

By the time Abraham arrives at the place where the angelic voice becomes audible, God's original command has released an alternative meaning—one that was till now quite inaccessible, locked into the words, like the smell of the hyacinth bulb. "Raise him up!" articulates a possibility that Abraham has now earned the right to understand.

This moment of sublimation is also a moment of knowledge. "Now," says the angel, "now I know that you fear God" (Gen. 22:12). A cathartic process has given birth to knowledge, eliminating compulsive wishes and terrors. Now, God knows what to answer the critical voices that interrogate His tender relations with Abraham. By the same measure, too, Abraham knows—for this is his angel—how to respond to these persecuting voices. The knowledge precipitated by rigorous experience allows the angel to describe him as *fearing God:* a very different mode from the visceral fear that motivates primitive religious experience. *Fear* has evolved into *fear of God,* the twin of love of God.

At the heart of civilization is darkness. In Joseph Conrad's novel *Heart of Darkness,* his tormented and tormenting antihero dies with the words "The horror! The horror!" on his lips. Abraham loves and is loved by a God who takes him through a cathartic journey to that horror, so that his love can lose its anxious misgivings.

All the tests of Abraham's life are approaches to the crisis that he has not yet experienced. All involve some measure of breakdown of apparent integrations, some intimate access to the heart of darkness. His journey from Ur of the Chaldeans has had the purpose of possessing the Land: so God promised him, "Oh Lord God," he cries out, "*how shall I know* that I am to possess it?" (Gen. 15:8). He wants knowledge that will connect his past with his future. God's answer—the vision of dread and darkness, furnace and fire, with vultures hanging menacingly over all—is summarized by Rashi: "Your children will endure in the Land *by virtue of sacrifice.*"[57]

When he is compelled to send his son Ishmael to a probable death in the desert, he again approaches the original madness. When God challenges him, "Become whole!" he falls on his face, as spurious convictions of wholeness disintegrate. The paradox of diminishing himself in order to become whole means confronting himself without defense. "The original experience of primitive agony cannot get into the past tense unless the ego can first gather it into its own present time experience."[58]

Introducing his essay on the breakdown that belongs in the past, Winnicott writes: "Naturally, if what I say has truth in it, this will already have been dealt with by the world's poets." Perhaps we can read T. S. Eliot's lines in "Little Gidding" as giving haunting poetic expression to Winnicott's "queer kind of truth, that what is not yet experienced did nevertheless happen in the past":[59]

> We shall not cease from exploration
> And the end of all our exploring

Will be to arrive where we started
And know the place for the first time.

ENIGMATIC MESSAGES

The *Akedah,* then, returns Abraham to the past so that he may know it as he never knew it before. This is a narrative of *afterwardness:* "And it was *after these things. . . .*" In order to understand God's command, the midrash asks: "What lies *behind* it, *before* it? What is the necessary history of this moment?" We have focused on a childhood trauma that is totally repressed in the Torah text. The fact of this absence, combined with its pervasive presence in midrashic and medieval writings, intimates an archaic memory that leaves its traces in Abraham's imagery of thought and speech. The fiery furnace and the father who kills two sons become the foundational narrative of his life. In this sense, the *Akedah* is the inevitable confrontation, the *test,* that is to define his inner world.

The foundational reality in Abraham's life is, then, primarily a psychic reality. But what of historical reality? If the *Akedah* is a story of *afterwardness,* this means that it enacts a later version of a primal event. The awkward English expression is in fact a translation of Freud's *Nachtraglichkeit:* sometimes translated as "deferred action," it refers to a significant early moment that is later remembered with a difference. The classic example is of the infant at the breast seen by the adult from the perspective of sexual experience: two different experiences of the breast, past and present, overlap.

Jean Laplanche[60] discusses two views of this relation between past and present moments. On the determinist view, the primary experience is retained within the adult, who registers it anew at the sight of the nursing baby; on the hermeneutic view, the adult retrospectively imagines all that he could have experienced if he had only had his present knowledge. The adult either *reconstructs* a memory whose trace is within him, or *constructs* it, creates it in his interpretation.

Against both these views, Laplanche offers his own understanding. A third party has been overlooked—the wet nurse. Her subjective reality, unconscious desires, and actual pleasure in her role constitute a third term: the nurse's message to the infant. There is always an other, who is prior to the life of the infant and whose unconscious experience is conveyed in enigmatic ways to the infant. The adult does not fully know what he is conveying, and the child receives traumatizing messages, which have to be repeatedly remastered, translated, and retranslated.

The enigmatic, traumatizing message forms the kernel of otherness in the child's world. The child attempts to metabolize this "foreign body hard as iron"[61] within him, to break down and reassemble it into a different entity. Analysis, writes Laplanche, offers "a reopening of the dimension of alterity,"[62] an opportunity to respond to the terrors and desires roused by the other, to de-translate the old translations, the old formations of identity.

On this view, Abraham's earliest past—the narrative of the fiery furnace—may be a historical event reaccessed in later life, or it may be a later construction projected backward—a kind of retrospective fantasy. The essential factor, however, is the presence of *others* whose unconscious reality has implanted within him a "foreign body" that he must repeatedly attempt to master. His habit of *hirhurim* speaks of enigmatic messages, from his family and his culture, which, by definition, cannot be totally understood or mastered.

At the *Akedah*, God plays the role of analyst, reopening the dimension of otherness, inviting Abraham's transferential love and fear. For as Laplanche most challengingly suggests, God, too, is enigmatic:

> That God is a god who speaks and compels the hearer to listen is obvious throughout the Book, which is but a variant of the paradigm "Hear, O Israel!" That God is enigmatic, that He compels one to translate, seems obvious to the entire Judaeo-Christian tradition of exegesis. Whether enigma pre-supposes that the message is opaque to Himself is plainly a different question.[63]

God's address to Abraham is not exhausted by its consciously understood meanings. "He compels one to translate." Laplanche cites Job as providing a fine example of enigmatic messages, which give rise to "repeated attempts at translation, justification, delimitation and mastery, which are the main points at issue between Job and his questioners." The tantalizing question, however, as Laplanche indicates, is whether God's message is, in any sense, opaque to Himself. "Does God have an unconscious?"

The *Akedah* is the archetypal example, it seems to me, of the divine enigmatic message, the address to the human being that traumatizes and compels one to translate. Here, God reopens the primal mystery of the Other—this time with therapeutic intent. An opportunity to loosen the bonds of trauma is offered. But for this metaphor to be imaginable, God, as a character in the narrative, must be perceived by Abraham and perhaps even by the reader as speaking out of depths that are, in some sense, opaque to His own consciousness. He speaks as *Elohim,* not as YHWH: the light is clouded, the revelation is incapable of paraphrase. He will never explain, resolve the mystery. It is left to Abraham to submit, to master by submitting to the enigma: that is, to de-translate the old translations, retranslate the enigma into forms that will allow history to arise.

But Abraham's work is endless, extended through history. The culmination that is the *Akedah* is not a final resolution: after Abraham comes Job. For God's meanings remain opaque, even, in a sense, to Himself. That is, even to the particular dimension of divinity by which God addresses a particular person at a particular moment of revelation. The task of translation is never finished: fundamental enigmas are constantly to be reelaborated.

ABRAHAM UNAPPEASED

And Abraham? He is not appeased, neither by the first angel nor by the second. Midrashic versions listen for the protest with which he breaks his long *Akedah* silence. Finally, God hears Abraham's voice in argumentative, even aggressive mode:

> At that time, Abraham declared before God: Master of the worlds, a man tests his friend, if he does not know what is in his heart. But You—who know what the heart and the kidneys counsel—did You have to treat me in this way? God answered:

Now I know that you fear God. Immediately, God opened the heavens and the deep darkness, and said: By Myself I swear, says God. . . . Abraham interrupted: *You* swear! *I* swear that I will not descend from the altar until I have said all that I need to say! God told him: Speak!

Abraham said: Did You not tell me, "Count the stars, if you are capable of counting them—so many will be your seed!"? God said: I did. Abraham continued: My seed from whom? God answered: From Isaac. And Abraham declared: I had answers for You in my heart: yesterday You told me, "In Isaac your seed will be named"; now, You tell me, "Take your son and offer him as a burnt offering." But I suppressed my impulses and I did not answer You. So, when Isaac's children sin and are involved in suffering, remember Isaac's *Akedah* to their credit, and let it be accounted before You as though his ashes were gathered upon the altar, and forgive them and redeem them from their suffering.

Then God replied: You have had your say, now I will have Mine. Isaac's children will indeed sin before Me, and I will judge them on Rosh Hashanah [the New Year]. But if they wish Me to seek out merit for them and remember to their credit Isaac's *Akedah*, then let them blow the shofar of this one before Me. Abraham asked: What is the shofar? God told him: Turn around and look behind you! "And Abraham lifted up his eyes and he saw—behold!—a ram—behind—caught in the thicket by its horns" (Gen. 22:13).[64]

The biblical text celebrates closure, with the angel swearing in the name of God to bestow bounteous blessings on Abraham's children, "because you have listened to My voice." The midrash undermines closure, by imagining Abraham's angry, even irreverent appropriation of God's words: " 'I swear by Myself,' says God. . . . Abraham interrupted: '*You* swear! *I* swear that I shall not descend. . . .' " Abraham will have his say. Urgently, and with God intently listening, the enigmas and inconsistencies of God's messages erupt from him, becoming the burden of what he *did not say* at the time of the *Akedah*.

Abraham wants permanent credit for his silent restraint, *as though* the sacrifice had in fact been consummated; the credit is to be transferred as prophylactic atonement for the sins of future generations.

So explosive is his protest at the mystery of God's messages that it is difficult to imagine God resisting his demand. In the rhetorical balance of the midrash, Abraham now holds the high moral ground. But God's answer is qualified. Essentially, He denies Abraham the closure he asks for—the absolution that will inoculate his children against future sin, indeed against the traumas of history. Instead, He refers him to the shofar as the means of evoking forgiveness. By blowing the shofar, future generations will continue Abraham's work, rather than simply banking on it.

The midrash undermines the closure offered in the biblical narrative, as well as the theological closure claimed by Abraham. If the past is to redeem the present and future, it can do so only by being worked through in the present. If Abraham's sacrifice is to affect the future, it can do so not by purchasing, with its consummated beauty, an immunity from sin and suffering, but precisely by modeling a process, necessarily incomplete, to be resumed in every life.

Abraham did *not* consummate the sacrificial command: that is his greatness and his gift, his true consummation. We remember Bataille's discussion of the meaning of sacrifice: "it is gift and relinquishment. . . . This is the meaning of 'sacrificing to the deity,' whose sacred essence is comparable to a fire. To sacrifice is to give as one gives coal to the furnace."[65] In his readiness to confront and metabolize the complexity of his life, Abraham has relinquished an insistence on the "lasting order," in which all values are subordinated to the value of duration; he has affirmed the value of constant translation, which submits the past to the fire of the present.

The closure offered by the midrash is a vision of an animal caught in a thicket, a tangle (in modern Hebrew, *sevakh* indicates psychological complexity) by its horns. Here, the ram substitutes for Isaac, but the emphasis is on the shofar, the instrument wrought of these complicated horns, and on the animal's position—"behind." The shofar blown on Rosh Hashanah to evoke God's forgiveness may not be straight, or "simple" *(pashut)*. And it should be directed upward. As emblem for the complex human being, subject of many attempts to de-translate and retranslate his experience, the shofar cries with a human cry, produced by human breath.

Most strikingly, however, the midrash focuses on the ram's position: "And Abraham lifted up his eyes and he saw—behold!—a ram—*behind (achar)*. . . ." In order to see it, he is told, "*Chazor l'achorekha*—Turn around! Look *behind* you!" In this way, the midrash addresses the anomalous use of *achar*—behind—as though it were syntactically detached from its context: not *acharav*—behind him—but simply and enigmatically *achar*. The flow of the sentence halts; questions gather. Does this refer to space—the space *behind* Abraham, hidden, other? Or to time—*after*? The ram whose horns will offer atonement for the future is to be found in the world of *achar ha-devarim ha-eileh*, of *after these things*, where what lies behind the apparent facts, what happened before, the residues of the past, suffuse the present.

Abraham has wished to make something enduring of his sacrifice. That will be his recompense for his restraint in the face of God's enigmas. The *Akedah* is simply to undo the rigors of the future. God responds by turning Abraham back to the world of behind, of *afterwardness*. What lies behind him is the future of his past, the once inevitable consequences of those traumatizing messages; and a dynamic possibility—that his children, like him, will work to transform and translate the enigmas of their own past. This is God's offer: the perpetual return of the shofar cry, for memory and transfiguration.

SEVEN

"Her Own Foreigner"
Rebecca's Pregnancy

THE PREGNANT INTERIM

Rebecca is the first biblical character to question the limits and meaning of her subjectivity, and to go in quest of God. Reflecting on her life, she twice asks, "Why?" The first time God responds, but He does not assuage her desire. This "Why?" is a question born in pregnancy; it will haunt her to the end.

Rebecca's pregnancy is in a sense the only biblical pregnancy. As a condition in itself, a human experience to be questioned and constructed into meaning, this pregnancy is unique in the entire range of biblical narratives.[1]

Of course, the *achievement* of pregnancy constitutes a triumphant crisis in many narratives. It is only after long barrenness that, typically, biblical heroines conceive. In order to attain this moment of consummation Sarah, Rachel, Hannah, and Rebecca herself have had to suffer and pray. But the movement from conception to birth is generally seamless: *va-tahar va-teled*—"she conceived and gave birth"—becomes a formula that covers almost all accounts of pregnancy. Between the two dramatic moments, the pregnant interim disappears.

To give birth is to continue and extend God's creation. When Adam reproduces, he creates in God's image, which is the human image:

> This is the book of human generation: on the day that God created the human being, He made him *in the divine image;* male and female He created them. . . . And when Adam was 130 years old, he gave birth in his image after his form. (Gen. 5:1–3)

Such proliferation of the divine image is attended with difficulties from the beginning. According to the Talmud,[2] Adam did not even attempt this task for 130 years: alienated from God after his expulsion from Eden, his progeny at first lacked the divine image. Only at a certain moment of maturity, a fully human conception becomes possible. From then on, generations of children are born with apparent ease and recounted in genealogical lists, dense with names. These passages are succeeded by very different ones in which barren women endure the anguish and the triumph of this delayed moment. Once the child is conceived, however, birth follows instantaneously. The space and time of pregnancy are effectively absent from these narratives.

Rebecca's is the one exceptional experience of a troubled period that moves her to speak strange words, and to seek God:

> The children struggled within her, and she said, "If so, why do I exist?" And she went to inquire of God. And God said to her, "Two nations are in your belly, two peoples shall separate from your bowels; One people shall be mightier than the other, and the older shall serve the younger." (Gen. 25:22–23)

In these two verses, an inner history is unfolded, enigmatic meanings intimated. On the biological level, there is the struggle of twins in her womb. But does she know that the turbulence is caused by twins? There is the radical, almost nihilistic force of her question: *Lamah zeh anokhi?*—which essentially translates as *"Why I?"* (*Zeh* indicates emphasis.) Does this express her anxiety that she may miscarry, or even die in childbirth?[3] Does she regret her desire to become pregnant, if she is to suffer such pain?[4] Does she even wish for death to escape her suffering?[5] Or is she asking something more primal, more violently existential?[6]

And there is the quest for God. Does she simply go to inquire of God, to elicit answers from some oracular source, to allay her anxiety about the outcome of her pregnancy?[7] Or is she seeking a relationship, rather than an oracle?[8]

WHY I?

It is striking that she immediately undermines her achievement of pregnancy—the conventional "happy ending" of her story of barrenness—by her enigmatic question: *"Why I?"* Starkly, she inter-rogates the meaning of her *anokhi*, her *I-ness*.[9]

Her question resounds strangely, too, on the lips of the woman who had, in a sense, created a new register for *anokhi*, the "I" of sub-jectivity. She was the first biblical character to speak the word *anokhi* as a term of identity. *Bat Betuel anokhi*—"I am the daughter of Betuel" (Gen. 24:24)—she had declared to Abraham's servant, defining her past and her future.[10] With total assurance, she had initiated the con-struction of the human subject as *anokhi*. And when her family had asked her with a shade of skepticism, "Will you go with this man?" she had replied fearlessly, perhaps defiantly, *"Elekh*—I will go!" (24:58). (Rashi glosses: "Of my own will *[me-atzmi]*—even if you do not wish it.") Firmly centered in her family, she equally firmly sepa-rates from them, her intentionality ringing clear. But now—*"Why I?"* speaks from an altered self. What has eroded her confident subjec-tivity? What has her pregnancy generated within her that finds such poignant voice?

This pregnancy is the direct offspring of prayer: Isaac's prayer for his barren wife has, with uncanny directness, taken root in her.

> And Isaac pleaded *[va-ye'etar]* with God on behalf of his wife, because she was barren; and God responded to his plea *[va-yei'ater]*, and his wife Rebecca conceived. (Gen. 25:21)

The Hebrew for "pleaded" signifies great intensity; like a laser beam, Isaac focuses his prayer *le-nokhach ishto*—upon his wife, fac-ing her, desiring only her to bear his child. Unlike the other patri-archs, Isaac is monogamous, all his love, his desire for children, set on this one wife. And God responds with a mirroring fulfillment of his prayer, so that "his wife Rebecca" becomes pregnant. The nuance is eloquent: he prays for *his wife*, but it is *Rebecca* his wife who becomes pregnant. Rebecca, the personal name, does not entirely coincide with her status as Isaac's wife. There is a surplus, an excess: the woman who conceives is also a subject who will immediately complicate the "happy ending" of a history of barrenness.

· · ·

THE ENIGMATIC QUESTION

Instead of signifying a conventional conclusion to a troubled story, then, Rebecca's pregnancy becomes the beginning of a new concept of conception. The physical fulfillment of desire—a prayer answered in her body—opens up unforeseen questions about the *anokhi,* the experience of *I-ness,* of that body. The question "What does Rebecca want?" strangely arises. But how can there be any question about what a barren woman wants? The very reference to her barrenness, in the context of her husband's prayer, indicates a distortion that will be made straight. The history of frustration will be consummated in fertility: "He sets the childless woman among her household as a happy mother of children. Hallelujah" (Ps. 113:9). Here, however, the blissful resolution modulates into tragic questioning: *"Why I?"*

Everyone wanted this pregnancy: Isaac prayed for it, Rebecca's family blessed her that she would become "thousands of myriads" (Gen. 24:60). But why does Rebecca not pray, too?[11] Where is her desire? Is it too obvious to narrate? Or is its silence significant, eloquent of a conflict, a wish of a less obvious kind?[12]

Freud famously asks a similar question: "What does a woman want?"[13] Here, too, from a male viewpoint, woman's desire may be regarded as obvious. Raising the issue as a persistent enigma, Freud allows the woman's experience of her desire to emerge in all its irreducible difference. Setting aside his own wisdoms about female desire, he acknowledges a limit to his mastery: he places in focus woman's *want* as the unresolved question of psychoanalysis. Shoshana Felman argues that Freud *lives* the question by dreaming the Irma dream—the crisis that gives birth to a new recognition of otherness.[14] We will return to this crisis later.

Rebecca's pregnancy, too, is set in the context of a question that reopens, beyond biology and society, the enigma of woman's desire. She, too, lives the question *"Why I?"* so that it challenges her relationship to herself.

A history of her desire—What happened to her *anokhi,* to her lived experience of *I-ness?*—must pause, I suggest, at the earlier moment when she first meets Isaac. Her future husband is meditating in the field toward evening when Rebecca comes upon him unexpectedly.

> And he lifted up his eyes and saw camels coming. And Rebecca lifted up her eyes, and saw Isaac; and she fell from the camel. And she said to the servant, Who is that man who is walking in the field toward us? And the servant said, That is my master. And she took her veil and covered herself. (Gen. 24:63–65)

Isaac sees camels approaching; Rebecca sees Isaac. And she falls off her camel.[15] Some crisis of seeing destabilizes her. Her vision of Isaac absorbs her and in some mysterious way wounds her. She does not yet know who this man is who so deeply affects her: "Who is *that man (ha-lazeh)?*" she asks, her language implying her sense of wonder, of otherness. And when she is answered, she covers herself with a veil.

What creates the tension of this moment, its unique focus on veiling and vision? This is Rebecca's first encounter with the otherness that is embodied here in Isaac, and that affects her to the point of trauma.[16] The midrash intimates this: "She saw him majestic, and she was confounded, astonished, in his presence."[17] She receives the shock of his otherness, and is forever veiled before him. Something of the pride and energy of her *anokhi* is obscured. Isaac takes her and loves her and is comforted after his mother. But Rebecca—her lived experience of self—is wounded, less sure.

In this crisis, she is totally engrossed in her vision of Isaac. And we, reading her absorption, are empathically engrossed in her experience. Rebecca becomes real for us precisely because of this moment of conflicted intensity when what she sees is in some sense excessive—as though she cannot bear either to look at Isaac or to look away from him. So she falls from her camel and veils herself. Dumbfounded by ambiguous experience, she evokes our own experience of such moments. More than anyone before her, she engages the depth of our inwardness.[18]

It is against this background that Rebecca's pregnancy cry—"*Why I?*"—is to be heard. She has defined herself so assuredly in her difference from her family—*Elekh!*—*I shall go!*—that her blinding encounter with her husband astonishes her with its penetration of her own being. By the time she veils herself, it is already, in a sense, too late. Something alien has been implanted within her: a vision of Isaac—perhaps rapt in prayer, as the midrash narrates, radiantly beautiful, with angelic escort—has now become uncannily part of her. She has her first experience of being *decentered.* A "stranger" inside her is activated by this experience:

> With the Freudian notion of the unconscious the involution of the strange in the psyche loses its pathological aspect and integrates within the assumed unity of human beings an *otherness* that is both biological *and* symbolic and becomes an integral part of the *same.* . . . Uncanny foreignness is within us: we are our own foreigners, we are divided.[19]

TO BE OR NOT TO BE—REBECCA AND JOB

With her pregnancy, the other within her takes on overwhelming reality. This is the blessing that her husband and her family have desired: "Our sister, may you *[att]* become thousands of myriads . . ." (Gen. 24:60). *Att*—the second-person equivalent of *anokhi*—emphatically places her both as subject, the one who will become myriads, within whom myriads *already have their potential being,* and as object, in her family's world of language and desire.

Doubly situated, she cries, *Why I?* The simplest reading is that she is in pain at the churning in her womb, and anxious about the fate of her pregnancy. Or does she, as the midrash suggests, ask around among her friends: Is this your experience, too? Realizing that she is alone in her distress, she asks, *Why I?* and turns to prophet or oracle for answers. On this reading, *Why I?* becomes a social question— Why am I different from you all? What she seeks is information that will explain her suffering, her difference. Her pregnant experience is a narrative strategy designed to introduce the oracular statement about the "two nations" of the future; the struggling twins in her womb foreshadow a complex future.

Ramban, however, reads differently:

I think the real meaning is that she said, "If this is my fate, why then am I *in the world*? Would that I were not, that I would die, or had never been," as in "Better had I been as though I never was" (Job 10:19).

Startlingly, Rebecca becomes Job. Her question resonates with his anguish as he interrogates the meaning of his life:

Why did You bring me forth from the womb? Better had I expired before any eye saw me, had I been as though I never was, had I been carried from the womb to the grave. (Job 10:18–19)

The little space between womb and tomb has become senseless to him. Wishing he had never been born, or even conceived, Job, too, asks, *Why?*

Why did I not die immediately I emerged from the womb, expire as I came forth from the belly? (Job 3:10)

Obsessively, Job articulates the problem of *natality*. "To be or not to be" is the question that haunts Hamlet: whether to affirm or deny one's existence, the fact of having been born. As Stanley Cavell puts it, the unacceptable choice is rooted in the discovery that "there is no getting even for the oddity of being born, hence of being and becoming the one poor creature it is given to you to be."[20] He names the alternative, "world-consuming doubt," the skepticism that wants annihilation: rejecting partings, departures, parturition, separation, the skeptic wants "not to count," "not to be natal, hence not mortal." To see ourselves "as apart from everything of which we are part, always already dissevered,"[21] is to determine the issue of natality that Job breaches with his *Why?* questions. It is striking that his questions are generally phrased in the future tense, as though challenging his incipient life from the very moment of birth, or of conception. ("Why *should* I not die immediately I emerge from the womb?") By an intricate act of *Nachtraglichkeit*,[22] he revisits the crisis of his birth, interrogating the now-known future.

Rebecca's *Why I?* can be heard in the same register of skeptical anguish as Job's. Both, strikingly, turn to God in their suffering. In the face of his friends' disapproval, Job demands answers of God. He should, says Eliphaz, seek out God in a very different spirit: "I would seek out *(edrosh)* God, I would lay my case before God" (Job 5:8). He should be begging forgiveness for his sins, not making transgressive demands. But God vindicates Job and his meanings, preferring his radical challenges to his friends' humility; preferring, too, the spirit in which he seeks out God.

Essentially, Job's anguish and his quest originate in Rebecca's. She is the first human being to have sought out God. The pain that threatens to tear her apart seems to signify some destructive conflict raging in that secret place within her.[23] A new desire moves her: not simply for the oracular answer, but for the God who will hear and even vindicate her question. For, after all, her experience of the problem of natality is of a different order than Job's. If he represents the human strangeness of being born from a woman's belly, Rebecca's relation to that belly, that womb, is more complex. For she *is* the womb, the belly, the entrails. She not only questions her natal condition, but *is* the body in which human life uncannily originates.

If Job, or the Psalmist, or Ecclesiastes contemplates that place where he was fashioned, where consciousness brushes against its limits, Rebecca embodies that place at her center. The Psalmist, in wonder and terror, speaks of the unfathomable matrix of his being: "I was shaped in a hidden place, knit together in the recesses of the earth" (Ps. 139:15). In Rashi's reading, the "hidden place" is the uncanny place of the parents' desire. Ecclesiastes focuses on the inscrutable contents—unknowable, absent from consciousness—of the full belly of the pregnant woman—so protuberant, so present— as a metonymy for the mystery of God's world: "Just as you do not know the path of the wind, or the contents of the full belly, so you do not know the actions of God who causes all things to happen" (Eccles. 11:5). But Rebecca is that belly and that consciousness both. Simultaneously, she experiences the presence and the absence of meaning.

. . .

DISUNITY OF BEING

The disunity of being that is the pregnant condition is exacerbated, of course, in the case of twins. These twins—quintessentially divided—internally replicate the simultaneous sameness and difference that belongs to pregnancy. This explosive disunity is contained within Rebecca; but she experiences it as also containing her, isolating her from a knowable world.

Elaine Scarry writes powerfully about the sense of being "swallowed alive" by one's body. Intense pain, she argues, has the power to "unmake the world." One's own pain, so engrossing to oneself, may seem to another person "to have the remote character of some deep subterranean fact, belonging to an invisible geography that . . . has no reality" because it is inexpressible and therefore unshareable.[24] She quotes Virginia Woolf: "English which can express the thoughts of Hamlet and the tragedy of Lear has no words for the shiver or the headache. . . . The merest schoolgirl when she falls in love has Shakespeare or Keats to speak her mind for her, but let a sufferer try to describe a pain in his head to a doctor and language at once runs dry."[25]

Similarly, Bergman's film *Cries and Whispers* begins with a woman's diary entry, "It is Monday morning and I am in pain,"[26] and attempts to find ways to represent the interior facts of bodily sentience: two hundred different background shades of red, for instance, give the "shrill sentience" of the body a voice and extended human presence. Lacking such a voice, "pain engulfs the one in pain but remains unsensed by anyone else." For this reason, artists like Edvard Munch, Francis Bacon, and Grunewald paint the open mouth, with no sound emerging, to represent the human scream that goes unheard.[27]

Rebecca's words—*Why I?*—represent her interior experience in the barest, most cryptic form. Fragmentary, hermetic, they resemble the open mouth whose pain is inaudible to others. This is language attempting to convey its own constriction, the "unmaking" of a rich world of meaning.

In pregnancy, the body grows, fills space—and breaks in two.

Julia Kristeva describes the paradoxical state of the mother, before and after birth. "A mother is a continuous separation, a division of the very flesh." Birth is an

> abyss that opens up between the body and what had been its inside. . . . What connection is there between myself. . . and this internal graft and fold, which, once the umbilical cord has been severed, is an inaccessible other? My body and . . . him. No connection.

Kristeva confronts "the *flash that bedazzles me* when I confront the abyss between *what was mine and is henceforth but irreparably alien.* . . . No identity holds up"[28](emphasis added). Maternal love is "a surge of anguish at the very moment when the identity of thought and living body collapses."[29] "The other is inevitable . . . for such an other has come out of myself, which is yet not myself but a flow of unending germinations, an eternal cosmos. The other goes much without saying."[30]

THE UNCANNY INTERIOR

"What was mine and is henceforth but irreparably alien": for Rebecca, the invisible geography of her body is both hers and doubly alien. Twins struggle "within her," *be-kirbah,* in her *kerev,* the site of the entrails—in Latin, the *viscera,* in Greek, the *splanchna,* in Yiddish, the *kischkes.*[31] In biblical language, the *kerev* of the animal sacrifice, for instance, includes the heart, the kidneys, the stomach and intestines. Only dimly imaginable to their human owner, these organs have a tactile, slippery, unseizable physicality. If she is a woman, that interior becomes the source of pain, blood, fluids; the source, also, of life. In the womb, of course, hysteria originates. This intimate, alien world both fascinates and repels others—men—who, in Kristeva's expression, "abject" it, repudiate its horrifying humanity as nonhuman.

These same organs also deliver passion and thought, yearning and prayer: "My heart is hollow within me *[b'kirbi]*" (Ps. 109:22); "My heart turned over within me" (Lam. 1:20); "And Jonah prayed from the bowels of the fish" (Jon. 2:2); "My bowels yearned for him" (Jer. 31:20); "He probes the heart and the kidneys" (Ps. 7:10).

"Has any god ventured to go and take one nation from the midst [mi-kerev—from the innards] of another nation?" (Deut. 4:34). The imagery is of birth—a difficult birth, as the midrash describes it, involving forceps and trauma, and indicating a radical connection between emergent Israel and the Egyptian host body.[32] The birth of the subject is fraught with pain.

However, in a frequent reversal, it is Israel that becomes the maternal body, in whose kerev, that spongy, unfathomable interior, many objects may live. God may live there, in their midst [middest] (Num. 14:14), guide His people from there (Exod. 34:9), create signs and wonders there (3:20). The Israelites may reject God from His residence there (Num. 11:20). Or it may be the spirit of harlotry that takes up residence (Hosea 5:4), or strange gods (Judg. 10:16). Most perplexingly, Israel may be uncertain whether God is, or is not, within her: "Is God in our midst or not?" (Exod. 17:7).

The interior of the body constitutes a subterranean region of psychosomatic experience. Here, Israel is imagined as alienated from its own interiority, from its subjectivity, ambivalent about God's position in its life. According to one midrash, the people set the stakes high: "If we harbor doubts in our hearts, and He knows our qualms, then we will serve Him. If not, we will rebel."[33] The people wish for a God who can contain their uncertainties, who intimately knows that which does not know Him. The proper place for God is in the heart, in the human innards; if God is not present there, then ayin—nothingness.[34] This visceral place, uncanny, intimate, and alien, has the power to make and unmake the world.

If this unconscious world could find benign conscious expression, the Psalmist's dearest wish would be fulfilled. "May my nefesh bless God, and all that is within me [k'rovai] His holy Name!" (Ps. 103:1): the Psalmist wishes that his nefesh, his lungs, his breath, his spirit, and his kirbayim, his innards, his visceral life, may praise God's name. He asks, that is, for his whole uncanny interior world to find expression in a world of communicable knowledge. He yearns for the separate parts of the self to be fused, reintegrated. In this way, he will become, at least as long as the blessing lasts, real to himself.

Within Rebecca, there is a struggle of unknown forces. Strikingly, the expression *kerev* sometimes refers to "battle."[35] What is most intimate may also be violently divided. The biological reality may be that the twins are already at war, but in terms of fantasy her very interior *(kirba)*, it seems, is embroiled in conflict.

Suddenly, the young woman who had provided an object lesson in gratuitous and loving energy can barely bring herself into words at all. Language fails her; in Jacqueline Rose's poignant phrase, it "brushes against its limits." Commenting on Kristeva's essay on maternity, Rose characterizes the "felt catastrophe" of "the fact that there is an unconscious, that we cannot fully know . . . either the other or ourselves." It is the mother, she claims, who is made responsible for this "zone of anguish," known as "femininity, non-language, body." But it is precisely the mother who forces us to confront the limits of our being. She quotes Sylvia Plath: "I am breaking apart like the world."[36] The fantasy of primary union of mother and child hides the conflicts and tensions that elude conscious awareness.[37]

ALIEN GUESTS

Rebecca is the biblical character, woman, mother, whose turbulent pregnancy issues in a question—*Why I?*—that interrogates the limits of knowledge. Her very name in Hebrew represents the enigma of subjectivity: *Rivkah* is an anagram of *kirbah* (her interior). All that is within her, in its presence and in its absence, is to become Rebecca.

But not without struggle. "The ego is not master of its own house," declared Freud, thus undermining one of the vestiges of human narcissism. Man can no longer experience himself as absolute ruler of his own mind: "Come, let yourself be taught something on this one point! What is in your mind does not coincide with what you are conscious of." The subject is decentered from his own experience of consciousness: "Thoughts emerge suddenly without one's knowing where they come from. . . . These alien guests even seem to be more powerful than those which are at the ego's command."[38]

Decentered from her early confidence, Rebecca in pregnancy experiences a new sense of subjectivity, baffling intimations of "alien guests" within her. She lives between two worlds: she must find herself in the relation between consciousness and unconsciousness.

In his discussion of the Freudian view of subjectivity, Thomas Ogden argues that these qualities of experience are created in a discourse between the two, each dialectically defining, negating, and preserving the other.

> [A] psychoanalytic theory of experiencing "I-ness" must incorporate into its own structure and language a recognition of the ineffable, constantly moving and evolving nature of subjectivity.[39]

Within this kinetic model, the ego plays its part, but only as part of a dialectical whole. Interplay, movement, mystery create the "stereoscopic illusion" of a unified experience.

"Inside" Rebecca, located in her belly, her innards *(b'kirbah)*, are twin babies, mutually destructive. What this evokes in Rebecca, associated with her physical pain, is a sense of incoherence, an "I-ness" now unfathomable, dynamic, its unconscious elements in palpable conflict.

Rivkah/*kirbah:* her alien interior agitates, mystifies, and isolates her. Her response—*Why I?*—*Lamah zeh anokhi*—seems to ask for some explanation for her existence. "And she went to inquire of God." Seeking answers to her own mystery, she consults a prophet, or an oracle. This is one classic understanding of her response.

However, the biblical question, *Lamah—Why?*—almost always introduces a rhetorical question: "*Why* did Sarah laugh?" (Gen. 18:11); "*Why* did You bring us up out of Egypt?" (Exod. 17:3); "My God, my God! *Why* have you abandoned me?" (Ps. 22:2); "*Why* do You hide Your face?" (Ps. 44:25; Job 20:24). Often, such rhetorical questions shade off into a mode of complaint, or accusation. A harsh taste of futility infuses the demand for meaning. No answer can subsume the question.

"WHY?"—LAMENT AND PRAISE

In relation to Psalm 22 ("My God, my God! Why have You abandoned me?"), Paul Ricoeur discusses the paradoxical force of the *Why?* question. He focuses on the reversal in the psalm from lament to praise: "Just as the poetic 'I' is open to whoever says 'I,' the intratextual reversal is offered to every suppliant invited to trace out the pathway from lament to praise."[40] Beginning as lament, bordering on accusation, the psalm is at the same time addressed to God, "held within the space of prayer. . . . It is by asking 'why?' that the *Urleiden* of being 'abandoned by God' is addressed to God." Praise and lament, Ricoeur asserts, are "imbricated" with each other, since the praise already announces itself from the initial address to God, while the lament is sustained throughout: "the praise remains a lament right to the end."[41]

In Ricoeur's eloquent reading of the psalm, the "questioning address"—the radical *Why?* question, addressed to God, modulating between praise and lament—offers itself "to whoever says 'I.' " In a similar vein, I suggest that Rebecca's "questioning address," her "*Why I?*"—at first a soliloquy of unshared and unshareable pain—becomes part of her trajectory, the expanded reach of her quest for God. This dynamic turn from a bleak sense of a world unmade to a possibility for remaking enfolds her poignant *lamah* question into a form of prayer.

Paradoxically, the *lamah-Why?* question seems to convey a quality of experience that excludes any possible relation to God. At its darkest, it expresses futility, emptiness, absence.[42] At this level, "*Why I?*" translates as, "This is not I. This is what I am not." In this mode, Rebecca is essentially repudiating any relationship between her visceral messages and any acceptable sense of self, between her unconscious and her conscious experience. And yet, "she went to inquire of God, to seek God." Has she turned her question toward God? And if so, how does this affect its meaning, its register of lament?

"WHY I?"—SEEKING GOD

Here, the history of exegesis yields ambiguous understandings. As we have noticed, the most common reading of "She went to inquire of God" is the oracular one: Rebecca goes to consult a prophet or seer, who will reveal endings to her. On this account, her question solicits an answer that will recenter her, return her conclusively to the realm of meaning. Ramban is alone in insisting that *lidrosh et Ha-Shem*—"to seek God"—always refers to prayer. Rebecca is not consulting an expert in outcomes; she seeks God.[43] And indeed, the common oracular interpretation ignores the many texts—including some cited by Ramban—in which *lidrosh et Ha-Shem*—holds no oracular implication: the quest for God holds its original meaning of a movement toward a solicitous, caring relation with God.[44]

If Rebecca is looking for a solution to her perplexity, the words of God, or the prophet, offer little in the way of clarity. She now knows that her inner sensations are the effect of a twin pregnancy and that the two children will split off from her and from each other and become nations eternally in tension with each other. But even the expression "The older will serve the younger," which seems to offer some clear prophecy about power relations between the two nations, is irreducibly ambiguous, as many commentaries notice.[45] In fact, the oracle speaks in the classic manner of oracles, leaving much interpretive work for the questioner. In this case, Rebecca is given some information about the outcome of her pregnancy, in terms that expand her constricted experience of pain. The remaking of the world in this mode, however, endows her uterine experience with the force of paradigm. Eternally, in the political world beyond her womb, the two children will struggle, each in turn dominating the other, each perhaps drawing strength from the other.[46]

On the other reading, however, Rebecca's question precipitates her into a quest for a new praxis of relationship with God. As we have noticed, she is the first human being to initiate such a quest. The disunity of her being, her decentered subjectivity, moves her to address her lament to God: to enter the space of prayer. Like Job, like the Psalmist, she solicits, by way of the aggressive *Why?* question, One who will hear her cry.

God's words to her communicate an elusive, ambiguous mirroring of her own disunity. In a sense, God is *confirming* her experience of fragmentation. ("Two nations shall split off from your bowels . . .")[47] Her children, her interiority, are to be both alien, separate, absent—from each other and from her—and eternally present to her. Her life is forever bound up with them, her "I-ness" constituted by the interplay of conscious and unconscious aspects of experience. If Rebecca's *"Why I?"* expresses a radical sense of "This is what I am not," it is answered by God's "This, these are you, yet not you."[48]

In this mode, the *Why?* question suspends any response of resolution; as Ricoeur argues, it sustains an inscrutable God against an encompassing theology of history. When the Psalmist cries, "My God, my God! Why have You abandoned me?" he testifies to the mystery of the hidden God and to the sense that it is the individual who suffers and who constantly reopens the question *"Why . . . ?"* The tension between prayer and theology, between the question of the Psalmist and the response of the prophets, is maintained in a continuous duality.

From Psalms to Job, *"Why?"* becomes a question answered ultimately by the inscrutable God who is beyond human conception. Why be born at all?—Job's insistent question of natality—is absorbed into God's mysterious final words "out of the tempest." These last words settle nothing. Compounded of rhetorical questions of His own, they implicitly require of Job some modulation of voice, some shift in posture:

> Who is this who darkens counsel,
> Speaking without knowledge?
> Gird your loins like a man;
> *I will ask and you will inform Me.*
> Where were you when I laid the earth's foundations?
> . . .
> Who set its cornerstone?
> . . .
> Who closed the sea behind doors?
>
> (Job 38:2–8)

Ineffable, God engages the ineffability of the human subject, in his "unbearable lightness of being." Job is left in silence, an inscrutable Job, his response to God's response—"I will ask and you will inform Me"—not yet born.

I-YET-NOT-I

Rebecca's *Why I?* and God's enigmatic response constitute the paradigm of such an encounter. God both confirms and disconfirms her experience of disunity. Now, she, like Job, is silent. "This green sprout why," her utmost statement, has been uttered.[49] How does she position herself in relation to God's words? By using ambiguous expressions such as *rav ya'avod tza'ir*—(lit.) "older shall work younger" (serve? or be served by?)—God has opened up dialectical possibilities, changing matrices of power, evolving each out of the ripeness of its contrary.[50] Space is made for constant interplay between two opposites—perhaps even for the creation of a kind of third area between them, composed of overlapping spheres of energy. For Rebecca, this might mean an evolving sense of *anokhi* as *I-yet-not-I*.

The phrase "I-yet-not-I" suggests the blurring of boundaries between self and other. Marion Milner draws two jugs, one set slightly in front of the other, so that they can be seen as two overlapping circles: this is an exercise in "observing how shadows cut across or bring about a *merging of boundaries*."[51] This image becomes for Winnicott a means to convey the potential space, the "interplay of edges," where new things are born.

"On the sea-shore of endless worlds, children play" (Tagore).[52] For both Winnicott and Milner, the seashore is the space of tension between the imaginative realities of the inner world and the tangible realities of the external world, as well as the meta-tension between the need for these boundaries and the equivalent need for "an overlap, a stage of illusion, intoxication, transfiguration."

At this point of overlap, "I-yet-not-I" both perceives and creates the world. Here, the subject may become willing to accept chaos and uncertainty as a part of the creative process. "We are poor indeed if we are only sane."[53] A kind of faith is involved in this willingness. Here, the mystic, the artist, and the analyst are agreed.

In thinking of the relationship between two people, however, the overlap may be seen as an entity of its own. Winnicott ponders the radical implications of this notion of potential space:

There is no interchange between the mother and the infant. Psychologically, the infant takes from a breast that is part of the infant, and the mother gives milk to an infant that is part of herself.[54]

In this intermediary area of experience, the perceptions and meanings of two people shape and color each other. A third area of consciousness is formed, which Samuel Gerson refers to as the *relational unconscious*.[55] Here, both participants experience new opportunities for previously unrealized elements of subjectivity, as well as limitations specific to their relationship.

MATRIX FOR THE UNTHINKABLE

In her encounter with God, Rebecca experiences a new—and potentially generative—confusion about the boundaries of identity. Her narrative of pregnancy—*Why I?*—raises the issue of subjectivity *as a problem*. Her psychic disunity is never, in fact, resolved. She carries it in her interior. On the level of fantasy, her question can be translated as, "Am I capable of bringing a whole live baby to birth?"[56] God's answer confirms, in a sense, her inner division: *"Two . . . two . . . split. . . ."* The otherness within her is acknowledged, possibilities for interplay are intimated. But His words are ambiguous; they withhold certainty, firm definition.

Between Rebecca and God, an intermediate space is created. Here, Rebecca knows herself as "I-yet-not-I." Her subjectivity, her *anokhi*, is invited to acknowledge previously unrealized possibilities. God speaks from the *Anokhi* that becomes His marker when He reveals Himself to Israel at Sinai: *"Anokhi*—I am the Lord your God who brought you out of the land of Egypt." One midrash, in fact, connects Rebecca's question with that moment of epiphany:

> *"Why then I?"*—To whom will You say on Mount Sinai, *"Anokhi—I am* the Lord your God . . ."? Immediately, she girded her loins in prayer.[57]

Sensing conflict within her, she fears that the destiny of Israel is at stake: who will survive to receive God's law at Sinai? Her prayer is her response to the catastrophe impending for *Anokhi,* the voice of God in communication with the human.

God answers her enigmatically. How indeed do His words relate to her anguish of identity? A powerful Hasidic reading of God's *Anokhi* offers a possible understanding. Mei Ha-Shilo'ach focuses on the uncertainty, the "I-yet-not-I" nature of God's representation of Himself at Sinai. The letter *khaf* in *anokhi* expresses the incomplete, provisional, metaphoric nature of this revelation. (As a prefix, *khaf* indicates likeness, similarity, approximation, imagination.) Identifying Himself as "I-yet-not-I," God opens for His seekers a future history of richer and fuller representations of divinity. The imaginative, provisional nature of God's *Anokhi* allows for the future development of human subjectivity and of a more capacious potential space, larger arcs of overlap with *"not-I."*

The message that Rebecca receives from God respects, in a similar way, the provisional nature of her *anokhi.* Her baffled question had been addressed to the God who would respond in an evocative mode, without inundating her, without even referring to His *Anokhi*—as one inexpressible being speaking to another. Included in His address is Rebecca's unconscious life—as well as, perhaps, the relational unconscious that is created by God and human together. His words provoke further deepenings of the human mind, always elusive to itself, only partly known.

In pregnancy, then, Rebecca is positioned at the place where she knows her difference from herself, as she struggles to express an unfathomable sense of "I-yet-not-I." Pregnancy becomes the matrix for that which is still unthinkable. Rather than assuring her that she is capable of birthing a whole baby, coherent, whose descendants will stand stably at Sinai to receive God's revelation, God implants in her a conviction of internal disunity, of opposites, in which the other is constantly implicated in the self. An internal otherness challenges her sense of autonomy and, paradoxically, establishes her subjectivity. The *anokhi* that has become questionable is precisely what brings her to seek God. Perhaps His otherness will help her with her own?

THE NAVEL OF THE DREAM

"In every dream," Freud writes, "there is at least one spot at which it is unplumbable—a navel, as it were, that is its point of contact with the unknown."[58] The navel, the place where the newborn is connected with the mother, evokes the pregnant belly, blatant, protuberant, uncanny; the cord of connection is cut on birth. In Shoshana Felman's brilliant reading of Freud, the navel thus marks both the disconnection and the connection between mother and child, and "embodies, thus, the way in which the dream is, all at once, *tied up* with the unknown and *disconnected* from its knowledge."[59] In the form of a *knot,* the navel suggests to Freud the "tangle of dream-thoughts which cannot be unraveled."[60] The dream resists full understanding.

In context, Freud's comment refers to the "unplumbable" strangeness of femininity. In a moment of revelation, Freud acknowledges that unknownness that can never be explained away, that female pain that is unspeakable in its difference, necessarily resistant to male solutions. Attempting unsuccessfully to heal Irma, he dreams his desire to overwhelm her resistance and wakes to a new sense of the unfathomable—the otherness that is woman comes to name and give shape to the otherness that he newly knows in himself. The "unknown woman"[61] becomes the catalyst for a new apprehension of the unknown self.

In the larger dynamic of the biblical family narrative, I suggest, Rebecca comes to represent the pathos of the "unknown woman." God challenges her to accept her own strangeness, to find a space within herself, as well as in the external world, for that "I-yet-not-I" condition in which boundaries are blurred so that imaginative possibilities of connection can emerge. How far can she be seen to appropriate this message?

Her twin children are, as foretold, radically different from each other; and so is the relationship of each parent to them: "And Isaac loved Esau, because he gave him game in his mouth, while Rebecca loved [lit., was loving] Jacob" (Gen. 25:28). Love is at the center of this story—Isaac's love for Esau, Rebecca's love for Jacob. Strikingly, Isaac's love for Esau is explained; it is subject to understanding (though the explanation remains difficult). But Rebecca's love for Jacob is unexplained, perhaps inexplicable, situated in that navel of the dream that reaches into the unknown. In some sense, it resists interpretation—even as the verbal form *ohevet,* "was loving," implies a relationship without origin or cause. What is clear, however, is that Rebecca identifies with only one of her two children.

To Jacob, she gives Esau's clothes, and animal skins to simulate his very skin. Three times, she says to him, *"Listen to my voice,"* as she moves him to her will.[62] The union between them is to be complete. To this end, she herself maintains a listening posture: "And Rebecca *was listening* when Isaac spoke to Esau" (Gen. 27:5). Once, she had been the object of vision and speculation for Abraham's servant; then, she had become the subject of a traumatic vision of her future husband that had made her fall from her camel and cover herself with a veil. Seeing and being seen had perhaps proved unbearable; now, she listens and wills herself to be heard. In a sense, she matches herself to Isaac in his blindness. His voice, his blessing and curse, frame her world; so must her voice frame the world of Jacob whom she loves.

In the listening mode, it is easier to imagine the "I-yet-not-I" of her subjectivity, the overlap between herself and her son that can be reconstructed as her experience of pregnancy. Then, she was audible to him as a voice that merged two existences in the music of the womb. If she loves him now, this is, after all, explains the midrash, quite understandable: "Whenever she heard his voice, she would love him more."[63] This is a love that accumulates, that feeds on the voice of the beloved who is one's twin self.[64]

But this love has forgotten the disconcerting truth of pregnancy in favor of a retrospective fantasy. Rebecca has refashioned her pregnancy to authorize her wish for wholeness, for a concerted identity. In this sense, God's message to her has not been taken in. She places Jacob at the center; he always was at her center, alone, harmonious. Esau is censored from her intimate narrative.

THE UNKNOWN WOMAN

Between the lines of the narrative, Rebecca's tragedy is intimated. It is brought to light at the last moment, in the midrashic account of her death. In the biblical text, however, we listen to her voice, as she again cries: *"Lamah?—Why* should I be bereaved of you both in one day?" (Gen. 27:45). And again: "I am disgusted with my life because of the Hittite women. If Jacob marries a Hittite woman like these, from among the native women, *lamah?—why should I have life?"* (27:46). Here, she speaks to Isaac in subterfuge; her true fear she expresses only to Jacob. But the rhetoric of pain, the interrogation of her life's meaning, remains recognizable; it is her idiom, and these are the last words we hear her speak.

As for her death, that is absent from the biblical narrative. By the time Jacob returns home twenty-two years later, rich in wives, children, and livestock, she has disappeared. But she haunts Jacob and his family with her absence, her unknownness. On their journey home, a woman, Rebecca's wet nurse, Deborah, dies and is buried "under the oak below Beth-el; so it was named Allon-bacut (the oak of weeping)" (Gen. 35:8). Intense weeping saturates and names the place. But who was she, this unknown woman?

> *"And Deborah died"*: How does Deborah belong in Jacob's family? But since Rebecca had told Jacob, ". . . then I will send and bring you back from there" (Gen. 27:45), she sent Deborah to him in Padan Aram with the message to return—and she died on the journey back.
>
> " . . . *below Betel"*: The city was on the mountain, and she was buried in the foothills.
>
> " . . . *under the oak"*: in the foothills of the plain, which was called *Allon*. But the *aggadah* tells that Jacob was given the news of a second mourning—that his mother had died. *Allon* in Greek is *other*. Because the day of her death was concealed, so that people should not curse the belly from which Esau was born, the text too did not reveal it.[65]

In Rashi's source, Midrash Tanchuma, Rebecca is buried surreptitiously by night. The midrash reads the burial narrative of Deborah as a covert reference to the suppressed narrative of Rebecca's death and burial. Rebecca's only mourner would have been her wicked son, Esau, her disavowed son. As his mother, she would have become the object of popular calumny: "Cursed be the belly from which he was born, the breasts that suckled him."[66] Rebecca's secretive burial is displaced, then, represented by the public burial of her nurse, Deborah, who had been sent as her emissary to bring Jacob back home.

Deborah is symbolically associated with Rebecca by way of a history that goes back to Padan Aram, Rebecca's childhood home. Accompanied by her nurse,[67] Rebecca had traveled to Canaan to marry Isaac. Now, in old age, this same nurse dies on her journey, again returning to Canaan, after representing her mistress in a mission to reunite mother and son.

Deborah's death thus comes to represent *another* death: Rashi puns on the Greek word *allon* (other) to hint at the unspeakable, repressed death of the mother. Rebecca is lost to the narrative, absent in her death as, largely, in her life. This woman is fundamentally unknown to her husband and to her son Esau. She dies alone and is buried without honorable escort: a private death, signifying her alienation from Esau and Isaac.[68] Even Jacob, the avowed son of her desire, represses her memory. His tears are shed for the old family retainer, whose breasts had suckled his mother. Rebecca has vanished from the surface of his narrative.

But the excess of his tears tells another story:

> One who mourns excessively for his dead is mourning for *another death*.[69]

Through the banal cover story, *another* death makes itself felt. The word *tachat*—under, instead—is used twice in this verse, suggesting substitution, a hidden grief. On this other level, eluding consciousness, Jacob weeps for his mother. She is lost to him, but he cannot fully mourn her, or know what he has lost. By the strange logic of the emotions, then, he cannot stop mourning for her. Something unthinkable hides in this loss.

Perhaps it is his very bond with her, the total complicity that Rebecca has imposed on him, that prevents him from engaging with her and disengaging from her. He has not confronted her difference—her own *difference from herself*. That which is unthinkable *in her to herself* keeps him in thrall.

As a young woman, she had separated from her family. Incisively, she had cut the bond with them, perhaps particularly with her father. *Bat Betuel anokhi*—"I am the daughter of Betuel," she had said; and then, *Elekh*—"I will go—of my own will, whether you agree or not."

But, mysteriously, her father has disappeared from the narrative by the time she makes this brave declaration (Gen. 24:55). The midrash conjectures: he intended to prevent Rebecca from leaving and was killed during the night.[70] Or he was killed because he tried to poison the servant to prevent Rebecca from leaving. Or because he intended to have relations with his daughter, as he did with all the local virgins on their first night of marriage.[71]

These traditions clearly read Betuel as endangering Rebecca's ability to break decisively with her past. The sexual corruption that threatens her identity—Betuel is connected in these sources with the word *betulah,* virgin—is removed by her father's death, allowing her to declare with perfect clarity, *Elekh,* I will go! The midrash intimates, nevertheless, a world of sexual violence that makes such surgical separations plausible only on the conscious level.

The classic midrashic image for her relation to that world is that she was like "a rose among thorns."[72] The simile conveys her sublime difference, her corrupt background a dramatic setting for her moral beauty. A different simile would be necessary to accommodate the psychological sense in which otherness is primary and penetrates the self with enigmatic messages.[73] From this perspective, she is connected with her father and his meanings, even as she repudiates them.

In brave simplicity, she selects a different identity, only to encounter the otherness of Isaac, and the decentering enigma of her pregnancy. *Im ken, lamah zeh anokhi,* she cried, baffled; and sought God. Repudiating otherness—her father, her husband, her wild son Esau—she loved Jacob. But—to borrow from Kristeva—she is her own foreigner. Unable to accept this otherness, she is unknown to herself, and uncanny—familiar but alien—to Jacob as well. For her divided being has become part of him; she is, after all, internal to him, as he was to her; she is lodged in his unknown inner life. "*She* was what he had missed."[74] In losing her, he has lost something unfathomable.

NEGOTIATING WITH LEOPARDS

The acknowledgment of otherness—in others and in himself—will remain the spiritual task of Jacob's life. From Rebecca, he will inherit an experience of *I-ness—I-yet-not-I*—that will constitute a problem of relationship with the stranger, outside and within. Merged with her, he, too, rejects Esau's otherness, puts it out of his mind. But when his blind father questions him, he identifies himself: "*Anokhi—I am Esau your firstborn.*" This split identity—Jacob/Esau—will haunt him, generating questions and dreams. Waking at Bet-El, he will cry out in wonder and confusion: "Indeed, there is God in this place—and *anokhi—I* did not know!" "My self, my *anokhi*, my *I-ness*, I have never known," reads the Zohar. Fragments of self will jostle over a lifetime for a measure of integration.

The paradox, however, of Jacob's life is that in order to bring these fragments into relation with each other, he will have, first, to acknowledge them in all their essential alienness. For him, this story begins with Rebecca, with her inner world in which wild things hide. Through her experience of pregnancy, she had glimpsed the terror of the leopards described by Kafka:

> Leopards break into the temple and drink to the dregs what is in the sacrificial pitchers; this is repeated over and over again; finally, it can be calculated in advance, and it becomes part of the ceremony.[75]

What had been a violation has been tamed, its otherness absorbed into a personal ritual. Decentered, Rebecca had sought God, and partially retreated from her own experience, to a fantasy of wholeness embodied in Jacob (the *tam*, as the Torah at first calls him—simple, wholesome, uncomplicated [Gen. 25:27]). She had lost her radical vision, lost herself, the turbulent subjectivity that had barely been born.

"*She* was what he had missed." If the mourner in James's story is seized too late by the beast of his own blindness, Jacob is given a larger space to negotiate with his leopards. Joseph, the fantasy child with whom he identifies, will, in thought, be torn apart by a wild beast. But even before that, his other "unknown women," his wife Rachel and his daughter Dinah, will be lost to him, as he fails to acknowledge their otherness and his own.

"Am I *(anokhi)* in God's place," he will respond to Rachel's bitter appeal, "who has withheld from you fruit of the womb?" (Gen. 30:2). God who filled his mother's womb with uncanny fruit has left his wife empty: Jacob can find no words, no prayer in the face of the woman's pain. If he allowed it entry, it would lacerate him from within. So when his daughter is raped, he seems strangely apathetic. And he ignores Rachel's last will and testament, her naming of the child born in her death: "son of my pain," she had called him. "But his father named him Benjamin, son of strength [lit., the right hand]" (35:18). Rachel's passion is silenced in its last living utterance.

For Jacob, she is the navel of his dream, unfathomable, unthinkable. He loves her but cannot acknowledge her. Apart from the conversation about her fruitless womb, he never—in the biblical text—speaks to her or, after her death and till just before his own, of her.

But seventeen years later, her son Joseph will dream of sun, moon, and stars bowing down to him. Jacob will interpret the dream and at the same time, apparently, mock it: "What is this dream you have dreamed? Shall we indeed come, I, your mother and your brothers, to bow down to the ground before you?" (Gen. 37:10). In Rashi's reading, Jacob is apparently disparaging the dream, in order to protect Joseph from his brothers' jealous rage. Your dream is absurd, he says, since your mother is long dead. How can she bow down to you? Really, though, Jacob takes the dream seriously: "His father kept the matter in mind." But in that case, what does he make of Rachel's presence in Joseph's dream?

The midrash assigns the Rachel element in the dream to a category it calls *devarim betelim*—meaningless things:

Our Rabbis learned from here that there is no dream without meaningless, void things. Jacob intended to dismiss the dream so that his other sons would not be jealous of Joseph: "Just as the part about your mother is absurd, so is the rest of it."[76]

In this fascinating comment, the Rabbis use Jacob's response to arrive at an observation similar to Freud's: every dream has a navel—a place at which it is unplumbable, that is its point of contact with the unknown. In Joseph's dream, that uncanny place is the image of the moon, his mother Rachel. This is the spot that resists interpretation. Like the navel, it was connected with the unknown but is now disconnected. This female place, uncanny, *unheimlich*, in Freud's terminology, "is the entrance to the former *heimat* [home] of all human beings, to the place where everyone dwelt once upon a time and in the beginning." This is the mother's body that "was once *heimisch*, homelike, familiar; the prefix 'un' is the token of repression."[77] For Joseph, Rachel represents birth and death, a nostalgia that can only be coded in dreams. For Jacob, Rachel is the *davar batel*, the element that cannot be thought, the disturbing feminine otherness that was once so familiar.

THE UNTHOUGHT KNOWN

Here, Rachel and Rebecca meet, as they never do in life. Jacob is assailed by thoughts that lie too deep for tears. Rachel's death in childbirth, her desperate plea for a child, "or else I die," her dying claim on the infant as she names him *Ben oni, Son of my pain*—all must be suppressed, as they link with those other thoughts: Rebecca's questioning of her life's meaning, her relentless claim on him to be the only total child—"My son, *listen to my voice*"—her lonely death and repressed burial.

But then, Joseph, with whose being Jacob is bound up, is savaged by a wild beast. And within Jacob, a space is forced open where the wild beast is allowed imaginative range. We remember his pride that no sheep of Laban's had ever fallen prey to a wild beast: "No savaged animal did I ever bring you. I myself—*anokhi*—made good the loss [*achatena*—lit., I corrected the error, the sin]" (Gen. 31:39).

Zealously guarding his integrity, his coherence, he has perhaps, as the midrash startlingly remarks, *sinned* against the law of the wild:

the lion has been *robbed* of its savage rights.[78] Something unfathomable in his own narrative can now no longer be discounted. This rupture cannot be absorbed into the household; it defies his mastery. The leopard can become a part of the ceremony only if, in some sense, it retains its uncanniness.

As he himself prepares to die, Jacob will eventually allow Rachel to return to him: "And as for me, when I was returning from Paddan, Rachel died *alai*—upon me, for me, to my cost" (Gen. 48:7). Jacob's language expresses a sense that he is *possessed* by Rachel and his loss of her. She baffles him and his deepest desires. Just as he is returning home, "on the road . . . there, on the road . . . ," she dies an *outside* death, in no place, unhoused in the family grave.

Rashi conveys the outrage of this, as well as its rationale:

> *And as for me, when I was returning from Paddan:* Although I trouble you to carry me to be buried in the land of Canaan, and I did not do so for your mother, for she died near Bethlehem . . .
>
> *And I buried her there:* and I did not carry her even to Bethlehem to bring her into the Land of Israel. And I know that you have a complaint in your heart against me. However, know that by the word of God did I bury her there, so that she might be of aid to her children when Nebusaradan exiles them and they pass by there. There Rachel will emerge upon her grave, crying and pleading for mercy for them, as it is said, "A voice is heard in Ramah, wailing, bitter weeping, Rachel weeping for her children. She refuses to be comforted for her children, who are not. Thus said God, Restrain your voice from weeping, your eyes from shedding tears. For there is a reward for your labor, declares God; they shall return from the enemy's land. And there is hope for your future, declares God; your children shall return to their country [lit., boundary]" (Jer. 31:15–17).

Beyond boundaries and identities, Rachel's burial place will become a transit point for her exiled children as they disperse to their unimaginable destinations. In this transitional space, she will weep for them and, in Jeremiah's words, she will receive reward for her tears. Her tears are privileged because they know about bitterness and separation. And ultimately, Jacob allows that otherness a place inside his narrative, *al pi Ha-Shem, by the word of God.* No longer, in Kristeva's expression, *abjecting* all that challenges his mastery, he acknowledges that which haunts him.

Essentially, he acknowledges not only his wife but—another unknown woman—his mother. The history of Rebecca's *anokhi,* the vanishing point of knowledge, had turned out to be endless. *"She* was what he had missed"—her subjectivity, like his, had been premised on intense bonds that could barely be recognized: with her father, with Isaac, with Esau, with Jacob. Excessive, threatening her identity, these bonds had also created and sustained her.

The abyss of separation from "what was mine and is henceforth but irreparably alien," the flash that bedazzled her—that is one dimension of her history. But, always, she will remain the Rebecca who confronted that blinding knowledge and "went to seek God." Seeking what no one had sought before her, she finds the God who affirms her disunity of being. She recognizes Him because He brings her internal otherness to life, giving it words, a future. He positions her, eternally pregnant, to intimate a rich ambiguity: *I-yet-not-I.*

EIGHT

Blindness and Blessing

Isaac Trembles Twice

TEARING OPEN AND TURNING OVER TIME

Isaac is the inscrutable patriarch. He neither journeys in quest toward the Holy Land nor in exile from it; his life is spent within its borders, cultivating its soil. Unlike his father and his son, he lives out his life with one wife; and although, like them, he experiences difficulty in procreation, his narrative of infertility is, unlike theirs, encompassed in the brief space of one verse. The two major episodes of his life represent him in a passive role: in the *Akedah,* he is the bound one, silent and immobilized, while Abraham lives the test and the drama; and when he bestows the family blessing on his son Jacob, he does so unwittingly, deceived by his own blindness and Jacob's manipulations.

This general sketch of Isaac suggests a figure set in low relief, lacking the energy proper to a hero. Yet the word *love* appears for the first time in the biblical text to describe his relation to his wife. And he alone of the patriarchs is described in intimate "play" with Rebecca. If erotic energy unexpectedly characterizes him, so, too, does material success: he sows seed and the earth yields him "a hundred-fold" on his investment. We remember Freud's criterion for a well-realized life—success in love and work. By this measure, he lives a vigorous life. And yet, his figure remains mysterious, deeply ambiguous.

His first autonomous act is his prayer for children. Rebecca is barren. "And Isaac pleaded with God on behalf of his wife, for she was barren. And God responded to his plea and his wife Rebecca conceived" (Gen. 25:21). The word used here for prayer is unusual: *va-ye'etar.* Rashi translates this as intense, persistent prayer. It is striking, however, that, unlike Abraham, Isaac is never heard to pray for children. Abraham pleads with God on several occasions, even after

Ishmael is born: he wants a child from Sarah. We hear the words of his desire, his debate with God. In other words, he prays. Yet these speeches are not formally described as "prayer."[1]

Isaac's voice in prayer is silent in the text. Yet he is described as *pleading*, and, unlike Abraham, he is immediately answered: *Va-yei'ater lo*—a striking expression in which God responds to his plea by accepting the passive position—"He was entreated": that is, He accepted Isaac's prayer. The power of Isaac's wordless prayer is unique and instantaneous.

The Talmud offers a remarkable image for the peculiar power of prayer:

> R. Isaac stated: Why is the prayer of the righteous compared to a pitchfork *[attar]*? As a pitchfork turns the sheaves of grain from one position to another, so does the prayer of the righteous turn the dispensations of God from the attribute of anger to the attribute of mercy.[2]

The transformative energy of prayer can move God from anger to mercy. The pitchfork tosses the grain sheaves, changing their position and place. The act of *turning, inverting*, is *revolutionary*; it reveals what was hidden. The word *attar*, a pitchfork, is also the term for a plough, which turns over the sods of earth to create a newly fertile surface. The motion of pitchfork or plough tears open, enters darkness to bring to light something that had been buried. The prayer of the righteous, the midrash claims, has this transfigurative effect; but it is specifically Isaac's prayer that works through the resonances of the pun—*va-ye'etar*—plead/pitchfork—to suggest a descent into darkness, an upheaval that inverts the previous order.

Similarly, the notion of *turning* is central to a classic midrash on the study of Torah: "Turn it over and over, for all is in it."[3] Precisely because it contains all, the Torah requires this kind of transfigurative study: the plough exposes new surfaces of earth to the light and the student reveals unexpected, or long-buried facets of meaning.

The turning plough offers Osip Mandelstam a metaphor for the way poetry can penetrate the past:

Poetry is the plough tearing open and turning over time so that the deep layers of it, its rich black undersoil, ends up on the surface. . . . Mankind . . . craves, like a ploughman, for the virgin soil of time.[4]

Here, the past is an object of desire; its resources yield to poetry's work of "tearing open and turning over time." The plough tears fragments from the depths and sets them in new alignments with one another. It disturbs a basic position of "immobilized totality."[5] Both in the study of Torah and in prayer, the plough image suggests new ways of connecting the present with the past.

As a description of Isaac's mode of prayer, however, the image holds peculiar force. Beit Ya'akov makes a radical suggestion: Isaac's wordless prayer expresses an intense surrender, a prayerful pressure, that accumulates as he refrains from particular, articulated requests. His prayers form deep grooves within his heart, accessing unconscious seams of experience. The passion of that life beyond conscious expression is what he brings to God: an inner darkness of surrender.

Isaac is here imagined as sustaining his essential life in the depths, in the dark. Indeed, his meeting with his future wife, Rebecca, happens at a moment *lifnot erev*—"at the turn of the evening"—when he has emerged *lasu'ach basadeh,* to meditate in the field, or, according to the midrashic reading, to pray the afternoon prayer.[6] Darkness has just cast its first shadows as Isaac initiates a new genre of prayer: *tefillat minchah,* the afternoon prayer, at the turn of the evening. Here, already, is the model of an unarticulated prayer, provoking the reader's imagination: Isaac's darkness is turned, quickly, to love.

When Isaac prays his underground prayer, God comes to meet him. Like tunnels meeting, God responds to his prayer:

Vayei'ater lo—"And God responded to his plea . . ." As in the parable of the prince who dug *[hattar]* a tunnel into his father's palace to gain a gold treasure: the one excavated from within while the other excavated from outside.[7]

Attar (pleading, ploughing) resonates with *hattar* (underground burrowing that opens a passage for prayer): God subversively aids Isaac in his efforts to break into the palace. In Rashi's version, God allows himself to be urged, persuaded, seduced *(nitpateh)* by Isaac's prayer: He desires Isaac's wordless desire.

In his work in the world, too, Isaac plays at the seam between the hidden and the manifest. His two main activities are digging wells and sowing seed. His servants dig in the wadi; "And they found there a well of living water" (Gen. 26:19). The wonder of life emerging from the depths is reflected in a Rabbinic teaching: "If one dreams of a well, one should rise early and say, 'A well of living water.' "[8] The dream of a well holds sinister as well as vital possibilities: interpreting the dream, therefore, giving words to what was wordless, becomes an urgent task. "All dreams follow the mouth":[9] meaning is created in the telling.

As sower of seed, too, Isaac is successful beyond measure: in a time of famine, "Isaac sowed in that land and reaped [lit., found] a hundredfold that year; and God blessed him" (Gen. 26:12). Again, blessing comes in the form of subterranean activity: he deposits seed into the soil only to find a hundredfold. His world of food and water issues from the resources of darkness: from the depths, life repeatedly surprises him.[10]

THE *AKEDAH*—AN IMPENDING DARKNESS

The imagery of pitchfork, plough, subversive tunneling in the dark, digging wells, and sowing seed creates a characteristic intimate tonality. Ultimately, a literal darkness falls on his eyes: "And when Isaac grew old, his eyes were too dim to see" (Gen. 27:1). Although old age fully accounts for his blindness, the midrash offers a poignant history of a different sort: *mei're'ot* ("Too dim to see") is read, quite literally, "from seeing . . .":

His eyes became dim *from the impact of that seeing.* When Abraham bound his son on the altar, the angels wept; as it is written, "Hark! The Arielites cry aloud" (Isa. 33:7). And the tears dropped from their eyes into his eyes and were imprinted within his eyes till he became old and his eyes became dim.[11]

Isaac becomes blind as a result of the angels' tears that fell into his eyes at the moment of the *Akedah*. This classic midrash connects the two major events of his life, the *Akedah* and the stolen blessing. Between these two moments, underground, as it were, unconsciously, the wound made by the angels' tears has been developing, till in old age it seals him in darkness. On the altar, he did not weep for himself: he lay with open eyes staring upward. The angels weep in protest and pity at the impending sacrifice. Isaac becomes an object of outraged compassion.

With that sense of himself as seen by angels at the moment of death, he lives his life. It becomes his "unthought known":[12] imprinted deep, unfathomed, until, in old age, he decides to bless his son Esau. An always impending darkness falls. What is it in this later narrative that precipitates the full impact of the earlier narrative?

Another midrash focuses on the moment of death on the altar:

When the knife touched his neck, his soul departed [lit., took wing]. And when God made His voice heard from among the angels, saying, "Do not lay your hand on the boy," his soul returned to his body. And Isaac rose to his feet and Isaac knew that in this way the dead would return to life. And he opened his mouth and declared, "Blessed are you, God who revives the dead."[13]

"His soul took wing and left him." Is this the jolt of terror that anticipates death? Or is it, simply, a notation for dying? Although a certain ambiguity hangs over the midrashic expression, here it clearly refers to death. For an instant, Isaac departs; and returns. His blessing as he stands solidly on his feet again marks his passage from death to life: he *knows* that the dead will be revived—not through prophetic knowledge, but through physical experience. To thank God for his resurrection, he coins the blessing that is said three times daily in the *Amidah* prayer.

The midrash takes him one breath further than the biblical narrative: he returns to life not at the last moment before death, but after dying. A margin is crossed and recrossed. With the effect of *knowledge,* his world of vision disappears and reappears. Fear, *yir'ah,* becomes his modality, a distinct sensibility and idiom. What is it that he now knows about resurrection? How does he live with his knowledge that God revives the dead?

The *Akedah* is, literally, the *Binding of Isaac.* In several midrashic sources, it is Isaac's own request that he be bound—in a posture of total helplessness, trussed like an animal for the slaughter, arms and legs behind. He explains his wish: he is afraid of the involuntary movements of his body under the terror of death. Physical convulsion of his limbs may invalidate the sacrifice; perhaps he will kick out at his father, disgracing his last moment; he may even curse his father.[14] To prevent such involuntary acts of violence, he asks to be bound hand and foot.

To prevent verbal violence—cursing his father—he would of course have to be gagged; but the binding becomes a graphic expression of a single idea. Isaac knows about the limits of conscious resolution. In the moment of extremity, his body may act involuntarily, "for the life instinct is irrepressible" *(ha-nefesh hatzufah).*[15] Only if his body is bound will he be able to prevent such unwilled movements. Precisely because he respects those dimensions of life that are not controllable by will, he demands to be bound.

Poignantly, the image of Isaac, bound hand and foot, draws attention to his eyes—the only "free" part of his body. Whether it is the angels' tears, or the experience of the world gone dark and restored to light, his eyes alone register a knowledge that will shape his sensibility forever.

THE ENIGMA OF SURVIVAL

After the *Akedah,* when Abraham returns to his waiting servants, he returns, strangely, alone (Gen. 22:19). Where is Isaac? He disappears from the narrative, returning only to encounter his bride, Rebecca: "Isaac had just come back from the vicinity of Beer-lahai-roi, for he was settled in the region of the Negev" (Gen. 24:62). This well is the only clue that the narrative offers as to Isaac's whereabouts since the *Akedah*. This, we remember, was the place where Hagar, in flight from Sarah, encountered the angel who announced the birth and destiny of her future child, Ishmael (16:13). She had named it "the well of *my living God who sees me*," recording her experience of the God who "sees unseen"[16]—the God who has answered her prayer and restored her son to life remains unfathomable.

Why has Isaac just come from this well? Ramban suggests that it had become his habitual place of prayer.[17] This well, perhaps, becomes a displacement for his own encounter with angels on Mount Moriah. There, he experienced a vision that later blinded him; there, he lay with open eyes searing the heavens, and seared by them. Incomprehensibly, he has survived; he has died and been revived from death. He, too, has been seen by the God whom he cannot fathom.

What does it mean to survive death? Or to be revived from death? In recent years, the phenomenon of trauma, and particularly of posttraumatic stress disorder, has received much attention. In the fields of psychiatry, psychoanalysis, and neurobiology, many studies have examined the impact of the violent event on the mind. Cathy Caruth eloquently argues that trauma is not simply the effect of external violence but of an essential *incomprehensibility*: it constitutes

> an enigma of survival. It is only in recognizing traumatic experience as a paradoxical relation between destructiveness and survival that we can also recognize the legacy of incomprehensibility at the heart of catastrophic experience.[18]

Freud first addressed the issue of trauma in relation to the war neuroses suffered by soldiers in the First World War. In Caruth's reading of his *Beyond the Pleasure Principle,* the sufferer is understood to be repeating—in dream and flashback—the traumatic event in order to engage with the incomprehensible moment of survival. Often, no physical harm has been suffered, so that the wound—the meaning of the Greek *trauma*—is not directly perceptible. The shock is "a break in the mind's experience of time." The mind has in fact *missed* the experience of the threat of death: it has not yet been fully known. The return of the traumatic crisis in dream is "an attempt to master what was not fully grasped in the first place."[19]

Survival, then, means the "endless *inherent necessity* of repetition" of the trauma. Caruth cites the high suicide rate of survivors of Vietnam or of the Nazi concentration camps. She suggests that the trauma "consists not only in having confronted death, but in *having survived precisely, without knowing it.*" It is the incomprehensibility of one's own survival that impels one to return to the scene, to attempt to claim one's own survival.[20]

Caruth reads Freud's *Moses and Monotheism* as connecting the individual experience of trauma with the national history of the Jewish people. Both are centrally concerned with something ungrasped and endlessly returning in experience. The victim of an accident, who gets away unharmed, suffers not only from "the unexperienced event of the crash, but the non-experiencing of the fact that the person has indeed remained 'unharmed.' " As bearers of an experience that they cannot fully claim as their own, the Jewish people become an exemplar of the historical sense of having been incomprehensibly chosen to survive. What returns, then, in both the individual psyche and the structure of Jewish historical experience, is the sense of *"being chosen for* a future that remains, in its promise, yet to be understood. Chosenness is thus not simply a fact of the past but the experience of being shot into a future that is not entirely one's own."[21]

What does it mean for Isaac to survive? Perhaps we can say that it means to know the limits of his mind's experience, to live with the enigma of a past and a future that are not entirely his own. He remains with a deepened awareness of the seam line between conscious and unconscious experience. Apparently unscathed, he descends from the altar. But his eyes are intimately scarred; an essential blindness has begun to gather.

VITAL BLINDNESS

His blindness, then, develops in response to his experience of the unfathomable in his own life. His own death and life both exceed his grasp, so that the usual platitudes of knowledge become inaccessible. Claude Lanzmann, writing about his approach to the making of *Shoah,* repudiates the very project of understanding. "There is an absolute obscenity in the very project of understanding. Not to understand was my iron law during all the eleven years of the production of *Shoah.*"[22] This refusal "opens up the space for a testimony that can speak beyond what is already understood." The refusal of understanding, indeed, may become a fundamentally creative act: *"this blindness was for me,"* Lanzmann writes, *"the vital condition of creation.* Blindness has to be understood here as the purest mode of looking, of the gaze, the only way to not turn from a reality which is *literally blinding"*[23] (my emphasis).

If blindness can be the vital condition of creation, perhaps we can think of Isaac's delayed blindness—his response to the trauma of the *Akedah*—as the vital condition of his blessing of Jacob. Blessing, in some sense, requires blindness. The terror of the *Akedah,* of the death and resurrection that the midrash narrates, bears strange fruit. We remember that, according to *Pirkei de-Rabbi Eliezer,* his first act on leaving the altar is to *bless,* to coin the blessing "Blessed are You, God who revives the dead."

After many years, trauma and blessing again appear together, as if for the first time, when Isaac confronts the incomprehensible nature of his act of blessing Esau, the *other* son. After being deprived of his blessing, Esau tearfully identifies himself to Isaac, who "was seized with very violent trembling" (Gen. 27:33). He is shaken, *traumatized* to the roots of his being, incapable of framing a plausible speculation about the identity of the son he has blessed. The midrash comments on the intensity of his *charadah,* his trembling, that it is worse than that other *charadah* that he experienced while bound on the altar.[24] The second episode allows Isaac, for the first time, to claim his own experience of the *Akedah.* The time lag between the two events allows the *Akedah* now to enter consciousness.

If trauma as trembling represents the impact of an incomprehensible death and resurrection, the midrash anticipates Freud in describing the historical trauma of the Jewish people:

R. Levi said: Israel asked of God two things—that they should see His glory and hear His voice; and they did see His glory and hear His voice, for it says, "And you said: Behold, God has shown us His glory and His greatness, and we have heard His voice out of the midst of the fire" (Deut. 5:21). But they had no strength to endure it, for when they came to Sinai and God revealed Himself to them, their souls took wing because He spoke with them, as it says, "My soul left me when he spoke" (Songs 5:6). It was the Torah that pleaded for mercy for them before God: "Is there a king who gives his daughter away in marriage and slays his own family? The whole world is now rejoicing, yet Your own children are dead." So their souls immediately returned, for it says, "The law of God is perfect, restoring the soul" (Ps. 19:8).[25]

At the moment when God spoke at Sinai, a whole nation lost consciousness and regained it. In anticipation of this moment, "the whole people trembled" (Exod. 19:16); "the whole mountain trembled violently" (19:18). In Caruth's terms, the Jewish people passed through death without knowing it. This traumatic experience generates a desire to master the moment of resurrection. Failing to return to that moment, the Jewish people are impelled to seek other ways to appropriate their own survival.

One such way is, of course, precisely the midrashic enterprise. By telling the story of departure and return at Sinai, the author of the midrash seeks to master the incomprehensible. "Their souls took wing because He spoke with them": the shock of God's voice inflicts a trauma of departure. How is one to grasp this moment, or the equally mysterious return of the soul when the Torah asks God for mercy? By quoting from the Song of Songs, the midrash evokes the traumatic impact of the lover whose voice penetrates and destabilizes one's being. The people have no strength to stand. Like Isaac, who stands on his feet when his soul returns, like the beloved in the Song of Songs, the people experience a loss of stability, and a restoration. In all three cases, there is the terror of intimate invasion, by death, or by love, which also deals a kind of death.

In the midrashic narrative, the Torah appeals to God's compassion and stability is restored. The Torah is God's daughter, on whose wedding day the king's family mysteriously die. Specifically, his *children* are dying. The imagery is both conventional and obscure: the wedding becomes the focus of both joy and mourning—the bride's joy at her marriage, her mourning at the deaths of the Israelites, her brothers. The groom is absent from the scene; but, in many midrashic sources, the Israelites are the groom who marries the Torah. An impossible, self-contradictory narrative is resolved when the Torah asks for compassion—compassion precisely for this ungraspable complexity of relationships and roles, of joy and sadness. The proof text from Psalms gives the Torah all credit for resurrection: the Torah "restores the soul."

Here is the moment of national trauma at Sinai, the ravishing and fatal impact of God's voice upon human beings; here, too, is the healing power of Torah, which speaks for life and order, for a bearable passion. The Torah and its commandments, one might say, allow God's voice to be absorbed into the particulars of a human life, for the sake of life.

This is the narrative that the midrash rehearses and attempts to master. But this moment of national trauma is repeated and interrogated throughout Jewish history. "What does it mean to survive?" becomes, "What does it mean to be chosen?"[26]

Departure and return lie at the heart of Freud's famous example of the child's *fort-da* game. He observed his grandson reenacting the departure and return of his mother by repeatedly throwing a wooden spool on a string into his cot, uttering the sound "oo-oo," and retrieving it, uttering "a-a-a." Freud interprets these sounds as meaning *"fort"* ("gone") and *"da"* ("here"). As Caruth points out, the game seems mostly concerned with repeating the "gone" phase, while the entire episode, with its pleasurable ending, is far less frequently enacted. The game becomes, simply, a game of departure.[27]

In the midrash, too, the heart of the matter is clearly the fatal rapture of the people. The return to life and order is less resonant than the sudden impinging violence that eludes the comprehension of the survivors. It is this mystery that repeatedly demands rehearsal, some attempt at mastery. The narrative passion of the midrash is drawn precisely from the *departure*—from the collapse of understanding that accompanies survival.

Isaac, then, becomes the paradigm in midrashic thinking for the experience of enigmatic survival. He *knows* about the life that disappears and reappears; and about the God who sees and cannot be seen. He has trembled, twice. But only the second time, after he realizes that it is Jacob he has blessed, is this trembling registered in the Torah, in his consciousness. The first time, after the *Akedah,* he coins a blessing to be repeated endlessly by the Jewish people. The second time, the whole future hangs on his response to the traumatic moment: How will he record his now-double knowledge, in blessing or curse?

Jacques Derrida writes of this moment:

> I tremble at what exceeds my seeing and my knowing although it concerns the innermost parts of me, right down to my soul, down to the bone. . . . Another secret, another enigma, or another mystery comes on top of the unlivable experience. . . . One doesn't know *why one trembles.* This limit to knowledge no longer only relates to the cause or unknown event, the unseen or unknown that makes us tremble. . . . What does *the body mean to say* by trembling . . . ? . . . What is it that makes us tremble in the *mysterium tremendum?* It is the . . . dissymmetry that exists between the divine regard that sees me, and myself, who doesn't see what is looking at me.[28]

Isaac experiences the traumatic moments of his life as an irrepressible agitation that records mystery, dissymmetry in his relation to God who "sees, unseen." Between those moments, what does he see? How do the tears of the angels imprint within his eyes, before they appear as blindness?

DENSITY OF ASSEMBLED MOMENTS

In a poignant essay on departure and return, death and resurrection, John Berger tells a story about the Polish artist Kokoschka, who was teaching a life class and instructed the model to pretend to collapse. Kokoschka then announced to his shocked students that the model was dead. A little later, the model got to his feet and resumed his pose. "Now draw him," said Kokoschka, "as though you were aware that he was alive and not dead!"

A cruel game to shock the half-living to life. In the same essay, John Berger tells an intimate story about his last moments with his father. Beside his father's coffin, he did several drawings of his face and head. In the urgency of death, impelled by the intensity of seeing for the last time, he attempted to save a likeness. "I was making a record and his face was already only a record of his life. Each drawing then was nothing but the site of a departure." Over time, however, this finality changed. "The drawing, instead of marking the site of a departure, began to mark the site of an arrival. . . . The drawing was no longer deserted but inhabited."[29] Memories were drawn to that face. "My father came back to give the image of his death mask a kind of life."

Berger reflects on the meaning of the static image: it records "an appearance which will disappear." "The visual is always the result of an unrepeatable momentary encounter." The image is constructed from the "debris of all that has previously appeared . . . the drawing challenges disappearance."[30]

The drawing that challenges disappearance is always a construction with a history. "To draw is to look. . . . A drawing of a tree shows, not a tree, but a tree-being-looked-at." Examining this drawing takes hours; "it also involves, derives from, and refers back to, much previous experience of looking. Within the instant of the sight of a tree is established a life-experience. . . . What is unchanging in a drawing consists of so many assembled moments that they constitute a totality rather than a fragment." This has to do with the "density per square millimeter of assembled moments," caught by the vision of the artist. "Every day," he concludes "more of my father's life returns to the drawing in front of me."[31]

In this account, the sense of sight constitutes an *active* response to the continually changing world. The intensity of seeing for the last time draws to itself a lifetime of moments. I suggest that from the moment of the *Akedah,* a density of seeing gathers into Isaac's eyes. The vision of the weeping angels has imprinted him with a searing sense of himself and of his world, so that his eyes sear whatever they see. Deepest in his life is the knowledge of departure and return, of a mystery that cannot be encompassed by consciousness. This becomes an inchoate prayer, an internal murmur. In the space

between the *Akedah* and his full blindness—the space of a lifetime—
he marries, loves, laughs,[32] digs wells, plants seed, while his eyes
gather the density of moments with which he will confront the final
issue: the blessing of his son.

Blindness, then, comes to represent the cumulative knowledge of
a survival, a revival, that Isaac cannot fully claim as his own. "This
blindness was for me a vital condition of creation" (Lanzmann). It
constitutes knowledge of a vital gap in consciousness, and it imbues
him with resistance to the platitudes of knowledge.

CHOOSING ESAU

In this condition, Isaac will bless his son with the blessing of family
destiny. Alone of the three patriarchs, he must choose: Esau or Jacob.
Abraham had not needed to choose, since God had clearly indicated
that Isaac was the chosen son ("For it is through Isaac that offspring
shall be named for you" [Gen. 21:12]). And Jacob will, in the end,
include all his children in his blessings: "His bed," says the midrash,
"was whole, without debris."[33] Isaac, though, must choose, since
Esau and Jacob, children of his only wife, Rebecca, are similar and
different in ways that make choice necessary. As Abarbanel puts it,
there is a situation of ambiguity that must be resolved.

Isaac chooses Esau. His choice is explained: as the twins begin
their different lives, the narrative declares, "Isaac loved Esau . . ."
(Gen. 27:28). His love has an absolute ring; nevertheless it is immediately accounted for: *ki tzayid b'fiv*—"for he brought game to his
mouth." As an explanation for love, this explains nothing. Are we to
understand that Isaac's love is contingent on the food that Esau
brings him? Or on some seduction (*tzayid*—the hunt) that Esau
knows how achieve with his words ("by his mouth"[34])? Isaac, as we
noted previously, is the first *lover* in the Torah: he loves his wife, he
loves his son Esau—and he loves food ("Make me delicacies such as I
love" [27:4]). Love has a force that defies explanation, as absolute and
idiosyncratic as food preferences. For this dimension of affinity that
is not subject to will, Isaac has a special respect. A kernel of reality is
manifested in loves and hates, a sensual base beyond rational
appraisal.[35]

When the Zohar wishes to account for this love Isaac bears for
Esau, it states simply: "Love comes *from affinity*." This aphorism
seems strangely applied to Isaac and Esau, perhaps indicating how
unpredictable such affinities can be. In which way does Isaac identify with his hunter son?

It is remarkable that, in different ways, both Isaac and Esau are
preoccupied with death. Isaac twice declares that his death is imminent: this becomes the urgent occasion for his blessing (Gen. 27:2,4).
So powerful is this note of mortality that Rebecca, reporting to
Jacob, adds her own editorial warning about the "blessing before
death" to her report of Isaac's speech (27:7,10). The historical fact is
that Isaac has sixty years to live. But death looms large in his mind,
giving urgency to his blessing.

Esau, too, lives in close proximity to death. Avid for the stew that
Jacob is cooking, he cries, "I am at the point of death, so of what use
is the birthright to me!" (Gen. 25:32). This can be read simply as, "I am
dying of hunger!" In the midrash, however, it is heard as an existential cry that robs the birthright of meaning. In one haunting
midrash, Esau meditates on the starkness of human fate:

> "Jacob was cooking a stew" (Gen. 25:29): Esau asked him, "What
> is this stew for?" He answered, "I made it because that old man
> [Abraham] has died." "Judgment has overtaken that righteous
> man!" Esau exclaimed. "Then there is neither reward nor resur-
> rection!" But the Holy Spirit cries out, "Weep not for the dead,
> nor bemoan him" (Jer. 22:10) "Weep not for the dead," applies to
> Abraham; "but weep sore for him who goes," applies to Esau.[36]

The death of his beloved grandfather overwhelms Esau with a
sense of the remorseless nature of *middat ha-din*—the judgment that
strikes down all living things. Esau, the hunter who lives among the
spasms and blood of animal death, is driven to see human life as animal life. With a bleak realism, he discards the figments of religious
hope: ultimate reward for the righteous, and the resurrection of
the dead. His world cannot be morally explained or existentially
redeemed. The midrash ends by poignantly rereading Jeremiah to
declare that Esau, who is "going to die," going toward death without

further margin of hope, is more pitiable than Abraham, whose death is no cause for tears. In Esau's words, "I am going to die," the midrash detects the anguish of the human animal knowingly living toward death.

But it is specifically Esau's repudiation of "the resurrection of the dead" that, I suggest, defines the affinity that Isaac feels for him. Isaac knows that darkness: he has lain trussed like an animal with the knife raised over his throat. He recognizes Esau's idiom of the hunter immersed in the dark welter of blood. But Isaac has disappeared and reappeared; there is a rhythm of departure and return that he wishes to convey particularly to this son.[37]

BLESSING OF THE *NEFESH*

The central narrative question, however, concerns the very meaning of blessing. What happens in the scene between Isaac and Jacob? Is Isaac duped by Jacob's masquerade? If so, how are we to understand his state of consciousness at the moment of blessing? What would a blessing given in error bestow on its recipient?

Isaac himself strikingly describes the dynamics of blessing: he asks Esau to bring him food, "so that my *nefesh* may bless you before I die" (Gen. 27:7). In fact, all the protagonists in this drama speak of the blessing of the *nefesh*,[38] except Rebecca, who instead speaks of the blessing "in the presence of God." The singular music of Isaac's idiom is transformed in Rebecca's version; reporting to Jacob, she quotes Isaac: "so that I may bless you *in the presence of God,* before I die" (27:7).

What is the nature of the blessing that flows from the *nefesh*? We notice that each time the expression is used, it is in the context of Isaac's favorite food, which is essential, apparently, to inspire him to this blessing.

In biblical usage, *nefesh* usually refers simply to life; in Genesis, often to animal life, physical survival, or, for purposes of counting, to the individual organism.[39] The root meaning seems to refer to the breathing apparatus or the digestive system. It is therefore somewhat ironic that it is often translated *soul*. However, in Psalms and the Prophets, the term does modulate in meaning toward the mental experience of the individual, becoming an expression of the whole being of a person, breath, appetite, desire of all kinds.[40]

Isaac, then, repeatedly declares that he wants his blessing to flow from his whole being, to be an expression of a desire that encompasses body and soul. Rebecca understands this to mean that such a blessing will be inspired by the divine will (on Ramban's reading);[41] or that its effectiveness will depend on God's assent (on Rashi's reading).[42]

Rashi's reading compels our attention. On the face of it, it seems to set theologically correct limits to the "magical" pretensions of Isaac's blessing: it will take effect only if God consents. But if Rebecca is relating to Isaac's own expression—"that my *nefesh*, my appetitive self, may bless you"—she is saying that his most authentic blessing arises from his instinctual self and represents a loss of conscious autonomy: his blessing arises from a knowledge that he is now in the *reshut*, in the hands of God.

Rashi translates Rebecca *(in the presence of God)*, who translates Isaac *(that my* nefesh *may bless you)*. In my reading of this chain of meaning, the central issue is the nature of blessing. For, in an obvious sense, this is a problematic idea. Is it simply a prayer, a wish? Why, then, are Rebecca and Jacob so anxious to appropriate it? If, on the other hand, the words of blessing have a real effectiveness, a theurgic or "magical" power, then their desire to "take" this power to themselves becomes intelligible. Both theologically and dramatically, however, this notion is fraught with difficulties. Once Isaac realizes—as eventually he must—that he has been duped, he will inevitably withdraw the blessing, or even convert it into a curse—as Jacob himself fears (Gen. 27:12). What do the conspirators then stand to gain from their plot?

A second question follows from Ramban's reading of "in the presence of God." What is the experience of divine inspiration that, according to Ramban, will give power to Isaac's blessing? Will it spontaneously characterize his words? Or will it require God's assent, His corroboration?

. . .

BLINDNESS AND BLESSING

These questions connect with the central narrative question: What happens in the scene between Isaac and Jacob? Is Isaac really duped? Or does he recognize Jacob and bless him with full intent? Abarbanel, the medieval Spanish commentator of the Torah, offers a subtle reading. "There is no doubt in my mind," he writes, "that Isaac was confused about whether it was Esau or Jacob." This reigning doubt in Isaac's mind informs the whole scene. Isaac is not duped; he knows that he does not know. At first, in a state of agitated confusion, he attempts to determine who it is that stands before him. In the end, he blesses Jacob without any clear resolution as to his identity.

Repeatedly, Isaac verbally and physically interrogates his son's identity: "Who are you, my son?" (Gen. 27:18); "How is it that you succeeded so quickly, my son?" (27:20); "Come close so I can touch you, my son—Is this really you, my son Esau, or not?" (27:21); "Is this you, my son, Esau?" (27:24); "Come close and kiss me, my son." (27:26). Isaac's ambivalence is sustained throughout the scene. He uses all his senses, including taste (eating his son's food) and smell (the kiss), as means of identification; but at each stage his doubt remains.

Strikingly, Abarbanel reads the famous line: "The voice is the voice of Jacob, but the hands are the hands of Esau" (Gen. 27:22) as expressing radical confusion: he experiences a hybrid creature, with the hands of one son and the voice of the other. "And he could not identify him" as Jacob—in spite of the evidence of his voice—because of the evidence of his hands. As he repeatedly seeks to identify his son, one sense cancels out the other, so that definitive knowledge eludes him. In the end, he gives his blessing to the unknown being in front of him: his *fragrance* indicates that God has blessed him ("See! The fragrance of my son is like the fragrance of the field—which shows that God has blessed him!" [27:27]). *"He blessed him in doubt,"* concludes Abarbanel, *"simply with the conviction that this was God's will."*

In this reading, Abarbanel achieves one important aim. If Isaac is *mistaken* in the identity of the son he blesses, the blessing is misdirected and can be repudiated. But if Isaac, while not identifying

Jacob, is in a state of ambivalence (doubt, confusion) throughout the scene, this opens up the possibility of a valid blessing, given in full awareness of *not knowing*. He simply *smells* the hybrid being in front of him and, regardless of his identity, he blesses him: a visceral *nefesh* response to an unknown presence. In such a narrative, God inspires him precisely through his body experience. Such a blessing cannot be repudiated; an authentic transaction has taken place.

On this basis, we may notice that, in the end, after using all his senses to decode the mystery—he listens, touches, tastes, smells—he cries out, "*See!* The smell of my son . . ." At this moment, the visual world symbolically returns in a density of assembled moments. Seeing fragrance, he is carried beyond the limitations of the senses. The foul-smelling goatskins become paradisal; an intimation, sensual-spiritual, of blessing surges into words. Meshekh Hokhmah incorporates the Zohar to affirm that "God spoke out of Isaac's mouth: 'See! The fragrance of my son.' " Isaac is divinely inspired to see without anxiety or rational inhibition.

In a strange way, this moment fuses with the *Akedah* moment, recovering the gap, the experience of departure and return. For this moment, too, is one where consciousness fails him, where the ambiguity of Jacob/Esau moves him to surrender to unconscious sources of knowledge. The scene is played out, of course, in subjective darkness. Eight times, he addresses his son as *b'ni*, "my son," intimating a presence unidentified. The text gives the reader the effect of Jacob's identity gradually shading off into namelessness: at first, Jacob is clearly named (Gen. 27:19, 21, 22), but he then becomes a pronoun (27:23–27); the name *Jacob* vanishes from the text. Clarity returns only after Isaac has finished his blessing, when the narrative focuses on the plot irony of Jacob and Esau almost meeting in the doorway. "And it was when Isaac had finished blessing Jacob, that Jacob had just left his father's presence when his brother Esau came back from his hunt" (27:30). The punctilious naming of the characters at this point marks the reader's return to ordinary consciousness, with the clash of identities and desires that is about to become manifest.

For the space of the blessing scene, however, a different reality prevails. When Jacob addresses his father—*Avi!* ("Father!")—and is answered—*Hineni!* ("Here I am!")—Isaac is precipitated back to the

Akedah, to the fraught dialogue that he had initiated with his father as they approached the mountain. The unfathomed possibilities of what can happen between a father and a son are again intimated. Here, however, Isaac struggles to break the spell, to master his situation and know it. The more he struggles, however, the more surely he knows that he does not know what he most needs to know. In the end, he surrenders to another kind of knowledge that prevails precisely in ambiguity.

Isaac had always intended his blessing to be *birkhat ha-nefesh,* finding its inspiration in the physical knowledge that baffles consciousness. Three times, he uses the word *zeh,* "this." Twice he asks, "Is this—*zeh*—you, my son?" and again, "How is it—*zeh*—that you succeeded so quickly, my son?" In all three cases, the word *zeh* plays an enigmatic role in his questions, alluding to an uncanny, unknowable, yet deeply known presence, which is neither Jacob nor Esau. In the end, he blesses *"this* one who is in front of him."[43]

Blindness becomes a condition of blessing. We remember Lanzmann's "This blindness was for me a vital condition of creation." In Isaac's confrontation with Jacob-Esau, platitudes of knowledge break down as he discovers a language for what cannot yet be understood.

A VITAL CONDITION OF CREATION

Essential to this experience is the ambiguity of the Jacob-Esau hybrid that eludes naming. Addressing famous examples of visual ambiguity, like the duck-rabbit figure, or Escher engravings such as *Night and Day,* Ernest Gombrich points out that the two interpretations—duck or rabbit? black or white birds?—are mutually exclusive. One can see one *or* the other, not both at once, since clues oscillate, serving one or the other reading in an equally plausible way. This creates a stalemate situation, a visual deadlock, in which figure and ground keep reversing. The figure thus remains irresolubly ambiguous, an impossible object, an artificial construct, outside the range of normal experience.

The effect of such figures is to break up the passivity of the interpreter. Habitual perspectives on ducks and rabbits are challenged and the reading process becomes dynamic, involving perpetual oscillation from one alternative to the other. Our interpretation "can never come to rest and our 'imitative faculty' will be kept busy as long as we join in the game."[44] One becomes aware of the movements and fluctuations of one's own mind, of the constant flux of consciousness. The effect is to prolong and complicate the reading process.

Visual ambiguity thus undermines habitual perception, the automatisms of routine reactions. Victor Shklovsky, the Russian formalist, writes:

> Habit devours everything, objects, clothes, furniture, your wife and the fear of war. . . . That which we call "art" exists in order to remedy our perception of life, to make things felt, to make the stone stony. The purpose of art is to evoke in man a sensation of things, to make him perceive things rather than merely recognize them. In order to do so art uses two devices: making things strange and complicating the form, so as to increase the duration and the difficulty of perception.[45]

The irresoluble ambiguity, the impossible object that confronts Isaac, is the figure of Jacob-Esau. Habitual meanings are suddenly disrupted; Isaac becomes newly aware of the sound of the words spoken, the touch, the taste and smell that create a new field of perceptions, not belonging to the already known world. Whatever his perception of Jacob had previously been, it now takes on an uncanny quality as he attends to the reality of an uncanny presence.

Doubt generates a fuller blessing, which is both *birkhat ha-nefesh*, a surrender to his whole experience, and "in the presence of God," a sense of being possessed by a blessing that flows through him. Seforno identifies this state—induced, ultimately, by a sensuous-spiritual rapture of smell—as *k'naggen ha-menagen*—the musical rapture that inspires Elisha with prophecy.[46]

The expression is used in later literature as a code for a state of ecstatic passiveness. The Maggid of Mezritz, the charismatic disciple of Israel Baal Shem Tov, the founder of Hasidism, for instance, writes: "As the minstrel, the servant of God, becomes like his instrument, then the spirit of God comes upon him."[47] Inspiration comes when one allows the spirit to play upon one. One becomes a harp, or an organ, or a shofar: the latter motif appears throughout early Hasidic literature. In prayer, or in preaching, the Hasid opens himself to a form of involuntary speech. No longer regulating himself, he becomes the instrument of God. This divine infusion produces words of inspired improvisation: coherent, well developed, but dictated from above. The condition that allows this to happen is one in which *"one is not aware of oneself."*[48] By narrowing down the field of consciousness and thus intensifying the activity of thinking, the mystic recognizes his own radical passivity and yields to the divine musician.[49]

Isaac's experience of blessing, I suggest, has a "proto-Hasidic" quality. Blindness has grown in him since the *Akedah:* his traumatic awareness of having *missed* an experience of death and resurrection, of his own departure and return, lays the ground for some future event when he may come to own his own experience. But in facing the "impossible object" that is Jacob-Esau, mastery is again baffled. Again, Isaac knows the incomprehensible and surrenders to knowledge that he does not own. Without consciously naming Jacob, he senses that blessing flows through him.

INSTRUMENTAL RAPTURE

However, this passivity has something of the experience that Caruth describes as "being shot into a future that is not entirely one's own."[50] As with the early Hasidic masters, it is an ecstatic passivity, in which unconscious energy is granted free passage. Unlike the habitual perception that freezes the movement of perception, it resembles rather the state that generates art or mystic contemplation. The "impossible" ambiguity of Jacob-Esau releases Isaac from his prejudices.

This notion of ecstatic passivity appears not only in prophetic sources and Hasidic homilies, but also in classic midrashic accounts of Isaac's state, during the blessing and after it:

R. Levi said: Six organs serve a human being: over three he is master, and over three he is not. Over the eye, ear, and nose he is not master, for he sees what he does not wish to see, hears and smells what he does not wish to hear and smell. Over the mouth, hand, and foot he is master. If he desires, he studies the Torah, while if he wishes he engages in slander, and if he wishes, he blasphemes and reviles. With the hand he can dispense charity if he wishes, while he can rob and murder if he so desires. With his feet he can go to theaters and circuses, while if he wishes he can go to synagogues and houses of study. But when one merits it, God puts those over which a person is normally master out of his power. The hand: "And his hand, which he put forth against him, dried up" (1 Kings 13:4); the mouth: "And he shall indeed be blessed!"; the feet: "My son, walk not in the way with them . . . for their feet run to evil" (Prov. 1:15f).[51]

The three voluntary organs—hand, foot, mouth—give the human being mastery, the possibility of free choice in action, movement, and speech. Beginning with a simple contrast between voluntary and involuntary responses, however, the midrash modulates beyond the obvious moral imperative of free will to make a startling claim: when one *merits* it, God takes the voluntary organs out of one's power. Apparently, losing control of hands, feet, and mouth can be a privileged condition.

The example of the unmastered mouth is Isaac's cry: "And indeed he shall be blessed!" (Gen. 27:33). With these words, Isaac ratifies his blessing in the face of his outraged and beloved son Esau. Implicitly, the midrash claims that these words—so ill-advised as a rational and placatory response to Esau—are spoken through him rather than by him. He is not in possession of his own words; and, in some sense, this is a sign of his "merit."

Ramban comments on the irrational nature of Isaac's declaration:

"And indeed he shall be blessed": this means "against my will, since it is impossible for me transfer the blessing from him." From the moment he blessed him, Isaac knew by divine inspiration that his blessings indeed rested upon Jacob. This then is the reason for his violent trembling; he knew that his beloved son Esau had lost his blessing forever.

In spite of himself, and in spite of his conscious intention, Isaac knows that his blessing has an absolute validity. Seforno articulates this conviction as Isaac's palpable experience, in the act of blessing, that his words engage precisely with their object. Both commentators indicate the gap between Isaac's conscious and even moral intention and the state of inspired passivity in which one's words mean more than one can fully understand.

In this condition, Isaac experiences yet again a transformative reversal of consciousness. Speaking with a kind of free association, he allows unconscious knowledge, the fruit of darkness, to be born. He testifies to a musical truth, like the musician who has become the instrument.

"WHAT IS ESSENTIAL IS INVISIBLE TO THE EYE"

Uttering the words, "And indeed he shall be blessed," Isaac hears himself articulate a counterintuitive truth. Instead of reassuring Esau, he ratifies the blessing. Some midrashic sources, indeed, explicitly spell out a repressed desire: Isaac had the conscious intention of *cursing* Jacob for deceiving him, only to find that he has instead confirmed the blessing.[52] Precisely this outcome—that Isaac would curse instead of bless—had been foreseen by Jacob when he attempted to ward off his mother's plot (Gen. 27:12). The blessing should, by rights, have turned into a curse; instead, the curse turns again to blessing.

This midrashic narrative resonates with associations from the story of Balaam, whose conscious intention to curse the Israelites is transformed into blessing. "And God turned the curse into a blessing for you" (Deut. 23:6). The classic understanding of both "turnings" is that God places His words in the human mouth, even against the grain of conscious desire.[53] Perhaps we can say that in this uncanny moment a version of the "Freudian slip" is played out. An unavowed wish, a blocked awareness informs the unintended words: Isaac *really* wants to bless Jacob; a repressed desire finds unwitting expression in the words "And indeed he shall be blessed." And, more strangely, perhaps even Balaam, possessed by God's words, gives expression to his own disowned desire.

The inner world of a human being is dense with unheard voices. Christopher Bollas writes:

Indeed, I would like to strengthen the image of being lost in thought. I think these are the moments when we are in the heart of darkness, dispersed into so many elements that constitute being that from the point of view of consciousness we are no longer present. These absences, or abstentions from alert existence, are, in my view, vital to the elaboration of one's idiom. . . . We can enter a form of solitude in which we are lost in thought, and lost to thought.[54]

Lost in thought, lost to thought, Isaac moves through the doubt and confusion of his failure to identify his son. The ambiguity of Jacob-Esau compels him to yield mastery, giving him access to a more radical perception. "What is essential is invisible to the eye."[55] This blindness delivers stark revelations.

Writing of his clinical approach to the knowledge of another human being, Freud declared, "I blind myself artificially to focus all the light on one dark spot." The encounter with another requires a kind of blindness, if one is to catch the drift of the other, in his underground life. When unconscious meets unconscious, a different recognition becomes possible. "It is as if people can only meet in anonymous encounters," writes Adam Phillips.[56]

When the prophet or the poet is inspired, he is "uttering something which he does not wholly understand—or which he may even misinterpret when the inspiration has departed from him."[57] What emerges from Isaac's words of blessing, and, again, in the words with which he confirms the blessing, is a recognition of Jacob, the son whom Isaac had *not loved*. The midrashic and Hasidic sources that speak of divine inspiration may be translated into terms that register the innermost movements of the human spirit. Here, surprise reigns. Surprise and terror resonate in Isaac's voice, as Esau abruptly rouses him to the world of consciousness:

And Isaac was seized with very violent trembling. "Who was it then," he demanded, "that hunted game and brought it to me? And I ate freely of it before you came, and I blessed him. And indeed he shall be blessed." (Gen. 27:33)

Isaac's cry registers the stages of his response: bewilderment, detailed memory of his experience, in all its plenitude, recognition of an irrefutable encounter. Perhaps this is the most poignant moment in his story.

For Isaac to release the other voices within himself, a certain uncertainty is necessary: a return to that other *charadah,* the trauma of the *Akedah* when the incomprehensible left its brand on his eyes and his mind. Then, too, hands and feet and mouth had to be immobilized, stripped of their voluntary power, so that his eyes could register, searingly, another encounter. Now, he trembles "in that strange repetition," described by Jacques Derrida, "that ties an irrefutable past . . . to a future that cannot be anticipated; anticipated but unpredictable; *apprehended,* but, and this is why there is a future, apprehended precisely *as* unforeseeable."[58]

The Hasidic master Mei Ha-Shilo'ach portrays Isaac as possessed by unaccountable words, reluctant to end the blessing. "And it was when Isaac had finished blessing Jacob . . ." (Gen. 27:30). He invites us to listen to the melody within the words—to the traditional cantillation[59] with which biblical narrative is performed and informed. The trill notation here delays the words, conveying Isaac's unwillingness to end the blessing. The words are sweet in his mouth, infused by God. Lingering in the inspired moment, Isaac knows an otherness within himself.[60] Mei Ha-Shilo'ach communicates that inner complexity by enacting it: the reader can hear the otherness within the Torah words by simply *listening,* when the Torah is read in the synagogue, to the trills of uncanny sweetness. Such a reading, based on such a listening, opens within the reader questions about his/her own other voices.

If Isaac's blessing is the gift of darkness, however, it survives in the light of consciousness, so that he can retransmit it to Jacob, in translated form, this time willingly and wittingly. Before Jacob leaves home to escape Esau's revenge, his father gives him the "blessing of Abraham": inheritance of the land promised to Abraham, to him and his seed after him. At this moment, he ratifies, in full consciousness, the gifts of darkness.

In this drama of voices, Jacob's voice has been at the margin of our attention. We have not considered his perspective, nor attempted to judge the moral status of his role. I would like to make one suggestion, however. We have noticed that he resists Rebecca's plan to deceive Isaac: "Perhaps [*ullai*] my father will touch me and I will appear to him as a trickster, and bring upon myself a curse and not a blessing" (Gen. 27:12). Clearly, Jacob fears exposure under his father's touch. Remarkably, though, he uses the expression *ullai*, which implies a *wishful* possibility. We can perhaps detect a nuance of desire: though consciously he dreads his father's touch, a longing emerges from his words—"*Perhaps* he will fondle me"—and an intimation of the ambiguity that his father will experience. This is Jacob's only real chance to have his father reconsider him as heir to the family destiny. Only if Isaac is compelled to relinquish his unequivocal certainties can Jacob come to be known differently: through the senses, through the traumatic encounter with the unknowable.

The hint of a wish underlying Jacob's apprehension speaks of a desire *to be known*. For this meeting to be one where "Deep calls unto deep,"[61] Jacob has to surrender himself, his need to be intelligible to himself; he must assume treacherous garments. The risks are great; but perhaps misrecognition will release Isaac to a new recognition.

PART THREE

Between Self and Other

NINE

"And I Did Not Know . . ."

The Secret of Prayer

"I AM NOT LIKE MY FATHER"

In the lives of the patriarchs, the narrative of generation—becoming a father—is never simple. Abraham has to endure a hundred barren years before the promised son is born to his wife, Sarah; Isaac prays strenuously for his wife, Rebecca, to bear children. In Jacob's life, however, the theme of stalled fertility takes a different form. On the one hand, parenthood comes easily: he fathers thirteen children within a period of twenty-two years, without any physical difficulty. On the other hand, unlike his father and grandfather, he lives a complex history before he marries; and his marriage story is itself fraught with conflict, deception, love and hate and jealousy. Later, his relations with his children are also complicated: the saga of Joseph and his brothers will torment Jacob until the last period of his life.

For Jacob, then, fatherhood may be physically easy, but much of his narrative is concerned with the psychological turmoil that is the breeding ground of his family. In other words, before he can become a father in the fullest sense, he has much to undergo.[1]

In one midrashic tradition, he himself, with almost brutal clarity, articulates the unique quality of his history. When Rachel desperately pleads, "Give me children, or I shall die!"[2] he fends her off: *"I am not like my father."* He cannot pray for children because, unlike his father and his grandfather, he is fertile. By the time Rachel bears her first child, he will have fathered seven children from Leah, his other wife—as well as two from Bilha, Rachel's maidservant, and two from Zilpah, Leah's maidservant. In this midrashic version, Jacob emphasizes this disparity between his fertility and Rachel's barrenness ("God has withheld *from you* fruit of the womb") to explain why, unlike his father, he cannot pray for her. His physical fertility sets him apart from both his ancestors and his wife; in a sense, it disables him from undertaking the spiritual act of prayer for a child from his beloved wife.[3]

"I am not like my father." Despite his physical fertility, Jacob is almost one hundred years old by the time his family is established. His marriage history reflects the spiritual complexity that haunts his life. His issue—what will issue from him—will be bound up with his intimate vicissitudes. This narrative will be the subject of the second half of Genesis.

MARRIED, ALONE

Jacob's marriage history begins, we remember, with a journey. Unlike his twin brother—who marries promptly though, from his parents' viewpoint, unfortunately[4]—Jacob marries late,[5] and only after his father sends him abroad to Haran, to Rebecca's family. In this, Isaac is moved by Rebecca's passionate complaint: " 'I am disgusted with my life because of the Hittite women. If Jacob marries a Hittite woman like these, from among the native women, what good will life be to me?' "

In speaking to Jacob, however, Rebecca had not used the marriage argument to spur him to leave home. A different fear inspires her words to him: Esau plots to kill Jacob, who must, therefore, immediately flee. Jacob listens to the complex messages of both his parents and embarks on his journey with a double purpose: to marry and to escape death at his brother's hands. Desire and fear, *eros* and *thanatos*, create a force field that will repeatedly imperil and transfigure his identity.

By the time he marries, then, he has already lived a turbulent narrative: he has incurred his brother's murderous hatred by depriving him of both birthright and blessing. He has yet to encounter God at Bethel, to dream of a ladder reaching into the heavens and wake to find "God in this place," to meet Rachel in a fraught scene by a blocked well, to work seven years for her only to lose her on their wedding night. Unlike Abraham and Isaac, he will love his wife Rachel before he marries her.

The shape of Jacob's history, then, suggests a powerful paradox.

Much married and father of many children, he lives many years single, palpably alone. His narrative conveys a sense of solitude and inwardness. More than anyone before him, he lives in a large register of turbulence, of error and revelation. He, alone of the patriarchs, leaves the Holy Land for an extended period of time and, obeying two different parental voices, travels into a twenty-year exile. And even when he returns, heavy with family and possessions, he is pointedly described as *levado—alone:*[6] though he is married—to four wives—he has reverted to the condition of Adam before God creates his helpmate. In this condition, he struggles with a man-angel who changes his name. Then, strangely, after all the early vicissitudes of his married life, his wives disappear from the narrative: Rachel dies in childbirth, and no further mention is made of his other wives. Alone, he endures the anguish of Joseph's loss; unpartnered, he brings his children down to Egypt; and alone, he blesses them on his deathbed. From this perspective, Jacob's essential aloneness is palliated for a relatively brief segment of his life.

Before he departs on his journey, Isaac blesses him. In full consciousness, he transmits to him "the blessing of Abraham": " 'that you may possess the land where you are sojourning, which God assigned to Abraham' " (Gen. 28:40). Meshekh Hokhmah connects this expression with the words of God's complex promise to Abraham—"Your *seed* shall be *sojourners* in a land not theirs . . . to your *seed* I assign this land" (15:13, 18). The promise has a dialectical character: Abraham's heir, who will possess the land, will be the one who knows the life of the sojourner, of the stranger. Isaac realizes that the seed of destiny is borne by Jacob, who is embarking on a long *gerut*—a stranger in a foreign land. Jacob has thus identified himself as the bearer of Abraham's seed: a fate of *gerut*, of homelessness, will paradoxically qualify him to inherit the promised homeland.

In this nuanced reading, a dialectical tension is set up between the experience of the stranger and that of the entitled heir. By some paradoxical spiritual law, the painful destiny of the wanderer, the foreigner, will mark him as the rightful inheritor of the Promised Land. In the legal imagery of the midrash, Jacob here pays off a historic *bill of debt.*[7]

The burden of Abraham's blessing, then, signifies physical wan-

dering and homelessness. Perhaps, too, it invokes other kinds of dispossession, an existential otherness that characterizes all the patriarchs. In fact, it is striking that the fate of *gerut* is attributed to all
three patriarchs, even to Isaac, who never leaves the country. But
Jacob's destiny will be saturated with this marker of Abraham's seed;
the founder of the House of Israel will know homelessness in all
its variations.[8] Before he can enter into his own, he is destined to
travel far.

> In order to arrive at what you do not know
> You must go by a way which is the way of ignorance.
> In order to possess what you do not possess
> You must go by the way of dispossession.
>
> T. S. Eliot, "East Coker"

GOD IN THIS PLACE

The night at Bethel is the heart of his journey, the dream interim
between Be'er Sheva and Haran. There, he dreams and wakens with
the words "Surely, God is in this place. And I did not know." He wakens, that is, with the deep conviction that he *did not know*. He has
brushed against a knowledge that could arise only from the way of
ignorance. In such profound shifts of experience, the revelation is
the not-knowing; the sense of previous darkness itself intimates a
dawning light. In a startled moment, Jacob recognizes the shape of
his own ignorance: "Surely, God is in this place." Why is it so unexpected that God should be *in this place*? What strange beauty has just
touched him?

Jacob's journey into dispossession and ignorance begins with a
violent encounter with *the* place: *"Va-yifga ba-makom"*—"He came
upon a certain place" (Gen. 28:11). A faithful translation of the
Hebrew would yield, inelegantly, "He *crashed* into, *collided* with *the*
place." What place is indicated in this way, with the definite article?
Rashi writes: "This refers to that place mentioned elsewhere—that is,
Mount Moriah, of which it is said, 'He saw *the place* from afar' " (22:4).

In Rashi's midrashic reading, clouds begin to gather: this place is none other than the place where Jacob's father, Isaac, lay on the altar, bound for sacrifice. Rashi will return to this extraordinary claim. Now, he comments on *Va-yifga:*

> Most plainly, it means, "he arrived." But the Rabbis explained it to mean, "he prayed," as in "Do not beseech me" (Jer. 7:16). From here, we learn that Jacob composed the Evening Prayer [*Arvit*]. The text did not use the ordinary word for prayer [*va-yitpallel*] in order to teach you that the earth shrank under him—that is, that he arrived at his destination with miraculous speed.

The resonances of the biblical words assemble a rich and allusive narrative. In the world of space, the abrasive collision between Jacob and the place conveys the effect of a precipitate arrival: the earth shrinks and deposits him suddenly, shockingly, in *the place:* Mount Moriah. On another level, Jacob registers this precipitate arrival by creating a new genre of prayer, the evening prayer, the prayer of darkness. For in the world of time, too, the sun sets unexpectedly, disrupting the sequence of the hours:

> "He spent the night there, for the sun had set" (Gen. 28:11): It should have read, "And the sun set, and he spent the night there." The precipitate "for the sun had set" indicates that the sun set for him, suddenly, not at its proper time, so that he should spend the night there.

In this surrealistic account, Jacob finds himself hurtled through shrinking space and accelerated time to land in *this place,* which is Mount Moriah, just as darkness has fallen. God has extinguished *(kivah)* the sun two hours early, claims the midrash—punning on *ki va* ("the sun *had set*")—so as to have a private conversation with Jacob. This personal sunset allows a darkness in which Jacob will encounter God. *Va-yifga* conveys Jacob's traumatic engulfment in the darkness, in the place of his father's binding; and the night prayer that is his response.

Rashi again addresses the theme of *the place,* this time raising the obvious problem: the place is clearly named Luz, which Jacob renames Bethel (House of God) (Gen. 28:19). How then can the Rabbis identify it as Jerusalem, or, specifically, Mount Moriah? Rashi answers emphatically:

> I say that Mount Moriah was uprooted from its place and came here [to Luz]! That is what is meant by the "shrinking" of the earth that is mentioned in B. *Hullin* 91b: the site of the future Temple came toward him as far as Bethel. This too is what is meant by *Va-yifga ba-makom:* he collided with the place, as two people clash who are moving toward each other. Now, if you should ask, When Jacob passed the Temple, why did God not make him stop there?—If it never entered his mind to pray at the spot where his fathers had prayed, should God force him to stop there? In fact, he had reached as far as Haran, as Scripture proves: "He went to Haran." When he arrived at Haran, he said, Is it possible that I have passed the place where my fathers prayed—and I did not pray there? He decided to return and got as far as Bethel, when the ground "shrank" for him.[9]

Jacob has bypassed the sacred place—Mount Moriah, where the future Temple will be built—and omitted an essential prayer, which would have linked him with his fathers. Unawares, in a kind of daydream, he reaches his destination, only to be visited by remorse: "Is it possible that I have passed the place where my fathers prayed—and I did not pray there?" *How could I have bypassed that place, forgotten that past?* He turns back, only to find himself shockingly precipitated through time and space into abrasive impact with *the place.* "Like a man," says the Talmud, "who crashes into his friend who is also moving toward him." An unexpected double momentum gives the meeting the quality of a blow: the place toward which he is traveling turns out to have been *traveling toward him.* Before he can compose himself, he has "collided" with Mount Moriah. The lights of the world are unexpectedly extinguished. He has arrived too early, unprepared, at *the place.*

. . .

AVOIDANCES

Mount Moriah becomes, in Rashi's narrative, a place in Jacob's mind, uncannily overwhelming him, just as the sudden sunset becomes his personal syncope, a kind of blackout, which moves him to a new genre of prayer—*arvit*—the prayer in darkness. This is the place he unwittingly bypassed on his journey: "How could I have forgotten to pray?"

The moment is intensely serious but not without its humor: clearly, the "accident" of Jacob's omission is no accident. It represents an evasion, a gesture of "motivated irrationality."[10] Mount Moriah, I suggest, holds a form of unconscious meaning for him. The place where "his fathers had prayed" is the place where his father had lived through a scene of terror: an altar, wood, bound limbs, a knife, an angel's cry. The physical details have, in Jacob's imagination, become subsumed into a pious abstraction. Perhaps the reality of the scene is something that Jacob cannot bear to acknowledge? To let his mind dwell on his father's experience as he lay bound on the altar—this is the unbearable possibility that he bypasses. That place has become the focus of a lifelong avoidance.

Jacob's relation with his father is subtly indicated in the biblical narrative. In his mind, he characterizes his father's God as *Pachad Yitzhak*—Isaac's *Fear*. Significantly, he invokes the "God of my father, the God of Abraham, and the Fear of Isaac" (Gen. 31:42)—identifying Abraham as his father. In his imagination, Isaac, engulfed in the terror of the *Akedah*, has become unapproachable. In other words, the *Akedah* has, in a sense, left Jacob fatherless. The father he adopts is Abraham, the grandfather whose God sent an angel to restore the world to sanity, and who then sent his servant to choose a bride for Isaac to regenerate Abraham's world of loving-kindness.[11]

I suggest that, for Jacob, the *Akedah* is the unreachable place. His prayers cannot find inspiration in the thought of that terror. But, having unwittingly traveled past Mount Moriah, guilt assails him: "How could I have passed by the place where my fathers prayed, without praying there?" He sets himself to return, and finds himself abrasively hurtling against that place, that darkness. A new prayer is born: *arvit,* which represents an unimaginable possibility—that divine light can be revealed in the dark.[12] The world of darkness, of sleep and dream, of loss of consciousness, vulnerability, passivity— all this is associated with the *Akedah* and his father's helplessness from which he has long recoiled.

No simple oversight, then, carried him unwittingly past Mount Moriah. When he decides to return, he discovers that self and place are moving toward a violent and dreamlike collision. In a sense, even before he lies down in that place to sleep and dream, he is already caught up in a kind of dream. Every path ends in darkness. "The whole world," says the midrash, "became a kind of wall up against him."[13] This place will not let him pass: it blocks the world from him. There *is* no world for him other than this place: if he will not surrender to this encounter, there is nowhere else for him to go. If he is to be born into a world of his own, he must confront his father's place of terror.

What he has avoided now compels his presence and—strikingly— his loss of consciousness. Now, God has him in the posture that, strangely, He desires: "This righteous man has come to My lodging-place: Shall he get off without spending the night?" This place has become a *lodging place,* essential for a traveling human life: here, he is to sleep, perchance to dream. . . .

"And he took of the stones of the place, and put them under his head. *And he lay down in that place.*" The counterintuitive act—to lie down in that place where his father had lain on the altar—has a dreamlike inevitability. Even the tempo of reading slows, conveying an uncanny fatedness.[14]

This core narrative in which Jacob lies on his father's altar is unfolded in *Pirkei de-Rabbi Eliezer:*

> Jacob took twelve stones *from the altar where his father Isaac had been bound,* and placed them under his head *in that place.*[15]

Jacob surrenders his body and his dreaming self to the place he has avoided. Ultimately, his surrender is *in his head:* his mental and imaginative world are, however unwillingly, set to engage with his father's experience.

In this condition, he dreams. Opening himself to the uncanny encounter with his father's terror, he dreams of angels ascending and descending a ladder that spans the distance between earth and heaven. In his dream, too, God stands over him and promises him the land, protection, safe return from exile: "Behold, I am with you . . . I will not abandon you till I have completed what I have spoken to you" (Gen. 28:15).

Strikingly, the divine promises are addressed to him by "the God of *Abraham your father* and the God of Isaac." God's address reflects Jacob's nervous distance from his father: Abraham, rather than Isaac, is his father. In the link between Isaac and Jacob, something has gone awry. If the Torah can declare, at the very outset of the story, "Isaac loved Esau, for he put food in his mouth, while Rebecca loved Jacob" (Gen. 25:28), a bias exists in the love dynamics of the family: unlike Esau, Jacob has not known how to "feed" his father; a filial intimacy has failed to take hold. And, strikingly, God acknowledges the bias in Jacob's feeling as a son: He announces Himself as "God of Abraham your father, and God of Isaac."

CONTRAPUNTAL ANGELS

The imagery of Jacob's dream speaks louder than words. The ladder, set firmly in the earth (lit., *toward* the earth), with its head reaching toward heaven, expresses a double energy, an intentionality equally drawn in both directions. The angels ascend and descend: it is clear that they begin on earth—they take their impetus from below and create a flow of movement upward and downward. How does this energy flow affect the image of the ladder that joins heaven and earth? And—asks a powerful midrash—what is the *it (bo)* that the angels move upon?

> R. Hiyya the Elder and R. Yannai disagreed. One maintained: They were ascending and descending *the ladder;* while the other said: they were ascending and descending *on Jacob.* The first view is clear. But that they were ascending and descending *on Jacob* must mean that some were exalting him and others chiding him, dancing, leaping, and maligning him. Thus it says,

"Israel in whom I will be glorified" (Isa. 49:3); it is you [said the angels] whose features are engraved on high; they ascended on high and saw his features and they descended below and found him sleeping. This can be compared to a king who was found sitting in his council chamber in judgment, while at the same time he lay asleep in the corridor.[16]

R. Yannai reads *bo* to mean that the angels are moving up and down on *Jacob,* the sleeper, and subject of the dream. He appears in his own dream in the guise of the ladder stretched between heaven and earth; in one direction, angels sing his praises, extolling his heavenly dimension, while, in the other, they chide him, malign him, mock him. Jacob-in-the-dream becomes a split being: on the one hand, he is the very image of ideal humanity that adorns God's throne;[17] on the other, a sleeping body, supine, shamefully torpid. The restless energy of the angels acquires a dissociated quality: clearly, they are agitated by these two versions, ceaselessly returning to both images in the attempt to integrate such contrary identities. How can the king be in two places at the same time? Dignified in his council chamber and prostrate in the corridor? The split baffles the angelic imagination: angels are famously capable of fulfilling only one mission at a time. Single-minded, they are ill-equipped to comprehend human complexity.

DISSONANT SELVES

This midrashic version of Jacob's dream represents his turbulent consciousness. At this moment of his life, Jacob is in conflict about his very self. In fact, the last words that have passed his lips were his answer to his father's question "Who are you, my son?"—"I am *(anokhi)* Esau your firstborn." Once spoken, the words acquire a life of their own. Who am I? Jacob or Esau? Who was it that received Isaac's blessing? An original simplicity has been disrupted. If the Torah describes him at first as a simple man, that may represent the beginning of his evolution; but at this point simplicity has become a troubling fantasy, perhaps an outgrown ideal. The restless angels express an ambiguous energy, as the two poles of Jacob's experience of himself, of his *anokhi,* pull apart.

Jacob wakes from his sleep. In a sense, it is the dream itself that wakes him. Within the dream, the contrapuntal angels offer him no refuge; the more acutely he experiences the dissonance between the higher and the lower *anokhi,* the more he is impelled to waken and play out the tension revealed in the dream. Even God's promises of protection and safe return can be fulfilled only if he wakes and embarks on his journey. If God is to fulfill His promise of fertility and inheritance, Jacob must engage with the waking, working, marrying world. The dream itself calls him to awaken; but it is only within sleep that the call can be heard.

In other words, the moment of awakening marks the real distance between the Jacob who is dreaming and the Jacob who is the subject of the dream. As Maurice Blanchot eloquently puts it:

> There is a fissure, a hint of an interval, a difference in structure; clearly it's not someone else, an entirely different person, but what exactly is it? And if, upon waking, we hastily and greedily take possession of the night's adventures as if they belonged to us, do we not do so with a certain sense of usurpation (as well as gratitude), do we not carry with us the memory of an irreducible distance, a peculiar sort of distance, a distance between self and self.[18]

A distance is traveled: What does Jacob "usurp" from his dream, for what is he grateful, when he wakes?—"And Jacob woke from his sleep and said, 'Indeed, there is God in this place. And I did not know.'"

The sense of God-in-this-place is clearly a revelation to Jacob. This refers, paradoxically, to the intensity of his dream experience of a divided self that now fuels his waking consciousness. For, as Christopher Bollas puts it, a dream "is not an event external to the self that awakening . . . can dispel, but an internal event, entirely sponsored by the . . . mind." This recognition plays a significant role in Jacob's revelation. "The bittersweet fate one suffers in *having a mind,* one that is only ever partly known" (my emphasis),[19] is part of his new awareness as he wakes from sleep. He knows that he is profoundly the author of his dream: that its uneasiness is born of him.

God's presence *in this place* is, then, surprising. Both as the place of his father's terror and as the site where a dismaying inner dissonance calls him to wake from his sleep, this place is not where he expected to encounter God. The disenchantment of his simplicity happens in his dream; but only on waking does he realize God's presence. "And I did not know." What is it that he did not know? That God could be *here*?

Knowing now that he did not know, Jacob begins to know. The Zohar reads his waking speech—*va-anokhi lo yadati*—"I—I did not know," as referring to his own selfhood: "I have not known my *anokhi*—my self." The emphatic *I,* the subject of his insight, also becomes the object. As object of reflection, *anokhi,* a new awareness of self, generates a profound sense of past ignorance. Jacob is able to surrender to the mystery of his own mind, to lose himself in an immediate experience: this in itself constitutes his new awareness. For the first time, he knows that he has never known himself, never integrated the fragmented perspectives that so agitate the angels.

It is also striking that with this new focus on a previously invisible *anokhi,* Jacob unconsciously echoes his mother's language, when her pregnancy agitates her to a new existential awareness: "If so, why then *am I [Lamah zeh anokhi]?*" A curiosity about the *anokhi,* about the self, engenders a new kind of question. Jacob, one of the children then in her womb, grows to a similar moment of curiosity.

THE SECRET OF PRAYER

Waking from sleep, Jacob senses God's presence. The midrash elaborates: with cryptic restraint, it adds one letter to the word *mi-shnato*—"from his sleep": *mi-mishnato, "from his learning."* The nineteenth-century Hasidic commentator on the Torah R. Kalonymus Kalman Epstein (the Ma'or Va-Shemesh) meditates on the possible meaning of this baffling midrash.[20] The main elements in worship of God are study (Torah) and prayer *(tefillah).* These two modes are in dialectical relation: in the words of the Talmud, "An ignorant person cannot be a pious one," on the one hand; on the other, "One who says, I need nothing but Torah, has no Torah." Splitting the spheres of Torah and prayer, intellect and piety, is impossible. A true piety involves knowledge, while intellectual knowledge uninformed by spiritual yearning is sterile and cannot even properly be called Torah.

At this moment, therefore, Jacob "wakes from his learning"—from an intellectual dream—from a life absorbed in study,[21] to invent a new prayer and to wonder at a new awareness: "Till now, I never knew the *secret of prayer!*" Well-versed in the *secret of Torah,* he encounters God only now, for the first time, in the essential mode of prayer. "Indeed, God is in this place—and I never knew Him!" His first revelation of God comes to him only with this first prayer.

The *secret of prayer* implies that beyond the *practice* of prayer there lies a mystery, which only now opens itself to him. What lies at the heart of Jacob's prayer—the prayer in darkness—and therefore at the heart of his new sense of God? An intense sense of paradox informs his cry: "There is *God in this place!*" Unimaginable till this moment was the idea that one could encounter God with such immediacy in this place, of all places. This is the place that he had resisted all his life—the binding-place of his father's terror. In avoiding this place, he had, in a sense, lost his father. In recognizing God's presence *here,* he discovers the secret of prayer. What then is implied about this mystery? Does his revelation in some way heal his unfathered condition? How does this healing relate to his new knowledge of himself? And, finally, how might this development relate to the problem of Jacob's own fatherhood? How does such a recognition, revelation, healing, self-knowledge prepare him for marriage and parenthood, which—as we have noticed—come so late in his life story?

TWO MODELS OF MARRIAGE

Suspending these questions, we turn now to the narrative of Jacob's marriages. A famous midrash describes him as the archetype of the man who actively seeks out his mate:

Said R. Phinehas in R. Abbahu's name: We find in the Torah, the
Prophets, and the Writings that a man's marriage partner is
from God. In the Torah: "Then Laban and Betuel answered and
said: The thing comes from God" (Gen. 24:50). In the Prophets:
"But his father and mother knew not that it was of God" (Judg.
14:4). In the Writings: "Houses and riches are the inheritance of
fathers; but a prudent wife is from God" (Prov. 14:14). Sometimes, a man goes to his spouse, and sometimes his spouse
comes to him. In the case of Isaac, his spouse came to him, as it
says, "And he saw and, behold, there were camels coming" (Gen.
24:63). Jacob, however, went to his spouse, as it is written, "And
Jacob left Be'er Sheva and went to Haran" (28:10).[22]

Whether one takes the more passive approach like Isaac, whose
spouse, Rebecca, left her world and came into his, or the more active
approach of Jacob, who travels far to find his spouse, the main message of the midrash is clearly that one's spouse is ordained by God.
Proof texts from all three sections of Scripture establish this theology of marriage. What, then, is the point of the distinction between
active and passive approaches to the choice of a spouse?

R. Isaac Luria, the great sixteenth-century mystic, offers a powerful rereading of this midrash. Engaging with the complexity of
Jacob's marriage story, he discerns *both* patterns—going to one's
spouse and having one's spouse come to one—in Jacob's two marriages, to Rachel and to Leah, respectively. Rachel is the wife that he
came for, the wife of his choice. Leah "comes to him," unbidden, in
the dark of night. We will return to this notion of the double marriage. But first, let us examine the early history of these two marriages from a midrashic perspective.

PASSION AND SOCIETY

Sent by his father to find *a wife*, he encounters her immediately as he
arrives at his destination. In the scene by the well, Jacob single-
handedly removes the stone blocking the well—just as Rachel arrives
shepherding her father's sheep. "And it was when Jacob saw Rachel,

the daughter of Laban, his mother's brother, and the sheep of Laban, his mother's brother, Jacob approached and rolled the stone off the mouth of the well, and watered the sheep of Laban, his mother's brother" (Gen. 29:10).

The repeated reference to *Laban, his mother's brother,* reveals his sense of having arrived at the family homestead. Happy to be on familiar ground, he expresses his kinship by watering the sheep— and by kissing Rachel.[23] A sense of completing his journey is sealed by these acts that link him with his mother. What, though, are we to make of his next act: "And he lifted up his voice and wept" (Gen. 29:11)? In terms of family feeling, these tears are mysterious, excessive; they rupture the public scene of family reunion.

Rashi offers a midrashic explanation: "He foresaw by divine inspiration that she would not be buried together with him." At the moment of first meeting, he has an intimation of death—death as separation from Rachel. In an instant, the narrative shifts from the register of family greetings to one of passion. Retrospectively, indeed, all Jacob's acts shift to a new register; they all now express the love that is, from its dawning, haunted with death. The intimation that he and Rachel will be divided in death engenders *passion,* which, paradoxically, will bind him to her as the wife of his quest. As *thanatos* enters his imagination, *eros* comes to life. The suffering that informs passionate love gives it eternal resonance.[24]

The narrative reverts immediately to the register of family talk, hospitality, work conditions. It is in this register that we learn that Laban has two daughters: "the elder was named Leah and the younger Rachel. Leah's eyes were weak, but Rachel was shapely and beautiful" (Gen. 29:17). And, explicitly, we are told, "Jacob loved Rachel; so he said, I will serve you seven years for your younger daughter Rachel." As though we had not witnessed the tears by the well, the narrative reintroduces Rachel as merely one of two marital possibilities, with Jacob's love and declaration for Rachel firmly lodged in the familial, economic context. An alternative narrative might have continued directly from the well scene to Jacob's proposal. Instead, the Torah sets Rachel in her context: since there are two daughters, Leah, the elder with the strangely weak, or soft, eyes, becomes significant. Jacob's single-minded love of Rachel is thus complicated from the outset—by Leah's being the elder, by the enigmatic message carried by her soft eyes.

LEAH'S DESIRE

The Talmud offers a history of those eyes:

> Rav said: Her eyes were indeed actually weak, but that was no disgrace to her but a credit; for at the crossroads she heard people saying: Rebecca has two sons, and Laban has two daughters; the elder daughter should be married to the elder son and the younger daughter should be married to the younger son. And she sat at the crossroads and inquired: "How does the elder son conduct himself?" And the answer came that he was a wicked man, a highway robber. "How does the younger man conduct himself?"—"A simple man dwelling in tents." And she wept until her eyelashes dropped off.[25]

Before Leah ever sees him, Jacob has already been established as the object of her passion—an ethical passion, to be sure, for the cousin whose behavior is exemplary, but nevertheless a forbidden passion, for the younger son whom society and fate has assigned to Rachel. Jacob's love for Rachel, then, has already been constructed by Leah as the fate that frustrates her own desire. In this sense, Jacob arrives in a world already dense with expectation and conflict.

Leah is depicted as sitting at the crossroads, refusing to accept her fate, interrogating its meaning, aspiring to her own desire. She protests her fate with such passion that, in the unsparing imagery of the midrash, "her eyelashes dropped off." The description leaves the reader compassionate, but also *appalled* by the self-destruction implicit in it.[26] So deep a protest makes her willing to *undo* herself, to deface, efface herself—to be not-Leah: her permanently reddened, blurred eyes make of her face a kind of tragic mask.

Such passionate will, claims Rav, is a credit to her. Unequivocally aligning herself with Jacob, she is, then, presumably not entirely pas-

sive in the wedding-night deception. It is true that the biblical narrative emphasizes Laban as the sole actor:

> When evening came, he took his daughter Leah and brought her
> to him; and he came in unto her.—Laban had given his maidser-
> vant Zilpah to his daughter Leah as her maid—When morning
> came, behold, she was Leah! So he said to Laban, "What is this
> you have done to me? I was in your service for Rachel! Why did
> you deceive me?" (Gen. 29:23–25)

All the verbs relate to Laban, except for Jacob's two acts of cohab-
iting with Leah and complaining about the deception. And Jacob's
reproach is addressed only to Laban. Leah figures as the object
whom Laban brings to Jacob. The apparent passivity of her role,
however, is powerfully questioned in an arresting midrash:

> All that night he called her Rachel, and she answered him. In the
> morning, however, "Behold, it was Leah!" He said to her: "You
> are a deceiver, daughter of a deceiver!" She replied: "Is there a
> teacher without pupils? Did not your father call you Esau, and
> you answered him! So too did you call me, and I answered
> you!"[27]

Jacob's reproach to Leah goes unrecorded in the Torah. The
midrash spells out a disregarded dimension of the story of woman's
desire: far from passive, Leah *answered* Jacob when he called her
Rachel in the darkness. Strikingly, this is the focus of his complaint:
not her physical participation in the deception, but her act of naming, misnaming, self-naming. In his mind, he was uniting with his
beloved Rachel: he is outraged by Leah's success in duping his imagination. As though, in some sense, she had *become* Rachel during the
night, a phantom of Jacob's desire. "And when morning came,
behold, she was Leah!" By the uncompromising light of day, she was
Leah. "But at night," Rashi asserts, "at night, *she was not Leah*."[28] The
formidable energy of Leah's desire makes her over into the object of
his desire.

Leah's response to Jacob's reproach is startling. He has condemned her as congenitally sly, a true daughter of her notorious father, Laban. She replies with another affiliation: Is there a teacher without pupils! Implicitly, she names Jacob as her model, chosen like a teacher, rather than genetically determined like a father. She is referring, of course, to Jacob's deception of Isaac. Her satirical answer effectively silences him: he has become the teacher of all who impersonate a rival, who use the darkness to deceive.

THE TRUTH OF IMPROVISATION

Perhaps, however, Leah's answer holds more than satirical intent. Jacob's betrayal, like Leah's, had been in the realm of language: not so much the farcical goatskins as the misnaming: "I am Esau your firstborn." Masquerading as his brother, he has defied the values of the daylight world: the rights of the firstborn, the fact of Isaac's choice. He has employed what George Steiner calls the "alternative powers of language," to create a counterworld informed by desire.

This, perhaps, is the burden of Leah's riposte: "I am your kin, an apt student, for we both know the fascination with masks, the impulse to reinvent, redefine ourselves." In discussing this midrashic interchange, Sefat Emet evokes a similar theme: Jacob and Leah share a sensibility; both appropriate what, in the given world, is not theirs. Jacob answers his father's searching question "Who are you, my son?": "I am—*anokhi*—Esau your firstborn."

The lie is an embarrassment to commentators from Rashi onward. He attempts to close the gap between word and fact, by opening another gap: he reads, "I am *[pause]* . . . Esau is your firstborn." Sefat Emet, however, uncompromisingly claims: "Jacob *spoke truth* when he said, I am Esau your firstborn."[29] The truth Jacob speaks, I suggest, is the truth of improvisation, of self-invention. He assumes a dimension of Esau's identity, an Esau mask, in order to release within himself his Esau potential. "Every profound spirit needs a mask" (Nietzsche).

In *Sincerity and Authenticity*, Lionel Trilling explores the paradoxes of truth and masking. He cites Oscar Wilde: "Man is least himself when he talks in his own person. Give him a mask and he will tell you the truth."[30] Emerson, similarly, wrote: "There is no deeper dissembler than the sincerest man." And, "Many men can write better in a mask than for themselves." The problem of truthfulness becomes one of being *true to a complexity,* of being authentic rather than sincere. Oscar Wilde, again, attacks a direct, simple model of sincerity when he says that "all bad poetry springs from genuine feeling." Trilling explains the paradox: "He means that the direct conscious confrontation of experience and the direct public expression of it do not necessarily yield the truth, and indeed that they are likely to pervert it." A certain ironic posture emerges from such reflections. As Trilling points out, irony derives from the Greek word for a *dissembler;*[31] the wearer of masks is *ironically* aware that only in this way can he perform aspects of a complex and dynamic identity.

Improvisation and playfulness become, then, oblique means of expressing truth. George Steiner explores the interface between truth and lying from a different angle. Focusing on the relations between language and performance, he declares: *"Language is the main instrument of man's refusal to accept the world as it is."*[32] Language is used to describe and create counterworlds; using counterfactual and optative grammatical forms, we "gainsay or 'un-say' " the world. The brute literalism of the unsaid world must be refused; otherwise, "we would turn forever on the treadmill of the present." "Feigning" is rooted in "shaping" *(fingere):* to speak is to shape reality, to create a *fiction.*

Steiner discusses Swift's account of the Houyhnyhnms in *Gulliver's Travels:* these noble horse-men cannot fathom the prevalence of *"Lying, and false Representation"* in the human world. Since the purpose of language is to convey information, if anyone *"said the Thing which was not,"* he subverted that purpose. The resulting "impropriety" is both moral and semantic. In this way, the Houyhnyhnms have dismissed all uses of language that are not strictly factual. However, Steiner argues, the great mass of speech acts are not of this kind: "The current of language is intentional, it is instinct with purpose in regard to audience and situation. It aims at attitude and assent."[33] We speak not "the things which are . . . but those which might be, which we would bring about."

Desire, memory, creativity inundate language, creating an im-

mense repertoire of counterfactual expressiveness. Steiner translates the French concept of *altérité* as "alternity"[34] to describe this
fictional thrust of language. Naming oneself, for example, or withholding one's real name, is a significant theme in world literature,
folklore, and legend. Steiner touches on a few examples—from
Odysseus to Roland to Rumpelstiltskin to Turandot—where the
alternative powers of language are employed in a potentially liberating way. The Houyhnyhnms "inhabit a tautology of coherent self:
they are only what they are."[35] Human beings play with masks to give
voice to an otherness that is essential to their humanity.

SINCERITY AND AUTHENTICITY

Returning now to Jacob, I suggest that he, too, is working with an
"improvisational truth": "I am Esau your firstborn." In the discussion
of Sefat Emet, Jacob has the conviction that he can appropriate
Esau's identity to good purpose. Perhaps the twins, for the sake of
differentiation, have divided the territory of identity too neatly,
Jacob assuming the role of the "simple man, dwelling in tents," while
Esau becomes the hunter, the man of the field. Rashi offers a
midrashic understanding of the "hunter" role:

> He knew how to hunt and deceive his father *with his mouth* [i.e.,
> in language]. He would ask, for instance, "Father, how should
> salt and straw be tithed?" [although he knew full well that these
> are not subject to the law of tithe]. Consequently, his father
> believed him to be meticulous in keeping the commandments.[36]

Esau is ingratiating, manipulative, representing himself in language so as to create a false impression. This Machiavellian portrait,
however, predetermines a complex issue: Esau's question, his false
representation, has, after all, the effect of beguiling, captivating[37] his
father. Such attention to Isaac's wishes, to his sensibility, surely
deserves some credit; at the very least, it creates love: "And Isaac
loved Esau, for he put food in his mouth" (Gen. 25:28). (Rashi: "Esau
deceived Isaac *with his mouth,* with his beguiling words.")

If "saying the Thing which is not" is improper, then Jacob is described, conversely, as a "simple man," *ish tam*. Here is Rashi's comment:

> He was not expert *[baki]* in all these things [i.e., Esau's hunting practices]: he spoke what was in his heart. One who is not sharp *[harif]* in deception is called a *tam*, a simple, straight person.

Jacob emerges as the truthful brother, the polar opposite of Esau. However, to be a *tam*—whole, simple, innocent, sincere—may eventually be felt to restrict a richer consciousness of self. Even in Rashi's approving account of Jacob's difference from Esau, a subtle counterpoint can be heard. The words he uses to describe Jacob's shortcomings as a deceiver are elsewhere associated with desirable intellectual qualities: to be *baki* is to be expert, well versed in a complex body of material, while to be *harif* is to be sharp, perceptive, acute, inclined to raise questions, capable of transformative understandings. As attributes of the scholar, the *talmid chakham*, these terms represent essential powers, the capacity to master texts and to reason beyond obvious meanings. A certain ingenuity, a capacity to invoke alternative frames of thought, characterizes the Rabbinic view of the human mind at its best. To be a *tam*, then, could be a seriously limiting fate, within the internal register of Rabbinic associations.[38]

Perhaps, then, Jacob becomes dissatisfied with his earlier construction of self, with its exclusion of rhetoric and of improvised versions. In impersonating his brother, he has begun to experiment with a hazardous redefinition of self. Isaac reacts to Esau's pain by diagnosing the situation: "Your brother came in guile *[mirmah]* and took your blessing" (Gen. 27:35). But this critical description of Jacob is startlingly transformed in Rashi's translation: "In *mirmah*—in *chokhmah*, in wisdom, cleverness." This translation is, in fact, derived from the classic Aramaic translation, Targum Onkelos. Is this simply to whitewash Jacob's deception? Or can we say that Isaac is acknowledging an area of "creative falsehood," of ingenuity dangerously overlapping with duplicity?

Jacob has adopted the improvisational mode of language in order to elaborate his own repertoire of identity; "I am Esau your firstborn" is spoken with a new and perilous ambition of self-creation.

The unequivocal innocence and sincerity of an earlier stage yields to a more complex struggle for authenticity. The Sages strikingly express the moral and developmental issue: "When *chokhmah* [wisdom] enters a person, cunning enters with it."[39]

If Jacob is to move from simplicity to wisdom, his identity, his *anokhi*, will have to be exposed to the duplicities, the improvisations of consciousness. No longer all of a piece, he will bring imagination and desire to bear on shaping a self that may often seem incoherent, troubling, enigmatic. Moral discriminations will have to be made—between ingenuity and duplicity, for example—in particular situations. But the dynamic sense of the *anokhi*, the instinct to elaborate himself, can no longer be denied.

THE MIRRORING MARRIAGE

It is this situation that Leah mirrors back to him, the morning after the wedding. "Is there a teacher without pupils?" Birds of a feather, both bride and groom share the proclivity for masks, for words that reshape identity, opening to transformation. In the midrashic narrative, the heart of the deception is not the physical act—taking the brother's blessing, usurping the sister's bed—but the language of self-invention.

In the Sefat Emet's account, Jacob and Leah become fit for each other, by an almost mathematical shift of identities. Since Jacob has appropriated Esau's identity (his *chelek*), he has become the older son who is fated to marry the older daughter. What unites them is the Esau dimension in both of them, which they will play with a difference. In kabbalistic language, they will achieve *tikkun*, correction, redemptive revision of the Esau mode. Jacob's connection with Rachel, on the other hand, is that she was fundamentally *(mamash)* destined for him; without complication, he simply loves her.

"And God saw that Leah was hated" (Gen. 29:31). Faced with his own image in Leah's impersonation, Jacob hates her. He hates her, of course, for not being Rachel, for depriving him of Rachel. But, more subtly, he hates her for revealing himself to himself. This is a hatred that perhaps only God can discern. Perhaps he behaves with perfect propriety to Leah as his wife. Perhaps he is genuinely unaware of his own hatred. But God sees his real aversion to his own complexity, his own unobservable self. A simply coherent self has cracked up, and he does not know himself.

In this situation, Jacob fathers his first children with Leah. Four children are born, and their names become Leah's record of the inner history of the marriage: first, Reuben—"for God has seen my affliction" and also, "Now my husband will love me"; then, Shimeon—"for God has heard that I am hated"; then, Levi—"This time my husband will become attached to me"; and then, Yehuda—"This time I will praise God." The cryptic simplicity of the fourth name—without explanation of the reason for her gratitude—becomes eloquent when set against the emotionally explicit record of loneliness, rejection, and painful hope. Perhaps, in this journal of her relations with Jacob, Leah intimates a movement toward harmony—between Jacob and herself, and between Jacob and himself. If Jacob grows to accept Leah, in all her mirroring complexity, then perhaps that indicates a growing acceptance of himself, of the *anokhi* that he had never known.

REFORMULATING EXPERIENCE

In his dream at Bethel, God had spoken to Jacob words of reassurance and promise. He had not specifically addressed the vision of the restless angels, who praise and castigate him. Responding to Jacob's fear, God had said: "Behold, I—*anokhi*—am with you" (Gen. 28:15).

Mei Ha-Shilo'ach elaborates the meaning of *anokhi*, as opposed to its apparent synonym, *ani*.[40] The difference lies in the letter *kaf*, which, as a prefix, denotes approximation—"like," "as if." God here reveals Himself as only incompletely, provisionally knowable. If Jacob is to develop a larger capacity for comprehending God, he will need to unfold the latent dimensions of his own *anokhi*.

God shows Jacob the *birurin*, the many stages of clarification he has yet to endure: the moments in which the past is revisited, rethought, and newly comprehended. Through recurring episodes of uncertainty, Jacob will develop a sensitivity to constructions of self that were never before visible. Mei Ha-Shilo'ach invokes the Talmudic aphorism: "One cannot comprehend [lit., stand upon] words of

Torah unless one has stumbled over them."[41] This dynamic vision of Jacob's future centers on an *anokhi*, a self, that grows with God and is willing to stumble, to attempt provisional solutions so as to surpass them. The movement of such a history runs through crises of ignorance and incoherence. Jacob's amplified awareness of *anokhi*, of all that he cannot yet grasp in himself and in God, is to become a *source of endless life*; errors and obstacles will be transmuted into a larger desire. The mere facts of the past, its dead weight, will be transformed into a significant history.

In Jacob's evolving sense of self, Leah plays a crucial role. She comes to him unbidden, and with her comes agitation and disorder. We remember the midrash about the "one who goes to his spouse."[42] This is Jacob, says R. Isaac Luria, in his relation to Rachel; she was the single object of his quest, the purpose of his journey.[43] Leah, on the other hand, "comes to him," undesired, unbidden. "And when morning came, she was Leah."

In his commentary to the Torah, *Beit Ya'akov*, R. Ya'akov Leiner[44] writes of these two types of marriage relationship as types of "helpmate that God sends a person." In one, a human being seeks out in full intentionality the object that will satisfy his desire, his sense of a coherent life. Rachel is the archetype of this mode, and in this sense, she remains forever Jacob's true wife. Even after the narrative of jealousy and hatred has moved, with catastrophic results, to the next generation, after Jacob has had ample opportunity to reflect on the fate of favorite sons, he will allow himself to tell Judah, son of Leah, "Two sons *my wife* bore me"; and Judah will become capable of bearing this fundamental truth of his father's life.

The other mode, however, is represented by Leah: unwittingly and unwillingly, Jacob finds her lodged in his life. She has been sent by God, she comes to him; but Jacob experiences her as a grotesque disruption of his design. Such forms of "helpmate," which appear *shelo mi-da'at*, as incoherent, inscrutable elements of experience, often bring a sense of moral dissonance with them. Paradoxically, writes R. Leiner, precisely this sort of relationship may later be understood as a source of vital power.

He cites the case of Eve—"And God *brought her* to Adam" (Gen. 2:22)—as the spouse who is experienced as intervening, even disruptive: she does, after all, bring death into Adam's world. But, in the end, he acknowledges her paradoxical vitality by naming her Chavah—"Mother of all life" (3:20). She comes to represent an uncanny value, baffling and transcending his own framework of understanding.

Jacob and Leah thus represent a turbulent matching that disrupts Jacob's world of desire. Their children, too, are problematic, the protagonists of troubling narratives: Judah and Tamar, Reuben and Bilha, Dina and Shechem. But, significantly, it is from this marriage that the Davidic—and messianic—dynasty eventually emerges.

The theme that runs through Beit Ya'akov's analysis, then, is of an apparently anomalous relationship, originally experienced as baffling and "not good," that ultimately is "clarified" as good. The *birur,* the clarification, is the transformative later revision of the narrative, when new perspectives have become visible and when one is moved to pursue different forms of meaning.

Such reformulations of experience mobilize a vital energy around the most enigmatic phenomena. Leah comes to symbolize this power of the "hidden world," in Beit Ya'akov's kabbalistic terminology. A grotesque event—like the unveiling of the *wrong* sister the morning after the wedding—may eventually be transformed in Jacob's mind; he may even come to see beauty—a generative beauty—in this complex relationship.

This use of the *birur* has a similar function to Freud's *nachtraglichkeit*—the "afterwardness," or "deferred action," by which "experiences, impressions and memory traces may be revised at a later date to fit in with fresh experiences or with the development of a new stage of development."[45] The *birur* retrospectively allows one to see what before was imperceptible. The new formulation does more than register meaning: it retranscribes memory, creating new possibilities for questioning, for reflecting on the "unthought known."[46]

A GARDEN IS NOT A TAPESTRY . . .

In her classic work, *Purity and Danger,* Mary Douglas discusses a similar phenomenon in an anthropological frame. Using the body as a basic symbolic scheme for social systems, she discusses pollution taboos as attempts by the social organism to protect itself against the dangers of boundary transgression. Vulnerable at its margins and its openings, the organism excludes forces that would disrupt internal order. Purity and coherence are compromised by anomalies of all kinds, intrusions from beyond the boundary, or bodily emissions and parings that blur the boundary in either direction. Pollution laws thus ban anything that threatens the rigid world of distinctions that defines the social structure. Dirt, defined as "matter out of place," is dangerous when it impairs the clarity of forms and meanings.

The Lele culture, for example, represents its cosmology and social order by separating and classifying certain animals and parts of animals as appropriate for men to eat, others for women, children, or pregnant women. Rejected animals, Douglas claims, turn out to be ambiguous according to their scheme of classification. Flying squirrels, for instance—neither birds nor animals—are avoided by discriminating adults. Concepts of fertility define normal human births as single, while animal births normally occur in couples or litters. Human twins are thus anomalous.

Here, however, Douglas describes the paradoxical vision of such societies: "a series of cults allow their initiates to eat what is normally dangerous, forbidden." Even the hybrid monster, the pangolin or scaly anteater, which transgresses all categories, is "reverently eaten by initiates and taken to be the most powerful source of fertility."[47] In the same way, human twin parents are ritualized as sources of fertility.

Douglas movingly discusses the "sorrowful mysteries" of such practices. Such cults "invite their initiates to turn round and confront the categories on which their whole surrounding culture has been built up and to recognize them for the fictive, man-made, arbitrary creations that they are."[48] Ambiguity is shunned and yet confronted; the dangerous anomaly releases its power for good.

A garden is not a tapestry; if all the weeds are removed, the soil is impoverished. Somehow the gardener must preserve fertility by returning what he has taken out. The special kind of treatment which some religions accord to anomalies and abominations to make them powerful for good is like turning weeds and lawn cuttings into compost.[49]

Normally, dirt, as "matter out of place," threatens order; it is "the by-product of a systematic ordering and classification of matter."[50] Since ordering involves rejecting inappropriate elements, elements that make no rational whole of experience are excluded. And yet, precisely such anomalies can be fed back into the organism and be made powerful for good. The composting metaphor exploits the paradox of two opposite yet related ways of looking at an object: the weed is pollutant, dangerous, but also a source of enrichment.

Jacob's marriage to Leah can be viewed through the prism of this metaphor. Jacob first perceives Leah as, literally, "out of place": an alien element in his life. But "a garden is not a tapestry." Two different models of beauty set up a field of tension. Immaculate purity of design occurs rarely in human experience. As against Rachel's harmonious beauty, which evokes a tapestry world of perfect design, Leah comes to represent the world of ambiguity that disrupts his conscious ordering. She and her children will release their power for good: weeds turned into compost strangely enrich the garden. What has been avoided, repudiated, becomes a source of fertility, and, perhaps, of a different aesthetic. Her "soft eyes" evade classic norms of beauty, telling of danger and desire.

It is striking that the midrash imputes to Jacob a fundamental concern that there should be no *p'solet*, no foreign body, no "matter out of place," in his family life. This is a concern that all his children, without exception, should form part of the complex organism of Israel. His father and grandfather both fathered children who were not included in the family destiny; he wishes that none of his many, varied offspring may be repudiated. His bed is to be whole.[51] Its integrity remains his concern till the end of his life. But the ideal of integrity comes to include the work of integration. From the night when Leah is given to him, the notion of purity is constantly challenged.

"Purity is the enemy of change," writes Douglas. She quotes Sartre's bitter attack on the anti-Semite and his old yearning for impermeability . . . there are people who are attracted by the permanence of stone. They would like to be solid and impenetrable, they do not want change: for who knows what change might bring? . . . They have no wish to acquire ideas, they want them to be innate . . . they want to adopt a mode of life in which reasoning and the quest for truth play only a subordinate part . . . in which one never becomes anything else but what one already was.[52]

If this fantasy yearning for rigidity characterizes the anti-Semite, that is because, for Sartre, the Jew represents precisely the contrary mode of life, in which "reasoning and the quest for truth" play a decisive role. But Douglas is critical of Sartre's too-clear division between the anti-Semite and the rest of humanity: "The yearning for rigidity is in us all."

THE WAY OF IGNORANCE

In Jacob, who will become Israel, precisely this yearning for impermeability—in which "one never becomes anything else but what one already was"—is repeatedly challenged. He encounters the darkness of the night at Bethel and of the night in which Leah comes to him. Both nights bring him to acknowledge the way of ignorance, the way of dispossession. Incoherence and discontinuity compel him beyond the limits of his conscious understanding.

At Bethel, he woke from his sleep with a revelation: "God is in this place! And I—I did not know." We remember the Zohar's reading: "I have never known my self." Jacob's *anokhi*, which could identify itself so promptly as Esau, is a stranger to the "simple man living in tents." He has never known, never integrated his *anokhi*, composed its conflicts, its different voices.

Jacob's first awareness of a ladder in tension between heaven and earth, of the agitated angels, comes to him in *this place*, the place he has avoided all his life, the site of his father's terror. Essentially, his fear of his father's *Akedah* experience has deprived him of a father. Metaphorically, Abraham has become his father. Perhaps he would rather identify with the father who will survive than with the son who almost died before he could himself become a father. In a sense, therefore, Jacob has resisted imagining himself as the son of a father who was almost killed before Jacob could be born. Mount Moriah has become the unthinkable place where Jacob's very being is in question.

According to Rashi and his midrashic sources, this is the place toward which Jacob finally returns, consenting but violently dislocated, in a rush of time and space. An abrasive collision takes place and his perception shifts. Suddenly, he is praying his own original prayer. According to Ma'or Va-Shemesh, he suddenly becomes aware of a gap, a "shape of absence"[53] in his perception. The "secret of Torah" had been his, but the "secret of prayer" had not; and only now, because of God-in-this-place, does he begin to know that absence, whose shape has been waiting, unfelt, to be filled.

The secret of prayer begins to reveal itself to him in this place. I suggest that the secret of Torah and the secret of prayer represent a polarity similar to that of Rachel and Leah. The secret of Torah is the experience of intellectual mastery; in the life of study, one aims to discern significant structures, to classify knowledge and compose it into harmonious relation. The power of the intellect controls chaos and creates meaning. This is an aesthetic as well as an intellectual experience. One goes toward one's spouse, according to one's best lights. The secret of prayer, on the other hand, is constituted by the unwilled collision with the avoided place, with the unknown self, with the unchosen bride. Here, consciousness and control fail, and a fastidious, predetermined sense of beauty may receive a jolt. In this place, one can only sleep and dream of restless angels and of a God whose *anokhi* remains always provisional, always "as though."

Out of this experience, a new prayer—*arvit*—is generated. The prayer in darkness is the essential prayer,[54] in which a human *anokhi*—too complex for easy composure—meets the divine *anokhi*. In such a prayer, conflict, terror, vulnerability—the knowledge that one is not master in one's own house—may strangely become a "source of endless life."

In the course of two dark nights, Jacob confronts the self that will endure many revisitings and revisions in the course of a turbulent life. His recurrent experience of darkness, of ignorance and dispos-

session, will enter into generative interplay with that masterful
sense of self that is represented by the secret of Torah. Since he has
lain on Isaac's altar, he has regained for himself a father. "And he was
afraid and said, 'How fearful is this place!' " (Gen. 28:17). Through the
very experience of fear, he has gained access both to his father and to
God. The way of ignorance brings Jacob to a place of encounter with
himself, his father, and God. " 'He collided with *the place [Ha-
Makom]': God* encountered him."[55]

The abrasive impact alters him, breaks him open: becoming a son
to his father releases him to father his own children. No longer
flinching from the secret of prayer, he can move into the complex
world of his two marriages. Leah brings him to the gate of fatherhood: a more intimate acceptance of what has come to him unbidden, a willingness to revise his sense of beauty, so that it can become
fertile.

TEN

The Pit and the Rope

Recovering Joseph

*His desire to set a beginning to the chain of events to which he
belonged encountered the same difficulty that it always does:
the fact that everybody has a father, that nothing comes first
and of itself, its own cause, but that everybody is begotten and
points backwards, deeper down into the depths of beginnings,
the bottoms and abysses of the well of the past.*

Thomas Mann, *Joseph and His Brothers*

THE PACT OF SILENCE

Perhaps the most poignant moment in the saga of Joseph and his
brothers is the moment when Jacob is confronted with his son
Joseph's bloodied coat:

And he said, "It is my son's coat! A wild beast has devoured
him—Joseph has been torn by a beast!" (Gen. 37:33)

Rashi comments, hauntingly and cryptically:

The Holy Spirit flickered in him; for these words may be taken
to mean that Potiphar's wife would attack Joseph. Why did God
not reveal to him that Joseph was still alive? Because the brothers had placed a ban or a curse on anyone who would reveal the
truth, and they had included God in their pact of silence.[1]

On this reading, Jacob is not unequivocally convinced of Joseph's
death. Against the grain of the biblical narrative, in which Jacob falls
into the pit his sons have dug for him, emphatically identifying the
coat and interpreting its unavoidable meaning—"A wild beast has
devoured him—Joseph has been torn by a beast!"—Rashi tells of

Jacob tormented by "flickers" of uncanny intuition. He experiences sporadic "flashes" of "the Holy Spirit," moments of piercing vision of an alternative reality. Here, Joseph is alive, vulnerable to another "wild beast"—Potiphar's wife. This metaphorical understanding of his own words visits Jacob implausibly but compellingly. From now on, he will be unable to reconcile himself to Joseph's death ("And he refused to be comforted" [Gen. 37:35]): his own words will stammer in ambiguity, as visions appear and disappear.[2]

Why does God torment him in this way? Why these spasms of vision, rather than a clear divine communication? Rashi's midrashic answer baffles and intrigues the reader: the brothers have framed a pact of silence that includes God Himself. In what sense is God compelled by a human silence? How is His freedom to speak curbed by the brothers' ban?

The narrative continues:

Jacob rent his clothes, put sackcloth on his loins, and mourned for his son many days. All his sons and daughters sought to comfort him; but he refused to be comforted, saying, "No, I will go down mourning to my son in Sheol." And his father wept for him. (Gen. 37:34–36)

The description of Jacob's inconsolable mourning comes to a climax in the last sentence: "And his father wept for him." Is this not rather anticlimactic? Who weeps here and for whom? Even the syntax suggests a doubt: if the subject of the passage is Jacob, perhaps it is *Jacob's* father who weeps for *him*?

This is Rashi's midrashic narrative:

"And his father wept for him": Isaac would weep at Jacob's pain. But he did not mourn, for he knew that Joseph was alive.

The source midrash continues:

And why did Isaac not reveal the truth to him? He said: If God has not revealed it, should I reveal it?[3]

An uncanny silence now surrounds Jacob. His children, his father, and his God all know the truth, but all are bonded in a pact of silence. Mysterious and absolute, this silence isolates Jacob for the next twenty-two years, until Joseph finally reveals himself in Egypt. Then, we read, "And Jacob's spirit came to life" (Gen. 45:27). These words describe a resurrection. Jacob has been walled up in a silence that has separated him from God and from human beings; as the silence of his children, and of his God, fell on him twenty-two years ago, his spiritual life went into limbo.[4]

TESTIMONIES

In a sense, the pact of silence around Joseph's fate and around that day at the pit affects the reader, too. Indeed, the story of that day and its horrors is strangely blurred, even, at some points, contradictory. The Bible testifies to a confusion that leaves the reader unable to envision a clear narrative sequence. Most striking are the inconsistencies that inform the narrative of Joseph's sale: Judah proposes to sell him to the Ishmaelites, his brothers agree, and then we read:

> And *Midianite* traders passed by and drew Joseph up out of the pit and sold Joseph to the *Ishmaelites* for twenty pieces of silver, and they brought Joseph to Egypt. . . . And the *Midanites* sold him to Egypt. (Gen. 37:28,36)[5]

Passed from hand to hand, Joseph disappears in the contradictions of the story. What, in fact, happened to him on that fateful day?

A more subtle, and more significant, ambiguity informs the question of Joseph's reaction to his brothers' rage. This ambiguity is connected with the conflicting accounts of the sequence of events by the pit. Reuben modifies the brothers' original plan (" 'Let us kill him and throw him into one of the pits' " [Gen. 37:20]). Testifying to his good intentions ("And Reuben heard them and saved Joseph from their hands" [37:21]), the Bible records his words: " 'Let us not take his life.' And Reuben went on, 'Do not shed blood! Throw him into that pit in the wilderness, but do not touch him with your own hands!' " (37:22). His brothers comply. They strip Joseph of his coat of many colors and throw him into the pit. Reuben's plea is principled but impersonal: the taboo of murder, of blood-on-the-hands, inspires him. There is little personal feeling for Joseph. To throw him into a pit is simply "white-collar murder," a more elegant form of bloodshed.[6]

Twenty-two years later, the brothers stand in Joseph's court. Accused of spying, they speak among themselves:

> "Indeed, we are guilty because of our brother, because we saw the anguish of his spirit as he pleaded with us and yet we did not listen. That is why this distress has come upon us." And Reuben said to them, "Did I not tell you, 'Do not sin against the child'? But you would not listen. Now comes the reckoning for his blood." (Gen. 42:21–22)

Now Reuben tells a different story: by the pit, he pleaded with them not to "sin against the child," and they refused to listen to him. He remembers speaking with a religious pathos and a compassion for "the child" that was quite absent from the original account. Which version of that day's events is the true one?

Ramban suggests that both versions are true: the biblical account of Reuben's impersonal plea omitted an earlier plea in which Reuben spoke more passionately and compassionately. But it was only the later, minimal appeal that was "heard" by the brothers; and therefore it is only that appeal that is recorded in the biblical narrative. Twenty-two years later, Reuben's "unheard" plea suddenly returns to memory. It is "heard" for the first time, by the brothers, by Reuben himself, by the reader. For the first time, therefore, it can be entered into the record as testimony; at the traumatic moment by the pit, it simply fell on deaf ears.

Similarly, Joseph's response as his brothers hurl him into the pit is unrecorded in the original account. Only after twenty-two years, his brothers suddenly "hear," *for the first time*, what then they had merely "seen, but not heard": "the anguish of his spirit as he pleaded with us." The guilt they suddenly perceive is for a callousness so total that it obliterates the scream even as they register it visually. (Edvard Munch's painting *The Scream* comes to mind.)

Why, indeed, does the original account not tell of Joseph's desperate entreaties for his own life? Ramban answers that it is quite obvious that the victim, gripped by mortal terror, would beseech in this way: the obvious does not need to be narrated. Or—alternatively—that, in the interests of narrative economy, the Bible distributes the details of the story between the two accounts (chapters 37, 42). Or—most interestingly—that the narrative condenses the tale of horror in its most horrifying aspect, so that the brothers' crime is left somewhat obscured. To have dwelt on Joseph's anguish of terror would have irreparably damned the brothers in the eyes of the reader.

I suggest that Joseph's anguish by the pit goes unrecorded *precisely because* the brothers did not hear it. No testimony can be offered to cries that fell on deaf ears. Only after twenty-two years, and triggered by an almost fortuitous set of circumstances, the brothers suddenly hear *for the first time* how their brother cried for his life. " '*Indeed [aval]* we are guilty,' " evokes a startled sense of contingency about this perception: a chance concatenation of events—Joseph's demand that one of their number be imprisoned (Gen. 42:18–20)—triggers a sudden retrieval of the past.[7]

"JOSEPH IS NOT"

Strictly speaking, however, the past has not been retrieved: it has been encountered for the first time. In some real sense, Joseph and his screams had been absent from the historical moment by the pit. Indeed, to be thrown into a pit in the wilderness is to have one's cries go unheard: one disappears and one's voice is lost.[8] In an uncanny figuration of this absence, the biblical text gives us Reuben's horrified reaction when he returns to the pit: "and behold there was *no Joseph [ein yosef]* in the pit; and he tore his garments. And he turned to his brothers and said, 'The child *is not [einenu]*, and as for me, where shall I go?' " (Gen. 37:29–30). The Zohar comments: Reuben is not told of Joseph's sale; he therefore experiences the pure horror of the empty pit. There is no body, nothing to bear witness to, no basis for a narrative. A corpse is the minimal residue of a "speakable" murder. Now, what testimony to his brother's fate can Reuben offer? He tears his clothes in token of mourning; but this mourning is for an absence, a scotoma, a loss of voice.

Joseph is not. At the narrative level, Joseph is indeed blanked out, his responses silenced. In the end, not only his brothers but his readers are deaf to his anguish. Deliberately, he is excised from the record of that day. For the most part, the reader remains unaware of a scotoma, of an anguished absence. The midrashic reader, however, is, with a cunning ferocity, reminded of Joseph's pain:

> The brothers said, "Let us sell him to the Ishmaelites who will carry him off to the end of the wilderness." So they sold him for twenty silver pieces—that is, two silver pieces each, enough to buy shoes for their feet. But can you imagine that such a beautiful boy was sold for only twenty silver pieces? But when he was thrown into the pit, terror of its serpents and scorpions transformed his face—all color fled and it turned green. That is why he was sold for only twenty silver pieces for ten pairs of shoes.[9]

As a result of the terror of the pit, Joseph's market value has plunged. With satirical and unsentimental circumstantiality, the midrash intimates the unspeakable: an experience that leaves Joseph almost unrecognizable. His pallor and his financial worth registers an inferno survived. What has been lost is his face, his blood, his market value. What, then, has survived?

That this is a real question is indicated by certain sparse clues in the narrative, which the midrash amplifies. Joseph, archetype of success, of a life charmed by God's presence, emerges with apparent triumph from every pit. In Potiphar's house, and, later, in prison,[10] he rises to power; finally, he finds himself on the viceregal throne of Egypt. But when he comes to name his firstborn son, he calls him Menasseh—forgetfulness: " 'for God has made me forget completely my suffering and the house of my father' " (Gen. 41:51). Joseph has forgotten his history, himself. Strange occasion for celebration!

The midrash amplifies:

"And his master saw that God was with him" (Gen. 39:3). But in the end he forgot, as it is written, " 'for God has made me forget completely my suffering and the house of my father.' " R. Huna in the name of R. Acha said, "He whispered to himself as he walked in and out of his master's house."[11]

The Rabbis describe a losing battle. Joseph tries to keep God with him. According to R. Huna, he even mutters constantly the words of his father's house as he moves through his master's house. But in the end, he forgot. And he names his first child for that oblivion. For if he is to survive his own unwitnessed death in the pit, he must forget his father's house, his past, himself. He must "bury the dead witness" inside himself.[12] Or that, at least, is part of the truth of such survival. The other part is intimated in the irony of naming one's child Amnesia! A will to forget lives in tension with a project of memory. A conscious strategy of mute survival is undercut as it enacts itself.

The anguish of memory and forgetting in Joseph's history is re-evoked at the moment when he sees his brothers again, twenty-two years after the pit:

And Joseph saw his brothers and he recognized them. And he made himself strange to them and spoke harshly to them. . . . And Joseph recognized his brothers, but they did not recognize him. (Gen. 42:7–8)

Beyond the asymmetrical drama of recognition and nonrecognition, there is the enigma of "He made himself strange to them." This reflexive verb suggests a more-than-tactical move of self-disguise on Joseph's part. Within himself, he becomes alien to himself. It is striking that the Hebrew word for "self-estrangement" *(va-yitnaker)* shares the same root as the word for "recognition" *(va-yaker)*. As Rashi points out, the brothers had not "recognized" him at the pit, had had no compassion for him. The result is that he cannot know himself, cannot relate to his past in compassion for himself. Only through a radical act of self-cauterization can he proceed to a limited experience of memory: "And Joseph remembered the dreams he had dreamt about them" (Gen. 42:9). But if he is to have compassion for them, to "recognize" them as his brothers, he will have to retrieve himself from the pit, to recognize himself, have compassion for himself.

EXILE OF THE WORD

For Joseph has experienced a primal scene of horror that has, effectively, annihilated him as witness to his own experience. Testimony has become, in a real sense, impossible; where there is no imaginable "Thou" to whom to tell the story, one cannot say "Thou" even to oneself. God Himself falls mute, turns His face aside.

The sense of belonging to a "secret order" that is sworn to silence lies at the very heart of Joseph's trauma.[13] We remember the pact of silence ordained by Joseph's brothers, a pact that bonds and bounds all alike, victim, perpetrator, bystanders, God himself. Here, by the pit, exile begins; in the most intimate sense, one's own experience falls mute, unexperienced, unthought.

The muteness that is born of the pit is, I suggest, the muteness of Joseph unable to send word to his father of his survival. The question is an old one, most famously framed by Ramban: Why, at least from the time of his rise to power, does he not communicate with his father whom he knows to be suffering the anguish of bereavement?[14] The question is never raised in the text itself. And yet, buried, silenced, it rises irrepressibly, endangering the plot and the reader's conception of the characters of this narrative. Many answers have been offered; but Joseph's silence will not be explained away. It is the very heart of the story. For he, too, is involved in the pact that his brothers have imposed on their world. One midrashic source articulates this essential silence precisely in terms of the enigmatic power of the pact:

> Why did Joseph not let his father know at once that he was alive in Egypt all those twenty-two years? When his brothers declared their ban on revealing the truth, they included Joseph, too: he, too, would not reveal the truth. They also included God Himself.[15]

Bonded and bounded in a silence in which God Himself is implicated, Joseph has lost his voice; he has lost himself, as witness, as survivor. The traumatic void is, for Freud, the result of survival itself: the victim of a "shocking accident" is never fully conscious at the time of the accident. The void exists within the experience itself, so that it is not simply forgotten and later repeated, but it is first experienced at all only in and through its forgetting. The victim, says Freud, "gets away apparently unharmed."[16] Joseph escapes the pit, all the pits of his life, and rises irrepressibly to success: at least in the eyes of the observer, "God is with him." But his traumatic history is beyond access. Accompanied by an amnesia, it has not been integrated into consciousness. Indeed, flashbacks ("And Joseph remembered his dreams"), the "unerring 'engraving' on the mind," the " 'etching into the brain' of an event in trauma" may, modern neurobiologists have suggested, be associated with the elision of its normal encoding in memory. The event cannot be placed within the schemes of intelligence, of the "wisdom" for which Joseph is so celebrated.[17] The "history that a flashback tells . . . is, therefore, a history that literally *has no place,* neither in the past, in which it was not fully experienced, nor in the present, in which its precise images and enactments are not fully understood."[18]

Ultimately, Joseph's history raises the question, "What does it mean to survive?" If he has, in some essential way, missed the experience of his own death and survival, how is he to return to life and to language? In a most poignant passage, Primo Levi narrates a recurring nightmare in Auschwitz. He has survived and is telling his story, "this very story." But his listeners do not follow him; they are indifferent. "My sister looks at me, gets up and goes away without a word." The desolating grief that is now born in him makes him waken with some relief to the defined suffering of Auschwitz. Awake, he remembers that this is the dream of many others, perhaps of everyone. This is "pain in its pure state," says Levi, "like certain barely remembered pains of one's early infancy."[19]

For such pain, what healing? Paul Celan, the poet of the Holocaust whose lifework focuses, precisely, on the loss of voice, on the exile of the word, nevertheless maintains with a rigorous hope,

"This, the language, was not lost but remained, yes, in spite of everything. But it had to pass through its own answerlessness, pass through a frightful falling mute, pass through the thousand darknesses of death-bringing speech. . . . These are the efforts of someone . . . also shelterless in a sense undreamt-of till now and thus most uncannily out in the open, who *goes with his very being to language, stricken by and seeking reality*"[20] (emphasis added).

Only by turning toward one's wound—the wound of reality— only from within that wound—can the event become accessible. "Shelterless," vulnerable, "answerless," language must "pass through the thousand darknesses of death-bringing speech." For the testimonial power of language to work, however, a listening Other is required. "The history of a trauma . . . can only take place through the listening of another."[21] For Joseph, does such a healing moment occur?

THE PIT AND THE ROPE

I suggest that it does occur, but in a fragmentary, suspended manner. The moment of healing is precipitated by Judah, as he breaks through the line of his brothers ("And Judah came close to him" [Gen. 44:18]) and speaks with passion into Joseph's ear. This speech, a long, poignant account of the history of the bereaved father, has the ultimate effect of making Joseph break down: "And Joseph could no longer restrain himself" (45:1). A long silence, the silence of survival, collapses, and Joseph gives his sole testimony to the past: " 'I am Joseph your brother whom you sold to Egypt' " (45:3). These are the only words in which Joseph ever bears witness to that day in the pit. With them, there begins the passage through answerlessness, through the exile of the word.

What makes Joseph's testimony possible? What, in Judah's story, collapses the structure of an old pact? Objectively, his account lacks novelty. It focuses on Jacob's suffering: "our father" and "my father" recur endlessly. But the sentence that accesses Joseph's pain is the final one: " 'For how can I go back to my father if the boy is not with me? Let me not be witness to the evil that would befall my father!' "

(Gen. 44:34). With this sentence, Judah speaks his own strong testimony—to himself, to the past, to a kind of witnessing that he now knows to be unbearable. For the first time after the years of silence, Judah finds a way of using language to access an intimate reality. Essentially, his plea to the enigmatic Egyptian viceroy is: "Keep me here in prison, in place of Benjamin—for I *could not bear* the alternative—to witness my father's pain, if Benjamin, too, disappears." That is, he imagines himself as eyewitness to his father's anguish and, in a language of broken pathos, discovers a new truth: this is simply not bearable.

Not bearable, that is, for him, who, thereby, bears witness to the past and its unbearableness. Judah's language has passed through its own "answerlessness": " 'What shall we say to my lord, what shall we speak, and how shall we justify ourselves?' " (Gen. 44:16). He begins his speech by abandoning mastery, the glib narrative of understanding. "A strange lostness / Was palpably present" (Celan). He passes through the crisis of language, by going "with his very being to language, stricken by and seeking reality."[22]

But this is language that has lost possession of the truth and that performs its own capacity to come upon truth. This unpredictable truth that Judah comes upon (" 'How can I witness the evil that would befall my father?' ") is personal and transformative. Nowhere does he use the privileged vocabulary of religious authority: the name of God is not mentioned in his speech. But as the Talmud points out, his own name contains the letters of God's name:[23] through his wrenching act of testimony, he makes God palpable within the lostness of the world.

The Hasidic master Sefat Emet describes this transformative moment:

> "And Judah came close to him" (Gen. 44:18): "To him"—to Joseph. But also, "to his own Self—to himself." And also, "to Him—to God." For indeed, Judah said nothing new in his speech, had no legal plea to make to Joseph. Nevertheless, since he accessed the reality of his narrative, salvation came to him, as in "Truth springs up from the earth" (Ps. 85:12).[24]

The midrash tells that Truth is splintered into a thousand pieces when God throws it to the earth.[25] It is now to be found within the human world piecemeal, fragmented, often in the form of broken narratives of personal struggle. Judah's speech to Joseph becomes the prototype of such narratives. Ultimately, Sefat Emet daringly affirms, Judah accesses Joseph, and himself, and God—as though these are three dimensions of the same act. To come to his own self is to come to God. And to come to Joseph is to save both himself and God from the deadly muteness of the past.

It is this enigmatic effect of Judah on Joseph that the midrash addresses most powerfully:

> It is written, "Deep waters are counsel in a man's heart" (Prov. 20:5). This can be compared to a deep well full of cold water—its water was cold and fresh, but no one could drink it. Then someone came and tied rope to rope, cord to cord, string to string, and drew the water and drank. Then, everyone began to draw the water and drink. In the same way, Judah did not stir till he had responded to Joseph, word by word, and had reached his heart.[26]

In order to retrieve the fresh, cold water at the bottom of the deep well, all the improvizations of a Judah are necessary. He approaches the hiddenness, the silent absence of Joseph with an intuition about deep pits and deep wells. Cognitively, he knows nothing of Joseph's identity. But, the midrash affirms, Joseph is a pent-up spirit, spellbound by a twenty-year silence. Paradoxically, the depth of his silence intimates his potential power for good, if the water can only be brought to the surface. Only by a process of words, by Judah's willingness to live through an unpredictable trial of language (rope to rope, cord to cord), is Joseph to be released, to the benefit of all. Unconsciously, Judah frames his words to access Joseph's hidden heart. Rope by rope, cord by cord, he speaks precociously, beyond his means; he feeds his testimony downward into the listening of another.

The effect of such a testimony is to restore Joseph to the world of language, to the possibilities of a redemptive connection with his past, his family, and his future. He utters a brief—too brief—testimony to the past. But "his brothers could not answer him, for they were dumbfounded before him" (Gen. 45:3). A dangerous silence greets his testimony. Instead of triumphal closure, mutual confessions, and admissions, the Torah gives us a confounded silence that Joseph tries to break with a long speech of forgiveness. But this speech, I suggest, is precisely not the kind of witness to himself and to the past that might have retrieved the true selves of Joseph, his brothers, and God. The old pact of silence is not broken. Indeed, after Joseph speaks, the silence endures. It is only when he embraces his brothers and "cries over them" that they respond: "And *after that,* his brothers spoke with him" (45:15).

THE LIGHT OF HIS FACE?

It seems that Joseph's noble speech of forgiveness does nothing to dispel the silence. Its very nobility perhaps represents an avoidance of pain, of reality. It is only when he abandons the moral high ground and cries *for them* that the current of language is released between them.[27]

What is it that sustains the dangerous silence between him and his brothers? We read that "His brothers could not answer him, for they were dumbfounded before him." In Hebrew, however, "they were dumbfounded before *his face [mi-panav]*." It is something in his face that affects them. The great Hasidic commentator R. Zadok Ha-Cohen reads: "When Joseph revealed himself to them, he no longer hid the light of his face from them. At that moment, they truly recognized him, and were dumbfounded by the light in his face."[28]

This is an apocalyptic moment, when the light of Joseph's face, so long obscured, is suddenly unveiled. In other words, Joseph, who, in some real sense, *was not,* who had been lost to all, even to himself, is suddenly present again. Sefat Emet, reading the unnecessary emphasis on *Joseph's* making himself known to his brothers,[29] goes as far as to claim, "Apparently, Joseph had previously not been Joseph at all!"[30]

It seems that the light of the face can recede, making way for another face. This may even be a normal, cyclical occurrence: "The light of a person's face on Shabbat is not the same as during the week."[31] Perhaps it is part of the human accommodation with the world to bear a dual identity, in which full inwardness is revealed to a greater or lesser extent.

In Joseph's case, the long-hidden light suddenly flares out, with blinding, or "dumbfounding," effect. For his father, Jacob, the survival of Joseph's face is occasion for joy: "Now I can die, since I have seen your face, that you are still alive" (Gen. 46:30). But what does it mean for the light of one's face to survive? For the survivor to be able to witness to himself?

That this question is not redundant in relation to Joseph is indicated in a deeply ambiguous midrash. Joseph has sent his brothers home to his father with news of Joseph's survival, and with wagons—*agalot*. Jacob's "heart went numb, for he did not believe them. But when they recounted all that Joseph had said to them, and when he saw the wagons that Joseph had sent to transport him, the spirit of their father Jacob revived." (Gen. 45:27). This is Rashi's version of the midrash:[32]

> "All that Joseph had said to them": He had given them a sign, as evidence of his identity—what he had been studying with his father at the time they parted: the law of the Heifer *(eglah)* that had its neck broken (Deut. 21:6). That is why the text says, "He saw the wagons [*agalot*—here meaning Heifer] that Joseph had sent," instead of "that Pharaoh had sent."

In the midrash, Joseph is indicating to his father that he remembers what they were studying together on that fateful day when his father sent him to Shechem, to the pit. "When I separated from you, was it not the teaching of the Heifer whose neck is to be broken that I was studying?" On one level, the midrash represents Joseph as testifying to his past, to what unites him with his father. He is not only identifying himself but intimating that the light of his face is still present; that he remembers the essential words that give purpose to his family's life; that he is still Joseph.

However, as the version of the midrash found in the Zohar makes clear, Joseph testifies also to rupture and anguish. For the law of the

Heifer refers to the case of an unidentified corpse, found between cities, the murderer unknown: in this case, the elders of the nearest city break a heifer's neck, wash their hands over the heifer, and declare, "Our hands did not shed this blood." Commenting on the act of absolution, the Talmud in *Sotah* adds to the elders' speech, "We did not let this man depart without provisions or proper escort."[33] One can be absolved of responsibility for the anonymous death only if every humane, civilized norm of behavior toward the traveler was observed. Otherwise, one's hands are stained with his blood.

The Zohar picks up on this Talmudic requirement and reads Joseph's coded message to his father as a bitter complaint: "He sent him a *remez*, a hint to be decoded . . . 'No one accompanied me on my way, nor did anyone feed me, on that day I parted from you.' "[34] In a veiled and encoded manner, Joseph is testifying to himself, to the abandoned boy whom even his father had not protected. Since the message is contained in an elaborate pun on wagon/Heifer (*agalah/eglah*) and on a visual impression carried over to a name that evokes a different name, it is cryptic. It is also ambiguous, readable, as we have seen, either as a message of reassurance and continuity or as one of rupture. In the Zohar's version, Joseph gives testimony from inside the world of death; essentially, he tells Jacob, "I am that dead body." By conveying his testimony through the displaced imagery of wagons and heifers, he brings it home in the shared language of family law and culture.

The Joseph who sends such a message knows death from within. His face cannot be the same face that parted from Jacob twenty-two years ago; nor can its light be the same light. As we have seen, the midrash conveys the sense of a face transformed by terror, its beauty effaced in the pit. If his *panim* is barely recognizable, that surely represents something of his *p'nim*, his inward being.

In this narrative, there is no retrieving that pristine light. But like the shattered Truth that God throws down to earth, the fragments of Joseph's light can be recomposed. By improvising, by following the thread of truth, "stricken by and seeking reality," Joseph may access a new, darker light. Or will he, in spite of everything, simply retrieve his true self, so that his face shines with the old light, while his deathly history drops away? In the midrash, this is perhaps the optimistic message of the wagons: I remember the Torah we shared, I am unchanged, we will resume where we left off.

But in the Zohar's darker reading, too, there is hope. For if Joseph cannot bear explicit witness to his death and resurrection, his language can, through the words of Torah, and within the intimacy of two—father and son—who learn Torah together, pass through its own answerlessness. And if the original light of his face is irretrievable, the light born of the "thousand darknesses" has its own brilliance. It can strike his brothers dumb with its radiant and dangerous testimony. It can also pierce his father's heart, with the conviction that Joseph has survived.

ELEVEN

"What If Joseph Hates Us?"

Closing the Book

INSCRUTABLE REVELATION

Genesis ends with a formal sense of closure. In the only deathbed scene in the Torah, Jacob blesses his twelve sons; with deliberate gravity, he repeats his final wish to be buried in the Cave of Machpelah in the Holy Land. In a potent physical gesture as he utters his parting words, he draws his legs into the bed and expires. The language is ceremonious and poetical and permeated with a sense of history. Joseph, too, expresses his mourning in an unprecedentedly lavish scene of grief, flinging himself on his father's face, weeping over him, kissing him. And, in obeying his father's instructions, he emphasizes that he is fulfilling an oath, that this is an act of piety that consummates his filial relation to Jacob. The burial, too, is enacted in a public and "heavy"[1] style. Like a stone on a grave, these descriptions communicate closure: no ghosts will rise from this place. Jacob's life is over, the time of the patriarchs is past, and the book of Genesis can be closed.

However, a more ominous version of closure arises from Rashi's first comment on this *parashah*. He comments on a graphic peculiarity in the way the text is inscribed in the *sefer Torah* (the Scroll of the Law):

> Why is this *parashah* totally closed? Because as soon as our father Jacob departed this life, the hearts and eyes of Israel were closed [their eyes became dim and their hearts troubled], because of the misery of the slavery that began at that time. Another reason is: because he wished to reveal to his sons the date of the End of Days, but the vision was closed [obscured] from him.[2]

The new *parashah* is written without a break from the end of the previous one. Normally, an "open" *parashah* begins on a new line, while a "closed" (*satum*—blocked) *parashah* allows only nine letter spaces to mark the gap. Here the lack of any space between readings makes this *parashah* the "most closed" in the entire Torah.³ No punctuation marks the beginning of this new section of the Torah. This technical peculiarity becomes the basis of two metaphorical stories of "closings." In the first, Jacob's death brings about the beginning of slavery, which "closes the heart and eyes" of his children; in the second, a revelation is blocked at the very moment that Jacob attempts to tell it. In both versions, a vision is obscured, a kind of blank descends.

The Egyptian slavery, of course, began only after Jacob's children had themselves died. Exodus begins with an account of the process by which that slavery came about. What Rashi is suggesting is that even during their own lifetime, Jacob's children already sense the beginning of slavery; at Jacob's death, a fog settles over their heart and eyes. This purely internal sense of vital blockage is intensified in the Zohar's account, where slavery is not mentioned at all, only the blockage of heart and eyes.⁴

In Rashi's second explanation, it is Jacob himself who is blocked, as he attempts to *reveal the end*. This theme—the withdrawal of the Shekhinah (God's presence), the withdrawal of vision, the sudden disappearance of words of blessing or prophecy—becomes a repeated motif in Rashi's commentary on Jacob's death. It recurs when he blesses his grandchildren;⁵ and again as he begins his deathbed blessings.⁶ There, too, Jacob is described as wishing to *reveal the end,* to communicate prophecy rather than blessing, in the usual sense. To *reveal the end* is to give definite form to the endlessness of history, to date the end of days, to shed light on the darkness of exile. And indeed, Jacob begins to communicate just this: " 'Gather round that I may tell you what is to befall you in the end of days' " (Gen. 49:1). But his vision is occluded; "he began to speak of other things." Jacob's last words to his children, emerging from the blank that descends upon him, are *other things*. In essence, they are neither prophecy nor blessing; they are defined as absence—absence of the Shekhinah, absence of revelation.

Our original sense of Jacob's death as ceremonious closure, then, is significantly qualified by Rashi's midrashic reading. Instead of closure—the formal speeches in which Jacob's living will is communicated—there is the sense of a vision that eludes Jacob's grasp. Instead of a coherent ending to a life and a book, there are intimations already of the new epoch of exile.

The graphic clue to these inchoate experiences is the run-on writing in the *sefer Torah*. Unlike a book, however, which can be closed as it ends and replaced by the next volume, the *sefer Torah* is a scroll, with volumes winding continuously out of one another. To mark the end of a *parashah*, a minimal space is normally required. This is the space that makes reading possible, breaking the text into readable portions. An "open" *parashah* allows more space than a "closed" one; but, in this "most closed" *parashah*, the density of the writing is unrelieved by any gap. What is hidden, blocked, then, is the *parashah* break. The very meaning of the word *parashah* is "separateness": the run-on text obscures this separateness, the thinkable unit of meaning.

Like punctuation marks, the spaces allow meaning to be constructed.

> What purpose did the pauses serve? To give Moses an interval to contemplate between one teaching and another, and between one issue and another. If one who listened to the mouth of God and who spoke by divine inspiration yet needed to contemplate between teaching and teaching, and between issue and issue, how much more does an ordinary person who listens to another person![7]

An interval to contemplate between . . . This human cognitive need is frustrated by the graphic layout of this "most closed" *parashah*. For Rashi and his midrashic sources, the effect on the reader conveys something of the experience of the protagonists in the narrative: Jacob's children feel a darkness descend on their ability to read the world; Jacob himself can no longer *reveal the end*. Quite literally, he can no longer read the ending of the story of exile. In this condition, without space or breath, exile becomes endless, resists meaningful construction or interpretation.

Even before physical slavery begins, then, Jacob and his children already have intimations of a wilderness world, unmarked, meaningless. Sefat Emet articulates the paradox:[8] if Jacob had been able to reveal that *there is an end* to exile, then exile would have lost its grip on them. But since they had to experience exile, he could not reveal that *there is an end*. The secret—that there is a structure, a meaning to the condition of exile—cannot be revealed; but Jacob's desire to reveal it *is* revealed, together with the fact that he is blocked. Obliquely, then, as the Zohar intimates, the secret is revealed:[9] by speaking of *other things,* Jacob communicates, however obscurely, that the history of exile *has an end*. Now begins the condition of *hester* (hiddenness), where meaning is inscrutable—and yet, in some sense, readable in its very inscrutability.

Read in this obscure light, the ending of Genesis becomes problematic. A "blocked" world, without punctuation, offers itself, and threatens to block the eyes and the heart. How is meaning to be read in such a text? How is the secret—that there is an ending—to be accessed in the world of exile?

UNNERVING POSSIBILITIES

On the surface, all is clear: a life comes to an end, many words are spoken—blessing, prophecy, burial instructions. But all these words are *other words,* other things. Something has been hidden, so that it can no longer be communicated. An impossible word haunts these many *other* words.

After the death and burial of the father what remains is, once again, Joseph and his brothers. In this relationship, there remains a secret, long buried. While Jacob was alive, it could remain buried, forgotten. But once he is gone, the ground begins to stir:

> After burying his father, Joseph returned to Egypt, he and his brothers, and all who had gone up with him to bury his father. When Joseph's brothers saw that their father was dead, they said, "What if Joseph hates us and pays us back for all the evil that we did to him!" (Gen. 50:14–15)

After fulfilling his oath to his father, and burying his father in the family crypt, Joseph returns with the procession of dignitaries to Egypt. In this whole narrative, Joseph has, essentially, acted alone. It is true that many Egyptian dignitaries accompany him, as well as his family, and a significant cavalry escort: all in all, a very *heavy* camp. But it is he who initiates the journey to Canaan. Burying his father is, in a sense, his personal mission.

He returns, adds the text, *after* burying his father. What does the last phrase add to a narrative that has amply described the burial ceremonies? A note of black humor, one might almost say, infiltrates the somber account. The closure is overemphatic: the father is buried, a life and its stories are brought to a close. But there is the sense of something suppressed—"Methinks the lady doth protest too much?"

Suddenly, there emerges a last-minute qualm. For the first time, the brothers articulate a fear of Joseph's vengeance for that long-buried day in the pit. What brings this fear to the surface is that they "saw that their father was dead." Again, the repeated reference to the departure of the father makes one wonder what symbolic meaning this has for the brothers. In this vein, Rashi responds to the apparent banality of the observation:

> What is the meaning of "they saw . . ."? They realized the mean-
> ing of his death in Joseph's behavior. Previously, they used to
> dine at Joseph's table and he used to receive them with open
> arms out of respect for his father; after Jacob's death, however,
> he no longer treated them in a friendly manner.

Rashi's scenario explains the brothers' sudden eruption of fear. Joseph's behavior has changed ominously since Jacob's death. Death—even burial—is not necessarily closure: on the contrary, this death seems to open up unnerving possibilities. The brothers begin to conjecture about the meaning—for Joseph, for their own future—of this death. Even the slight expression *loo—what if . . .* —has a conjectural resonance: *what if* Jacob's death means hatred and revenge?

The word for "hatred" here is the unusual *yistemenu,* rather than *yisn'enu.* This rather rare expression occurs three times in Genesis. The first occasion is immediately after Esau loses his blessing to his brother Jacob: "And Esau hated Jacob because of the blessing which his father had given him, and Esau said to himself, 'Let but the mourning period of my father come, and I will kill my brother Jacob'" (Gen. 27:41). Esau's resentment is not at all allayed by the alternative blessing that he has received from his father; on the contrary, this blessing seems to trigger his hatred, as though reminding him of Jacob's usurpation. He waits only for his father's death to vent this by killing Jacob. This is revenge-hatred, unappeasable, biding its time till the father dies.

The second time this hatred appears is in Jacob's blessing of Joseph: "The archers hated him" (Gen. 49:23). This refers to the brothers' hatred of Joseph and uses the metaphor of archery for their malicious language (Rashi).

From these three uses of *sitma* in Genesis, a particular genre of hatred emerges: sibling hatred, repressed in the father's lifetime, biding its time for the fratricidal moment.[10] The brothers clearly assume that Joseph has been nursing his hatred against the day he will be free to express it. This is the dreaded implication of Jacob's death. Midrash Tanchuma, in fact, translates the term to refer to the "repressed malice in Joseph's heart."[11] And it requires nothing more sinister than a cooling in Joseph's behavior to stir up his brothers' worst apprehensions.

The trigger for the brothers' dread becomes more dramatic in another midrashic narrative:

> "And Joseph's brothers saw that their father was dead." What did they now see that they were afraid? When they returned from burying their father, they saw that Joseph went to make a blessing over that pit where his brothers had thrown him. He made a blessing, as a person should do over a place where a miracle was done for him: "Blessed be God, who made me a miracle in this place!" When they saw this, they said, "Now that our father is dead, what if Joseph hates us and pays us back for all the evil that we did him!" So they sent a message to Joseph, saying: "Your

father left this instruction . . . 'So shall you say to Joseph.' " We
have searched but we have not found that Jacob left any such
instruction! But see the power of peace, that God wrote such
things in His Torah about the power of peace.[12]

Implicitly, the midrash reads "They *saw [va-yir'u]* that their father
was dead" as "They *feared [va-yira'u]*." Their fear is stirred by the scenario of the return to the pit. Joseph stares down into "that pit."
Apparently, they misread his intentions, which are of the purest: he
has gone to the trouble of returning to that place of his terror in
order to bring closure to the old narrative. He makes the blessing for
a personal miracle, claiming the site of his trauma as the site of
redemption. By this act, he rereads the pit as a space of rebirth, transforming pain into hope. The grave has become a womb. Jacob's
death and burial have become an occasion for blessing. Joseph's act
of redemptive narrative, however, is misinterpreted by his brothers:
they do not hear his blessing, they merely watch him as he stands
staring into his pit. And immediately their dread flares up: "What if
Joseph hates us."

Here, however, the midrash suspends its judgment. Their fear,
after all, is not implausible. Why, indeed, has Joseph taken them on
this journey to that long-forgotten pit, without imparting to them
his benign intentions? He has silently led them directly from a grave
to a pit: a burial is followed by a cryptic gesture of excavation. Is he
truly laying the past to rest? Perhaps his conscious intentions were
of the best, but his silent action speaks louder than words. Suddenly,
his brothers realize the full implications of their fatherless condition. Without any delay at all, Joseph has flung them back into the
passion of the past. Is he totally unaware of the storm of fear that
now assails them? In an ironic comment, the midrash cites: "You
shall be innocent before God and before Israel" (Num. 32:22), and
notes: "One's innocence should be as clear to other human beings, as
it is to God."[13]

The midrash ends by recounting the brothers' response—they
send Joseph a message, conveying Jacob's dying instructions to
Joseph to forgive his brothers—and remarks ingenuously: "We have
searched but we have not found that Jacob left any such instruc-

tion." In a word, the supposed testament is a fabrication. The brothers have invented it, putting into their dying father's mouth words that they hope will protect them from Joseph's vengeance. Almost all midrashic sources, indeed, assume that this is the case: Jacob never left such a testament, and the words quoted from the grave are sheer invention.[14]

Strikingly, however, the midrash adopts a naive pose: as though only thorough scanning could have produced such a finding, as though a lie in the divine narrative would constitute a theological problem. The midrash seems to affirm a dramatic judgment—the superiority of peace over truth—which justifies the brothers' lie. But the strident rhetoric itself raises questions: it draws attention to the lie, to the fear out of which it emerges, and to Joseph's role in generating that fear. Subtly, it undermines the closure, the "peace," that it claims to vindicate.

BLOCKED CHANNELS: JOSEPH WEEPS

They sent this message to Joseph: "Before his death your father left this instruction: 'So shall you say to Joseph, "Forgive, I pray you, the offense and guilt of your brothers who did evil to you."' Therefore, please forgive the offense of the servants of the God of your father." And Joseph wept as they spoke to him.

His brothers went to him themselves, flung themselves before him, and said, "We are prepared to be your slaves." But Joseph said to them, "Have no fear! Am I in God's place? You thought evil against me, but God thought it for good, so as to bring about the present result—the survival of so many people. And so, have no fear, I will sustain you and your little children." And he comforted them and spoke hearteningly to them. (Gen. 50:16–21)

Joseph weeps. Of all the many tears he sheds in the course of his narrative, these are the most mysterious. Indeed, tears by their nature are mysterious, overdetermined; they cause confusion or embarrassment in the social world, whose language offers no adequate translation.

And Joseph's tears have always had an enigmatic quality. Three times in the course of his masquerade with his brothers, he wept. Accusing them of being spies, demanding they bring him their youngest brother, while he keeps Shimeon as hostage, he brings them to a moment of guilty recognition of their own callousness. As they remind one another of that day by the pit, unaware that Joseph can understand their language, Joseph turns aside and weeps—and returns to his cruel role, chaining Shimeon before their eyes (Gen. 42:24). Again, he weeps on seeing his brother Benjamin: this time, he has to withdraw to another room and wash his face after his paroxysm of tears (43:30–31). The process of resuming his bizarre role is obviously more difficult now: his weeping is described in full emotional and physical detail, culminating in the word *va-yit'apak* (he restrained himself). The third time he weeps, he can no longer restrain himself: *lo yakhol l'hit'apek* (45:1). This time, his weeping is public and uninhibited, audible throughout the palace and beyond. His effort to restrain himself evokes the masculine imagery of *afak*—water channel—so called, according to one view, because it flows powerfully within its bounds. When this fluid but contained strength fails to sustain itself, Joseph breaks down in tears.

His paroxysms continue: he weeps twice more in the same scene, as he falls on Benjamin's neck and as he kisses all his brothers (Gen. 45:14–15). And again, when he is reunited with his father, he weeps *persistently* (46:30).[15] And when his father dies, he falls on his father's face and weeps (50:1).

The history of Joseph's tears is a history of loneliness. Seven times he weeps alone; only when he weeps over Benjamin does his younger brother respond by weeping, too. During the masquerade, in revealing himself, in reassuring his brothers, his tears are not met by theirs. Even in meeting his father, it seems that he alone weeps.[16] On each occasion, a private world of powerful but inscrutable emotion breaks through. Only with Benjamin, his true brother, his tears act as a language, opening a dialogue.

Perhaps his tears represent the tears he never shed in the horror of the pit—the tears that his brothers remember twenty years later but that they could not hear at the moment he wept them. Falling on deaf ears, they gave him no relief. Till his brothers *hear* them for the first time, twenty years later, it is as though they were never shed. At that moment, Joseph begins to weep, seven times, endlessly, as though to drain some bottomless pit. And indeed, that pit was empty, it had no water in it; according to Rashi, however, it held serpents and scorpions.[17]

In this final scene, Joseph weeps his most enigmatic tears. "He wept *be-dabram eilav*"—lit., *"at their speaking to him."* Perhaps he weeps at the distance of suspicion that still divides him from his brothers; sure of his own good intentions, he weeps at their fear. Or perhaps he weeps *at the manner of their addressing him*. For, actually, they are *not speaking to him:* they communicate through a messenger, who reports a fabricated message containing deathbed instructions, in their father's name and words, to ask Joseph for forgiveness. If one were to write the verse, the core of the message—the confession and plea for forgiveness—would be hedged about with a forest of quotation marks. In other words, the brothers' plea is indirect and equivocal to the point of absurdity. This is the only way, it seems, that they can *speak to him*. Joseph weeps, then, at the failure of language to maintain itself in the family after Jacob's death.

If language breaks down between Joseph and his brothers, then, Joseph knows that this is no trivial failure. The tragic history began with such a breakdown ("They hated him so they could not speak to him peaceably" [Gen. 37:4]). Where brothers cannot speak their animosity, blood may yet be shed. The precedent of Cain and Abel cries to high heaven: "And Cain said to his brother Abel . . . and when they were in the field, Cain rose up against his brother Abel and killed him" (4:8). Cain apparently makes an attempt to speak, which is aborted and becomes the physical act of murder. Abel's blood then *cries out* from the earth (4:10). The fratricidal impulse is played out in the Joseph story in disguised forms; but, in the end, even after Joseph has revealed himself, the residue of past passion silences his brothers: "they could not answer him, for they were dumbfounded before him" (45:3). In order to open the flow of words between them, Joseph has to reassure them at great length, and kiss them and cry over them: "only then were his brothers able to speak to him" (45:15). Only now can the family be reunited for the last seventeen years of Jacob's life.

Against this background, then, the failure of language—the indirection and equivocation with which his brothers now speak to him—wounds Joseph to the quick. It is as though nothing has changed; the forty years since the pit vanish; channels of communication seem to close up once more.

However, the scene ends with apparent reconciliation: the brothers, perhaps on hearing of Joseph's tears, do come in person and offer themselves as slaves. Clearly, they are still filled with fear: better lose their freedom than their lives. And Joseph reassures them one final time. He specifically addresses their fear, rereading their story to display its providential meaning: all that anger and jealousy has led to a benign conclusion, now that he is positioned to save the lives of so many who might have starved in the famine. " 'And so, have no fear, I will sustain you and your little children.' Thus, he comforted them and spoke hearteningly to them." In this way, Joseph brings the turbulent family narrative to a peaceful close. By speaking encouragingly to them (lit., "he spoke upon their heart"), he reopens the blocked channels.

NO CLOSURE?

Precisely here, though, uneasiness becomes palpable. For one thing, the brothers are not heard to speak; only Joseph's voice is heard, even in the coda in which he speaks his last words, making them swear to carry up his bones to the family grave. No dialogue in fact follows on his encouraging speech; rather than opening them to language, he seems to have silenced them.

His encouragement is expressed as "He spoke upon their hearts"; he raises their morale, bidding them take heart. Twice, indeed, he urges them, "Have no fear." But Rashi comments:

> "He spoke upon their heart": means that he spoke words that found ready entrance into their heart: "Before you came down here, people spread rumors about me that I was born a slave; through you, it became public that I am a freeman by birth. If I were to kill you, what would people say?" He saw a group of fine young men and he boasted of his relationship with them, say-

ing, "These are my brothers; but afterward he killed them. Have you ever heard of a man who kills his brothers?!"[18]

Rashi emphasizes that Joseph is willing to use any argument that his brothers will find plausible. This is Joseph, the effective orator, who dispenses heartening words from the high ground of power and providential wisdom. It is striking that "speaking upon the heart" occurs only once more in Genesis, in the story of Dinah and Shechem: the prince first rapes Dinah, then *speaks upon her heart*. There, too, Rashi comments: "words that found ready entrance to her heart" (Gen. 34:3). He seduces her with promises of benefits to her family. The narrative conveys Shechem's impassioned sincerity, but does not blur the grotesqueness of a seduction that follows a rape. Here, too, Joseph's seductive words cannot disguise the power imbalance and the fact of the pit. Even his promise to sustain their "little children" only reminds them of their infantile status, as indeed the expression "He spoke *upon* their heart" reminds the reader of his superiority. Ambiguity—reassurance and intimidation both— hovers over his speech.

This ambiguity emerges acutely from the specific argument that, according to Rashi, Joseph deploys. His sophistical claim—"I would lose my credibility if I were to kill you, after acknowledging you as my brothers: how could one kill one's brothers?"—achieves a moment of black humor. Consciously, perhaps, he intends to convince his brothers by using a pragmatic rather than a sentimental argument. But, by a kind of Freudian slip, he finds himself turning the knife in their wound: "Have you ever heard of a man who kills his brothers?!"

Rashi's sample of Joseph's reassuring rhetoric conveys a prevailing midrashic ambivalence about Joseph. He does wish to allay his brothers' anxiety, but his rhetoric lays him open to ironic readings. Here is one such reading:

> "I will sustain you . . . ": It was not fitting to use this expression, for it is God who "sustains all life and living creatures." For this reason, Joseph died before all his brothers.[19]

The fact that Joseph is the first among his brothers to die—in spite of being second to youngest—becomes a trigger for subtle critiques. Here, his language betrays him: unawares, he adopts the idiom of divinity. Even the redundant *anokhi*—"I will sustain you"—expresses the narcissistic tone of his reassurance.

Again, the Talmud notes:

> Why did Joseph die before his brothers? Because he gave himself superior airs.[20]

"Superior airs" refers to the general tenor of Joseph's conduct. His masterful temperament affects even this last speech, in which he attempts to restore communication: even here, as he administers a rhetoric of consolation, he—unwittingly?—slips a blade between their ribs. It is as though the anger and hatred he is so efficiently denying makes a lightning appearance in spite of himself. In the same Talmudic passage, R. Judah claims that this haughty temperament manifests itself even in relation to his father: he fails to interrupt Judah who repeatedly refers to *"your servant* our father." Subtly reading his silence, his failure to protest, the Talmud raises a question about his moral sensitivity.

And, again, we remember the midrashic comment on Joseph's journey back to the pit:

> "You shall be innocent before God and before Israel": One's innocence should be as clear to other human beings as it is to God."[21]

Joseph is not entirely cleared of responsibility for his brothers' apprehension. Even if his motive is not consciously vindictive, he nevertheless behaves in such a way as to alarm them.

The following midrash makes the most incisive statement about this last dialogue between Joseph and his brothers:

> Why did Joseph not forgive his brothers, in spite of their plea ("Please forgive the offense and guilt of your brothers")?

Because a person cannot be forgiven unless he pleads face-to-face; and the brothers sent a messenger; they did not speak for themselves, but through the device of "Your father left this instruction."[22]

The startling assumption here is that Joseph did not forgive his brothers. Since they never confronted him with a personal confession, but instead wrapped their plea for forgiveness in layers of indirection and fabrication, forgiveness is impossible. Astonishingly, the brothers never actually confess and apologize for the past *to Joseph's face*.[23] That is one side of the situation. But the brothers' failure is implicitly matched with Joseph's; what they do not do mirrors what Joseph does not do. For complex reasons, some of which I would like to explore, Joseph does not actually forgive his brothers. The tangled dynamics of their relationship make it all but impossible for him to do so. The midrash, then, is claiming that there is *no closure* to this anguished saga. The channels of language are never fully opened; a blockage persists through the apparent reconciliation of the last passage.

Communication is informed, it seems, by a dialectic of open and closed: if language flows freely, openly, closure of the traumas of the past may be achieved. But this balance may be disturbed. Too great an insistence on closure, for example, may close off those channels that must remain open. This is the issue with which the story of Joseph and his brothers ends. And this, I would suggest, is an immediate dimension of the blockage that Jacob senses, as he tries to reveal meaning—the end—to his children. The manifest rituals of closure barely contain the forces that thrust up against them.

Jacob's burial is constructed by his sons as an ending to his power to protect his children. Newly exposed to Joseph's presumed hatred, they are, however, at liberty to use their father's death to fabricate a *postmortem* plea: since he is dead and buried, they make him protect them despite himself. But their invention backfires; it exposes their fear to Joseph and, obliquely, aborts the very closure they desire.

· · ·

"IF ONLY JOSEPH HATES US"

Perhaps the central indication that all is not as it seems in this closing narrative is to be heard in the brothers' cry: "What if *[loo]* Joseph hates us?" The Hebrew word *loo* strikes a discordant note since, most commonly, it refers to a *wish* ("Would that *[loo]* we had died in the land of Egypt!" [Num. 14:2]; "If only *[loo]* you would listen to me!" [Gen. 23:13]). Nowhere else is it used to denote apprehension; for that, the usual biblical expression is *pen*—"*lest* Joseph hate us." Here, however, the context seems too clear for doubt: the brothers dread Joseph's hatred. So clear, indeed, that Rashi feels justified in asserting that *loo* can bear a negative meaning ("lest"), using as proof text this very verse that is under discussion. But in this usage, Rashi admits, it has no biblical parallel.

The eighteenth-century commentator Or Ha-Chaim offers a brilliant reading of the brothers' unconscious wish:

Why would the text use an expression the usual meaning of which is the opposite of its meaning in this context? Since here, unmistakably, the meaning is *"lest* Joseph hate us," the appropriate word would be *pen* or *ulai*. But there is another level of meaning: they *hope* that he will pay them back . . . and that they will suffer in some way commensurate with the suffering that they caused him. In such a case, they would not have been condemned to the exiles and sufferings that were the consequence of this sin—as the Sages have said of the Egyptian exile and of our present exile. See, for example, the midrash about the Ten Martyrs.

In spite of their conscious apprehension about Joseph's vengeance, the brothers, on some level, *wish* for him to express a hatred that, unpurged, will poison the fate of the family for many generations. Or Ha-Chaim associates the recurrent exiles and sufferings of the Jewish people with this foundational narrative, invoking midrashic links between the Joseph saga and the Egyptian slavery, the first and paradigmatic exile. He even invokes the uncanny story of the Ten Martyrs, the great sages led by R. Akiva, whose lives are claimed by the Roman emperor; who argues that since Joseph's ten brothers never paid for their crime—and since kidnapping is a capital offense—the ten Sages must now pay with their lives. This midrashic narrative becomes part of the liturgy for Yom Kippur (*Eileh ezkerah*), raising troubling questions about the transgenerational nature of the workings of justice.[24]

The story of the Ten Martyrs is one of the most poignant episodes during the destruction of the Second Temple, which, according to a famous midrash, was caused by *sin'at hinam*—causeless hatred. Or Ha-Chaim is thus making a large claim: that Joseph's failure to engage with his own hatred leaves a toxic residue in the family. Unresolved, it results in the destruction of sages and Temple. " 'If only Joseph would hate us!' " An enactment of authentic resentment at this juncture might have prevented the traumas of exile.

On this reading, the brothers wish for Joseph's healing hatred, even as they fear it. A painful confrontation might have opened the wounds of the past, making real cure possible. But Joseph cannot allow that old anguish to resurface. That would involve an *unsettling* of old scores that he is as anxious as they are to leave untouched. "*If only* Joseph would hate us." The counterfactual *loo* acknowledges an unlikely outcome: that Joseph will be able to resist the temptation to make sense—premature sense—of the whole painful story. But instead, Joseph tells a story of meaning that leaves the real wrongs of the past unredressed and unresolved.

REVEALING THE END

The brothers' ambivalence about such a confrontation is not hard to understand: they dread it, even as they wish for it. But Joseph's providential narrative—a briefer version of the one he had immediately produced on revealing his identity[25]—also carries the marks of an anxious desire to suppress conflict. He tells God's story, which coincides with his own: God benignly reweaves his brothers' evil intentions into a providential plot that positions Joseph as the Egyptian viceroy. The meaning of history—God's thought—is entirely accessible to Joseph; beautifully, it has transformed fratricide into the survival of so many people who might have starved in the famine. This overarching narrative literally *reveals the end:* it retells the human story of suffering as an apocalyptic narrative whose governing meaning is gathered into its conclusion. But what of the human story lived by the jealous brothers and the crying boy hurled into a pit? What has Joseph done to the cries of the past? And why is he anxious to keep the old scores well settled?

D. A. Miller offers a provocative discussion of the "narrative of happiness": of the paradoxical relation between narratives and endings in the traditional novel:

> The narrative of happiness is inevitably frustrated by the fact that only insufficiencies, defaults, deferrals, can be "told." Even when a narrative "prepares for" happiness, it remains in this state of lack, which can only be liquidated along with the narrative itself.[26]

Miller is interested in the internal conflict between the narrative—kept going by instability, confusion, error—and the claims of closure: full and final meaning. The very conditions under which a story is possible are to be removed in the ending:

> Traditional narrative is a quest after that which will end questing; ... or a distortion of what will be made straight; a holding in suspense or a putting into question of what will be resolved or answered.[27]

The traditional novel, therefore, is a "perverse" project, in which the underlying instability that generates the narrative is threatened by the very possibility of the perfect ending.

If Sartre claims in *La Nausée,* "Une chose commence pour finir," Miller argues nevertheless that novels are never fully or finally governed by closure. He quotes George Eliot's famous "pier-glass image" as expressive of the problem of closure:

> An eminent philosopher among my friends, who can dignify even your ugly furniture by lifting it into the serene light of science, has shown me this pregnant little fact. Your pier-glass or

extensive surface of polished steel made to be rubbed by a
housemaid, will be minutely and multitudinously scratched in
all directions; but place now against it a lighted candle as a centre of illumination, and lo! The scratches will seem to arrange
themselves in a fine series of concentric circles round that little
sun. . . . These things are a parable. The scratches are events, and
the candle is the egoism of any person now absent.[28]

Any person now absent, Miller notes, refers ironically to the narrator himself, who is fully engaged in centering the novel: "And what
else does he center it on but an insight that undermines the validity
of centers?"[29] By centering the novel in the very metaphor that casts
most doubt on such centering, George Eliot implies that her own
attempt to achieve mastery over the insufficiencies of narrative is
like the distorting candle flame. A subtle epistemological doubt
affects the narrator: "every attempt to grasp reality in narrative form
involve[s] a distortion by desire, ideology, language itself."[30] "Closure
is an act of 'make-believe,' a postulation that closure is possible."[31]
The candle flame that creates the illusory circles of ordered meaning
is an inevitable feature of such postulates.

Miller's discussion yields a provocative view of Joseph and his
candle flame, his narratives of full and final meaning. His original
dreams stage, of course, such acts of centering: "Suddenly, my sheaf
stood up and remained upright, and your sheaves *gathered around*
and bowed low to my sheaf" (Gen. 37:7). His brothers' sheaves surround his *(tissubena)* like satellites—an image at least as revealing of
Joseph's desire as the image of *bowing low* that follows, and prevails,
without the centering motif, in his second dream. Centering his narrative on himself, Joseph finds support in dreams to which even his
father gives credence: he "kept the thing in mind" (37:11).

Here, precisely, is the problem with biblical closure. For Joseph, a
character in the drama, to read so fully and unfailingly the meaning
of his own narrative creates problems and tensions not only for his
brothers, but for his readers as well. Thomas Mann puts it succinctly:
"It is possible to be in a plot and not understand it." Joseph is in the
troubling position of "always knowing far too well what was being
played."

In this final speech to his brothers, his analysis of the "God story" is perhaps too confident, ignoring his own participation in the turbulence and insufficiency, the deferrals and distortions of the narrative world. He tells a story in which a hidden necessity informs everything, and in which a final state of total coherence offers to release the narrative world from error and equivocation.

If he is a character in this play, he also writes and directs it. He "reveals the end," imposes the final fiction, as though no gap exists between God's thought and his own. Of course, he often disclaims such identification: "Am I in place of God?"[32] But the very denial arouses the suspicion of the reader. As Freud pointed out in his essay "Negation," "the content of a repressed image or idea can make its way into consciousness, on condition that it is *negated*."[33] In negation, the repression is "lifted," while what is repressed remains unacceptable.[34]

IF JOSEPH SAYS, "Am I in place of God?" he is saying: "This is what I am not," in this way revealing what he is. On an unacceptable level, he is undifferentiated from God. Why else would he constantly refer to himself and God in the same breath? In conscious terms, clearly, he is acknowledging an absolute difference. But a dialectic of affirmed and disavowed meaning is being played out. How, for instance, are we to read his modest disclaimer to the butler and the baker in the Egyptian prison: "Do not all interpretations belong to God? Tell me your dreams!" (Gen. 39:8). Joseph's intimacy, if not identity, with God is exposed, even as he denies it.

A similar dialectically constituted experience speaks out of "Am in the place of God?" With this rhetorical question, he reassures his brothers—"Have no fear, for am I in place of God?—vengeance is not mine to exact"—while at the same time he conveys a sense of his own godlike power. In other words, he both soothes and arouses his brothers' fears.

The syntax alone alerts the reader—"Have no fear, for am I in place of God?"—suggesting that his modest disclaimer is, in fact, an aphorism. Theologically correct, his words deny the madness of omnipotence. But this impeccable sentiment is not his own. He is, in fact, quoting his father's words to Rachel, in answer to her desperate plea: "Give me children, or I shall die!"—"Am I in place of God, who has withheld from you fruit of the womb?" (Gen. 30:1–2). These are, in fact, the *only* recorded words that Jacob ever speaks to his beloved wife, Joseph's mother. This fact is chilling, since his response to her passionate need is so chilling. Traditional commentaries attempt to justify him. If she is asking him to pray for her, he refuses on theological grounds: he already has children, and therefore cannot pray for offspring with full authenticity (Rashi). Or, she has no need of an intercessor—since God's relationship is solely with her in her barrenness, it is her prayer that He desires (Ramban). Theologically these arguments are interesting, even generative. Nevertheless, Ramban includes the scathing comment of the Rabbis: "God said to Jacob: Is this how you respond to a woman in distress?"[35]

The Rabbinic critique of Jacob has the ring of truth. Regardless of the theological value of his disclaimer, it remains inadequate as an emotional response. The chill quality of his words is exacerbated by the fact that the Torah chooses to record these alone. What they say may be true, may even express humility; but what they perform, what they *do*, is callous, even arrogant.[36] By preaching humility— "I am not God"—Jacob effectively removes himself from the heat and turbulence of the human narrative, assuming a godlike aloofness as he interprets God's acts. The Torah has testified to Jacob's love for Rachel; here, soberingly, it acknowledges the poignant ambiguities of human relationship.

It is, then, supremely ironic that Joseph—the son born in response to Rachel's prayer—comes to speak the same words. Joseph has inherited much of Jacob,[37] including a certain "violent innocence," to use Christopher Bollas's expression.[38] Both father and son utter a truism about human limitation; but this has the paradoxical effect of isolating them in godlike detachment from the emotional needs of wife and brothers. Joseph responds to his brothers' fear by dismissing all grounds for fear, and effectively defends himself against unsettling his own anger and hate. Instead, perhaps unwittingly, he uses his father's words, hallowed by tradition, transparently correct; he assumes the high moral ground, and leaves his brothers relieved but, in some barely conscious sense, frustrated.

Like the "Never mind" response to an apology, Joseph's providential speech disturbs even as it purports to soothe. A hope of redress withers. The narratable anguish of the past is subsumed in a fiction of closure. And precisely here is the core of the irony: in his anxiety to *reveal the end,* to resolve the narrative in full meaning, Joseph suppresses the conflicts in his family and within himself. Stridently humble, he asserts a superiority that makes him untouchable and his brothers unredeemable.

SUPPRESSING THE CONFLICT

A famous midrash tells how Joseph, at the moment of temptation with Potiphar's wife, is visited by a vision of his father's face.[39] Haunted by his father's image at moments that threaten his mastery, Joseph is always striving to be equal to him—or to himself at his least ambivalent. His superiority to conflicting voices within or without is essential to him—a superiority that is guaranteed in advance of any actual encounter. Losing his superiority would be unthinkable for Joseph. As interpreter of dreams, he is accorded the status of Wise Man *(chakham)* by Pharaoh: "There is none so discerning and wise as you" (Gen. 41:39). He is, at root, the *poter*—the dream analyst: the word is coined for him, occurring fourteen times within his narrative. To be a *poter* is to crack the code, to isolate the inherent meaning within the turbulence and displacements of the dream. It is to *reveal the end,* to resolve conflicting evidence, to find a solution that simplifies, makes sense of the data. Such a person is of the utmost value to society, making wise decisions possible. But, by the same token, such a person is hardly willing to sustain disagreement.

Or Ha-Chaim defines Joseph's interpretive role: "He meant to impose the words of the interpretation upon thought." Joseph recognizes that dreams need to be mastered in words that fix one among many possible meanings. In this way, chaos is avoided; closure is brought to the narrative of endless discontent. His analytic competence is celebrated by Pharaoh: "I have heard about you, that for you to hear a dream is to tell its meaning" (Gen. 41:15). Ha'amek Davar reads this: "you hear a dream—not as others do who wish to listen to a fascinating but pointless drama—but *in order to interpret it,* to decipher it." That is, Joseph's wisdom consists of his analytic *listening:* he is attuned to meaning, to endings, so that the dream as narrative, anarchic, passionate, and enigmatic is compelled to yield to an authorized translation. He is the expert who decides on the purpose of the dream in waking life. What must be suppressed in order to comply with such an interpretation? Perhaps other solutions could be found for the same dream? But Joseph says twice, unambiguously, to the butler and to the baker: *"This is its interpretation"* (40:12,18). For him, dreams are the way God communicates information about the future: nothing is redundant, everything in the dream is coherent, interpretable as part of a scheme of meaning.

The problem with Joseph's superiority, his problem-solving wisdom, is that he really is wise, and superior. His advice to Pharaoh is sound. But his authority suppresses conflict—a blessing perhaps when practical decisions have to be made. However, imposing a providential pattern over the raw dream of family relationships may settle too many old scores, without first sufficiently unsettling them.

The tragedy of this moment in the history of Joseph and his brothers is that conscious goodwill moves all the brothers to comply with a simple model of resolution. "It is indeed illuminating," remarks Adam Phillips, "to think of the super-ego not as the cause of conflict but as the *saboteur of conflict*" (my emphasis).[40] Joseph's competence and sexual restraint speak of a powerful superego, overriding conflict, haunted by the image of his father. But the tears that break out seven times in the course of his story tell of water channels that crack under pressure. The image of waters purposefully directing their energy informs *Va-yitapak,* the word used for Joseph's self-restraint. It is an image of masculine force. Joseph's tears are so poignant because they represent the pressure of his unacknowledged complexity.

His brothers do not witness his final paroxysm of tears, as he registers their absence, their fear of him. For them, he remains the puppeteer who manipulated their responses during the masquerade. At that time, he asked them certain questions. Rashi comments:

My lord asked his servants, "Have you a father or another brother?" From the beginning, you came upon us with a pretext [*b'alilah*, lit., with a plot]. What need had you to ask us all these questions? Were we asking for your daughter in marriage or were you asking for our sister?[41]

They sense his questions as designed to fit them into his scheme of meaning. Earlier, when the brothers found their money returned in their bags, they were filled with terror: "What is this that God has done to us?" (Gen. 42:28). Rashi elaborates: "To bring us into this plot [*alilah*]—for our money was returned only in order to torment us [*lehitolel*—to make us figures in his plot]." They do not recognize Joseph but they sense that they are being incorporated into a plot of meaning. Under his questioning, they feel their subjectivity drain away: they have become plot material in an unknown drama that Joseph is composing.

In the same vein, Rashi quotes a powerful midrash: "The man asked us many questions," the brothers tell Jacob, "about ourselves and our origins [*moledet*]" (Gen. 43:7). Rashi comments:

> "Our origins" means "our families." But the midrash translates *moledet*: "He asked us concerning the *circumstances of our birth*. He could even tell us of what kind of wood our cradles were made of—and we were compelled to answer him in terms of his questions."

Joseph's questions intimate an uncanny knowledge of the earliest life of his brothers—"even the wood of our cradles." He imposes on them a direction of thought and meaning. He is the master of contingency, of narrative. A transferential awe enforces their compliance. But resentment informs their version of events, and some residue of this makes it impossible for them, to the end, to confront Joseph with a full confession and plea for forgiveness. Their distrust only confirms Joseph's need to dominate, to the end, with kindness and noble understanding.

"What if/if only Joseph hates us!" Joseph does not reclaim his own hatred. And the effect of this is palpable even in the midst of the ceremonies of closure that characterize the final chapters of Genesis. When, for instance, Joseph brings his sons, Ephraim and

Menasseh, to his father for blessing, Jacob reacts with strange alienation: "Israel saw Joseph's sons and asked, 'Who are these?'" (Gen.
48:8). After seventeen years of living together in Egypt, he seems not
to recognize his grandsons. Two verses later, his failing vision is
offered as a possible explanation: "Israel's eyes were dim with age; he
could not see." But if blindness is responsible for his question, the
Torah should have *prefaced* the story by telling of his failing vision;
instead, it emphasizes that he *saw* Joseph's sons.

Rashi comments:

> He wished to bless them but the Divine Presence departed from
> him, because he saw that the wicked kings Jereboam and Ahab
> would be descended from Ephraim, and Jehu and his sons from
> Menasseh (Tanchuma).
>   "And he said, 'Who are these?'"—"Where do these come
> from who are unfit for blessing?"

Jacob experiences two things: a desire to bless his grandchildren
and a mysterious blank, as God's presence suddenly withdraws. The
reason for this loss of inspiration is given by Rashi: it is to be found
in the future, in the wicked descendants of Ephraim and Menasseh.
Something of those descendants is already implicit in his grandsons.
But when he asks, "Who are these?" and Rashi amplifies, "Where do
these come from who are unfit for blessing?"—he is asking about the
cause, the origin of the blank. Aware that his blessing has been
repressed, he is not looking to the future for an explanation, but to
the past. In the simplest sense, Ephraim and Menasseh come from
Joseph. Joseph is responsible for the lost blessing. Or, in other words,
Joseph himself acts as repression within the family dynamic, as the
force that knows, and masters, and represses the knowledge that
threatens his sense of coherent meaning.[42] Ironically, his children,
who come of him, are sensed by his father as unfit for blessing. At
least at first, Jacob can find no place for them within *his* world of
meaning.

The pressure of old turbulence affects Jacob's capacity to bless. It
is not that he is blind but that he sees too well. But what exactly does
Jacob know about the past? Ramban argues that he was never told

about the sale of Joseph: the brothers had no interest in revealing the truth, and Joseph restrained himself. Jacob's supposed testament to Joseph to forgive his brothers is adduced to support this: if Jacob had known the truth, he would surely have interceded with Joseph while he was still alive, and the brothers would not have felt forced to fabricate the testament story.

Assuming, then, that Jacob was never told the truth, how do we read the following midrash?

> Jacob said to Joseph: Why do you say, "This is the firstborn?" I know, my son, I know. What do you think? Because I asked you many times, "What did your brothers do to you?" and you would not tell me, did you think that I did not know? I knew, my son, I knew.[43]

As Jacob moves to bless his grandchildren, Joseph, assuming that his father is confused about his sons' birth order, tries to switch his father's hands. Jacob replies, "I know, my son, I know." What is it that Jacob knows? The midrash loads the rift with ore: Jacob implies that he knows everything about Joseph's trauma. The normal reading, of course, refers to the birth order of Ephraim and Menasseh: Jacob refuses Joseph's correction (*Lo ken avi*—"Not so, Father" [lit., not correct, not stable]), affirming that he is quite aware of reality. In context, this reading makes perfect sense, and, in miniature, displays Joseph's concern for stability, coherence—that things should make sense.

Against the grain of the text, however, the midrash detects a larger resonance in Jacob's answer. The particular situation of blessing his grandsons is unconsciously linked with the buried past. No one ever told Jacob the truth, but he knows, and his knowledge at first blocks his blessing. How does he know, if he was never told? The midrash need not explain; perhaps because it is obvious that in a secretive family atmosphere, it is difficult for a father not to know. Communication is never exhausted by conscious, explicit speech. Perhaps Jacob's ear has been fine-tuned by many years of yearning for the return of what has been repressed.

· · ·

SUSTAINING THE CONFLICT

When Jacob turns to bless his twelve sons on his deathbed, however, blessing again fails him. Or rather, as Rashi puts it: "He sought to reveal the end, and the Divine Presence departed from him" (Gen. 49:1). The cue to this reading is in Jacob's first words: "Gather round that I may tell you what will happen with you *at the end of days*." His project is prophecy; depending on divine inspiration, his last words are to prepare his children for the rigors of exile that are to begin at his death. But the eschatological purpose of his speech is undermined by the abandonment of the Shekhinah: he is blocked, *nistam mimenu*, as Rashi puts it. A dense blur affects his vision, without form or direction: he cannot even detect that there is an end to the exile, says Sefat Emet. No clear providential narrative presents itself. So he begins to speak of *other things*. What are these other things, neither prophecy nor blessing?

Mei Ha-Shilo'ach offers a profound reading of this deathbed speech, which, according to midrashic tradition, is born of repression:

> Jacob wished to bless his children, but was in doubt whether he ought to bless them since they had caused him so much pain over the sale of Joseph. And "any scholar who does not take revenge and bear a grudge, like a snake, is not a true scholar" (B. *Yoma* 22b). That is why the text says, "He called to his sons . . .": meaning that he cried out with hope in his heart. He turned his eyes and heart heavenwards, and cried out that whatever God would put in his mouth he would say.
>
> That is the meaning of the midrash that quotes the verse ["I call to God Most High, to God who is good to me"], as a cry to God to bring this moment to a good conclusion *[gomer]* for him.
>
> Moreover, he did not begin his speech with the word "blessing," since he had no clarity about what he would say to them. Moses, however, did begin immediately with the words: "This is the blessing." The word *ve-zot* ("this"), too, implies that his intention was clear, fully focused on blessing from the moment he began to speak. Jacob, on the contrary, could not begin with the

word *ve-zot;* only after he had finished his whole speech—and not before—had his mind become totally clear that his blessings were indeed from God.

The core midrash[44] is based on a verse in Psalms: "I call to God Most High, to God who is good to me" (Ps. 57:3), and meditates on the human desire to know God's will. On Yom Kippur, the fate of the two goats depends on the throwing of lots; so Jacob here cries to God to make it clear that He agrees with Jacob's wish to give each son his own proper blessing. Underlying the passage, then, is the issue of fate, the fate of each son, as delineated in Jacob's last words. He prays to know that God is with him in these fateful words, that his blessings have some prophetic force.

Mei Ha-Shilo'ach elaborates: Jacob is blocked by a real conflict, between his desire to bless his children and his anger at the torment they put him through for so many years. In this situation, he cannot simply dismiss his anger. As the extraordinary passage from the Talmud suggests, in order to fulfill the commandment "You shall not take revenge" (Lev. 19:18), a scholar—a person of deep seriousness— will need, in some sense, to take revenge; or, at least, to listen to the inner voices of anger, without hastening to repress them.

In this quandary, Jacob places his whole being, and particularly his *mouth,* the language that will emerge from it, in God's hands. Like Balaam, he will say whatever God puts in his mouth. He lays aside his sense of superiority, the coherent narratives that suppress conflict, and allows himself to say "whatever comes up," or, as Freud put it, whatever "comes to mind" *(Einfall).* He trusts that from his authentic words a truth will emerge that is not accessible to him before he begins to speak.

At first, there is no clarity *(ve-zot)* and no blessing *(berakhah).* Instead, he directs harsh words to his first three sons—who were the leaders in the plot against Joseph—modulating, by a process of *birur,* of catharsis, into blessing. By the end, he achieves both *ve-zot*—a clear focus on the truth of his words—and *berakhah*—genuine blessings, which can then flow toward all his sons: "And this *[ve-zot]* is what he spoke to them; and he blessed *[va-yivarekh]* them, each with the blessing appropriate to him" (Gen. 49:28).[45]

Mei Ha-Shilo'ach here offers an alternative to the repression, the willfully providential closure that tragically leaves the Joseph saga unclosed. Precisely because of his anxiety about closure, Joseph imposes a too meaningful ending upon the conflict-ridden narrative. Jacob, on the other hand—in this reading—allows authentic feeling full expression, till it plays itself out and he can access an equally authentic sense of blessing. His mind is at first deeply troubled by the consciousness of occluded meaning: "Who are *these* [eileh]?"[46] he asks, distracted by the diffuse voices of the buried past. There is no possibility of *ve-zot* with its focus and sense of intimate meaning, until he has surrendered to the freedom of authentic language.

In this process, strikingly, God is involved: for Jacob, free association means, at root, association with God. A willful pride must dissolve, the desire to make immediate moral sense must be suspended, so that God is given space and time to bring a profound process to consummation. From confusion to clarity, from conflict to a larger focus, Jacob's crisis of inspiration plays itself out "with hope in his heart."

The process of speaking itself generates clarity. The freedom to speak in this generative way, however, is possible only when the anxiety to *reveal the end* abates. Meaning emerges in the course of speaking. The apocalyptic mode, on the other hand, depends on knowing the end before history has yielded its data. In Rashi's brief comment, Jacob is compelled to turn away from his apocalyptic project—to *reveal the end*; instead, he speaks of *other things*. In this Hasidic reading, it is these *other things* that open a different path to blessing. Jacob imposes no authoritative resolution; he sustains the conflict—to bless or not to bless—so that the narrative comes to yield its intimate meanings.

Here, Mei Ha-Shilo'ach indicates a different relation to conflict than the one we have sensed in Joseph's words. Insisting on his providential narrative, Joseph blocks the organic possibility that his brothers themselves intuit: "If only Joseph would hate us!" *Loo yistemenu Yosef*. Although the two Hebrew roots for *hatred* and *blocking* are spelled differently, the verbal echo is compelling: repressing hatred *(sitmah)* in his will to closure, Joseph blocks *(satam)* the authentic meaning that might have emerged from a truer speaking. He weeps at the blockage still present in his brothers' speech to him—*b'dabram eilav;* but his anxiety to cure the malaise of language leads him to speak *upon* their hearts—*va-yidaber al libam:* soothingly, prudentially, providentially, but without ever engaging with the words that, unwittingly, slip out of his own mouth. Unaware, he conspires with his brothers to prevent the very closure they all desire.

KEEPING WATCH OVER ABSENT MEANING

Jacob comes to his clarity by accepting the world of *other things;* like Hamlet, he will "by indirection find direction out." In his original conflicted state, blessing is *nistam*—blocked, obscured. This state is the psychological experience of that condition of exile known as *hester panim:* God's face is hidden, so that one lives without clear inspiration for blessing. This fundamentally tragic state derives from Deuteronomy 31:18, where God warns the Israelites of the alienations of exile: *Haster astir panai*—"I will truly hide My face on that day." The double, emphatic reference to hiddenness casts a deep shadow over history. In Hasidic writings, Jacob's loss of inspiration is associated with this existential condition. Data crowd perception, unpunctuated, endless. Yet, Jacob finds a way of inviting blessing, obliquely, to return. This can happen, however, only when he has deeply acknowledged the anguish of conflict and the absence of conclusive meaning.

As Rabbi Nahman of Bratzlav expresses the paradox: If God is hidden in a single layer of hiddenness, it is possible, even if difficult, to labor till one finds Him. This is possible because one is aware that God is hidden. But where a double hiddenness exists—that is, where the fact that God is hidden is itself hidden—then it is impossible to find Him. This is the catastrophe of *haster astir,* where His hiddenness is hidden, so that one does not realize that He is to be sought.

If exile begins with Jacob's death—or even earlier, as he strives to reveal the end—the relationships within his family enact precisely that clouded sense of hidden meaning that is the climate of exile. Disavowing the hiddenness of God, Joseph triumphantly reveals

Him and His meanings. This is the darkest possibility, blocking the channels of language, leaving God, effectively, unfound in the human world. This is the condition in which language itself goes into exile. Jacob acknowledges God's hiddenness: conflict opens his eyes and heart to the absent God who may yet emerge obliquely in his words.

Jacob hopes that in acknowledging God's hiddenness he may give birth to blessing. Poignantly, abruptly, in the middle of his words, he cries out: *"For Your salvation I hope, O God!"* (Gen. 49:18). These three Hebrew words, occupying a whole sentence, sharply break with the rhythm and genre of Jacob's speech. But here, possibly, is the heart of his project: the profound need for salvation in a condition of absence. In fact, these three words, which center on hope, may have generated the reading of Mei Ha-Shilo'ach. Jacob prays for eventual clarity, for God, however obliquely, to show His face. He surrenders the superiority guaranteed in advance. Acknowledging that God's face is hidden, and casting off his preconceptions, Jacob allows himself free association with whatever God will place in his mouth.

A radical historical crisis is signaled here. Jacob leaves his children in exile. If they are to survive, they must yield their pretensions to full vision of meaning. The hidden face of God indicates an absence that must, first, be noticed. There is a desire to *reveal the end;* or, as Kierkegaard put it, to write the *last part* of one's book: in doing so, however, the writer "will make it thoroughly clear . . . that he makes a written renunciation to all claim to be an author. . . . To find the conclusion, it is necessary first of all to observe that it is lacking, and in turn to feel quite vividly the lack of it."[47] And, again, in the last of his pseudonymous works, the *Concluding Unscientific Postscript,* Kierkegaard writes of the sensibility that "constantly keeps the wound of the negative open, which in the bodily realm is sometimes the condition for a cure."[48]

This tension, which R. Nahman describes as acknowledging that God's face is hidden and setting oneself to find Him, haunts those who live in exile. At critical moments, absence of expressible meaning seems to engulf everything: "Suppose," writes the philosopher François Lyotard, "that an earthquake destroys not only lives, buildings, and objects but also instruments used to measure earthquakes."

Here, not only meaning is absent, but even its matrices; language falls silent; and the historian "must venture forth by lending his ear to *what is not presentable under the rules of knowledge*."[49] Here is a reality that defies the competence of historical knowledge. Here is silence that itself becomes a call.

For Joseph and his brothers, exile is a heritage from their father. It is also inherent in the way they speak to one another in their last scene, as channels of language are congested by old secrets. Language becomes *satum*—blocked and banal.[50] Even the graphic presentation of this final reading in Genesis displays this blockage, closing up the apertures that make reading possible. The brothers' attempts to make use of Jacob's death by fabricating a narrative that offers satisfactory closure tragically conspire with Joseph's love of solutions to thicken the plot of exile.

But, Mei Ha-Shilo'ach suggests, Jacob does have a final, redemptive bequest for his children. His death and burial remove him physically but create an ancestor from whom they can learn something about meaning and conflict. In the human act of burial,[51] the afterlife of the dead begins. Jacob offers both exile and an intricate path to meaning. All is blocked; but, the Hasidic writers insist, *there is an ending*. To access its knowledge, to find God's hidden face, it is necessary to acknowledge the blockage and, in Maurice Blanchot's beautiful phrase, to keep watch over absent meaning.

TWELVE

Law and Narrative in the Book of Ruth

LAW AND LOVE

R. Ze'ira said: This scroll [of Ruth] tells us nothing of purity or impurity, of prohibition or permission. For what purpose was it written? To teach how great is the reward of those who do deeds of loving-kindness [chasadim].[1]

The central message of the book of Ruth, declares R. Ze'ira, is not embodied in law but in narrative. The book tells a story about the good things that happen to good people. For modern readers, of course, whose assumptions have been shaped by empirical and cultural experience of the *bad* things that often happen to good people, this conventional moral theme is not a simple teaching. But R. Ze'ira is careful with his terms: he refers specifically to "those who do *chasadim*—deeds of loving-kindness": *chesed* is the elemental quality often translated as "love," in the expansive sense that opens out into kindness, loyalty, and courage. But the core meaning of the word resists translation. I suggest that Ruth is the narrative that displays that core meaning in dynamic form.

Here, *chesed* moves and breathes and generates; here, we can take the measure of its uncanny power. Here are Ruth and Orpah, in their devotion to their mother-in-law;[2] and Ruth in relation to Boaz (and perhaps to her dead husband, Machlon).[3] But here, too, is Boaz, encouraging Ruth to glean in his field, and instructing his reapers not to shame her but to leave the "forgotten" stalks for her gleaning. He, too, is one of the *chesed* people who, the midrash affirms, will receive great reward. His goodness, however, is precisely an expression of the *legal* requirements of his situation; that is, of the "prohibitions and permissions" that the midrash maintains are *not* the subject of the book. The laws of the field, as they are sketched out in Leviticus (19:9–10), are given dramatic form in Boaz's words of *chesed*.

In this narrative, then, law and *chesed* are not schematically opposed to each other. Indeed, law and custom inform many aspects of the narrative of *chesed*.[4] It is precisely the licit and the illicit—prohibition and permission—that provide a structure of meaning within which human desire and fear may resonate. Nevertheless, the *main* purpose of the book is "to teach how great is the reward of those who do deeds of *chasadim*." In the end, the book tells a tale of a certain kind of human being. How does this way of being human relate to the concept of law that defines the world of Ruth?

The law that most significantly defines this world is an exclusionary law that is never articulated in the text. Throughout the whole course of her narrative, its shadow looms over Ruth: "No Ammonite or Moabite may enter into the community of God; none of their descendants, even in the tenth generation, shall ever enter into the community of God."[5]

This law, repressed in the text, bans Ruth from ever marrying into the community that she has so passionately insisted on claiming as her own ("Your people are my people and your God my God" [Ruth 1:16]). In the presence of this law, the unguarded desire with which she solicits Naomi resonates poignantly. We will look more closely at this opening scene. For now, I suggest that if Ruth is described, repeatedly and redundantly, as Ruth *the Moabite*, this is a way of intimating the legal barriers that frame her world. If no explicit mention is made of this law, its presence nevertheless informs all the interactions, in speech and silence, of the narrative. Repressed, it is everywhere operative.

THE CONVERSATIONAL FABRIC AT RISK

However, perhaps the most radical claim that the midrash has to make about law in the world of this book is in its reading of the opening words: "And it was in the days when the Judges judged." As a historical framework for the narrative, the expression "when the Judges judged" *(b'shfot ha-shoftim)* has a tongue-twisting, ambiguous quality: "In the days of the Judges" would have served the purpose more simply. The mirroring noun/verb structure raises questions: Does it mean "when the Judges judged"? or "when the Judges were judged"?

> It was a generation that judged its judges. If the judge said to a man, "Take the splinter from between your teeth," he would retort, "Take the beam from between your eyes." If the judge said, "Your silver is dross," he would retort, "Your liquor is mixed with water."[6]

If the judge is subject to harsher criticism than the defendant, this signifies a breakdown in the rule of law. If judges cannot rule on the improprieties of those they judge without provoking much more serious charges against themselves, this indicates how seriously disabled the legal system has become. The images—the splinter between the defendant's teeth, the beam that grotesquely emerges from *between his eyes*—indicate the greater gravity of the judge's misdeeds. The splinter may be embarrassing, inappropriate, but the beam—massive, distorting the judge's vision—compromises the radar by which he evaluates the world.[7]

In another round of metaphors, the judge compares the defendant to alloyed silver: hidden acts have compromised his integrity. The latter responds with a counterimage: the judge is like watered-down liquor. At what point does diluted liquor stop being liquor? By imperceptible degrees, the judge has lost his claim to represent justice; or worse, in a world of such judges, the very concept of justice may lose all meaning.

From a sociological perspective, the corruption of judges signifies the collapse of a shared world of meaning. Peter Berger discusses the challenge posed by the sociology of knowledge to the maintenance of a particular worldview. Concerned with "studying the relationship between human thought and the social condition under which it occurs," this discipline proposes that "the plausibility . . . of views of reality depends upon the social support these receive." Individuals are subject to powerful pressures to conform to the views of others. "It is in conversation, in the broadest sense of the word, that we build up and keep going our view of the world."[8] Social networks or "conversational fabrics" produce practices and explanations to bolster conviction: controls, therapies, legitimations create the "plausibility structure of the conception in question."[9]

In this view, the mystery of faith disappears as the theologian's world becomes "one world among many," a community of faith constructed in a specific human history. Similarly, when judges lay themselves open to serious charges of personal corruption, a world of expectation and belief begins to crumble. "Woe to that generation," declares another midrash, "that judges its judges—who require judgment!"[10] The woe of this condition is socially determined but its effects endanger the survival of a world of meaning.

In a similar vein, the midrash indicates the reason for the catastrophe that befell the aristocratic house of Elimelekh. The death of father and sons, which effectively sets the narrative of Naomi and Ruth in motion, demands moral explanation. What was the family's sin that brought down such calamity?

It has been taught: In time of pestilence and in time of war, gather in your feet, but in time of famine, spread out your feet. Why then was Elimelekh punished? Because he struck despair into the hearts of Israel. He was like a prominent man who dwelt in a certain country, and the people of that country depended upon him and said that if a drought should come he could supply the whole country with food for ten years. When a drought came, however, his maidservant went out and stood in the marketplace with her basket in her hand. And the people of the country said, "This is the man upon whom we depended that if a drought should come he would supply our wants for ten years, and here his maidservant stands in the marketplace with her basket in her hand!" So with Elimelekh! He was one of the notables of his place and one of the leaders of his generation. But when the famine came he said, "Now all Israel will come knocking at my door [for help], each one with his basket." He therefore arose and fled before them. This is the meaning of the verse, "And a certain man of Bethlehem in Judah went . . ."[11]

Even though it is legitimate to flee the country in famine, Elimelekh bears responsibility for the social effect of abandoning his city. As a leader, a wealthy man, a *parnas* (lit., a feeder), he is the focus of economic expectations; when famine comes and his servant is found begging for bread in the market, this deals a blow to morale in Bethlehem. An unwritten contract has been betrayed; his power in the community had been based on an implicit network of social expectations.

The midrash emphasizes the inner world of the community, the narrative it has created around its feeder-leader. Beyond any specific law that might have prevented him from fleeing the country, his place in the "conversational fabric" of Bethlehem makes its own moral demand. Indeed, he flees not at the prompting of hunger, but in a kind of nervous recoil: he speaks of being besieged at every aperture by hands grasping begging bowls. What will remain of him? He flees, that is, in apprehensive fantasy of depletion, of loss of selfhood. To be a feeder means power; but it also raises the specter of the self consumed by the needs of others. In the face of this, Elimelekh abandons his position in his social world.

Nurturing life, maintaining vital connections with others, fulfilling needs—this is the world of *gomlei chasadim,* of "those who do deeds of kindness." In fleeing, Elimelekh removes not only his food resources but his role in the "plausibility structure" of his world. Essentially, he fails as a *father:* the death of his sons testifies to this larger failure.

"NOMOS AND NARRATIVE"

In his important essay "Nomos and Narrative," Robert Cover writes of the normative universe that is created and maintained by the interaction of law and narrative:

> We inhabit a *nomos*—a normative universe. We constantly create and maintain a world of right and wrong, of lawful and unlawful, of valid and void. . . . The rules and principles of justice, the formal institutions of the law, and the conventions of a social order are, indeed, important to that world; they are, how-

ever, but a small part of the normative universe that ought to claim our attention. No set of legal institutions or prescriptions exists apart from the narratives that locate it and give it meaning. For every constitution there is an epic, for each decalogue a scripture.[12]

The commitments of those who administer and live in this world determine what law means. Law may be viewed as a "bridge linking a conception of a reality to an imagined alternative—that is, as a connective between two states of affairs, both of which can be represented in their normative significance only through the devices of narrative."[13] This "alternity" is one element of a *nomos* that is

> a present world constituted by a system of tension between reality and vision. . . . Our visions hold our reality up to us as unredeemed. . . . But law gives a vision depth of field, by placing one part of it in the highlight of insistent and immediate demand while casting another part in the shadow of the millennium.[14]

Cover illustrates the tension between law and narrative by the example of the biblical law of inheritance, by which the eldest son receives a double portion of the family inheritance.[15] This is formulated as case history: the rights of the son of the less favored wife are pitted against those of the loved wife, already suggesting the human complexity that law addresses. But accompanying these legal texts are many significant biblical narratives, in which the firstborn is passed over in favor of the younger son: Cain and Abel, Ishmael and Isaac, Esau and Jacob, Joseph and his brothers, Moses, Solomon.

Cover argues that the formal precept is not ignored; indeed, these narratives owe their power to the fact that the rule was normally obeyed. However, in each narrative where succession is contested,

> there is a layer of meaning added to the event by virtue of the fact that the mythos of this people has associated the divine hand of destiny with the typology of reversal of this particular rule. . . . Revelation and . . . prophecy are the revolutionary chal-

lenges to an order founded on revelation. . . . The biblical narratives always retained their subversive force—the memory that
divine destiny is not lawful.[16]

NAOMI'S BITTERNESS

In terms of Cover's analysis, the normative world in which Ruth's
story plays out displays, from the start, symptoms of collapse. Law
no longer acts as the bridge linking reality and vision. The judge's
vision is skewed, yielding no depth of vision but mere fragmentation. Skeptical narratives are generated in this world, where the "is,"
the "ought," and the "what might be" are separated by impassable
gaps. Midrashic stories illustrate the failure to maintain a world of
meaning: stories of hypocrisy and resentment at norms that have
lost their power to inspire.

One such midrashic theme describes the famine at the beginning
of the narrative as a spiritual drought, a hunger for the word of
God.[17] Law has been rendered problematic by the way it is embedded
in narrative. The very idea of the world-builder, world-protector, the
feeder, the parent, has become hollow, and with it the sense of a normative universe. An unacknowledged "hunger" pervades the world
to which Naomi returns with her two Moabite daughters-in-law,
Ruth and Orpah.

All three are widows, childless, the wreckage cast up after the
storm. "She remained," we are twice told of Naomi—"the debris of
her husband's death, and then of her sons."[18] Eviscerated of meaning,
Naomi is compared in the midrash to the husk that is left over after
the meal offering goes up in smoke; after her sons die, she becomes
"the husk of a husk" (shiyarei shirayim).[19] Inessential, connected to
nothing, she returns with her daughters-in-law to Bethlehem. Like
the walking dead . . .

Naomi is absorbed in persuading the younger women to leave
her, to return to their proper place—ishah beit imah: "each woman to
her mother's house" (Ruth 1:8). "May God deal kindly with you, as you
have with the dead and with me! May God grant that each of you
finds security in the house of a husband!" Either within the mother's

world or within the husband's, a woman finds her home. Even the Hebrew wordplay (*ishah beit ishah*—lit., "each woman the house of her man") conveys the mirroring of identity that is to be sought. In this way, the hunger that these Moabite women bring with them may be appeased.

For their sakes, Naomi works to detach them from her. Speaking with affectionate gratitude, she calls them *b'nottai:* "my daughters." But in the same breath, tenderly, imperatively, she presses them: "*Shovna b'nottai*—Go back, my daughters!" Even as they link their destiny with hers—*ki ittakh nashuv:* "No, we will return with you"— she insists on the empirical meaning of "return": for them, this refers to Moab, for her to Bethlehem. Three times, she urges them, *Shovna,* pathos mounting as she demonstrates the absurdity of their journey.

At this point, Naomi's speech becomes charged with complex meaning: "It is very bitter to me because of you" (Ruth 1:13). Her passion to send them back to Moab is, on one level, concern for their future, for their sterile prospects if they attach themselves to one so wounded by fate. At the same time, however, she tells of her bitterness, which is *because* of them: these Moabite marriages have undone her sons, and the presence of these forbidden wives in her future life in Bethlehem would be a constant irritant and reminder of her losses. Naomi thus is driven by a real desire to rid herself of these clinging foreigners. She refuses their love, kissing them goodbye even as they weep, until Orpah returns her kisses, yielding to Naomi's bitter desire.

Naomi's bitterness is the main burden of her response to the women of Bethlehem. She repudiates her own name; she has outlived its meaning. ("Don't call me Naomi [sweetness]. Call me Mara, for God has made my lot very bitter" [Ruth 1:20]). Unrecognizable, now, as the wealthy patroness of an ordered world, she addresses those who had been abandoned by her family, telling them about her own inner world, grown rank and sterile. God is the agent of her bitterness. The taste in the mouth conveys an intimate experience, which comes from God. For if He is the God of justice, and the world is a world of law, her suffering must be a sign of guilt. "God has afflicted me *[anah bi],*" she declares (1:21); but also, "God has *testified* against me."[20] This alternative translation is offered by Rashi and Ibn Ezra: Naomi declares that her sufferings proclaim her failure; the bitterness of her fate becomes a source of humiliation.

Here, Naomi speaks like Job, justifying God and reproaching Him. Ibn Ezra in fact refers to Job's use of a similar metaphor of suffering as testimony to guilt. "You renew Your witnesses against me" (Job 10:17). But in Job's speech, we can clearly hear the complexity of his feeling:

> If I am wicked, woe is me; and if I am righteous, yet I will not lift up my head, for I am filled with disgrace, and I see my affliction;
>   If my head is lifted up proudly, you hunt me like a lion; and again work wonders against me:
>   *You renew Your witnesses against me,* and increase Your indignation against me; You bring fresh armies against me. (Job 10:15–17)

Job's state of mind, like Naomi's, is one of bitterness: "I will speak in the bitterness of my soul" (Job 10:1). Baffled by God's vindictiveness, Job wishes both to justify it and to reaffirm his innocence. Desiring a meaningful world, he searches for the law he has transgressed, but he can never quite convince himself that this accounting is true. Naomi similarly brings God into her narrative, as both rationale and enigma. If she is implicated in her husband's guilt, her sin is that she betrayed the expectations of her world, and her punishment that she is left empty, isolated: "I went away full, and God has brought me back empty" (Ruth 1:21). But if she is not to be held responsible for her husband's dereliction—if, that is, her status as a woman exonerates her from blame for his decisions—then she is wrecked indeed: of husband, children, and meaningful world.

Throughout her Job-like speech, Naomi ignores Ruth's silent presence—as, indeed, do the townspeople, the women of Bethlehem. Ruth's attachment does not at all, it seems, mitigate Naomi's emptiness. Nothing in her resonates to Ruth's equally passionate speech of devotion ("Where you go, I will go . . ."). Fiercely dedicated to her rhetoric of bitterness, Naomi had responded to Ruth's passion with silence: "And when Naomi saw that she was determined to go with her, she ceased speaking to her" (Ruth 1:18). Out of that silence came her testament of bitterness and utter loneliness. And now, Ruth stands silent and unnoticed, her loving words fallen on deaf ears. At this point in the narrative, Naomi allows Ruth to accompany her, but her silence becomes an attack on Ruth's consoling presence.

In a well-known anecdote, Freud describes his infant grandson playing with a reel and string, throwing it into the crib and pulling it back, at the same time uttering sounds that Freud interpreted as *Fort!—Da!: Gone!—Here!* In play, the child is enacting his mother's absence, repeatedly staging her disappearance and return.[21] Jonathan Lear comments that "the game is prompted by a rip in the fabric of life. . . . The outcome of the game is to convert what would otherwise be a nameless trauma into a loss."[22]

"In being able to get to 'da,' the child is able to bring his experience together." The game "creates a cultural space in which the child can play with loss: in this way he comes to be able to tolerate it and name it. . . . It is only now that the mind can wander around the idea of mother's absence. . . . Inventing the game, the child thereby creates the capacity *to think* about mother's absence. . . . This is courage-in-the-making.[23]

If, however, the child could never get to *"Da!,"* if he kept end-lessly repeating *"Fort!"* he "would never be able to get a thought together. . . . Rather than face his own loss, the child might opt to attack his own ability to understand what had happened to him."[24]

Naomi, I suggest, is engaged in such an attack on her own capacity for making meaning. Imaginative activity might link loss with recovery. Instead, Naomi's rhetoric isolates her in bitterness. For her, hope can mean only a grotesque scenario of the aged body giving birth to infant husbands for aging wives (Ruth 1:11–13).

THE PARADOX OF RUTH

The ironic aspect of this is that Naomi's one resource, that might have motivated her to hope, is Ruth—who is invisible, inaudible, and banned by law from entering the community of God. Because she is a Moabite, Ruth is excluded from Naomi's world. This is the law, and its reason is clear: "because they did not come out to greet you with bread and water on your journey after you left Egypt" (Deut. 23:5).

The Moabite stigma originates in a historical failure of *chesed,* of connectivity, of acknowledgment of the other's need.[25] The Moabites are not feeders, maintainers of the world. But in this narrative, as we have seen, it is precisely the Judean world that has failed to sustain the social networks, the conversational fabrics that keep faith alive. And it is Ruth the Moabite who has offered to be a link between past and future, a possible resource of meaning in Naomi's destitute condition.

Here, then, is the problem constituted by Ruth. Her situation is sharply defined by law: she can never find her place within the community of God. But, as every reader has always known, the book of Ruth will conclude in the way legislated by history: Ruth will marry Boaz, and their child will be grandfather to King David. In a sense, then, all the delays in the narrative, the episodes drawn out over a summer, the outrageous move that sends Ruth, dressed and scented, to the granary floor and to Boaz's feet on a harvest night—all contain a hidden necessity: the ending is legislated in advance.

NARRATIVE AND ITS DISCONTENTS

"Une chose," says Sartre, *"commence pour finir."*[26] Since everyone— writer and readers—knows that Ruth must marry Boaz, what is holding the narrative back? What, in fact, allows there to be a narrative at all? What makes this piece of history narratable? The answer is related to Ruth's identity, to the problem that she poses to the *nomos,* the normative world of law and story that, even before she arrived, had already been in palpable crisis.

Problems, crisis, conflict, instability—these are the very substance of narrative. Ruth constitutes the possibility of narrative, as well as the necessity of closure. But narrative is often radically at odds with the utopian state of closure. This central tension in the traditional novel, for instance, is the subject of D. A. Miller's *Narrative and Its Discontents.* Miller argues that "closure" and "narratability" are essentially in conflict. If the *ending* of a Jane Austen novel, for instance, yields "a state of absolute propriety: proper understanding expressed in proper erotic objects and proper social arrangements," her *narratives* are "generated precisely by an underlying instability of desire, language, and society, and, as such, they are inevitably felt to threaten the very possibility of this definitive, 'finalizing' state of affairs."[27]

Such a fiction, then, is a "perverse" project, since it longs to eliminate the narratable: it "is a quest after that which will end questing; or a distortion of what will be made straight." Since "only insufficiencies, defaults, deferrals, can be 'told,'" the very idea of a narrative of happiness is put in question.[28] For to bring the narrative to a state of fulfillment is, virtually, to end it. Miller argues, therefore, that narratives are never fully or finally governed by their endings.[29] There is an ongoing tension between the two states:

> One might say that the traditional novelist gives play to his discontent only to assuage it in the end, much as the child in Freud makes his toy temporarily disappear the better to enjoy its reinstated presence. . . . [It] would therefore work on the principle of vaccination; incorporating the narratable in safe doses to prevent it from breaking out.

If the novel attempts to master the narratable, it rarely succeeds. Even in Freud, the "anxiety of disappearance is intrinsically stronger than the gratification of return, for the former is not merely a moment in the game, it is the underlying inspiration of the game itself."[30]

In the book of Ruth, the narratable dimension is generated by Ruth herself, by the problem, the instability that she constitutes for the normative world that she enters. The resulting turbulence in some sense survives even the fulfillment, legislated in advance, of the ending. Simply by being Ruth, she raises questions and disrupts norms. She represents the "quest after that which will end questing," the "distortion of what will be made straight."

The "distortion of what will be made straight" embedded in Miller's rhetoric refers to the verse from Ecclesiastes that inaugurates the following midrash:

It is said, "That which is crooked cannot be made straight; and that which is wanting cannot be counted" (Eccles. 1:15). In this world, he who is crooked can be made straight, and he who is straight can become crooked; but in the hereafter he who is crooked cannot be made straight, nor can he who is straight become crooked. "And that which is wanting cannot be numbered." Consider two wicked men who associated with one another in this world. One of them repented of his evil deeds before his death while the other did not, with the result that the former stands in the company of the righteous while his fellow stands in the company of the wicked. Seeing him there, he says, "Woe is me, is there favoritism here? We both of us committed robberies, we both of us committed murders together, yet he stands in the company of the righteous and I in the company of the wicked!" And they [the angels] reply to him and say, "You fool! You were despicable after your death and lay for three days, and did not they drag you to your grave with ropes? 'The maggot is spread under you, and the worms cover you' (Isa. 14:11). But your old acquaintance understood and repented of his evil ways, while you too had the opportunity to repent but you did not take it."

He immediately replied, "Let me go and repent!" And they answer him, "You fool! Do you not know that this world is like the Sabbath and the world from which you have come is like the eve of the Sabbath? If a man does not prepare his meal on the eve of the Sabbath, what shall he eat on the Sabbath? And do you not know also that this world is like the sea, and the world from which you have come is like the dry land? If a man does not prepare his food on the dry land, what shall he eat at sea? And do you not know also that this world is like the wilderness and the world from which you have come is like cultivated land? If a man does not prepare his food on cultivated land, what shall he eat in the wilderness?"[31]

The verse from Ecclesiastes becomes a description of *olam ha-ba*, the world to come. There, the distorted can never be made straight. Herein lies a bittersweet paradox: our present world is the world for *teshuvah,* for repentance, while in the world to come, character and destiny are determined on arrival. The case of the two sinners, whose ways part so dramatically in the hereafter, stages the classic idea: repentance, transformation, is possible in this world only. Our hero is slow to comprehend this radical difference between worlds: he can no longer transform himself and his fate. The world he came from was the place and time for making the crooked straight. Three classic images conclude the midrash: the Sabbath, the sea, the wilderness—all must have food prepared in advance if one is to eat there. Or rather—from the perspective of the world to come, where the sinner now finds himself—if you want to eat *here,* you had to prepare *there.*

This midrash draws its narrative power from its shifted perspective. A classic notion about the relation between worlds looks different from the viewpoint of the hereafter. The world to come represents to the human being in this world a consummation devoutly to be wished, a prospect of clarity and fulfillment after the turbulence of this world. But it turns out that there is a sting in the sweetness. A melancholy limitation invests the hereafter: nothing there can change.

In Miller's terms, this world is the world of narrative, while the hereafter represents closure. Once instability and error have been resolved, one may find oneself at sea, or in a wilderness, or in the quiescence that is the Sabbath, without access to the "food" that can be prepared only in the energy of narrative. Narrative and closure are incongruous worlds; but they yearn for each other. In the world of narrative, ultimate meanings are veiled; desires and fears, multiple possibilities, suspense, insufficiency keep the story going. But when the end comes, nothing further can develop; all is arrested in the condition to which its turbulent history has brought it.

THE RIGORS OF NARRATIVE

From this midrashic perspective, Ruth and Orpah represent these two modalities. Ruth has the capacity to generate a story. Precisely because of her vulnerability, her "outsider" status, as well as her mysterious desire to find her way in, she sets episodes in motion. Lacking everything, she makes a decision to leave behind her the stability of family, nation, and religion, and to embark on a *narrative:* on a course that offers no visible fulfillment. Orpah starts out with her but soon yields to the blandishments of closure: "Return," Naomi urges, "*ishah beit ishah*—each woman *[ishah]* to the home of her man *[ishah]*" (Ruth 1:9). The play on words enacts closure, fulfillment. Orpah chooses the resolution that will liquidate a senseless journey.

But Ruth knowingly declares her commitment to a future that can bear no imaginable fruit. To Naomi's plea that she *go after* her sister-in-law, she responds, "Do not urge me to leave you, to turn back and not *go after* you. For wherever you go, I will go; wherever you lodge, I will lodge; your people shall be my people, and your God my God. Where you die, I will die, and there I will be buried. Thus and more may God do to me if anything but death parts me from you" (Ruth 1:16-17).

Her famous speech holds no hint of fantasy, of utopian closure. Her desire is to go with Naomi—or rather, to *go after* her—and to be with her unto death and burial. The dynamic of the moment is stark: urged to follow Orpah's lucid journey to womanly fulfillment, she redescribes this as a movement away from the essential magnetic connection to Naomi. *Going after* Naomi evokes an entranced state, an attachment blind to rational interest. *"I remember for you the devotion of your youth, your love as a bride—how you went after Me in the wilderness, in a land not sown"* (Jer. 2:2). Like the children who follow the Pied Piper into the mountain, she knows only the life she senses in this connection. This is the future she chooses, soberly, undeluded; it leads to the only plausible consummation, death, burial. She has no argument with Naomi's grim realism about the possibility of a conventional happy ending. Marriage and children do not figure in her expectations. Instead, she commits herself to the unmitigated rigors of her desire. Naomi is the essential clue in her labyrinth: for Ruth, she opens up a vista of movement and rest, of nation and God.

Orpah acts out the classic consummation of narrative: tearfully, she kisses her mother-in-law farewell and makes toward her foreseeable ending. Ruth, on the other hand, *clings* to Naomi (*davkah bah*). To cling is to affirm the passionate desire that constitutes its own gratification. It is to refuse to flee the rigors of narrative. The word *davak* is most resonantly used of erotic and of mystic connections: "Therefore, a man shall leave his father and mother and cling to his wife, so that they become one flesh" (Gen. 2:24). "And you who cling to God your God are all alive today" (Deut. 4:4). Implicitly, to cling is to move away from the given relationships of childhood, to desire a life beyond infantile fantasy.[32] At the same time, it evokes a risky persistence, a courage of desire that bears one through the drifts of the narratable. Ironically, this courage is subject to ambiguous judgments: it can be viewed as a clinging *to* infantile fantasy.

The tactile imagery of *devekut* (clinging, *stickiness*) accompanies Ruth throughout her narrative. She holds fast to Naomi, whose emptiness, as we have seen, is at first unappeased by her. Ignored by the women of Bethlehem, Ruth then proposes to find a field in which to glean—"following someone in whose eyes I may find favor." She is casting herself into the drift of chance and desire. In this world of narrative, the traveler has no guarantee of finding safe harbor. With unusual pungency, the narrative declares, *va-yiker mikrehah*—"*as luck would have it,* it was the land belonging to Boaz who was of Elimelekh's family" (Ruth 2:3). Unwittingly, she has fallen upon her destiny; her trajectory now holds out hope of a real "return" to Naomi's family. But, from Ruth's perspective, she is *taking her chances* (lit., *her chance chanced it*).

The coincidence that brings her to Boaz's field is of the kind that, retrospectively, can be read as an accident that was meant to happen. But Ruth has no knowledge of the ending of her story. In the drift of contingency, she enters a field; unknown to her, Boaz asks his servant about her: "Whose is this young woman?" And the servant answers: "She is the Moabite woman, who returned with Naomi from the fields of Moab" (Ruth 2:5–6).

The reader is caught in the subtle anguish of narrative. Ruth is being maligned: twice in one sentence, the servant has managed to refer to her Moabite origin—and this, after the narrator has reintroduced her at the beginning of the chapter as Ruth *the Moabite*. All the hopelessness of her situation is here, insult added to injury. What is the servant implying as he harps on her background?

"Whose is this young woman?" Did he not then recognize her? But when he saw how attractive she was, and how modest her comportment, he began to inquire about her. All the other women bend down to gather the ears of corn, but she sits and gathers; all the other women hitch up their skirts, and she keeps hers down; all the other women jest with the reapers, while she is reserved; all the other women gather from between the sheaves, while she gathers from that which is already abandoned.

In the same way one must understand the verse, "And when Saul saw David go forth against the Philistine, he said to Avner . . . 'Whose son is this youth?'" (1 Sam. 17:55). Did he not then recognize him? But yesterday he sent to Jesse saying, "Let David, I pray you, stand before me: for he has found favor in my sight" (16:22); and now he inquires about him? But when Saul saw the head of the Philistine [Goliath], he began to ask about David, "Is he a descendant of Perez, a king? Is he a descendant of Zerah, a judge?"

And Doeg the Edomite was present at that time, and he said to him, "Even if he is a descendant of Perez, is he not of impure descent? Is he not a descendant of Ruth the Moabitess?" Avner said to him, "But has the law not been revised: *Ammonite but not Ammonitess, Moabite but not Moabitess?*" He answered him: "But if so, we could also say *Edomite but not Edomitess, Egyptian men but not Egyptian women?* Why were the men repudiated? Was it not 'because they did not meet you with bread and water'? (Deut. 23:5). The women ought to have met the women!" And for the moment, Avner forgot the law.

Saul said to him, "Go and inquire about that law which you have forgotten from Samuel and his court." When he came to Samuel and his court, he said, "Where did this come from? Not from Doeg? Doeg is a heretic and will not leave this world in peace! And yet I cannot let you go without an answer: 'All glorious is the king's daughter within the palace' (Ps. 45:14)—It is not for a woman to go out and bring food [to foreign armies], but only for a man. 'And because they hired Balaam against you' (Deut. 17:5)—A man hires, but not a woman."

"And the servant who was in charge of the reapers answered and said, 'It is a Moabite woman'" (Ruth 2:6)—and yet you say that her conduct is praiseworthy and modest? Her mother-in-law has taught her well![33]

The midrash finely inflects the dialogue. Why did Boaz ask about Ruth? Surely he knew of her? Soon after, in fact, he will tell her of her admirable reputation for *chesed,* loving-kindness. His question, however, is *"Whose is she?"*—meaning that he is impressed by her bearing, her modesty and intelligence, and implying: "Could she be mine? Could she belong to my world?" Generations later, the same question will be asked by Saul about David, implicitly about his potential for positions of power. Immediately, David will be disparaged by Doeg, on the grounds of his impure descent from Ruth the Moabitess. A debate breaks out: on a closer look at the biblical text, it has become clear that only the male Moabite is banned from the community of God, not the female. The law has been revised, since this gender distinction makes room for Ruth to marry Boaz. But is this not a mere verbal quibble, which could be extended *ad absurdum* to all such marital bans? No, declares Samuel; here the issue of greeting and feeding strangers would exempt women on the grounds of modesty; the cultural codes of the time would make that obvious.

On Samuel's view, the biblical text always contained this nuanced gender distinction that might have been interpreted at any time. The fact remains that this interpretation was never made until Ruth came on the scene; she is the first Moabite woman to benefit from the change in the law.[34] It is striking, too, that in the time of David the issue is still controversial, so that the malicious counselor, Doeg, can still cast aspersions on David's ancestry, while even the honest counselor, Avner, forgets the law. The question has to be taken to Samuel, as the final court of appeal. He determines the gender functions in such a way as to make the new reading unassailable. But the midrash concludes by returning to Boaz and the servant in the field. His disparaging answer directly addresses Boaz's admiration of Ruth: she has merely benefited from good coaching (lit., *healing*) by Naomi. In other words, once a Moabite, always a Moabite. . . .

The midrash dramatizes the hostility of the social world that Ruth is trying to penetrate. The premise, both now and in the future, in the story of David, is that the law has been changed: otherwise, how could Boaz marry her? But the change has just happened, and society retains its sense of a normative world that excludes Moabites. Such classifications of inside/outside are hard to shift. One hears in the tone of the servant in the field, as well as of Doeg, generations later, a malicious satisfaction in ruling the other out. In Doeg's case, he himself is then paradoxically *ruled out* from the world ("He is a heretic and will not leave this world in peace")—precisely because of his rigidity. Revisions in the law constitute its organic life. But Ruth will nevertheless remain suspect; the taint of her ancestry will remain troubling in the narratives, if not in the law books, of her new people.

Moreover, the fact that the law is changed just as Ruth meets Boaz suggests that it is Ruth's presence that has made this change necessary. The servant's grudging answer defines her as merely *well coached*. But clearly it is her distinction that rouses Boaz's interest; in combination with her taboo status, it constitutes her as an irresoluble question. *Whose* is she? Her nation is under the stigma of lacking *chesed,* the instinct to nurture the vulnerable other. But this national character is not reflected in Ruth's bearing, which is charged with *chesed.* To what world, then, does she belong?

The law will make space for her inside the world of Judea. Boaz will beautifully describe her to her face in terms that evoke the epic heroes of his world.[35] Law and narrative both include her—and yet, poignantly, she remains an outsider, foreign in the eyes of others and in her own eyes.

POWERS OF HORROR

One specific dimension of her reviled status is the sexual notoriety of Moabite women. *Zenut,* sexual seduction, sexual waywardness, has marked the Moabite story from its origins. We remember how, after the destruction of Sodom, Lot's daughters made their father drunk and had sexual relations with him.[36] But it was the daughter who inscribed the incest into her son's name (Mo'av=Me-avi [from my father]) who exposed the act of darkness to the light. Later, it was the women of Moab who enticed Israel into the sin of Ba'al-peor (Num. 25:1).

This association of Moab—and, particularly of its women—with lasciviousness accompanies Ruth throughout her dealings with the world of Bethlehem. She becomes the embodiment of what Julia Kristeva calls *the abject:* that which is *cast out* of the self and considered loathsome:

> The abject confronts us, on the one hand, with those fragile states where man strays on the territory of *animal*. Thus by way of abjection, primitive societies have marked out a precise area of their culture in order to remove it from the threatening world of animals and animalism, which were imagined as representatives of sex and murder.
>
> The abject confronts us, on the other hand, and this time within our personal archeology, with our earliest attempts to release the hold of maternal entity even before existing outside of her, thanks to the autonomy of language.[37]

Both upheld by taboos and a focus of fascination, the abject rouses fear of the loss of boundaries.

Ruth's transactions with Boaz can be read as marked by such an ambiguity. After the servant has answered Boaz's question and Boaz has kindly opened up the field for her gleaning, her first speech transforms her from an object discussed by others into a linguistic being, neither animal nor the mother of early, preverbal life:

> And she fell upon her face and bowed down to the ground and she said to him, "Why have I found favor in your eyes to recognize me, though I am a stranger?" (Ruth 2:10)

In addressing him, she in a sense responds to his question: "Do you not hear me, my daughter?" (Ruth 2:8). Something unresponsive in her moves him to ask, *Do you hear? Do you understand my language?* But strikingly, her answer questions the very possibility of his *recognition* of her. The Gaon comments: Falling on her face expresses a certain dejection. Ruth sees that Boaz has spoken kindly to her, as though he means to marry her, and yet he adds, "So shall you cling to my servant girls," classing her with his servants and making no further move of courtship. Nevertheless, she bows down in gratitude for his kind words, and she says, "Why have I found favor in your eyes to recognize me, to single me out, as though you will know me as a wife?" But again, "I am a stranger": it is clear from your last words that I am a foreigner. I don't understand your meaning!

On this reading, Ruth is acutely sensitive to the ambivalence that Boaz displays toward her. The law may have been changed, but Ruth is depressingly conscious of the residues of the old boundaries: Boaz is blowing hot and cold. What might have been a moment of closure remains tantalizingly ambiguous—and keeps the narrative going in all its danger and possibility.

And yet, even as closure eludes her, Ruth speaks with a certain lucid pleasure in the sheer paradox of the moment. She plays with language: "Why have you acted as though you *know* me *[l'hakireini]*, as though I were recognizable to you, when I am a *stranger [nokhriyah]*?" To be known by the other, *as the other*—this, too, is recognition. Perhaps Ruth senses the hopefulness in being known in her very difference? Perhaps her foreignness can even become a gift that she can offer Boaz? As Edmond Jabès suggests, "The foreigner allows you to be yourself by making a foreigner of you."

At any rate, the Gaon notes a certain confidence in Ruth's tone, as she responds again to Boaz's second, and even more kindly, speech: "And she said, 'May I find favor in your eyes, my lord, for you have consoled me and you have spoken gently to your maidservant— *though I am not so much as one of your maidservants*'" (Ruth 2:13). Between this usual reading and the Gaon's *("I shall not be like one of your maidservants")*, the complexity of Ruth appears—modest and assertive, dejected but hopeful.

This complexity is her response to the ambivalence of Boaz and his world toward her. At the same time, we can say that it is precisely this complexity that arouses hostility and suspicion in a solidly demarcated world. As one who *clings*—serially, to Naomi, to the servants in the field, to Boaz during the night on the granary floor— Ruth is perceived as disturbingly anomalous.

In a classic essay, Sartre writes of the *viscosity,* stickiness, neither solid nor liquid, which is among our primary experiences. Mary Douglas amplifies Sartre's notion to discuss cultural categories and their relation to anomalies. She engages with the threatening quality of the viscous as "aberrant fluid or . . . melting solid":

> Its stickiness is a trap, it clings like a leech; it attacks the boundary between myself and it. Long columns falling off my fingers suggest my own substance flowing into the pool of stickiness. . . . In this way the first contact with stickiness enriches a child's experience. He has learnt something about himself and the properties of matter and the interrelation between self and other things. . . . It makes the point that we can and do reflect with profit on our main classifications and on experiences which do not exactly fit them. . . . So from these earliest tactile adventures we have always known that life does not conform to our most simple categories.[38]

The public character of a culture makes its categories more rigid, so that the anomalies that inevitably occur must generate new interpretations to reduce the threat to its definitions of reality.

In her *stickiness*—her persistent desire, her bold modesty—Ruth poses a disconcerting challenge to the world of Bethlehem. On the one hand, she is obedient, malleable: according to the midrash, she is submissive to all the legal stringencies with which Naomi tries to deter her. Even her great speech of devotion is read in this way, as a point-by-point response to the difficult demands of the law: Naomi warns her: "It is forbidden for us to go beyond the Shabbat boundary," and Ruth answers, *"Where you go, I will go."*[39] She accepts the boundaries of law, in its 613 forms: she will not visit theaters and circuses; she will not sleep in a house without a mezuzah; she acknowledges the sanctions for serious crimes—four types of executions and two types of ignominious burial. All these limitations she accepts.

On the other hand, her very existence challenges the imaginative boundaries that have defined the world she desires to penetrate. Moreover, in her poetic declaration of love for what she senses in and through Naomi, she has the courage to "play" with the imagin-ings of death, destruction, and loss. She not only *clings:* she *reflects* on *devekut* (the clinging posture), on the ways that language creates boundaries and dissolves them. Naomi acknowledges Ruth's capac-ity to play—but only, at first, by "ceasing to speak to her"—that is, she yields to Ruth's wish not to be separated from her, but she yields without any corresponding wish of her own.

Boaz acknowledges Ruth's spiritual parentage: like Abraham, she has left her father and mother in her quest for an unknown alterna-tive.[40] She belongs to the world of Abraham, which for her is repre-sented by Naomi. As a *mother,* however, Naomi is far from incarnating the soft mother of infancy. Her words create her as sep-arate, distinct, not the loving mother of primal desire, but the mother whom Christopher Bollas describes as a *process of transforma-tion.* From the mother who constantly alters the infant's environ-ment to meet her needs, the child is born into her own emerging capacities to transform the world, to handle and differentiate objects, to speak their distinctness. This transformational impact of the mother in early life is carried over into adulthood, when there will appear "the object that is pursued in order to surrender to it as a medium that alters the self."[41] The Ruth who is able to articulate her experience, to play in the potential space between desire and reality, is also the Ruth who seeks *devekut,* the transformative moment of uncanny fusion.[42]

It is at the hands of a somewhat austere mother, then, that Ruth seeks out her own transformation. Confronting the image of her own abjectness, she persists in her desire for the *devekut,* the unthinkable intimacy that is its other face. Treading a fine line, she assumes the risks of narrative: clinging to Naomi, seeking out some-one in whose eyes she will find favor, even twining herself around Boaz's feet on the granary floor. Haunted by racial stereotypes both of sexual license and of emotional stinginess, she neither acts them out nor violently repudiates them. If she is to find the transforma-tion she so devoutly wishes, she must open herself to the vagaries of narrative, and to its dangerous language of becoming.

. . .

THE WINGS OF THE DOVE

Ruth's process has its palpable effect on Naomi and Boaz. Naomi at first responds to Ruth's initiative of gleaning with just two words: "Go, my daughter." But at the end of the day, she greets Ruth returned from the field as *her mother-in-law*, three times repeated (Ruth 2:18,19). She speaks a language of blessing—that is, of wishfulness—previously unheard on her lips: "May the one who acknowledged you be blessed. . . . Blessed be he by God, who has not abandoned His love *(chesed)* to the living and the dead!" (2:19–20). She is now able to speak of God's love as persisting through all, as falling on the living and the dead. That is, where previously she had spoken dismissively of Ruth's *chesed* "with the dead and with me" (1:8), she now defines herself and Ruth as *the living*. God's love is now a sensed reality, affecting even the traumatic past. Redundantly, she addresses Ruth as her daughter-in-law (2:20,22), as well as her daughter (2:22). The increased vitality and warmth of Naomi's language is her tribute to Ruth's very being. Most strikingly, Ruth is once again named, both at the beginning of the chapter and at the end, as *Ruth the Moabite* (2:2,21). Outsider still, evoking complex associations, Ruth has palpably brought Naomi to life and to a language of attachment.

The dynamic effect on Naomi of Ruth's presence is felt most clearly in chapter 3. Here, Naomi takes the initiative and plots for Ruth the nighttime encounter with Boaz that will bring her narrative to its consummation: "And Naomi her mother-in-law said to her, 'My daughter, shall I not seek for you *a resting place* that shall be good for you' " (Ruth 3:1). Naomi declares the nature of her quest: an end to questing for Ruth, a full closure that will meet her desire.

The idea of *mano'ach*, a resting place, reminds us of Noach's dove, sent out to test the waters after the Flood: "And the dove did not find *a resting place* for the sole of its foot, so it returned to him to the ark, for there was water over all the earth" (Gen. 8:8). Like the dove, Ruth seeks a place of stability in the volatile world. By now, Naomi identifies sufficiently with Ruth's quest to wish it happily over.

But the dove's flight configures a question *(Have the waters abated?);* whether she returns to the ark or not will become the answer. Ruth's quest, too, raises an existential question, about the possibility of fulfillment for such desires as she harbors. Naomi demonstrates how deeply she has been affected by Ruth's courage, by her stamina in the face of danger. To find consummation for Ruth—and for herself—she adopts Ruth's "narrative" mode, endangering her reputation in the most Moabite way imaginable.

Naomi sends Ruth to the granary where Boaz lies during the night after the harvest, to uncover his feet and lie there. Ruth's preparations are to be those of a woman before a sexual encounter: washing, scenting, dressing, and secrecy. Boaz's acts are precisely foreseen: he will eat and drink and lie down—and he will tell her what to do. Ruth obediently replies, "Everything you tell me I will do"—her obedience including obedience to Boaz's instructions. Naomi, it seems, has entered into Ruth's risk-taking mode, coaching her for a role that unnervingly resembles the role of the harlots, the *zonot*, who haunt granary floors and who are the target of prophetic anger[43]—the role for which Ruth's Moabite background has prepared her. Only by such ambiguous means, it seems, can the world of law, of normative order, be accessed.

Ruth, in fact, follows Naomi's instructions, but not their timing: first, she goes down to the threshing floor and only then she makes her preparations. The Talmud notes the change: she prefers not to walk in public in her perfumed finery.[44] Another midrash adds that she fears being accosted by "one of the dogs."[45] Her own intelligence guides her to modify Naomi's instructions.[46]

Naomi thrusts Ruth into the eye of the storm, into all the turbulence of narrative. It is as though she now loves Ruth sufficiently to take risks with her. Indeed, she makes common cause with Ruth, referring to Boaz as *our kinsman*.[47] The Jerusalem Talmud indicates the depth of Naomi's identification with Ruth by noting her instructions—"Wash, perfume yourself, dress up, and go down to the granary . . . and lie down" (Ruth 3:3): the Hebrew verbs are read in the second person, but written, strangely, in the *first person*. "She told her: 'My merit shall go down there with you.' "[48] In other words, Ruth does not go alone: Naomi is with her as she moves into her moment of greatest narrative suspense.

In her relation with Boaz, too, Ruth displays a *chesed* quality that affects him profoundly. Here, too, the paradox is that the humble outsider, needy, suspect, abject, generates a movement of reciprocal recognition and gratitude in the other. The teacher is redeemed by the student, the older man is guided by the younger woman, Israel is regenerated by the woman from Moab.

Ruth is under Naomi's instructions to obey his wishes: "he will tell you what to do." But when he wakes at midnight, shuddering at the mysterious being who grips his feet, and asks, *"Who are you?"* she answers by identifying herself and, in the same breath, *giving him, too, an identity:* "I am Ruth your maidservant. Spread your robe over your maidservant, *for you are a redeemer"* (Ruth 3:9). She is, in fact, proposing marriage to him.[49] In a sense, too, she is answering his question to the servant in the field: *"Whose* is this woman?" She is his, she tells him, soliciting his care, protection, warmth, sexual intimacy; his concrete representation of the "wings[50] of the Lord God of Israel." He himself had described her as seeking refuge beneath those wings (2:12). Bringing his rhetoric in the field into intimate focus, she makes him the very emissary of the Lord God of Israel.

In soliciting him in this way, however, she is also expressing her solicitude for him: she is giving him an opportunity to be a redeemer. By redeeming Naomi's estate, in the legal sense, and by becoming Ruth's metaphorical redeemer—by taking her under his wing—Boaz will find his own redemption.[51] She has given him a place in her narrative, which, it will transpire, is to become *the* narrative. Through his connection with her, he will endow Elimelekh's family with a future. And as this connection takes form in her words, he is affected by the *chesed,* the beauty that her words create. He responds with strange gratitude: "Blessed are you of God, my daughter! Your latest deed of *chesed* is finer than the first, in that you have not gone after young men, whether poor or rich" (Ruth 3:10).

Boaz addresses Ruth as a source of blessing, and of *chesed*—precisely in her relation with him. He had woken, shuddering at the mysterious pressure at his feet; at first, he had not identified her as a woman—perhaps she is a demon embodied from his dream?[52] His initial terror modulates into acknowledgment of the loving energy that emanates from her. In soliciting his redemption, she has drawn out of him, with gentle force, a possibility of larger life. Demonic,

uncanny, speaking with numinous authority, she regenerates both
herself and him.

Chesed intimates, among other translations—love, kindness,
devotion, courage—*beauty*. The grace, the favor *(chen)* that she char-
acteristically hopes to find in the eyes of others is the twin of *chesed:*
a beauty of being and of language.[53]

In the potential space created by their words, they sleep till dawn.
She rises before the light, "so that none may know that the woman
came to the granary." And the next day, Boaz brings the work of narrative to its conclusion. What has been acknowledged in the darkness is publicly ratified in the daylight, at the gate of the city. Here, it
turns out, the other redeemer, Mr. X, is willing to undertake the legal
redemption of Naomi's estate—but not the metaphorical redemption of Ruth. His reason is clear: "lest I destroy my own estate" (Ruth
4:6). Ruth would bring confusion, anomaly to his condition. In economic terms, he would be investing his own resources in a son who
would legally be regarded as Machlon's. A banal and immediate
"happy ending" to his narrative is endangered by Ruth's ambiguity,
by her neediness, her viscosity. So Boaz consummates the narrative:
by legal transaction before witnesses, he claims both land and
woman, assuming responsibility, allowing intimacy, freeing all three
from limbo.

Ruth, meanwhile, returns unseen in the dark to her mother-in-
law, who asks her, "*Who are you,* my daughter?" What quality in Ruth
leads both Naomi and Boaz to ask this question? Boaz, of course,
asked it in a midnight daze, between sleep and waking. Naomi
knows her as "my daughter." And yet, for both, Ruth retains to the
end an *unknown* quality. Something in her remains strange. In both
cases, she has an answer. We have seen how deeply Boaz is affected
by the authority of her words. For Naomi, Ruth produces the barley
that Boaz has given her in token of promised plenitude. The dove has
found a resting place in the midst of many waters. But both answers
only partially eliminate the force of the question. There is a residue
of inscrutable *chesed,* of sheer unknownness, in the woman whose
impact they both know.

·   ·   ·

IF BOAZ HAD KNOWN . . .

The end of the story is, of course, triumphant. It is also public knowledge, an ending legislated in advance. A baby is born of the marriage of Boaz and Ruth, whose genealogy is then doubly traced: he is grandfather to David, and descendant, generation by generation, of Perez, son of Judah. The roll call of generations from Perez leads to Boaz and onward again to David. This is closure in its most utopic, definitive form: a list of male names, quasi-mythical, making for full and final meaning.

But what are we to make of the relation between this ending and the narrative that has come before? The midrash raises an uncanny question:

"And he reached her parched corn, and she ate and was satisfied and had some left over" (Ruth 2:14). R. Isaac ben Marion said: This verse can teach that if a person is going to perform a good deed, he should do it with all his heart. For had Reuben known that Scripture would record of him, "And Reuben heard it, and saved him from their hand" (Gen. 37:21), he would have borne Joseph on his shoulder to his father. And had Aaron known that Scripture would record of him, "And also, behold, he comes forth to you" (Exod. 4:14), he would have gone forth to meet him with timbrels and dances. And had Boaz known that Scripture would record of him, "And he reached her parched corn, and she ate and was satisfied and had some left over" (Ruth 2:14), he would have fed her fatted calves.

R. Cohen and R. Joshua of Siknin said in the name of R. Levi: In the past, when a person performed a good deed, the prophet placed it on record; but nowadays when a person performs a good deed, who records it? Elijah records it and the Messiah and the Holy One, blessed be He, add their seal to it. This is the meaning of the verse, "Then they who feared God spoke with one another; and God listened, and heard, and a book of remembrance was written before Him" (Mal. 3:16).[54]

If Boaz had known how his narrative would be written, he would have acted with greater panache—less equivocally, less hesitantly. Instead of a pinch of parched corn, he would have fed Ruth fatted calves! In the light of retrospective knowledge—that is, of full and final versions—how much better would we play our roles! If we knew the camera was focused on us, we would acknowledge one another with drums and dancing. The midrash seems to be advocating a kind of imaginative awareness that will intensify the good deed—*as if* we knew the final record.

However, in using the rhetoric of "If Boaz had known," the midrash paradoxically stages the unbridgeable gap that must exist between act and record, between narrative and closure. In the conditions of this world, the world of narrative, human beings struggle, ignorant on many levels, to act well, to "perform good deeds." The deeds of *chesed* in this world are often hesitant, partial, expressing the instability, complexity, insufficiency of narrative. Moreover, if Boaz had known how his story would be recorded, his act of kindness to Ruth might have been more fulsome; but it would have lost its human force, which was born precisely of the tensions of the situation that Ruth has precipitated. The fraught moment of his gift, the pinch of parched corn, if recorded on camera, would need an inspired director to communicate its mute expressiveness. The narrator of Ruth achieves just this in quietly observing, "And she ate and she was satisfied"—she was well satisfied by his gift. A pinch of corn has become an epiphany within this narrative world.

Narrative and closure constitute incompatible worlds. It is in the nature of narrative to be plagued by ignorance, oscillations, misunderstanding. Within these risky parameters, Ruth expresses, passionately but incompletely, her desire. Without knowing how the text will inscribe her, she clings, seeking that uncanny fusion, the *devekut* that her words can only intimate.

In fact, the midrash goes on to speak of the "nowadays" reality as one of pure narrative: when one does a good deed, who records it? In the past, the prophet was at hand to record such deeds—the gap between narrative and closure was narrowed, the prophet effecting almost simultaneous translation, so that full and final meanings were, to some extent, even in this world, to be understood. But now, such record is a matter of faith: Elijah, the Messiah, God Himself ensure that the significant moments of narrative are written, their meanings elucidated. But that writing happens in some other world. Here, now, Ruth must speak her desire without hearing its ultimate resonance.

The midrash ends with a verse from Malachi, the last prophet: "Then they that feared God spoke[55] with one another; and God listened, and heard, and a book of remembrance was written before Him." The conversation of the righteous is heard and recorded by God. In the reading of R. David Kimchi (Radak), the prophet is recording a contest of conversations: the disbelievers speak to one another, questioning God's appeals to them to consider their ways ("It is useless to serve God" [Mal. 3:14]); in response, "those who feared God and esteemed His name" maintain a conversation of faith. The constructive conversation is thus doubly recorded—by the prophet and, in his account, by God, too.

After the prophetic period, however, the existence of such a divine record becomes a matter of faith. We remain essentially uncorroborated in this world, with our various social networks, normative worlds, conversational fabrics. Although the midrash maintains that all is ultimately on record—signed by God—in this world we have no access to the divine text. Those who belong to the society of believers sustain their world of belief in God's providence and in the larger repercussions of human action. They may discuss theology and interpret reality; but final meaning—the divine writing—is not available to them. Like Reuven, and Aaron, and Boaz, they live in this world, which is the world of narrative. Here, a pinch of parched corn may have to do in place of fatted calves; Boaz's heart will have to be whole enough to sustain the energy of Ruth's desire.

In Ruth, even if theirs is only one among many conversations, those who seek meaning generate a world of meaning. In the end, Ruth's narrative is written, and brought to triumphant closure. All the emptiness is filled, the distortion made straight. The child that is born to Ruth and Boaz is set in a line of names that leads to David and to the Messiah himself. A world of narrative desire is consummated.

· · ·

RUTH EFFACED

But there remains one disturbing dimension to this fulfillment: Ruth disappears from the text. Just as the whole community seems to welcome her among them, ratifying Boaz's redemption, blessing her with the destiny of Rachel and Leah, the matriarchs who built the House of Israel, her disappearance begins. She becomes "the woman who is entering your home" (Ruth 4:11); "this young woman" (4:12). For the women who congratulate Naomi on the birth of the child, she is "your daughter-in-law who loved you" (4:15). It is they who name the child, after Naomi has taken him into her bosom and become his foster mother; deliberately, they displace Ruth: "A son is born to Naomi!" (4:17). Only for Boaz is she simply Ruth: "And Boaz took Ruth; she became his wife, and he came unto her" (4:13).

Ruth has faded out of this triumphant pageant. In uncanny fulfillment of her own absurd scenario of hope, Naomi has in old age given birth to this child and suckled him. Some translators evade this implication: in using the word *yulad* (born), the women may be referring simply to Naomi's fostering, rearing the child; so, too, the word *omenet* may refer to her nurturing role.[56] But these are metaphorical expansions; the literal meanings, with their strong physical base, shockingly displace Ruth and set Naomi at the center of the closing vignette, as mother and nurturer.

In a sense, Ruth's disappearance is inevitable. So powerfully is she associated with the turbulence and contingency of narrative that no place can be found for her in the world of full and final meaning. Perhaps her presence in the utopian pageant would be too disturbing; the ending might not fully govern the discomfort that Ruth arouses, the questions that her narrative has evoked. If there is to be a sense of total coherence at the close of her book, she must be effaced.

With the disclosure of the birth line that leads from Ruth to David, a hidden necessity comes to light; it has all been for this; *une chose commence pour finir*. But if all has been legislated in advance, how is it that this narrative remains readable, even strangely compelling? Perhaps we return to it again and again because its discontents, its drift of desire, are not totally assuaged? If the subversive questions that she evokes are not to get out of hand, Ruth must be effaced from the ending. Pressing against too many boundaries, she endangers the magnificent necessity of this closure.

CHOOSING RUTH

Might there have been an ending that read Ruth back into the text? The midrash offers such an alternative ending, where narrative and closure, desire and law, find, in all their tension, a moment of meeting:

> "There they dwelt, occupied in the king's work." On the strength of this verse, they said that Ruth the Moabite did not die until she saw her descendant Solomon sitting and judging the case of the harlots. That is the meaning of the verse, "And set a throne for the king's mother," that is, Bathsheba, "And she sat at his right hand" (1 Kings 2:19), referring to Ruth the Moabite.[57]

It seems that, after all, there is more to tell: another story about a mother and child. The midrashic writer begins by speaking of Ruth's death—the true closure of narrative—as deferred, so that she may see a narrative unfold which is not, properly, her narrative. "Ruth the Moabite did not die until she saw her descendant Solomon sitting and judging the case of the harlots." Till she witnesses this scene, she *cannot die*. Effaced from the public record at the moment she gives birth, she can be laid to rest only after she sees how Solomon her grandson stages her life in his judgment.[58]

In this last scene, Solomon, her grandson, is powerfully, and famously, maintaining a world of law: judging a case of disputed maternity, he sets a seat for his mother, Bathsheba. By midrashic license, the biblical description is complicated, its folds unfurled, to make room for Ruth. *"She sat at his right hand—that is, Ruth the Moabite."* A spectral presence, unable to die, she is read into the scene to witness the judicial narrative that now unfolds.

In what will become Solomon's flagship case, two harlots lay claim to the surviving baby. One woman narrates the circumstances of the case at great length: how both mothers gave birth, alone in the house, how the other woman lay upon her baby during the night and smothered him, how she switched the babies, how the speaker rose to nurse her baby in the morning, and "behold it was not my son, whom I did bear." The other woman disputes the narrative, creating a deadlock of versions: "No, the dead child is yours, mine is the living one" (1 Kings 3:16–23). The king repeats the deadlocked stories, calls for a sword, and commands that the live baby be cut in two, half for each mother. The true mother responds: *"Give her the living child— only don't kill him!"* But the other woman insists, "He shall be neither yours nor mine—cut him in two!" The king's verdict follows: *"Give her the living child—only don't kill him; she is his mother."*

With this judgment, Solomon gains his extraordinary reputation: "divine wisdom was within him to do justice" (1 Kings 3:28). This is the case that Ruth the Moabite witnesses before she dies. Here, like nesting boxes, narrative within narrative, we have Ruth's closure, Solomon's initiation into divine wisdom, the two harlots' stories, each excluding the other. Solomon orders the baby to be cut in two, a brutal gesture of justice,[59] which the false mother accepts: *gezoru—* Cut! It is only fair, evenhanded; in such a case of conflicting desires and versions, neither woman shall have the baby. The true mother prefers to lose the baby to her rival. Solomon's true verdict now emerges, once the counterfeit has done its work. But his majestic words of law simply repeat the words of the true mother, adding simply *hi imo—she is his mother*.

It turns out, then, that the first verdict, *Cut him in two!* was simply a charade, an incitement to extend the narrative. Apparently an expression of pure legality, his verdict acts performatively to generate a yet unknown justice. It provokes both women to show their true colors. Essentially, it provokes the true mother, in all her blind despair, to *frame the verdict*. It is as though Solomon is quoting her in a self-evident decision.[60] The true mother identifies herself in the very words with which she yields her child to the lying mother, in her readiness, that is, to live the confusion and anguish of narrative, rather than cut through to the inhumanly incisive gesture of law:

"Cut!" Solomon, in a sense, does no more than *listen* to the language of a woman struggling in and with her desire. Unwittingly, she speaks the words that he simply redirects to her.

Where did Solomon learn to listen so well? In the midrashic narrative, the two women who flank the king, Bathsheba and Ruth, become more than witnesses: both are associated with the issues that are brought into brutal focus in the case of the harlots. Solomon is in fact the child born of the illicit relationship between David and Bathsheba; he is also the great-great-grandson of Ruth *the Moabite,* once liminal, abject, full of desire. Perhaps Solomon has learned from these women to inform law with narrative, to bring the incompatible universes into dynamic relation.

Perhaps Ruth, in particular—who once chose for herself a new mother—has been chosen by Solomon as his ancestor. When he is faced with the challenge of recuperating and sustaining a viable normative world, his version of law seeks to bridge the reality and the vision, what is and what may be. As Robert Cover says, "Choosing ancestry is always a serious business." Solomon chooses Ruth the Moabite, as a constant reminder of the narrative anguish out of which transformations emerge.[61] Perhaps her willingness to be effaced from the written text of her own narrative, to give up her child as an act of devotion, is what gives her the grace of the "true mother" in the moment of Solomon's choice.

THE UNKNOWN WOMAN

In making this choice, Solomon has, in a sense, undermined the totality of closure. He has placed Ruth in a position where he can see her while he comes to his verdict. But perhaps more important, he is *seen by her:* "she did not die before *seeing* Solomon rendering judgment in the case of the harlots." To arrive at a true judgment that will reverse the anomie, the normative collapse with which Ruth's story began—*In the days when the judges judged*—Solomon must know himself as seen by the woman, the ultimately unknown woman, whose gaze has been acknowledged with such difficulty.

In the closing moment of Max Ophuls's film *Letter from an*

Unknown Woman, the man covers his eyes with both hands in horror and exhaustion, as images from earlier in the film assault him. Stanley Cavell suggests that this is

> an ambiguous gesture, between avoiding the horror of knowing the existence of others and avoiding the horror of not knowing it . . . he is in that gesture both warding off his seeing something and warding off at the same time his being seen by something, which is to say, his own existence being known, being seen, by the woman of the letter.[62]

As in the ending of Henry James's "The Beast in the Jungle," the "unknown woman" becomes a figure for the difficulty of seeing the other as other, of acknowledging her separate human existence. If the stupefied heroes of the Ophuls film and of the James tale survive the deaths of their unknown women, it is only to recognize, in a "horror of waking," that "*she* was what he had missed."[63] The essential point of view of the other, from the position of the feminine, is too late acknowledged. To have missed her would mean to have missed everything.

I suggest that the midrash responds to a similar concern with seeing and being seen in relation to Ruth. In the biblical story, this question animates her connections with Naomi, with Boaz, with the people of Bethlehem. She is the invisible heroine whose impact of *chesed,* of beauty, flows from her words.[64] The midrashic ending to her narrative allows her to see and to be seen in a mode of full acknowledgment.

Ruth's paradoxical closure comes when she sees Solomon *dan dinan shel zonot;* absorbing the voice of the harlot, the wayward voice of pure narrative, he regenerates a normative world that had lost plausibility. In some private sense, she presides over this scene; she is Solomon's teacher. Seeing this, she can die. As her grandson, Solomon learns from her a transformative dimension of Torah.

> R. Joshua b. Levi said: One who teaches his grandson Torah, is regarded by Scripture as though he had received it [direct] from Mount Sinai, for it is said, "And you shall make them [the things

your eyes have seen] known to your sons and your sons' sons"—
which is followed by, "the day you stood before God at Horeb"
(Deut. 4:9–10).[65]

The Torah one teaches a grandchild is the Torah of "the things
your eyes have seen" (Deut. 4:9). This is the Torah that flashes back to
Sinai, to the subversive moment of pure narrative. That foundational experience, before the Law was given, aroused "dread, fear,
shuddering and trembling."[66] Desire and fear sent the people plung-
ing back and forth at the base of the mountain, in overwhelming
attraction and recoil.[67] The grandparent teaches a Torah of r'iyah
(seeing), of personal experience, of oscillation, reversals, suspense,
insufficiency. Unlike the parent who transmits what has been
handed down, generation to generation, the grandparent, across a
gap, dares to tell a narrative of danger: how an unmediated vision of
great love, the impact of a passion, shook her being into movement,
unfurling it into a new language.[68]

Ruth's story makes it possible to reimagine Sinai. She becomes
the source of a teaching that Solomon acknowledges and makes his
own. She returns us, her grandchildren, across a gap, to that subversive force of narrative that is never lost. This is the Torah that, like its
teacher, can never be fully known, that is always discontinuous, of
which we ask, *Who are you?* and rejoice in the silence that animates
its response.

NOTES

INTRODUCTION: OF THE MURMURING DEEP

1. Cathy Caruth, "Traumatic Departures: Survival and History in Freud," in *Trauma and Self*, ed. Charles B. Strozier and Michael Flynn (Lanham, Md.: Rowman & Littlefield, 1996), 29.
2. Lionel Trilling, *Sincerity and Authenticity* (Cambridge, Mass.: Harvard University Press, 1972), 24.
3. Ibid., 25.
4. See chapter 10 of this volume.
5. Sefat Emet, *Bereshit*, 249.
6. The religious dimension of the Joseph narrative is framed significantly by this new silence: for the first time in the family history, God communicates with none of the protagonists. The patriarchal period is over. The Joseph story enacts rupture both within the family and between the family and God. (See chapter 10.) The effects on Joseph's relation to himself are the subject of chapter 11.
7. His own name (from the root *hoda*—to acknowledge) contains the letters of God's name (*B. Sotah* 10b). In admitting his responsibility for Tamar's pregnancy, and in acknowledging the difficult truths of his life with others, he comes into possession of his own name in which God's name is inscribed.
8. See Donnel B. Stern, *Unformulated Experience* (Hillsdale, N.J.: Analytic Press, 1997), 176.
9. Rashi to Genesis 2:15.
10. See chapter 1 of this volume.
11. Jean Laplanche, *Essays on Otherness* (London and New York: Routledge, 1999), 7–8.
12. Adam Phillips, *Promises, Promises* (New York: Basic Books, 2001), 205.
13. Laplanche, 82.
14. Christopher Bollas, *The Shadow of the Object* (London Free Association Books, 1987), 282.
15. Ibid., 283.
16. Jacqueline Rose, *On Not Being Able to Sleep* (Princeton, N.J.: Princeton University Press, 2003), 151.
17. Bollas, *Forces of Destiny* (London: Free Association Books, 1989), 63.
18. Maurice Blanchot, *The Unavowable Community*, trans. Pierre Joris (Barrytown, New York.: Station Hill Press, 1988), 25.
19. See chapter 6 of this volume.

20. Blanchot, *L'Entretien Infini*, quoted in Marc-Alain Ouaknine, *The Burnt Book* (Princeton, N.J.: Princeton University Press, 1995), 86–87.

21. Ibid., 283.

22. See Emor 28:16: "Indeed, there is God in this place, *and I did not know.*" The Zohar reads the emphatic *I* as both subject and object: "I have not known my Self."

23. *Likkutei Moharan*, 64:4.

24. Torat Kohanim to Leviticus 5:21. Thirdness has become a powerful idea in psychoanalytic thinking. Thomas Ogden, in *Subjects of Analysis* (Northvale, N.J.: Jason Aronson, 1994), describes the creation of the intersubjectivity of analyst-analysand as the "analytic third." This transcends the concrete presence of the two participants and constitutes an emergent complex presence. André Green and Jessica Benjamin, among other analysts, have developed this as a central concept. See also chapter 8 of the present volume.

25. Eric L. Santner, *On the Psychotheology of Everyday Life* (Chicago: University of Chicago Press, 2001), 6.

26. Lionel Trilling, *The Liberal Imagination* (New York: Viking Press, 1950), 221–22.

27. In an unpublished lecture, "Marginalia," presented at the London School of Jewish Studies, July 2007. My thanks to Jeremy Schonfield for his help in tracking down this information.

28. See A. M. Silbermann, trans., *Chumash with Rashi's Commentary* (Jerusalem: Silbermann Family, by arrangement with Routledge, Kegan, Paul Ltd., 1973). This translation is based on Abraham Benisch, *Jewish School and Family Bible* (London: James Darling, 1851), the first Jewish translation of the Bible into English.

29. Slavoj Žižek, *The Parallax View* (Cambridge, Mass.: Harvard University Press, 1992), 154.

30. Alphonso Lingis, *The Community of Those Who Have Nothing in Common* (Bloomington: Indiana University Press, 1994), 88, 91.

31. Ibid., 122.

32. This is reminiscent of the echo in the Malabar Caves in E. M. Forster's *A Passage to India*.

33. André Neher, *The Exile of the Word*, trans. David Maisel (Philadelphia: Jewish Publication Society of America, 1981), 68–69.

34. *Bereshit Rabbah* 2:4.

35. Ibid., 1:7.

36. Ibid., 3:4.

37. In a famous letter, Walter Benjamin writes to Gershon Scholem describing such revelations in Kafka's work: in the absence of any propositional content, the message has "validity without meaning," which creates a "nothingness of revelation." See Santner, 38–39.

38. Complex theological issues surround the order of creation. The notion that anything—light, *tohu va-vohu, tehom*—preexists God's creative words "Let there be light!" would be heretical. These midrashic passages, and many others, struggle with these issues.

39. See Pirkei Avot 5:1.

40. Mei Ha-Shilo'ach to Leviticus, *Emor*.

41. Caruth, 10–11.
42. Emily Dickinson, *The Complete Poems of Emily Dickinson* (Boston: Little, Brown, 1924), CVII.
43. Jean Laplanche, "Sublimation and/or Inspiration," in *Jean Laplanche and the Theory of Seduction,* ed. John Fletcher (*New Formations* 48, Winter 2002–2003), 48.
44. Gaston Bachelard, *Water and Dreams* (Dallas, Tex.: Pegasus Foundation, 1983), 92.
45. Ibid., 47.
46. William Wordsworth, "Lyrical Ballads," in *Wordsworth, Poetry and Prose* (London: Rupert Hart-Davis, 1955), 166, 154.
47. See chapter 3 of this volume. His prayer from the belly of the fish is couched in the past tense, becoming a prayer of thanksgiving for a resolved existential crisis. The *tehom* is not permitted to be present, profoundly experienced within him.
48. See Dickinson, CXIX.
49. Ann Carson, *Autobiography of Red* (New York: Vintage Contemporaries, 1999), 59.
50. Dickinson, CXXVII.
51. *B. Sukkah* 28a.
52. See Carson, 109.
53. Likkutei Yehudah, cited in *Torah Shelemah,* vol. 22 (Jerusalem, 1967), 182. A similar idea is attributed to the Kotzker: the veil is simply the face that masks its inner fire.
54. Pirkei Avot 2:15.
55. *Shir Ha-Shirim Rabbah* 1:52.

CHAPTER ONE: SEDUCED INTO EDEN: THE BEGINNING OF DESIRE

1. See, e.g., *Bereshit Rabbah* 8:7, 17:5.
2. See *Bereshit Rabbah* 8:7 and 8:8 for classic discussions of the heretical reading.
3. For a comparative account, see Nahum Sarna, *Etz Hayim: Torah and Commentary* (The Jewish Publication Society, 2001), to Genesis 1:26: "In the ancient Near East, the ruling king was often described as the 'image' of the 'likeness' of a god, which served to elevate the monarch above ordinary mortals. In the Bible, this idea became democratized. Every human being is created 'in the image of God'; each bears the stamp of royalty."
4. See Mei Ha-Shilo'ach, quoted on pp. 43–44.
5. See Rashi to Genesis 1:27: "And God created man in his image": in the mold which was made for him, since everything else was created by the word but he was created by the hands [of God], as it is said, "You set Your hand upon me" (Ps. 139:5).
6. Cf. Genesis 2:5: Immediately after his creation, the Garden is prepared for him and he is placed in it. Here, too, there is a cryptic emphasis on his being moved from one place to another. God could, after all, have prepared the Garden ahead of time, and formed Adam there.
7. See Exodus 22:15.
8. *Bereshit Rabbah* 15:5.
9. Rashi to Exodus 4:10.

10. Rashi to Genesis 16:3.

11. *Ashrei* is a wishful, counterfactual idiom.

12. Rashi to Numbers 20:25.

13. Rashi to Genesis 25:21. Lit., "lets Himself be seduced." This is the midrashic translation for *va-yei'ater lo*—"He accepted Isaac's prayer."

14. See Rashi to Genesis 2:20,21. Adam tries out the female animals—to no avail: "He did not find a helpmate."

15. See Rashi to Genesis 3:15.

16. *Bereshit Rabbah* 18:5.

17. Walter Benjamin, "On Language as Such and on the Language of Man," in *Reflections,* ed. Peter Demetz, trans. Edmund Jephcott (New York: Schocken Books, 1986), 318.

18. Seforno to Gen. 2:23

19. Cf. Macbeth's confident reaction to the prophecy that "none of woman born / Shall harm Macbeth" (act 4, scene 1, line 90). The large existential scope of the expression is reduced to a technicality—Macduff was born by cesarean section, which invalidates Macbeth's confidence.

20. "Born of woman" can be read to suggest that the frailty and indignity of the human situation is to be laid at woman's door. *Pirkei de-Rabbi Eliezer* 11 narrates that when God declares His intent of creating man, the Torah protests: "Master of all Worlds, the world is Yours, while the man whom You wish to create is *short-lived and sated with trouble;* he will fall into sin, and if you are not long-suffering, it would be better for him never to have entered the world." God answers: "Have I been called slow to anger and abounding in kindness without reason?" The midrashic description of man is quoted from Job (14:1): "Man, *born of woman, is short-lived and sated with trouble."* Radal, R. David Luria, comments that to be born of woman makes one prone to desire and therefore to sin; even Adam, who was not born of woman, sinned as soon as he was united with a woman. Contact with the feminine inevitably "humanizes" man to the point where God will require all His long-suffering love.

21. Bollas, *Being a Character* (New York: Hill and Wang, 1995), 239.

22. Ralph Waldo Emerson, "Nature," *Selected Essays,* ed. Larzer Ziff (New York: Penguin Classics, 1987), 38–39.

23. The single unequivocal appearance of this root in the Torah is the verse that introduces the narrative of the Golden Calf: "And the people saw that Moses *was late (boshesh)* in descending the mountain" (Exod. 32:1).

24. B. *Berakhot* 34b. Ha'amek Davar speaks from the world of nineteenth-century Lithuanian Judaism: sophisticated, cerebral, disenchanted, and conscious of the many complexities of the religious life. From a very different world, of course, the Hasidim found nothing more natural than praying to God in the open field.

25. Milan Kundera, *Slowness,* trans. Linda Asher (New York: HarperCollins, 1996), 39.

26. See Julia Kristeva, "Stabat Mater," in *The Kristeva Reader,* ed. Toril Moi (New York: Columbia University Press, 1986), 178–79.

27. T. S. Eliot "The Love Song of J. Alfred Prufrock" (London: The Egoist Ltd., 1917).

28. T. S. Eliot, "Virgil and the Christian World," in *On Poetry and Poets* (London: Faber and Faber, 1957), 122.
29. Adam Phillips, "The Soul of Man under Psychoanalysis," in *Equals* (New York: Basic Books, 2002), 100.
30. See, e.g., *Shemot Rabbah* 32:1.
31. Joseph Brodsky, *Less Than One* (New York: Farrar Straus Giroux, 1986), 7.
32. *Bereshit Rabbah* 17:5.
33. Walter Benjamin, "On Language as Such and on the Language of Man," in *Reflections*, ed. Peter Demetz, trans. Edmund Jephcott (New York: Schocken Books, 1896), 314–32.
34. Paul Celan, "Conversation in the Mountains." See John Felstiner, *Paul Celan: Poet, Survivor, Jew* (New Haven and London: Yale University Press, 1995), 142.
35. "The Meridian," Buchner prize speech, Darmstadt, October 22, 1960.
36. Hizkuni to 3:12.
37. See Mei Ha-Shilo'ach.
38. *Bereshit Rabbah* 29:22.
39. The midrash concludes: "God responded to this blasphemy by banishing him from the Garden."
40. *Standard Edition of the Complete Psychological Works of Sigmund Freud* XVII, ed. and trans. James Strachey (London: Hogarth Press, 1953–74), 141–42.
41. Eve, too, answers God in this mode, if more briefly: "The serpent duped me, and I ate *(va-okhel)*" (Gen. 3:13).
42. See Suzanne Fleischman, *The Future in Thought and Language,* cited in Malcolm Bowie, *Psychoanalysis and the Future of Theory* (Oxford, UK, and Cambridge, Mass.: Blackwell, 1993), 52–53: "future-tense forms . . . are rarely, if ever, employed exclusively for making subjectively neutral (factive) statements. . . . Futures appear commonly in a range of *nonfactive* utterances involving likelihood, supposition or inference, lack of knowledge, wishes and desires, intention and volition, obligation and command."
43. He suggests that "stretching out one's hand" holds the meaning of compulsive action. Cf. Genesis 22:10,12—the angel prevents Abraham from compulsively completing the sacrifice of Isaac.
44. *Ve-atta*—"And now"—is classically considered as introducing the theme of *teshuvah.*
45. *Eliyahu Rabba,* 1. This is a play on *garesh*—to drive out, to divorce.
46. Cf. the *bosh/boshesh* pun on which Ha'amek Davar based his meditation pp. 14–16).
47. Adam Phillips, *The Beast in the Nursery* (London: Faber and Faber, 1998), 45–49.
48. In this case, the past tense is converted to the future, perhaps suggesting a timeless quality to their intimacy, as though *he has always clung* to her.
49. Beit Ya'akov, *Bereshit,* 67.
50. The distinction is between "*upon* her heart" and "*to* her heart." See also the wordplay on *mefatehah* ("I will seduce her") and *petach tikvah* (opening of hope), in the next verse.
51. *Pirkei de-Rabbi Eliezer,* 41.
52. I am grateful to Jerome Gellman, whose discussion of *din* and *hesed* sparked

my formulation. See *Abraham! Abraham!* (Aldershot, Hants, UK, and Burlington, Vt.: Ashgate, 2003), 101.

53. *Da'at,* in Ramban's translation, is *ratzon*—intention, wish.
54. *B. Hullin* 60b.
55. *Bereshit Rabbah* 20:16.
56. Cf. *Shir Ha-Shirim Rabbah* 7:16, which inverts the statement: "The desire of Israel is for none but their Father in heaven."
57. Jean Laplanche, *Essays on Otherness* (London and New York: Routledge, 1999), 108.
58. See *Pachad Yitzhak,* Rosh Hashanah, 15. The Talmud (*Sanhedrin* 56b) derives all natural law (the Seven Noachide Commandments) from the word *va-yitzav*—"He commanded."
59. *Bereshit Rabbah* 8:8.
60. Proverbs 10:12. Mei Ha-Shilo'ach substitutes *rachmanut,* compassion, for *ahavah,* love.
61. See, e.g., Rashi to *B.Shabbat* 31a: " 'What is hateful to you, do not do to your friend': *Your friend* is God—just as you hate to be thwarted, so do not thwart Him."

CHAPTER TWO: DESPONDENT INTOXICATION: THE FLOOD

1. See Rashi to Genesis 4:1.
2. Rashi (Gen. 4:23) offers a bizarre midrashic account in which he is accidentally killed by his blind grandson, Lamekh, who then kills his own son for guiding his hands on the bow.
3. See W. B. Yeats, "Sailing to Byzantium," *The Collected Works of W. B. Yeats,* vol. 1, ed. Richard J. Finneran (New York: Simon & Schuster, Inc., 1924).
4. Franz Rosenzweig, *The Star of Redemption* (Notre Dame, Ind.: Notre Dame Press, 1985), 3.
5. See Genesis 11:10–25.
6. Ramban refers to the narrative of Shimei's suspended death sentence (1 Kings 2:36–46).
7. It is striking that Rashi makes no comment on the death theme.
8. Hizkuni explicitly comments on a *commutation* of the sentence (Gen. 3:17).
9. See Job 10:8.
10. *B. Shabbat* 147b.
11. Torah Temimah reads *itzbonekh v'heronekh:* the anguish *of* your pregnancy. Pregnancy becomes the prototype of this kind of anguish. He gives several examples of this rhetorical figure (known as hendiadys), where "and," linking two nouns in the expression of a single idea, is to be translated "of," or "in."
12. See Julia Kristeva, "Stabat Mater," in *The Kristeva Reader,* ed. Toril Moi (New York: Columbia University Press, 1986), 178–79:

    A mother is a continuous separation, a division of the very flesh. And consequently a division of language—and it has always been so.

    Then there is this other abyss that opens up between the body and what had been its inside: there is the abyss between the mother and child. What connection is there between myself, or even more unassumingly between my body and this internal graft and fold, which, once the umbilical cord has been severed, is an inaccessible other? My body and him. No connection. Nothing to do with it. And this, as early as the first gestures, cries, steps, long before *its* personality has become my opponent.

13. *Bereshit Rabbah* 25:2.
14. Ibid.
15. Ibn Ezra and Radak seem to refer to such a midrash. R. Kasher is skeptical about its existence: see *Torah Shelemah* to 5:29 [80].
16. See Rashbam, Hizkuni.
17. Tanchuma, *Bereshit* 11.
18. Rashbam strikes a different note when he emphasizes the *prayerful* nature of Lamekh's naming. See also Seforno.
19. Zohar 58b.
20. *Va-yit'atzev* is in the reflexive form: "He saddened Himself to the heart."
21. *Bereshit Rabbah* 3:9.
22. Zohar 69.
23. *Elohim* is used from the beginning of *parashat No'ach* (Gen. 6:9).
24. See Rashi to Genesis 6:4.
25. Cf. the potter image in Jeremiah 18:1–12, where the decision to remake the artifact occurs spontaneously, in response to a "corruption," something going wrong in the work.
26. *B. Sanhedrin* 108a.
27. See Or Ha-Chaim to Genesis 6:13.
28. No other figure in the Torah is praised so fulsomely.
29. *B. Sanhedrin* 108a.
30. See Genesis 6:22, 7:5.
31. Tanchuma, *Noach* 5. See also Rashi to Genesis 6:14.
32. Zohar 67b.
33. Ibid.
34. Søren Kierkegaard, *The Sickness unto Death,* ed. and trans. Howard V. Hong and Edna H. Hong (Princeton, N.J.: Princeton University Press, 1980), 33–34.
35. See, e.g., *J. Peah* 1:1. The phrase "They did exactly as God had commanded Moses," appears eighteen times in the final account *(parashat Pikudei)* of the building of the Tabernacle. This explains the eighteen blessings of the *Amidah* prayer.

    See also the punishment of Aaron's sons for offering "strange fire, which He had not commanded them" (Lev. 10:1). In the view of Ibn Ezra, Seforno, and R. Saadia Gaon, this refers to their merely "uncommanded" initiative. Hizkuni reads this as ordinary disobedience.
36. Or Ha-Chaim to Genesis 6:13.
37. See Rashi to Genesis 8:17.
38. Tanchuma, *No'ach* 9.
39. Tanchuma, *No'ach* 5.
40. Rashi to Genesis 8:16.
41. Rashi to Genesis 9:9.

42. William Shakespeare, *Hamlet* (Cambridge: Cambridge University Press, 1961), act 3, scene 1, line 65.
43. *Bereshit Rabbah* 34:5.
44. Anna Freud, "About Losing and Being Lost" (London: *Psychoanalytic Study of the Child*, 1967), 12.
45. *Bereshit Rabbah* 18:5.
46. André Neher, *The Exile of the Word*, trans. David Maisel (Philadelphia: Jewish Publication Society of America, 1981), 42.
47. Ibid., 48.
48. Ibid., 49.
49. Ibid., 51.
50. *Pirkei de-Rabbi Eliezer*, 13.
51. *Midrash Hagadol* 3:6.
52. *Bereshit Rabbah* 17:8.
53. *B. Berakhot* 40a.
54. See *B. Sanhedrin* 70a.
55. Ibid.
56. Kristeva, "Stabat Mater," 3.
57. Ibid., 33.
58. Ibid., 41.
59. Ibid., 42
60. Ibid., 5
61. Adam Phillips, *On Flirtation* (Cambridge, Mass.: Harvard University Press, 1994), 82.
62. Ibid., 83.
63. Ibid., 5.
64. Ibid., 53.
65. Ibid., 43–44.
66. *B. Sanhedrin* 70a.
67. *Pirkei de-Rabbi Eliezer*, 23.
68. Genesis 9:22, 24.
69. *B. Yoma* 75a.
70. Ibid.
71. *Pachad Yitzhak*, Pesach, 47.
72. See Rashi to Leviticus 10:2.
73. Marguerite Duras, *Practicalities* (New York: Grove Weidenfeld, 1990), 16–17.
74. *Hamlet*, act 1, scene 2, line 257.
75. The repeated form "Never again . . . never again" is read in the midrash as indicating an oath. See Rashi to Genesis 8:21: this is the oath that Isaiah refers to (Isa. 54:9).
76. Hizkuni to Genesis 8:21.
77. See Tanchuma, *Lekh* 10.
78. See Tanchuma, *No'ach* 9.
79. The term *amar* (say) is always used in these early chapters of the Torah; *dabber* (speak) is the form of address associated with "tough love."
80. Sefat Emet, *No'ach*, 30.
81. Or Ha-Chaim to Genesis 6:13.

82. See Ramban to Genesis 18:20.

83. In Lurianic kabbalah, *tzimtzum* is the primal movement of retraction by which God evacuates space where a world may be created.

84. A classic midrashic motif identifies "speaking *to* one's heart" as the mode of the righteous, as opposed to "speaking *within* one's heart." See *Bereshit Rabbah* 34:11.

85. See Ramban to Genesis 8:21. Ibn Ezra claims that God does inform Noach of His decision.

86. *B. Eruvin* 65a.

87. *Beit Ya'akov Noach*, 33.

88. In Jacques Lacan's famous phrase, the analyst is "the one who is supposed to know."

89. *Likkutei Moharan*, 1: 64.

90. R. Nahman compares the *klipot* to hair, fingernails, sweat.

91. See Don Handelman and David Shulman, *God Inside-Out* (New York: Oxford University Press, 1997), 185–201, for a brilliant articulation of similar tensions in Hindu mysticism.

92. Rashi to Genesis 8:21. He cites *B. Shavuot* 37, which quotes Isaiah 54:9—"as I swore that the waters of Noach would never again flood the earth"—and identifies the oath with the repeated biblical "Never again."

93. In the Jewish marriage ceremony, the words *Harei att mekudeshet* have the same effect.

94. Shoshana Felman, *The Scandal of the Speaking Body*, trans. Catherine Porter (Stanford, Calif.: Stanford University Press, 2002), 55–56.

95. She quotes Austin's metaphor about the miner's lamp on our forehead "which illuminates always just so far ahead as we go along. . . . The only general rule is that the illumination is always *limited*." (Felman, 70).

96. Felman, *Scandal*, 85.

97. "To breed an animal with the right to make promises—is not this the paradoxical problem nature has set itself with regard to man?" (Nietzsche, *Genealogy of Morals*, cited in Felman, 3).

98. *Bereshit Rabbah* 38:1.

99. *Tanchuma, Noach*, 18.

100. *B. Gittin* 43a.

101. Felman, *Scandal*, 93.

102. Ibid., 92.

103. Pirkei Avot 3:18.

CHAPTER THREE: JONAH: A FANTASY OF FLIGHT

1. Tarshish is identified by contemporary scholars as Tartesus in Southern Spain. See Uriel Simon, *Jonah* (in Hebrew) (Tel Aviv: Am Oved, 1992), 43–4.

2. The noun *tardema* signifies a comalike state. In this condition, Adam had Eve extracted from his side, and Abram had his vision of the Covenant between the Pieces.

3. The symmetry between the resolved evil and Jonah's rage is marked by the double *ra'ah* in each verse.

4. Abarbanel describes this as "a sickness: in the sadness of his heart, he fell sick with a great evil."

5. See Genesis 4:5–6.

6. The inversion of meaning is felt particularly since on other fast days the Thirteen Attributes passage from the Golden Calf narrative is the Torah reading for the *minchah* (afternoon) service. It is all the more striking that on Yom Kippur at this *minchah* service, when the community expects God's love and forgiveness to be invoked, Jonah's attack is read.

7. Freud's description of the Rat Man's prayers, in which, "like an inverted Balaam," he inserts curses and negations, is apposite here. As Jonathan Lear puts it, he is "launching a phantasized attack on his own prayer-making activity . . . primitively attacking his attempt at prayer. . . . He is actively disrupting his own thought." Jonathan Lear, *Open Minded* (Cambridge, Mass.: Harvard University Press, 1998), 107.

8. Classic interpretations of the narrative include, most prominently, the theory that Jonah deplores Nineveh's extraordinary repentance, since it shows up the recalcitrance of his own people, and the theory that he fears appearing as a false prophet, if his declaration of doom is not fulfilled. It is difficult to find support in the text for the first theory, while the second is rejected by Ibn Ezra on the grounds that the people of Nineveh are sophisticated enough to understand that the purpose of prophecies of doom is to rouse the population to repent—and to invalidate the prophecy. This more sophisticated understanding is presumed to be current already in Jonah's time; in its light, Jonah can only emerge as an *effective* prophet if his warning is heeded.

9. This is Jonathan Lear's expression, to be discussed later (see pp. 90–92).

10. See Lear, *Open Minded*, 64.

11. See Simon, 9–10. In *Ba-Midbar Rabbah* 18:17, Jonah is listed separately from the other eleven minor prophets, "since it is in a class of its own."

12. E.g., Psalms 69:3.

13. *Complete Poems* (New York: Macmillan, Penguin Books, 1994), 49–50.

14. Robert Pogue Harrison, *The Dominion of the Dead* (Chicago: University of Chicago Press, 2003), 8.

15. Adam Phillips, *Terrors and Experts* (Cambridge, Mass.: Harvard University Press, 1995), 48.

16. *Mechilta Shemot* 12:1.

17. B. *Brachot* 61a.

18. Emmanuel Levinas, *Nine Talmudic Readings* (Bloomington: Indiana University Press, 1990), 167.

19. This is the translation of R. Yehudah, cited by Ibn Ezra, for *v'nafshi yoda'at me'od* (Ps. 139:14). See also Metzudat David.

20. D. W. Winnicott, "On Communication," in *The Maturational Processes and the Facilitating Environment* (Madison, Conn.: International Universities Press, Inc., 1996), 185.

21. Ibid., 187.

22. *Pirkei de-Rabbi Eliezer*, 10.

23. Lear, *Open Minded*, 54.

24. Ibid., 29.

25. Ibid., 45–47.

26. Ibid., 46.

27. *Concluding Unscientific Postscript to the Philosophical Fragments: A Mimic-Pathetic-Dialectic Composition: An Existential Contribution*, by Johannes Climacus. Responsible for publication: S. Kierkegaard. Trans. D. F. Swenson and W. Lowrie (Princeton, N.J.: Princeton University Press, 1941). See Jonathan Lear, *Therapuetic Action* (London and New York: Karnac, 2003), 106–7.

28. Phillips, *Terrors and Experts*, 58.

29. Ibid., 58–59.

30. Ibid., 53.

31. It is striking that Josephus introduces this theme in his paraphrase of Jonah's prayer in his *Jewish Antiquities*, as do Philo and Sephardic *piyyutim* for Yom Kippur. See Simon, *Jonah*, 27.

32. See Psalms 107:27, where sailors are depicted as praying out of precisely this sense of the failure of any human ground of consciousness.

33. See *B. Berakhot* 34a.

34. Albert Hutter, "Poetry in Psychoanalysis," in *Transitional Objects and Potential Spaces*, ed. Peter L. Rudnytsky (New York: Columbia University Press, 1993), 75–76.

35. *Pirkei de-Rabbi Eliezer*, 10.

36. 1 Samuel 2:6.

37. *B. Berakhot* 31b.

38. See *J. Sukkah* 5:1; Midrash *Tehillim* 26; *Pirkei de-Rabbi Eliezer* 33; *Yalkut Shimoni* 550.

39. Zohar, *Hayyei Sarah*, 121b.

40. Cathy Caruth, "Traumatic Departures," in *Trauma and Self*, ed. Charles B. Strozier and Michael Flynn (Lanham, Md.: Rowman & Littlefield, 1996), 31–34.

41. Cathy Caruth, "Recapturing the Past: Introduction," in *Trauma: Explorations in Memory* (Baltimore: Johns Hopkins University Press, 1995), 153.

42. Ibid., 155.

43. Caruth notes "the high suicide rate of survivors, for example survivors of Vietnam or of concentration camps, who commit suicide only *after* they have found themselves completely in safety." *Trauma and Self*, 33.

44. The possibility that the first half of Jonah takes place in a dream is raised by R. Yosef ibn Caspi (1:1), who reports this as the view of some commentators. See Uriel Simon, *Jonah* (in Hebrew) (Tel Aviv: Am Oved, 1992), 10.

45. Christopher Bollas, *Cracking Up* (New York: Hill and Wang, 1995), 174–75.

46. Caruth, *Trauma and Self*, 38.

47. See Rashi on Ecclesiastes 7:1; *Kohelet Rabbah* 7:4.

48. It is significant that Moses, too, omits *Emet* when he first cites God's attributes in his plea for forgiveness after the sin of the spies (Num. 14:17–19). His purpose is clearly contrary to Jonah's.

49. In Flannery O'Connor's short story "A Good Man Is Hard to Find," an oversensitivity to the problem of an unintelligible world leads to psychopathic violence. My thanks to Eleanor Ehrenkrantz for this reference.

50. See Targum Yonatan: *Ha-lechada*—"Are you *very* angry?"

51. *Pachad Yitzhak*, Rosh Hashanah, 5.

52. See *B. Berakhot* 29b; *Mishnah Berurah* 122:5.

53. *B. Yoma* 53b; *B. Berakhot* 34a.

54. *B. Sotah* 22a.

55. *Netivot Olam,* Netiv Ha-Avodah, 5.

56. *B. Shabbat* 10a. See Rashi.

57. *B. Berakhot* 34a.

58. *Letters of John Keats* (December 21, 1817), 53.

59. Franz Rosenzweig, *Understanding the Sick and the Healthy* (Cambridge, Mass.: Harvard University Press, 1999), 98.

CHAPTER FOUR: ESTHER: "MERE ANARCHY IS LOOSED UPON THE WORLD"

1. David Weiss Halivni, "Prayer in the Shoah," *Judaism* 50, no. 3, Summer 2001, 268.

2. Ibid., 269.

3. Ibid., 287–88.

4. This is the kabbalistic notion that in creating the world, God *withdrew* Himself from His omnipresence, in order to make space for a world other than Himself.

5. See Deuteronomy 31:17–18 and Isaiah 59:2.

6. Esther instructs the Jewish population of Shushan to fast for her and with her, for three days (Esther 4:16). Implicitly, this means prayer. The absence of any clear reference to prayer, however, is all the more striking.

7. Deuteronomy 31:17–18.

8. See Rashi to Esther 2:22. The plotters, unaware that Mordecai knows all seventy languages, speak an obscure language (Thursi).

9. Franz Kafka, *Parables and Paradoxes* (New York: Schocken Books, 1961), 175.

10. *Melekh ha-fakhfakh*—in one scathing word, the Rabbis gesture at the central theme of reversed destinies (Esther 9:22). At the heart of this antic, "reversible" world reigns a "reversible" king.

11. See *Esther Rabbah* 1:12.

12. *Esther Rabbah* 2:11.

13. Frank Kermode, *The Sense of an Ending* (Oxford, UK, and New York: Oxford University Press, 2000), 45.

14. James Kugel, "Two Introductions to Midrash," in *Midrash and Literature,* ed. Geoffrey Hartman and Sanford Budick (New Haven, Conn.: Yale University Press, 1986), 89.

15. See *B. Megillah* 17a.

16. Sefat Emet, Purim, 179. His comment is based on the words *nizkarim v'na'asim* (Esther 9:28): the miracle is first *read,* then *practiced* in acts of celebration and feasting.

17. Rambam, *Laws of Purim,* 2:18.

18. Ravad emphasizes that it is the *public* reading of these texts that will cease to be practiced.

19. *B. Megillah* 13b.

20. See *Esther Rabbah* 7:24.

21. *Esther Rabbah* 6:10.

22. *B. Sotah* 12b–13a.
23. Cited in Adam Phillips, *The Beast in the Nursery* (London: Faber and Faber, 1998), 68.
24. *Pirke de-Rabbi Eliezer*, 50.
25. In modern Hebrew, *balash* is a detective.
26. *B. Megillah* 14a.
27. See Esther 4:4, 9, 10, 12, 15.
28. *Esther Rabbah* 8:6.
29. *B. Megillah* 15a.
30. The midrashic version of this concept has Esther acknowledge that in going *freely* to Ahasuerus, she loses all possibility of restoring her secret marital relationship with Mordecai. See Rashi to Esther 4:16: "As I am lost to my father's house, so I am lost to you."
31. See Ibn Ezra to Esther 4:16.
32. *Yalkut Shimoni*, 1056.
33. *B. Megillah* 14b.
34. *B. Megillah* 15b.
35. See *B. Sotah* 5b.
36. *Yalkut Shimoni*, Psalms 685, 22.
37. Maharal, *Or Chadash*, 54.
38. *Yalkut Shimoni*, Psalms 685, 22.
39. *B. Megillah* 14b.
40. See Meshekh Hokhmah to Exodus 19:17.
41. José Ortega, *The Revolt of the Masses*, quoted in Ernest Becker, *The Denial of Death* (New York: Free Press, 1997), 89.
42. See *Or Hadash*, 48.
43. Søren Kierkegaard, *The Concept of Dread*, quoted in Becker, *The Denial of Death*, 91.
44. William James, *Varieties of Religious Experience*, quoted in Becker, *The Denial of Death*, 88.
45. See Psalms 51:19; *B. Sotah* 5b.
46. J. M. Coetzee, *Foe* (New York: Viking, 1987), 30.
47. Marcel Proust, "Swann's Way," *Remembrance of Things Past*, trans. C. K. Scott Moncrieff and Terence Kilmartin (New York: First Vintage International Edition, 1989), 47–48.
48. Adam Phillips, *On Flirtation*, (Cambridge, Mass.: Harvard University Press, 1994), 15.
49. André Neher, *The Exile of the Word*, trans. Daniel Maisel (Philadelphia: Jewish Publication Society of America, 1981), 169.
50. Martin Buber, *On the Bible* (New York: Schocken Books, 1968), 186.
51. Ibid., 178.
52. Even in a leap year, since Purim is celebrated in Adar 2, it maintains its juxtaposition with Pesach.
53. See *Pachad Yitzhak*, Purim, 34. My text is a paraphrase of the original.
54. *B. Hagigah* 5b.
55. Cf. Freud's description of the place in every dream that eludes interpretation (Sigmund Freud, SE, *The Interpretation of Dreams*, vol. 4, pp. 111, 525.)

56. See Buber-Rosenzweig translation of Psalms 22:2–3:
    My God, My God, why dost Thou abandon me?
    . . .
    "Great God!" Is my one cry all the day, and Thou dost not answer.
57. "And at night, for me there is *no silence*" (Ps. 22:3).
58. Neher, 68.

CHAPTER FIVE: IN THE VALE OF SOUL-MAKING: ABRAHAM'S JOURNEY

1. For simplicity, I will refer to Abraham by his later, transformed name.
2. See, e.g., *B. Nedarim* 32b.
3. *The Oxford English Dictionary* glosses *travel:* "1. torment, distress, suffer afflictions, suffer pains of parturition. 2. make a journey, from one place to another."
4. See Gillian Beer's comment, associating this with a "travaillous history": "the ear does not discriminate between hardship and travel." *Open Fields: Science in Cultural Encounter* (New York: Oxford University Press, 1996), 55.
5. Ibid., 55.
6. *Y'lamdenu,* quoted in *Torah Shelemah* 12:107.
7. Tanchuma, *Lekh lekha,* 3.
8. Rambam describes Abraham as the epitome of that love of God in which one is totally *shogeh*—obsessed, "as though sick with love. . . . This is the meaning of the command, 'You shall love your God with all your heart and with all your soul. . . .' And also of King Solomon's allegory, 'for I am love-sick' (Songs 2:5): indeed the whole of Song of Songs is an allegory for this" (*Mishneh Torah, Hilkhot Teshuvah* 10:3).
9. Stanley Cavell describes Emerson's writing—and through him, Nietzsche's—as working out "the conditions for my recognizing my difference from others as a function of my recognizing my difference from myself." (*Conditions Handsome and Unhandsome* [Chicago: University of Chicago Press, 1990], 53.)
10. *The Visible and the Invisible,* 134–35. Quoted in Elizabeth Grosz, *Volatile Bodies* (Bloomington: Indiana University Press, 1994), 101.
11. Grosz, 100–102.
12. Ibid., 100.
13. The phrase is usually understood as referring to the household of servants.
14. Sigmund Freud, "Recommendations to Physicians Practicing Psycho-analysis." *SE* 12:114. (New York: Norton, 1955).
15. Paul Ricoeur, *Freud and Philosophy: An Essay on Interpretation* (New Haven, Conn.: Yale University Press, 1970), 409.
16. See Mei Ha-Shilo'ach on *Lekh lekha.*
17. *Bereshit Rabbah* 39:1.
18. Herbert Fingarette, *The Self in Transformation* (New York: Harper & Row, 1965), 86.
19. Ibid., 106–7.
20. Tanchuma, 3. *E'es'kha*—"I will make"—is read literally: "I will make, create you."

21. Ramban to Genesis 12:2–3.

22. Rambam, *Hilchot Avodat Kokhavim* 1:3.

23. Most midrashic sources have forty-eight as the age he achieved enlightenment.

24. John Holt, *Instead of Education: Ways to Help People Do Things Better* (New York: Dutton, 1976), 13.

25. On one understanding, the expression *talmid chakham*—scholar—refers to the student-sage, integrating the life of learning with that of teaching.

26. Jonathan Lear, *Open Minded* (Cambridge, Mass.: Harvard University Press, 1998), 57.

27. Abraham Joshua Heschel, *Man Is Not Alone* (New York: Noonday Press, 1976), 68.

28. *Mei Ha-Shilo'ach, Lekh lekha,* vol. 1.

29. Grosz, 101.

30. Adam Phillips, *Promises, Promises* (New York: Basic Books, 2001), 175.

31. Heschel, 128.

32. *Bereshit Rabbah* 39:2.

33. John Keats, *Letters,* April 21, 1819 (New York: Oxford University Press, 1965), 266.

34. This is more prosaically translated, "the household they had acquired."

35. *Shir Ha-Shirim Rabbah* 1:22.

36. A similar wordplay on *alamot/olamot*—with a third pun on *al mut* (beyond death)—is found in *Va-yikra Rabbah* 11:9.

37. Lear, *Open Minded,* 152.

38. Ibid., 57.

39. Ibid., 164.

40. Ibid., 166.

41. Sigmund Freud, "Fragment of an Analysis of a Case of Hysteria," *SE* 7:17, quoted in Lear, *Open Minded,* 154.

42. Heschel, 22.

43. Quoted in Adam Phillips, *The Beast in the Nursery* (London: Faber and Faber, 1998), 70.

44. Ibid., 72.

45. *Heh* is the prefix that indicates a question.

46. *Pachad Yitzhak,* Pesach, 17.

47. Rambam, *Laws of Hametz and Matzah,* haggadah text.

48. *B. Gittin* 43a.

49. *Yalkut Tehillim,* 628.

50. John Keats, *Letters,* April 21, 1819, pp. 266–67.

51. Ibid., May 3, 1818, pp. 115–16.

52. Ibid., p. 113.

53. *Bereshit Rabbah* 39:9.

54. *Lekh lekha,* 86–87.

55. *B. Ta'anit* 4a.

56. Robert Penn Warren, "I Am Dreaming of a White Christmas: The Natural History of a Vision." *Selected Poems of Robert Penn Warren,* ed. John Burtt (Baton Rouge: Louisiana State Univ. Press, 2001), 149–55.

57. Henry James, "The Art of Fiction," *Longman's Magazine*, 1884. Quoted in Adam Phillips, *The Beast in the Nursery*, 68. I am indebted to Adam Phillips whose chapter "A Stab at Hinting" provided the germ for my thinking about hints, and the three passages from Bouwsma (p. 160), James (p. 165), and Keats (p. 166).

58. John Keats, *Letters*, February 19, 1818 pp. 79–80.

59. B. *Berakhot* 7a.

60. *Rachamim*, compassion, has *rechem*, the womb, as its root.

61. Sefat Emet, *Lekh lekha*, 41.

62. Friedrich August Kekule, the chemist who discovered the structure of the benzene ring after years of work, dreamt of a snake swallowing its tail, and woke to his solution. This was his response to his students' envy.

63. Ralph Waldo Emerson, "Self-Reliance," *Selected Essays*, ed. Larzer Ziff (New York: Penguin Classics, 1987), 176.

64. Stanley Cavell, *Conditions Handsome and Unhandsome* (Chicago and London: University of Chicago Press, 1990), 57. I have appropriated Cavell's comment on Emerson: "Think of it this way: If the thoughts of a text . . . are yours, then you do not need them. If its thoughts are *not* yours, they will not do you good. The problem is that the text's thoughts are neither exactly mine nor not mine. In their sublimity as my rejected—say repressed—thoughts, they represent my further, next, unattained but attainable, self."

CHAPTER SIX: ABRAHAM BOUND AND UNBOUND: THE *AKEDAH*

1. See, e.g., Genesis 15:2, 3, 8; 17:18; 18:23. It is striking that even Abraham's unexpressed feelings are treated by God as legitimate occasions for response—e.g., Genesis 15:1; 21:12.

2. See, e.g., *Pirkei de-Rabbi Eliezer*, 26.

3. Ramban Genesis 22:1.

4. After the terrors of theophany at Mount Sinai, the people are told: "*Do not be afraid;* God has come only in order to *test* you, and in order that *the fear of Him may be ever with you*" (Exod. 20:17). One fear is to be replaced by another, through the medium of a transformative experience.

5. B. *Nedarim* 31b.

6. Rashi, Genesis 17:1.

7. Rashi is citing *Pirkei de-Rabbi Eliezer*, 29.

8. This has practical consequences only in relation to *terumah* (the heave offering), which is forbidden to an *arel*. See J. *Yevamot* 8:1 and Rambam, *Hilkhot Terumot* 11:7.

9. *Jokes and Their Relation to the Unconscious, SE* VIII, 26.

10. Malcolm Bowie, *Psychoanalysis and the Future of Theory* (Oxford, UK, and Cambridge, Mass.: B. Blackwell, 1993), 22.

11. *Bereshit Rabbah* 44:5.

12. Isaiah 33:12.

13. Psalms 31:20.

14. Rashi to Genesis 22:20.

15. *Bereshit Rabbah* 55:4.

16. See Genesis 12:7,8; 13:4.

17. Gaston Bachelard, *The Psychoanalysis of Fire,* trans. Alan C. M. Ross (Boston: Beacon Press, 1964), 18.

18. Ibid., 16.

19. Ibid., 17.

20. Ibid., 19.

21. Ibid., 20.

22. Marguerite Yourcenar, *That Mighty Sculptor, Time,* trans. Watter Kaiser (New York: Farrar, Straus and Giroux, 1992), 153.

23. Ibid., 154–55.

24. Georges Bataille, *Theory of Religion* (New York: Zone Books, 1992), 48–49.

25. Ibid., 52.

26. Ibid., 53.

27. Leviticus 16:1.

28. Leviticus 10:1.

29. *Sifra* 26.

30. *B. Avodah Zarah* 17a.

31. Tanchuma, *Lekh lekha,* 10.

32. See Rachel Adelman, "A Psychoanalytic Reading of the Covenant between the Pieces" (unpublished M.A. thesis, submitted to the Faculty of Baltimore Hebrew University, 2001).

33. Sigmund Freud, *Collected Works,* 23:43.

34. Cf. *Bereshit Rabbah* 44:5: "I descended to the fiery furnace and was saved; I descended in the war against the kings and I was saved."

35. *Tardema* may refer to sleep—in which case the vision would be in a dream— or to a coma, or some altered state of consciousness.

36. *Bereshit Rabbah* 38:19.

37. Midrash *Tehillim* 18:28.

38. *Bereshit Rabbah* 39:7.

39. See Jon D. Levenson, *The Death and Resurrection of the Beloved Son* (New Haven, Conn.: Yale University Press, 1993).

40. See, e.g., *Pirkei de-Rabbi Eliezer,* 24.

41. *B. Zevachim* 113b.

42. See Mei Ha-Shilo'ach, *No'ach,* Vol. 2.

43. *Bereshit Rabbah* 39:24.

44. Tanchuma, *Va-yera* 22.

45. "The Fear of Breakdown" and "The Psychology of Madness" in *Psychoanalytic Explorations,* ed. Clare Winnicott (Cambridge, Mass.: Harvard University Press, 1992).

46. Ibid., 91.

47. Ibid., 92.

48. Ibid., 127.

49. Rashi to Genesis 22:12.

50. Mei Ha-Shilo'ach *Va-yera,* vol. 1.

51. Rashi to Genesis 22:12.

52. Beit Ya'akov, *Va-yera,* 53.

53. See Rashi to Genesis 22:4.

54. Tanchuma, *Va-yera* 22.

398 Notes to Pages 199–211

55. See Rashi to Genesis 22:11.
56. Kedushat Levi. See Jacques Derrida, *The Gift of Death,* trans. David Willis (Chicago: University of Chicago Press, 1995), 78, note 6. He cites an objection made by Levinas to Kierkegaard: " 'In evoking Abraham he describes the meeting with God as occurring where subjectivity is raised to the level of the religious, that is to say above ethics. But one can posit the contrary: the attention Abraham pays to the voice that brings him back to the ethical order by forbidding him to carry out the human sacrifice, is the most intense moment of the drama. . . . It is there, in the ethical, that there is an appeal to the uniqueness of the subject. . . .' " (Emmanuel Levinas, *Noms propres* [Montpellier: Fata Morgana, 1976], 113; translated by David Wills).
57. Rashi to Genesis 15:8.
58. Winnicott, *Explorations,* 91.
59. Ibid.
60. Jean Laplanche, *Essays on Otherness,* (London and New York: Routledge, 1999), See, e.g., 263–65 and *passim.*
61. Ibid., 114.
62. Ibid., 230.
63. Ibid., 191.
64. Tanchuma, *Va-yera* 23.
65. Bataille, *Theory of Religion,* 48.

CHAPTER SEVEN: "HER OWN FOREIGNER": REBECCA'S PREGNANCY

1. Tamar's pregnancy—also a twin pregnancy—raises the question of the identity of the father and precipitates her "unveiled" confrontation with Judah. By contrast with Rebecca's pregnancy, it is a social and legal matter.
2. B. *Eruvin* 18b: "He begot spirits and demons." See also Rambam, *Moreh Nevukhim* 1:7.
3. See Seforno to Genesis 25:22.
4. See Rashi to Genesis 25:22.
5. See Hizkuni to Genesis 25:22.
6. See Ramban to Genesis 25:22.
7. Most of the medieval commentaries read in this way, with the oracular source, or prophet, being identified as Shem, or Abraham.
8. See Ramban to Genesis 25:23.
9. I borrow the expression from Thomas Ogden to convey the experience of subjectivity. See *Subjects of Analysis* (Northvale, N.J.: Jason Aronson, 1994), 14 and *passim.*
10. Soon after, the servant, too, identifies himself in the same style: "I am Abraham's servant"(Genesis 24:34).
11. According to Rashi, drawing on midrashic and Talmudic sources, both Isaac and Rebecca pray. It is his prayer, however, that is answered: he is "the righteous son of a righteous father," while she is "the righteous daughter of a wicked father." Her prayers are thus assumed to bear a more complex freight. In general, one who resists corrupting influences is accorded more

respect than one whose environment is morally congenial. (See Rashi on the previous verse—Genesis 25:20.) But prayer seems to constitute a special case, complicating Rebecca's position as Betuel's daughter.

12. See the extraordinary reading of Beit Ya'akov, 20: Rebecca's barrenness expresses her resistance to procreation as spiritual risk. Her anxiety is apparently validated when inward strife replaces her previously serene *anokhi*.

13. Sigmund Freud, letter to Marie Bonaparte, quoted in Ernest Jones, *The Life and Work of Sigmund Freud* (New York: Basic Books, 1955), 2:421.

14. Shoshana Felman, *What Does a Woman Want?* (Baltimore: Johns Hopkins University Press, 1993), 73–74.

15. Many translations and commentaries soften the drama of the moment. See, e.g., Rashi: "she slipped down from her camel."

16. See *Ha'amek Davar* to Genesis 24: 64–65. He uses the word *nivhal*—confused, disoriented, shocked—several times in this psychological reading of the traumatic potential of encounters.

17. Bereshit Rabbah 60:14. The midrash continues to explore the implications of *ha-lazeh*, suggesting a wordplay with the Greek word *allon*, other. An uncanny presence, perhaps an angel, seems to accompany Isaac. Cf. Genesis 37:19—"[Joseph's brothers] said to one another, Here is *that (ha-lazeh)* dreamer coming!"

18. See Michael Fried, *Realism, Writing, Disfiguration* (Chicago: University of Chicago Press, 1989), for an account of the "absorptive tradition" in painting that goes back to Caravaggio and Rembrandt and includes Chardin and Courbet. Fried argues that "the seeming obliviousness of one or more figures to everything but the objects of their absorption contributes to an overall impression of self-sufficiency and repleteness that functions as a decisive hallmark of the 'real' " (43).

19. Julia Kristeva, *Strangers to Ourselves* (New York: Columbia University Press, 1991), 181.

20. Stanley Cavell, *In Quest of the Ordinary* (Chicago: University of Chicago Press, 1988), 128.

21. Ibid., 88–89. Cavell discusses Leontes in Shakespeare's *The Winter's Tale* as a portrait of the skeptic as fanatic.

22. Translated as "afterwardness" or "deferred action," this refers to an early traumatic experience that is understood retroactively.

23. *Va-yitrotzetzu*—the "struggle" of the twins is constituted by two Hebrew roots: *ratzatz*—to crush; *rootz*—to run. The suggestion is of violent motion impelled by desire (see Rashi to Genesis 25:22).

24. Elaine Scarry, *The Body in Pain* (New York: Oxford University Press, 1985), 3.

25. Virginia Woolf, "On Being Ill," in *Collected Essays*, vol. 4 (New York: Harcourt, 1967), 194, quoted in Scarry, *The Body in Pain*, 4.

26. Scarry, 10.

27. Ibid., 51–52.

28. Kristeva, *Stangers to Ourselves*, 178–79.

29. Julia Kristeva, "Stabat Mater," in *The Kristeva Reader*, ed. Toril Moi (New York: Columbia University Press, 1986), 176.

30. Ibid., 184–85.
31. The Hebrew word *mei'ayim*—bowels—occurs in God's response to Rebecca: "and two nations shall separate out from your bowels" (Gen. 25:23).
32. *Yalkut Shimoni*, 828.
33. *Shemot Rabbah* 26:2.
34. *Ha-yesh Ha-Shem b'kirbenu im ayin*—"Is God in our midst—or else *nothing?*"
35. Psalm 144:1.
36. Sylvia Plath, "Three Women," in *Winter Trees* (London: Faber and Faber, 1971).
37. Jacqueline Rose, *On Not Being Able to Sleep* (Princeton, N.J.: Princeton University Press, 2003), 158–59.
38. Sigmund Freud, *A Difficulty in the Path of Psychoanalysis, SE,* 17, 141.
39. Ogden, 25.
40. Paul Ricoeur, "Lamentation as Prayer," in André LaCocque and Paul Ricoeur, *Thinking Biblically* (Chicago: University of Chicago Press, 1998), 217–18.
41. Ibid,, 218–19.
42. See the reading of *Ha-k'tav v'Ha-kabalah.* In Arabic and Aramaic, *lamah* means futility, emptiness.
43. To support his claim, he cites Ezekiel 20:3; Amos 5:4; Psalms 34:5. These quotations, however, can be countered by others that suggest precisely the inquiry from a prophet or an oracle (e.g., 2 Kings 1:2; 8:8). Ramban himself comments on Exodus 18:15, where the people besiege Moses from morning to night "to inquire of God": "they ask Moses to pray for their sick relatives and to tell them what they had lost." It is the prophet who fills this double role, praying for the sick and enlightening the troubled. Ramban accommodates the sense of consulting a prophetic source while insisting on his reading of *lidrosh et Ha-Shem* as prayer.
44. See Brown, Driver, Briggs: *Lidrosh*—to search, search out, research, investigate, tread, inquire, require, study, care, solicit.
45. See Rashi, Radak, Hizkuni, Ha'amek Davar. The ambiguity is a function of the meaning of "older" and "younger," as well as the lack of a clear indication of subject and object.
46. See Ha'amek Davar to Genesis 25:23.
47. In the Zohar, the term "the world of separation" is used to describe the fragmented condition of this world. This term implies a dialectical relation between fragmentation and integration, by way of absence and yearning.
48. Primo Levi describes one of his earliest realizations about Auschwitz: "Here there is no why" (*Survival in Auschwitz,* [London: Collier Macmillan Publishers, 1961], 25).
49. See Wallace Stevens, "Questions Are Remarks," *The Auroras of Autumn* (New York: Alfred A. Knopf, 1950), 104.
50. See Ha'amek Davar to Genesis 25:23.
51. Marian Milner, "Winnicott and Overlapping Circles," in *The Suppressed Madness of Sane Men* (London and New York: Taristock Publications, 1989), 279.
52. See D. W. Winnicott, *Playing and Reality* (Abingdon, Oxen, UK: Routledge, 1997), 95. Chapter 7, "The Location of Cultural Experience," begins with this quotation from Tagore.

53. Winnicott, "Primitive Emotional Development," in *Collected Papers: Through Pediatrics to Psycho-Analysis* (London: Tavistock; New York: Basic Books, 1958), 150.

54. Winnicott, *Playing*, 12.

55. Samuel Gerson, "The Relational Unconscious," *Psychoanalytic Quarterly* 73 (2004): 71.

56. See Winnicott's discussion of the mother-fetus relationship in terms of "her psychological ability to produce a whole, live child in fantasy": "A Note on the Mother-Foetus Relationship," in *Psycho-Analytic Explorations,* ed. Clare Winnicott (Cambridge, Mass.: Harvard University Press, 1992), 161.

57. Midrash Ha-Gadol to Genesis 25:22.

58. Sigmund Freud, *On the Interpretation of Dreams*, SE 4:111.

59. Shoshana Felman, *What Does a Woman Want?* 113.

60. Freud, 4:525.

61. Max Ophuls's film *Letter from an Unknown Woman* provides Stanley Cavell with a metaphor for the intimate stranger who is allowed full life only in a moment of horrified revelation. Cavell brings into play Henry James's story "The Beast in the Jungle," with its wrenching last paragraph: "*she* was what he had missed . . . he had been the man of his time, *the* man, to whom nothing on earth was to have happened. . . . This horror of waking—*this* was knowledge." ("The Melodrama of the Unknown Woman," in *The Trial(s) of Psychoanalysis*, ed. Françoise Meltzer [Chicago University of Chicago Press, 1988], 258.)

62. Genesis 27:8, 13, 43.

63. *Bereshit Rabbah* 63:15. The midrash picks up on the "present-continuous" usage in both verbs: *ohevet, mosefet ahavah.*

64. Midrash Ha-Gadol (37:3) detects a similarity with Jacob's love for Joseph.

65. Rashi to Genesis 35:8.

66. Tanchuma, *Teitzei,* 4.

67. See Genesis 24:59.

68. In the midrash, Isaac cannot accompany her body because he is blind and confined indoors. One can speculate, however, that Rebecca's deception of her husband and conspiracy against Esau are linked with her final isolation.

69. *B. Mo'ed Katan* 27b.

70. *Bereshit Rabbah* 60:12.

71. Midrash Aggadah. See also *Yalkut Shimoni,* 109.

72. *Bereshit Rabbah* 63:4.

73. See Jean Laplanche, *Essays on Otherness* (London and New York: Routledge, 1999).

74. Henry James, "The Beast in the Jungle," in *Selected Short Stories* (New York: Rinehart, 1995), 260. See note 69.

75. Franz Kafka, "Leopards in the Temple," in *Parables and Paradoxes,* (New York: Schocken Books, 1961), 93.

76. Rashi to Genesis 37:10.

77. Sigmund Freud, "The Uncanny," SE, 153.

78. *Bereshit Rabbah* 74:7. The midrash puns on Jacob's words, *achatena, g'noovti*

yom u-g'noovti laylah. See also *Sekhel Tov* 37:33: Jacob sets his scrupulous guarding of Laban's flocks from wild beasts against the fate of his beloved son: "My way is hidden from God!"

CHAPTER EIGHT: BLINDNESS AND BLESSING:
ISAAC TREMBLES TWICE

1. The expression *va-yitpallel,* the usual term for prayer, is used only once, of his prayer for Avimelekh (Gen. 20:17).
2. *B. Yevamot* 64a.
3. Avot 5:22.
4. Mandelstam, "Slovo i kul'tura," Sobranie *socinenij v dvux tomax,* vol. 2 (New York: 1966), 266. Quoted in Daniel Boyarin, *Intertextuality and the Reading of Midrash* (Bloomington: Indiana University Press, 1990), 37.
5. See Boyarin, 37–38, on Benjamin's practice of a "poetics of quotation, which breaches and continues a tradition," and on Arendt's description of his work of "tearing fragments out of their context and arranging them afresh in such a way that they illustrated one another." Boyarin argues that the intertextuality of midrash serves a similar recuperative purpose, "preserving the old by making it new."
6. See Rashi to Genesis 24:63.
7. *Bereshit Rabbah* 63:5.
8. *B. Berakhot* 56b.
9. *B. Berakhot* 55b.
10. See Rashi to Genesis 26:12: "That was a bad year in a bad land."
11. *Bereshit Rabbah* 65:5.
12. Christopher Bollas's expression, e.g., "a substantial part of our self [is] somehow deeply known . . . yet unthought." (*Being a Character* [New York: Hill and Wang: 1992], 51.)
13. *Pirkei de-Rabbi Eliezer,* 31.
14. See *Pesikta Rabbati, Targum Yonatan, Aggadat Bereshit,* cited in RaDaL on *Pirkei de-Rabbi Eliezer,* 31 [35] [36].
15. Yalkut Shimoni I, 101.
16. Rashi to Genesis 16:13.
17. Ramban to Genesis 24:62.
18. Cathy Caruth, "Traumatic Departures: Survival and History in Freud," in *Trauma and Self,* ed. Charles B. Strozier and Michael Flynn (Lanham, Md.: Rowman & Littlefield, 1996), 29.
19. Ibid., 32.
20. Ibid., 34.
21. Ibid., 38–39.
22. Cited in Caruth, "Recapturing the Past: Introduction," in *Trauma: Explorations in Memory,* ed. Cathy Caruth (Baltimore: Johns Hopkins University Press, 1995), 154–55.
23. Ibid., 204.
24. Tanchuma 13.
25. *Shemot Rabbah* 29:3.
26. See Caruth, "Traumatic Departures," 37, for a discussion of Freud's applica-

tion of these questions to the rather different material of *Moses and Monotheism*.

27. Caruth, "Traumatic Departures," 35.
28. Jacques Derrida, *The Gift of Death*, trans. David Willis (Chicago: University of Chicago Press, 1995), 54–56.
29. John Berger, "Drawn to That Moment," in *The Sense of Sight* (New York: Vintage International, 1993), 146–47.
30. Ibid., 148–49.
31. Ibid., 150–51.
32. Isaac is named after Abraham and Sarah's laughter (Gen. 17:17, 18:12) at his annunciation. His birth is celebrated by the joyful incredulity of Sarah's "God has brought me laughter; everyone who hears will laugh with me" (21:6). These moments are gathered into his own experience in his lovemaking, called *laughter* or *play (metzachek)*, with his wife (26:8).
33. See *Sifrei Devarim*, 31.
34. The game, in this midrashic reading, is Isaac; and it is Esau's mouth, his seductive words, that are the means of seduction. (See Rashi to Genesis 25:28.)
35. See Sefat Emet 103.
36. *Bereshit Rabbah* 63:16.
37. See Sefat Emet 103: the blessing is appropriate for one who has moved far from holiness and who needs blessing to find his own access point.
38. Jacob uses the idiom in Genesis 27:19; Isaac again in Genesis 27:25; Esau in Genesis 27:31.
39. See Genesis 1:20, 19:9, 46:15, 46:22.
40. See, e.g., Proverbs 13:4.
41. In Ramban's reading, Rebecca warns Jacob that his father's blessing will be divinely inspired, so that if Esau is blessed, Jacob will be left with no significant role in the family destiny. By inserting the idiom "in the presence of God" into her report, Rebecca is insisting on the gravity of this blessing.
42. Rashi translates: " 'In the presence of God': By His permission; that He may approve of my blessing." The power of Isaac's blessing is qualified here: he himself acknowledges that his words will take effect only if God consents. He wishes, or prays, that God may validate his blessing. His words have no enchanting power; their validity will depend entirely on God's assent.
43. See Or Ha-Chaim to Genesis 27:24.
44. Ernest Gombrich, *Art and Illusion: A Study in the Psychology of Pictorial Representation*, 240; quoted in Shlomith Rimmon, *The Concept of Ambiguity—The Example of James* (Chicago: University of Chicago Press, 1977), 229.
45. Shklovsky quoted in Rimmon, 229.
46. See 2 Kings 3:15: "As the musician played, the hand of God came upon him."
47. Joseph Weiss, *Studies in Eastern European Jewish Mysticism* (Oxford, UK: Oxford University Press, 1985), 71.
48. Ibid., 79.
49. Ibid., 83.
50. Caruth, "Traumatic Departures," 39.
51. *Bereshit Rabbah* 67:3.

52. See *Ruth Rabbah* 6:1, 2. This is merely implicit in the previously quoted source (*Bereshit Rabbah* 67:3).
53. See Numbers 23:5: "And God put a word in Balaam's mouth." This generates a disagreement in *B. Sanhedrin* 105b: R. Eliezer claims that an angel controlled his vocal organs, while R. Yonatan claims that it was an iron bit that God put in his mouth.
54. Christopher Bollas, *Cracking Up* (New York: Hill and Wang, 1995), 66–67.
55. Antoine de Saint-Exupéry, *The Little Prince* (London: Pan Books Ltd., 1974), 70.
56. Adam Phillips, *On Flirtation* (Cambridge, Mass.: Harvard University Press, 1994), 31.
57. T. S. Eliot, "Virgil and the Christian World," in *On Poetry and Poets* (London: Faber and Faber, 1957), 122.
58. Derrida, *The Gift of Death*, 54.
59. Known by the Yiddish term, *tropp*. The notation here is *zarka segol*—an elaborate trill.
60. Mei Ha-Shilo'ach has Isaac acknowledge that God is the source of the "fruit of his lips." The reference is to Isaiah 57:19: "He creates the fruit of the lips." In a vision of comfort and healing, God promises to create a new human language of blessing.
61. Psalms 42:8.

CHAPTER NINE: "AND I DID NOT KNOW . . .": THE SECRET OF PRAYER

1. This is reflected in the narrative space given to his early history: chapters 25–29 cover the period before he marries, and chapters 29–31 the complicated story of his marriages and the birth of his children.
2. See Rashi to Genesis 30:1–2.
3. Abraham does father Ishmael from Hagar—but only after many childless years. Ishmael, too, is clearly not the promised son of destiny.
4. See Genesis 26:34: "When Esau was forty years old, he took to wife Judith daughter of Beeri the Hittite, and Basemath daughter of Elon the Hittite; and they were a source of bitterness to Isaac and Rebecca."
5. According to Rashi (Gen. 29:21), he is eighty-four when he marries Leah.
6. See Genesis 32:25.
7. See Rashi to Numbers 20:14–17; *Ba-Midbar Rabbah* 19:7.
8. Esau, by contrast, is described as settling promptly in his own land (Gen. 36:6). See Rashi to Numbers 20:14. The midrashic tradition intuits in Esau an avoidance of the "bill of debt," which falls squarely on Jacob.
9. Rashi to Genesis 28:17.
10. This is Jonathan Lear's term for "the fundamental human phenomenon to which all of psychoanalysis is a response." See *Open Minded* (Cambridge, Mass.: Harvard University Press, 1998), 54.
11. See my *The Beginning of Desire* (New York: Doubleday, 1996), 139–41.
12. See *Sefat Emet*, 124–25.
13. *Bereshit Rabbah* 68:12.
14. According to the *tropp*, the traditional indications for chanting the Torah,

three Hebrew words fill the space of a half verse; the first half of the verse, composed of twelve words, would be read at a faster pace.

15. *Pirkei de-Rabbi Eliezer,* 35.
16. *Bereshit Rabbah* 68:18.
17. See Ezekiel 1:10.
18. Maurice Blanchot, *Nights as Day, Days as Night,* ed. Michael Leiris, trans. Richard Sieburth (Hygiene, Colo.: Eridanos Press, 1987), xxi.
19. Christopher Bollas, *Being a Character* (New York: Hill and Wang, 1992), 240.
20. See Ma'or Va-Shemesh to 28:16.
21. The reference here is to a midrash that describes Jacob as spending fourteen years studying Torah immediately after leaving home. (See Rashi to Genesis 28:9). This invisible gap in the story becomes the basis for this Hasidic critique of the imbalances inherent in the purely scholarly life.
22. *Bereshit Rabbah* 68:3.
23. The two verbs—*va-yashk* and *va-yishak,* "he watered" and "he kissed"—are almost identical.
24. See Denis de Rougemont, *Passion and Society,* trans. Montgomery Belgion (London: Faber and Faber, 1956). He argues that passionate love is originally a medieval European phenomenon, generated by the cultural trope of unconsummated and multiply forbidden love between the knight and his lady. The taboo—the sword laid between Tristan and Isolde in the forest—creates the intensity that married love cannot sustain.
25. *B. Bava Batra* 123a.
26. Tearing out eyebrows and eyelashes is a symptom of trichotillomania (TTM), a disorder that was first recognized by the Greek physician Hippocrates.
27. *Bereshit Rabbah* 80:17.
28. ". . . for Jacob had given Rachel signs to identify herself, but when Rachel saw that Leah was being married in her place, she said, 'Now, my sister will be put to shame.' So she rose up and gave Leah those signs." The figure of the signs speaks of sisterly love; but also supports the uncanny sense that, in the darkness, Leah becomes Rachel.
29. Sefat Emet, 132. See also p. 114.
30. Lionel Trilling, *Sincerity and Authenticity* (Cambridge, Mass.: Harvard University Press, 1973), 119.
31. Ibid., 120.
32. George Steiner, *After Babel* (New York: Oxford University Press, 1975), 228.
33. Ibid., 231.
34. Ibid., 232.
35. Ibid., 236.
36. Rashi to Genesis 25:27.
37. *Tzayid* (hunting, food) may well evoke the root *tzoded* (to captivate, beguile).
38. See Rashi on the question asked by the *tam* (one of the four sons in the haggadah, the text read on the seder night): "What is this?" (Exodus 13:14)—"This is a stupid child, who does not know how to deepen his question, and blocks *(sotem)* discussion." There is an implicit pun on *tam* and *sotem,* suggesting that this kind of simplicity has a stupefying effect.
39. *B. Sotah* 21b.

40. See *Mei Ha-Shilo'ach* 1, *Va-yetze*.
41. *B. Gittin* 43a.
42. See pp. 7–8 in this text.
43. In midrashic sources, Rachel is identified as *akeret ha-bayit*—the essence of the household. See, e.g., Rashi to Genesis 31:4 and to Ruth 4:11; Ibn Ezra to Hosea 12:13.
44. *Beit Ya'akov*, 63.
45. Jean Laplanche and J.-B. Pontalis, *The Language of Psycho-Analysis*, trans. Donald Nicholson-Smith (London: Hogarth Press, 1973).
46. This is Christopher Bollas's formulation. See *The Shadow of the Object* (London: Free Association Books, 1987).
47. Mary Douglas, *Purity and Danger* (London and Boston: Ark Paperback, 1984), 168.
48. Ibid., 171.
49. Ibid., 164.
50. Ibid., 36–37.
51. See *Sifrei Va-Etchanan*, 31; *Va-yikra Rabbah* 36:5; Rashi to Genesis 47:31.
52. Quoted in Douglas, 163.
53. See Donnel B. Stern, *Unformulated Experience* (Hillsdale, N.J.: Analytic Press, 2003), 176.
54. In purely halakhic terms, the evening prayer has a lesser status of obligation than the other two daily prayers.
55. *Pirkei de-Rabbi Eliezer*, 35. Ha-Makom is a common midrashic expression for God.

CHAPTER TEN: THE PIT AND THE ROPE: RECOVERING JOSEPH

1. Rashi to Genesis 37:33.
2. *Bereshit Rabbah* 84:19. See *Etz Yosef*.
3. *Bereshit Rabbah* 84:19. See Rashi to Genesis 37:33.
4. See Rashi to Genesis 45:27: "The Divine Presence which had departed from him again came to rest upon him." See *Targum Onkelos* and Tanchuma, *Va-yeshev* 2.
5. See Rashbam's interesting reading, in which the brothers do not actually sell Joseph at all: Judah proposes the idea, but the passing caravan of Midianites draw Joseph up out of the pit without his brothers' knowledge. Some textual problems remain but are not insoluble. Rashbam's reading vividly illustrates the difficulty of testimony, as, with disconcerting fidelity to the text, it undermines a received version of events.
6. See Ramban to Genesis 37:22. He points out that Reuben does not expostulate against "shedding *his* blood," but only, impersonally, against "shedding blood."
7. See Or Ha-Chaim to Genesis 42:21.
8. See Ramban to 37:22.
9. Tanchuma, *Va-yigash* 20.
10. See Joseph's ambiguous testimony to the butler about his pit/prison destiny: Genesis 40:15.
11. *Bereshit Rabbah* 86:6.

12. See Shoshana Felman and Dori Laub, *Testimony* (New York: Routledge, 1992), 225. My discussion of Joseph's implication in traumatic silence owes much to Felman and Laub's account of the Holocaust survivor experience of "a secret order that is sworn to silence."

13. See Felman and Laub, 82.

14. Ramban to Genesis 42:9.

15. Midrash, *Torah Shelemah* 45:9.

16. See Cathy Caruth, ed., *Trauma: Explorations in Memory* (Baltimore: Johns Hopkins University Press, 1995), 7–8.

17. See, e.g., Genesis 41:39.

18. See Caruth, *Trauma*, 153.

19. Primo Levi, *Survival in Auschwitz*, trans. Stuart Woolf (London: Collier Macmillan Publishers, 1961), 52–53.

20. Bremen Speech, *Gesammelte Werke*, 3 (1958). Quoted in Shoshana Felman and Dori Laub, *Testimony* (New York: Routledge, 1992), 28.

21. Caruth, *Trauma*, 11.

22. Celan, Bremen Speech. Quoted in Felman and Laub, p. 28.

23. *B. Sotah* 10b. Judah sanctifies God's name in public, by admitting his responsibility for Tamar's pregnancy (*hoda*—he admitted—represents the enactment of the inner meaning of his own name); therefore, his own name becomes entirely synonymous with God's name.

24. Sefat Emet, *Va-yigash*, 249.

25. *Bereshit Rabbah* 8:5.

26. *Bereshit Rabbah* 93:3

27. See Or Ha-Chaim's perceptive comment on Joseph's words "*And now,* it was not you who sent me here" (Gen. 45:8). Joseph emphasizes a *process* of transcending his original anger at the brothers' cruelty at the pit: *only now* is he able to be so high-minded. Joseph emphasizes this process, for otherwise such saintliness would appear unrealistic to his brothers. Essentially, Or Ha-Chaim acknowledges the emotional inadequacy of a providential perspective that takes no account of traumatic experience.

28. *Pri Tzaddik, Va-yigash*, 213. Similarly, he reads the reunion of Joseph and Jacob—" 'Joseph went up to greet his father Israel in Goshen, and *he appeared to him*' (Gen. 46:29): he *was revealed to him,* displaying the *light of his face*—that he had survived in his holiness."

29. "And Joseph could not restrain himself . . . and there was no one with him when *Joseph made himself known* to his brothers" (Gen. 45:1).

30. Sefat Emet, *Va-yigash*, 254.

31. *Bereshit Rabbah* 11:1.

32. *Bereshit Rabbah* 94:3.

33. *B. Sotah* 38b.

34. *Zohar Vayyigash*, 210.

CHAPTER ELEVEN: "WHAT IF JOSEPH HATES US?":
CLOSING THE BOOK

1. See Genesis 50:9, 50:11.

2. Rashi to Genesis 47:28.

3. See *Bereshit Rabbah* 96:1.

4. See R. Ya'akov's view: Zohar 209b.

5. See Rashi to Genesis 48:8.

6. See Rashi to Genesis 49:1.

7. *Torat Cohanim*, Leviticus 1:1.

8. Sefat Emet, *Bereshit*, 267.

9. Zohar 234b.

10. Five more uses of this root in later biblical texts yield a general meaning of persecutory behavior, bearing a grudge, cherishing animosity.

11. Tanchuma Yashan, *Shemot*, 2.

12. Tanchuma, *Va-yechi*, 17.

13. See Mishnat R. Eliezer, 7:94, 130.

14. Cf. *Bereshit Rabbah* 100:9. They are *devarim bedu'im*—invented words.

15. *Od* suggests excess.

16. The syntax bears this out; and Rashi reads in this way. But Ramban assumes, on general psychological grounds, that it is Jacob who cries.

17. Rashi to Genesis 37:24.

18. Rashi to Genesis 50:21.

19. Midrash Sekhel Tov.

20. *B. Sotah* 13b.

21. See note 13.

22. Midrash Hemdat Ha-Yamim.

23. They confess more or less obliquely among themselves: see Genesis 42:21–23, 44:16.

24. Since the Sages receive a cryptic message from God that seems to support the emperor's claim, the story makes a theological and not merely a historical statement.

25. Genesis 45:4–13.

26. D. A. Miller, *Narrative and Its Discontents* (Princeton, N.J.: Princeton University Press, 1981), 3.

27. Ibid., 4.

28. George Eliot, *Middlemarch* (London: Penguin English Library, 1965), 297.

29. Miller, 157.

30. Ibid., 158.

31. Ibid., 267.

32. See also Genesis 41:16; and Rashi to Genesis 39:3.

33. Sigmund Freud, "Negation," SE 19 (1925), 235–36.

34. "Freud's concept of negation represents a distinctively psychoanalytic conception of the constitution of the subject. The idea of a dialectic of affirmed and disavowed meaning played out phenomenologically in the form of the simultaneity of conscious and unconscious meaning is perhaps the most fundamental analytic proposition concerning the concept of mind." (Thomas Ogden, *Subjects of Analysis* [Northvale, N.J.: Jason Aronson, 1994], 21.)

35. *Bereshit Rabbah* 71:20.

36. See J. L. Austin's distinction between constative and performative language.

37. See Rashi to Genesis 37:2, 3 and *Bereshit Rabbah* 84:6, 8, which describe simi-

larities between both the facial features and the events of the lives of Jacob and Joseph.

38. See Christopher Bollas, *Being a Character* (New York: Hill and Wang, 1992), 165–92.
39. See Rashi to Genesis 39:11.
40. Adam Phillips, *Equals* (New York: Basic Books, 2002), 11.
41. Rashi to Genesis 44:19.
42. See B. *Sotah* 36b. His father's image appears to him with the threat of having his name erased from the priestly breastplate.
43. *Pesikta Rabbati, Va-yechi,* 1.
44. *Bereshit Rabbah* 98:1.
45. See Rashi, who emphasizes that all the blessings are free to flow to all the children, even the first three objects of his anger.
46. *Eileh* is the word that introduces the Israelites' acclaim of the Golden Calf: "*Eileh Elohekha Yisrael!*"—"*These* are your gods, O Israel!" (Exod. 32:4). It has acquired code status in Hasidic thought, connoting the diffuse world that requires human centering.
47. Kierkegaard, *On Authority and Revelation,* quoted in Gabriel Josipovici, *On Trust* (New Haven, Conn.: Yale University Press, 1999), 11.
48. Ibid., 17.
49. Lyotard, "The Differend," quoted in Felman and Laub, *Testimony*, 201–2.
50. The root of *satum* is *stam*—obvious, banal. The modern Hebrew translation of Freud's *id*—*Das Es* (the It)—is *ha-stam.*
51. See Robert Pogue Harrison, *The Dominion of the Dead* (Chicago: University of Chicago Press, 2003), xi: "Humanity is not a species . . . it is a way of being mortal and relating to the dead. To be human means above all to bury. Vico suggests as much when he reminds us that '*humanitas* in Latin comes first and properly from *humando,* burying.'"

CHAPTER TWELVE:
LAW AND NARRATIVE IN THE BOOK OF RUTH

1. *Ruth Rabbah* 2:15.
2. See Ruth 1:8.
3. See Ruth 3:10.
4. Beyond the details of the agricultural laws that shape the charitable responses of Boaz and his reapers, the text intimates other areas of law that engage with the proselyte, with the issues of redeeming land, and with the levirate problem: the law concerning the childless widow who is to marry her brother-in-law. Technically, this is not the situation in this narrative, but its moral residue creates a diffuse sense of obligation. Since Ploni Almoni (Mr. X) will not fulfill this obligation, Boaz assumes it as his own. These indications become the subject of many midrashic amplifications.
5. Deuteronomy 23:4.
6. B. *Baba Batra* 15b.
7. See the refrain that expresses the resulting anarchy in the book of Judges: "Each man did what was right *in his own eyes.*"

8. Peter L. Berger, *A Rumor of Angels* (Garden City, N.Y.: Anchor Books, 1970), 34.

9. Ibid., 36.

10. *Ruth Rabbah,* Preface *(Petichtah).*

11. *Ruth Rabbah* 1:4.

12. Robert Cover, *Narrative, Violence, and the Law* (Ann Arbor: University of Michigan Press, 1992), 95–96.

13. Ibid., 101.

14. Ibid., 101–2.

15. See Deuteronomy 21:15–17.

16. Cover, 117–20.

17. See Amos 8:11: "I will send a famine upon the land: not a hunger for bread or a thirst for water, but for hearing the words of God."

18. Ruth 1:3, 5.

19. See *Ruth Rabbah* 2:8, 10.

20. Ibn Ezra cites Exodus 20:13 for the root *anah:* to testify.

21. Sigmund Freud, *Beyond the Pleasure Principle,* SE 18:23.

22. Jonathan Lear, *Happiness, Death, and the Remainder of Life* (Cambridge, Mass.: Harvard University Press, 2000), 92.

23. Ibid., 94–95.

24. Ibid., 93.

25. Rashi comments: *"On your journey:* When you were exhausted" (*b'teruf*—in a state of madness, disarray). This emphasizes the need of the travelers for the symbols of an ordered world.

26. *La Nausée.* Quoted in D. A. Miller, *Narrative and Its Discontents* (Princeton, N.J.: Princeton University Press, 1981), xiii.

27. Ibid., x.

28. Ibid., 3.

29. Ibid., xiv.

30. Ibid., 265–66.

31. *Ruth Rabbah* 3:3.

32. See Targum Onkelos on Genesis 2:24: "a man shall leave his parents' bedroom."

33. *Ruth Rabbah* 4:8.

34. See *J. Yevamot* 8:3.

35. See Ruth 2:11. Boaz translates her narrative into the language of Abraham's election by God (Genesis 12:1).

36. According to the midrash, the incest is justified in the context of the apparent destruction of the world. Lot's daughters are moved to lie with their father to perpetuate the doomed human species.

37. Julia Kristeva, *Powers of Horror,* trans. Leon S. Roudiez (New York: Columbia University Press, 1982), 12–13.

38. Mary Douglas, *Purity and Danger* (London and Boston: Ark Paperback, 1984), 39.

39. *B. Yevamot* 47:2.

40. See Ruth 2:11.

41. Christopher Bollas, *The Shadow of the Object* (New York: Columbia University Press, 1987), 14.
42. See Ibid., 15–17.
43. See Hosea 9:1.
44. *B. Shabbat* 113b.
45. *Ruth Rabbah* 5:13.
46. "Everything you tell *me* I will do" is written with the word *li (me)* missing: the word is not written but it is read [the *kri u'ketiv* feature in the biblical text]. The midrash interprets this: "I will obey you—but it is *up to me* to make sense of your words." Ruth is deliberately reserving the right to her own interpretation.
47. Cf. Ruth 2:20, where Naomi uses a similar idiom.
48. *J. Pe'ah* 8:7. This is again the *kri u'ketiv* feature: written *you shall go down* and read, *I shall go down*. Some scholars note that this is an archaic form of the second person verb. Its arbitrary occurrence here still requires explanation.
49. Cf. Ezekiel 16:8.
50. The word for "wings" and for "robe" is the same: *kenafayim*.
51. Redemption of land and levirate marriage are distinct biblical categories.
52. See Rashi to Ruth 3:8.
53. I am grateful to Francis Landy for his eloquent discussion of Ruth as a "beautiful subject." See "Ruth and the Romance of Realism," in *Beauty and the Enigma* (Sheffield, UK: Sheffield Academic Press, 2001), 224–25 and *passim*.
54. *Ruth Rabbah* 5:6.
55. *Nidbaru* indicates continuous discourse.
56. The same chorus of women does refer to Ruth as "having given birth" to the child (Ruth 4:14). But even this is said in tribute to Naomi: Ruth is praised for loving her and producing the child as token of that love—he is "born for Naomi." At best, Ruth's role has become instrumental.
57. *Ruth Rabbah* 2:2.
58. My thanks to David Shulman for sharpening my reading of this point.
59. In Rabbinic Hebrew, the word for "decree" is *gezerah*, derived from the verb "to cut."
60. It is striking that Solomon's selection of the true mother at first appears ambiguous, since the last speaker before "She is his mother" was the *false* mother. However, his repetition of the true mother's speech leaves no doubt as to which woman he means. Judicial clarity is compromised to enact the performative point.
61. On a different level, of course, it is the Rabbis who have chosen Ruth by inserting her into a text that bears no indication of her. The effect is to admit her in a new way into their own world of law: as if to acknowledge that they see her, and know themselves seen by her.
62. Stanley Cavell, "The Melodrama of the Unknown Woman," in *The Trial(s) of Psychoanalysis*, ed. Françoise Meltzer (Chicago: University of Chicago Press, 1998), pp. 227–58.
63. Henry James, "The Beast in the Jungle," *The Complete Tales of Henry James*, vol. 2, ed. Leon Edel (Philadelphia: Lippincott, 1964), 397–402.

64. It is striking that the Hebrew word *ra'ah*, to see, is absent from Ruth, as are all references to physical beauty.
65. *B. Kiddushin* 30a.
66. *B. Berachot* 22a.
67. See Rashi to Exodus 20:15.
68. My reading is based on *Pachad Yitzhak*, Shavuot, 26.

GLOSSARY

Abarbanel, Don Isaac (1437–1508): Spanish Bible commentator, philosopher, and statesman.

aggadah: literally "telling," referring to the ethical imaginative and homiletic portions of talmudic literature, as opposed to the halakhic, the legal-ritual part.

Akedah: the Binding of Isaac, signifying Abraham's readiness to sacrifice his son at God's command.

Avot de-Rabbi Natan: tannaitic amplification on tractate Avot, by R. Natan, an older contemporary of R. Judah Ha'nassi.

B.C.E./C.E.: abbreviations for "Before the Common Era" and "Common Era," traditional Jewish designations for B.C. and A.D.

Beit Ya'akov: Rabbi Yaacov Leiner (1828–78), son of the Mei Ha-Shilo'ach, Rabbi Mordecai Yosef Leiner, inherited his father's position as Rebbe of Ishbitz, author of profound commentaries on the Torah.

Braita: Tannaitic tradition not included in the mishna of Rabbi Judah Ha'nassi.

Chesed: love, kindness.

Chokhmah: wisdom.

Gaon: Eliahu ben Shlomo, the Gaon of Vilna (1720–97), greatest of talmudic authorities of recent centuries.

Gur Arye: supercommentary to Rashi of Judah Loew ben Beẓalel, known as Maharal of Prague (1525–1609).

Ha'amek Davar: commentary on the Torah of Naftali Ẓvi Yehuda Berlin, known as the Netziv (1817–93).

Haftara: selection from the Prophets read in the syngogue after the Torah reading on Sabbaths and festivals.

Hasidism: religious movement founded by Israel ben Eliezer, known as the Ba'al Shem Tov, in the eighteenth century.

Hizkuni: Rabbi Hezekiah ben Manoah, mid-thirteenth-century commentary on the Pentateuch, probably of the school of Rashi.

Ibn Ezra, Abraham (1080–1164): Spanish Bible commentator, poet, and grammarian.

Ishbitzer: R. Mordecai Yosef Leiner (d. 1854), author of *Mei Ha-Shiloah,* a collection of his writings on the Parshiot of the Torah. Controversial in many of his theological positions, particularly in his skepticism about the existence of human freedom.

Kabbalah: Hebrew term for medieval Jewish mysticism.

Kedushat Levi: Rabbi Levi Yitzhak ben Meir of Berdichev (1740–1810), most famous of the third generation of Hasidism, author of commentary on the Torah.

Kli Yakar: homiletic commentary on the Torah of Ephraim Solomon ben Hayyim of Luntshitz (1550–1619).

Likkutei Moharan: see Nahman of Bratzlav.

Maharal: Judah Loew ben Beẓalel (1525–1609), author of philosophical, legal, and exegetical works; see Gur Arye.

Mei Ha-shiloah: see Ishbitzer.

Mekhilta: tannaitic midrash on Exodus, both halakhic and aggadic.

Meshekh Hokhmah: commentary on the Torah of Meir Simha Ha-Kohen of Dvinsk (1843–1926), Talmudist and rabbinic leader.

Midrash: from the root meaning "to seek out" or "to inquire": a term in rabbinic literature for the interpretive study of the Bible. The word is also used in two related senses: first, to refer to the results of that interpretive activity, the specific interpretations produced through midrashic exegesis; and, second, to describe the literary compilations in which the original interpretations, many of them first delivered and transmitted orally, were eventually collected.

Midrash Ha-Gadol: collection of midrashim on the Bible compiled from ancient tannaitic sources by David ben Amram Adani, a Yemenite scholar in the thirteenth century.

Midrash Rabbah: collection of ten midrashim, from various periods, on the five books of the Pentateuch and on the Five Scrolls (Ruth, Esther, Lamentations, Ecclesiastes, and Song of Songs).

Mitzvah: "commandment"—divine mandate in Jewish law.

Nahman of Bratzlav (1772–1811): author of *Likkutei Moharan,* a collection of theological teachings, in which he expounded a paradoxical concept of faith, the centrality of the tzaddik, and the importance of doubt and self-criticism, as well as of melody and dance, in the life of the spiritually aspiring.

Or Ha-Hayyim: commentary on the Torah of Hayyim ibn Attar (1696–1743), Moroccan Kabbalist, Talmudist, and leader of Moroccan-Jewish resettlement in Israel.

Pahad Yitzhak: collected discourses of R. Yitzhak Hutner (b. 1907), representing a synthesis of talmudic conciseness, hasidic mysticism, and ethical sensitivity.

Parsha: weekly Torah reading.

Peshat: the plain meaning or contextual sense among the different levels of interpretation.

Pesikta Rabbati: collection of midrashim for the festivals and special Sabbaths. According to Zunz, the work was "certainly not composed before the second half of the ninth century."

Pirkei d'Rabbi Eliezer: a midrashic description of the workings of God in creation and in the oldest history of Israel. The book was probably written in Palestine, sometime about the beginning of the ninth century.

Pri Zaddik: Rabbi Zadok Hacohen of Lublin (1823–1900), disciple of Rabbi Mordecai Yosef Leiner (the author of *Mei Ha-shiloah*), profound exponent of hasidism.

Radak: Rabbi David Kimchi (1160–1236), most influential Bible commentator of his time. He flourished in Provence. His commentary was reprinted along-side that of Rashi and Ibn Ezra.

Radal: Rabbi David ben Yehudah Luria (1798–1855), Lithuanian scholar, leading Rabbinic figure after the Gaon of Vilna, author of Talmudic glosses and notes and commentary on midrashic texts.

Rambam: Rabbi Moshe ben Maimon, or Maimonides, (1138–1204), author of a master code of Jewish law, *Mishneh Torah,* a philosophical handbook to Judaism, *Guide of the Perplexed,* and a compendium of the 613 command-ments, Sefer Ha-Mitzvot.

Ramban: Rabbi Moshe ben Nahman, or Nahmanides (1194–1270), Spanish biblical and talmudic commentator.

Rasag: Rabbi Saadia Gaon, born in Egypt in 880, philosopher, grammarian, one of the last and most illustrious of the Gaonim, the post–Talmudic authorities of the academies in Babylonia.

Rashbam: initials of Rabbi Shemuel ben Meir (1080–1158), member of Tosafist school, grandson of Rashi, renowned for his *peshat*—plain sense—commen-tary on the Torah.

Rashi: Rabbi Shelomo Yitzhaki, foremost commentator on the Torah (1040–1105). Lived in Troyes, France.

Ravad: Rabbi Avraham ben David of Posquieres (1125–98), outstanding French Rabbinic authority, chiefly noted for his commentaries on Rambam's *Code of Jewish Law.*

Sefat Emet: collected writings of Judah Aryeh Leib Alter (1847–1905), Polish Jew-ish leader and head of Hasidim of Gur. Characterized by wide scholarship, profundity of ideas, and clarity of exposition. Reflects the influence of Maharal.

Seforno, Ovadiah ben Ya'akov (1475–1550): Italian Talmudist, physician, and commentator on the Torah.

Shekhina: from the Hebrew for "dwell," it indicates the divine presence in the natural world.

Shofar: ram's horn used ritually in days of awe, especially on Rosh Hashanah, the New Year.

Sifrei: tannaitic midrashim on the books of Numbers and Deuteronomy, con-taining both halakhah and aggadah.

Talmud: code of Jewish law, lore, philosophy, and ethics, compiled between 200 and 500 C.E. in both Palestine and Babylon. Here, the two codices are referred to by J. and B.

Tanhuma: homiletic midrash on the Pentateuch known in a number of collec-tions.

Tannaim: mishnaic teachers, 20–200 C.E.

Targum: Hebrew for "translation." Any of the Aramaic translations of the Torah done in the last centuries B.C.E. and the early centuries C.E. Often exegetical in nature.

Tefilah: prayer.

Teshuvah: repentance.

Torah: Hebrew for "instruction." Designates the Five Books of Moses: Genesis, Exodus, Leviticus, Numbers, and Deuteronomy.

Torah Shelemah: compendium of early rabbinic commentary on the Torah, by Rabbi Menahem Kasher, begun in 1926.

Torah Temimah: commentary on the Torah of Rabbi Barukh Ha-Levi Epstein, Russian Talmudist (1860–1942), in which he appended to the written text his own selection of the main dicta of Oral Tradition selected from talmudic literature, with his commentary explaining their relevance.

Tzaddik: righteous person, saint.

Yalkut Shimeoni: a midrashic thesaurus on the whole of the Bible compiled from more than fifty works. Probably composed in the first half of the thirteenth century.

Yirah: fear. In mystical sources, psychological and spiritual attribute of Isaac.

Zohar: the Book of Splendor, the most important text of Jewish mysticism, purportedly written by R. Shimeon bar Yohai, but in fact composed in Spain in the thirteenth century.

ACKNOWLEDGMENTS

This collection of essays is the result of several years' thinking and teaching about the ways that unconscious life is intimated in biblical texts. ("Deep calls unto deep at the voice of Your cataracts . . ." [Psalms 42:8].) Issues of communication—seduction, trauma, and inspiration—arise between and within human beings, as well as between the human being and God. These enigmatic voices are often amplified in Rabbinic refractions of the Torah narratives, in midrash, and in Hasidic commentary. Ultimately, their resonance can be heard in the space between the Torah and those who read it, raising questions about the unconscious of the text itself.

In reflecting on these issues, I have been fortunate to have the conversation of friends in many fields, particularly literature and psychoanalysis. I am grateful to David Shulman for his profound listening and reading. Susan Shapiro read the entire manuscript; I owe her a heartfelt debt of gratitude for her wise and generous responses. I want to express my warmest appreciation for the conversation and encouragement of many people whose work has been invigorating for me: among others, Anna Antonovsky, Seth Aronson, Anna Birkenhauer, Judith Elkan, Shmuel Erlich, Stephen Frosh, Annette Furst, Maureen Kendler, Judy and Steve Klitsner, Ilana Kurshan, Peter Kussell, Jiska Mansfield, Debbie Masel Miller, Kenneth Reinhard, Betsy Rosenberg, Lison and Danny Schwartz, Chaim and Doreen Seidler-Feller, Paul Slater, Tamra Wright and Ian Gamse, and Linda Zisquit.

My deep appreciation to my students in Jerusalem; the reverberations of their responses have inspired me to continue teaching and writing. Invitations to lecture at venues in the United States, the United Kingdom, and Australia have given me the opportunity to try out my ideas in many different settings. I am particularly grateful for repeated invitations from the William Alanson White Institute to speak to the New York psychoanalytic community, as well from The Skirball Center for Adult Jewish Learning, the JCC in Manhattan, the Boston CJP, the UCLA Hillel, the London School of Jewish Studies, and the Shalom Hartman Institute in Jerusalem, who have also, year after year, offered me a forum to reach a wide range of students and engage in significant conversations.

I want to thank Adele and Ron Tauber, good friends and warm hosts, who have opened their home to me these many years for my American lecture tours. Thanks also to Sharon Friedman, my agent, and Altie Karper, my editor at Schocken, together with her colleagues, for their enthusiasm and energy in pursuing this project.

Living in a family makes me continuously aware of the murmurings of the deep. For that music, in all its rich complexity, I am grateful: to my children, Bracha, Moshe Yarden, Avi, and Tali, and my grandchildren, Miriam and Aluma; and to my husband, Eric, my partner in so much.

BIBLIOGRAPHY

Bachelard, Gaston. *The Psychoanalysis of Fire,* trans. Alan C. M. Ross. Boston: Beacon Press, 1964.

———. *Water and Dreams.* Dallas, Tex.: Pegasus Foundation, 1983.

Bataille, Georges. *Theory of Religion.* New York: Zone Books, 1992.

Becker, Ernest. *The Denial of Death.* New York: Free Press Paperbacks, 1997.

Benjamin, Walter. *Reflections,* ed. Peter Demetz, trans. Edmund Jephcott. New York: Schocken Books, 1986.

Berger, John. *The Sense of Sight.* New York: Vintage International, 1993.

Berger, Peter L. *A Rumor of Angels.* Garden City, N.Y.: Anchor Books, 1970.

Blanchot, Maurice. *The Unavowable Community,* trans. Pierre Joris. Barrytown, N.Y.: Station Hill Press, 1988.

Bollas, Christopher. *Being a Character.* New York: Hill and Wang, 1992.

———. *Cracking Up.* New York: Hill and Wang, 1995.

———. *Forces of Destiny.* London: Free Association Books, 1989.

———. *The Shadow of the Object.* New York: Columbia University Press, 1987.

Bowie, Malcolm. *Psychoanalysis and the Future of Theory.* Oxford, UK, and Cambridge, Mass.: B. Blackwell, 1993.

Boyarin, Daniel. *Intertextuality and the Reading of Midrash.* Bloomington: Indiana University Press, 1990.

Brodsky, Joseph. *Less Than One.* New York: Farrar Straus Giroux, 1986.

Buber, Martin. *On the Bible.* New York: Schocken Books, 1968.

Carson, Anne. *Autobiography of Red.* New York: Vintage Contemporaries, 1999.

Caruth, Cathy, ed. *Trauma: Explorations in Memory.* Baltimore: Johns Hopkins University Press, 1995.

———. "Traumatic Departures," in *Trauma and Self,* ed. Charles B. Strozier and Michael Flynn, 29–43. Lanham, Md.: Rowman & Littlefield, 1996.

Cavell, Stanley. *In Quest of the Ordinary.* Chicago: University of Chicago Press, 1988.

———. "The Melodrama of the Unknown Woman," in *The Trial(s) of Psychoanalysis,* ed. Françoise Meltzer, 227–58. Chicago: University of Chicago Press, 1988.

Celan, Paul. *The Bremen Speech.* In *Gesammelte Werke,* 3 (1958). Quoted in Shoshana Felman and Dori Laub, *Testimony,* 28. New York: Routledge, 1992.

———. "Conversation in the Mountains." See John Felstiner, *Paul Celan: Poet, Survivor, Jew,* 141–44. New York and London: Yale Univeristy Press, 1995.

Coetzee, J. M. *Foe.* New York: Viking, 1987.

Cover, Robert. *Narrative, Violence, and the Law.* Ann Arbor: University of Michigan Press, 1993.

de Rougemont, Denis. *Passion and Society,* trans. Montgomery Belgion. London: Faber and Faber, 1956.

de Saint-Exupéry, Antoine. *The Little Prince,* trans. Katherine Woods. London: Pan Books Ltd., 1974.

Derrida, Jacques. *The Gift of Death,* trans. David Willis. Chicago: University of Chicago Press, 1995.

Dickinson, Emily. *The Complete Poems of Emily Dickinson.* Boston: Little, Brown, 1924.

Douglas, Mary. *Purity and Danger.* London and Boston: Ark Paperback, 1984.

Duras, Marguerite. *Practicalities.* New York: Grove Weidenfeld, 1990.

Eliot, George. *Middlemarch.* London: Penguin English Library, 1965.

Eliot, T. S. *Four Quartets.* San Diego, New York, London: Harcourt Inc., 1943.

———. "Virgil and the Christian World," in *On Poetry and Poets,* pp. 121–31. London: Faber and Faber, 1957, 122.

Emerson, Ralph Waldo. *Selected Essays,* ed. Larzer Ziff. New York: Penguin Classics, 1987.

Felman, Shoshana. *The Scandal of the Speaking Body,* trans. Catherine Porter. Stanford, Calif.: Stanford University Press, 2003.

———. *What Does a Woman Want?* Baltimore: Johns Hopkins University Press, 1993.

Felman, Shoshana, and Dori Laub. *Testimony.* New York: Routledge, 1992.

Felstiner, John. *Paul Celan: Poet, Survivor, Jew.* New York and London: Yale University Press, 1995.

Fingarette, Herbert. *The Self in Transformation.* New York: Harper & Row, 1965.

Fletcher, John, ed. *Jean Laplanche and the Theory of Seduction, (New Formations* 48, Winter 2002–2003). London: Lawrence and Wishart, 2002.

Freud, Anna. "About Losing and Being Lost." London: Psychoanalytic Study of the Child, 1967, 9–19.

Freud, Sigmund. *Beyond the Pleasure Principle, SE,* 18.

———. *A Difficulty in the Path of Psychoanalysis, SE,* 17.

———. *The Interpretation of Dreams, SE,* 4.

———. *Jokes and Their Relation to the Unconscious, SE,* 8.

———. *Negation, SE,* 19.

———. "Recommendations to Physicians Practicing Psychoanalysis," *SE,* 12. New York: Norton, 1955.

Fried, Michael. *Realism, Writing, Disfiguration.* Chicago: University of Chicago Press, 1987.

Gellman, Jerome I. *Abraham! Abraham!* Aldershot, Hants, UK, and Burlington, Vt.: Ashgate, 2003.

Gerson, Samuel. "The Relational Unconscious," *Psychoanalytic Quarterly* 73, 2004: 71.

Grosz, Elizabeth. *Volatile Bodies.* Bloomington: Indiana University Press, 1994.

Handelman, Don, and David Shulman. *God Inside-Out.* New York: Oxford University Press, 1997.

Harrison, Robert Pogue. *The Dominion of the Dead.* Chicago: University of Chicago Press, 2003.

Heschel, Abraham Joshua. *Man Is Not Alone.* New York: Noonday Press, 1976.

Holt, John. *Instead of Education: Ways to Help People Do Things Better*. New York: Dutton, 1976.

Hutter, Albert. "Poetry in Psychoanalysis," in *Transitional Objects and Potential Spaces*, ed. Peter L. Rudnytsky, 63–86. New York: Columbia University Press, 1993.

James, Henry. "The Beast in the Jungle," in *Selected Short Stories*, ed. O. Anderson, 215–262. New York: Rinehart, 1955.

Jones, Ernest. *The Life and Work of Sigmund Freud*. New York: Basic Books, 1955.

Josipovici, Gabriel. *On Trust*. New Haven, Conn.: Yale University Press, 1999.

Kafka, Franz. *Parables and Paradoxes*. New York: Schocken Books, 1961.

Keats, John. *Letters*. New York: Oxford University Press, 1965.

Kermode, Frank. *The Sense of an Ending*. Oxford, UK, and New York: Oxford University Press, 2000.

Kierkegaard, Søren. *The Sickness unto Death*, ed. and trans. Howard V. Hong and Edna H. Hong. Princeton, N.J.: Princeton University Press, 1980.

Kristeva, Julia. *Powers of Horror*, trans. Leon S. Roudiez. New York: Columbia University Press, 1982.

———. "Stabat Mater," in *The Kristeva Reader*, ed. Toril Moi, pp. 161–86. New York: Columbia University Press, 1986.

———. *Strangers to Ourselves*, trans. Leon S. Roudiez. New York: Columbia University Press, 1991.

Kugel, James. "Two Introductions to Midrash," in *Midrash and Literature*, ed. Geoffrey Hartman and Sanford Budick, 77–103. New Haven, Conn.: Yale University Press, 1986.

LaCocque, André, and Paul Ricoeur. *Thinking Biblically*, trans. David Pellauer. Chicago: University of Chicago Press, 1998.

Landy, Francis. "Ruth and the Romance of Realism," in *Beauty and the Enigma*, pp. 218–51. Sheffield, UK: Sheffield Academic Press, 2001.

Laplanche, Jean. *Essays on Otherness*. London and New York: Routledge, 1999.

———. "Sublimation and/or Inspiration," in *Jean Laplanche and the Theory of Seduction*, ed. John Fletcher, 26–50. *New Formations* 48, Winter 2002–2003.

Lear, Jonathan. *Happiness, Death, and the Remainder of Life*. Cambridge, Mass.: Harvard University Press, 2000.

———. *Open Minded*. Cambridge, Mass.: Harvard University Press, 1998.

———. *Therapeutic Action*. London and New York: Karnac, 2003.

Levenson, Jon D. *The Death and Resurrection of the Beloved Son*. New Haven, Conn.: Yale University Press, 1993.

Levi, Primo. *Survival in Auschwitz*, trans. Stuart Woolf. London: Collier Macmillan Publishers, 1961.

Levinas, Emmanuel. *Nine Talmudic Readings*. Bloomington: Indiana University Press, 1990.

Lingis, Alphonso. *The Community of Those Who Have Nothing in Common*. Bloomington: Indiana University Press, 1994.

Miller, D. A. *Narrative and Its Discontents*. Princeton, N.J.: Princeton University Press, 1981.

Milner, Marion. "Winnicott and Overlapping Circles," in *The Suppressed Madness of Sane Men*, 279–86. London and New York: Tavistock Publications, 1987.

Moore, Marianne. *Complete Poems*. New York: Macmillan/Viking, 1967.

Muffs, Yochanan. *Love and Joy*. New York: Jewish Theological Seminary of America, 1992.

Neher, André. *The Exile of the Word*, trans. David Maisel. Philadelphia: Jewish Publication Society of America, 1981.

Ogden, Thomas H. *Subjects of Analysis*. Northvale, N.J.: Jason Aronson, 1994.

Ouaknin, Marc-Alain. *The Burnt Book*. Princeton, N.J.: Princeton University Press, 1995.

Phillips, Adam. *The Beast in the Nursery*. London: Faber and Faber, 1998.

————. *Equals*. New York: Basic Books, 2002.

————. *On Flirtation*. Cambridge, Mass.: Harvard University Press, 1994.

————. *Promises, Promises*. New York: Basic Books, 2001.

————. *Terrors and Experts*. Cambridge, Mass.: Harvard University Press, 1996.

Proust, Marcel. *Swann's Way, Remembrance of Things Past*, trans. C. K. Scott-Moncrieff and Terence Kilmartin. New York: First Vintage International Edition, 1989.

Ricoeur, Paul. *Freud and Philosphy: An Essay on Interpretation*. New Haven: Yale University Press, 1970.

Rimmon, Shlomith. *The Concept of Ambiguity—the Example of James*. Chicago: University of Chicago Press, 1977.

Rose, Jacqueline. *On Not Being Able to Sleep*. Princeton, N.J.: Princeton University Press, 2003.

Rosenzweig, Franz. *The Star of Redemption*. Notre Dame, Ind.: Notre Dame Press, 1985.

————. *Understanding the Sick and the Healthy*. Cambridge, Mass.: Harvard University Press, 1999.

Santner, Eric L. *On the Psychotheology of Everyday Life*. Chicago: University of Chicago Press, 2001.

Sarna, Nahum. *Torah and Commentary*. New York: The Jewish Publication Society, 2001.

Scarry, Elaine. *The Body in Pain*. New York: Oxford University Press, 1985.

Silbermann, A. M., trans. *Chumash with Rashi's Commentary*. Jerusalem: Silbermann family by arrangement with Routledge, Kegan, Paul Ltd., 1973.

Simon, Uriel. *Jonah* [in Hebrew]. Tel Aviv: Am Oved, 1992.

Steiner, George. *After Babel*. New York: Oxford University Press, 1975.

Stern, Donnel B. *Unformulated Experience*. Hillsdale, N.J.: Analytic Press, 1997.

Strozier, Charles B., and Michael Flynn, eds. *Trauma and Self*. Lanham, Md.: Rowman & Littlefield, 1996.

Trilling, Lionel. *The Liberal Imagination*. New York: Viking Press, 1950.

————. *Sincerity and Authenticity*. Cambridge, Mass.: Harvard Univeristy Press, 1972.

Weiss, Joseph. *Studies in East European Jewish Mysticism*. Oxford, UK, and New York: Oxford University Press, 1985.

Winnicott, D. W. "The Fear of Breakdown," in *Psycho-Analytic Explorations*, pp. 87–95, ed. Clare Winnicott. Cambridge, Mass.: Harvard University Press, 1992.

————. "A Note on the Mother-Foetus Relationship," in *Psycho-Analytic Explorations*, 161–62, ed. Clare Winnicott. Cambridge, Mass.: Harvard University Press, 1992.

———. "On Communication," in *The Maturational Processes and the Facilitating Environment*, 179–92. Madison, Conn.: International Universities Press, 1965.

———. *Playing and Reality*. Abingdon, Oxon, UK: Routledge, 1997.

———. "Primitive Emotional Development," in *Collected Papers: Through Pediatrics to Psycho-Analysis*. London: Tavistock; New York: Basic Books, 1958.

———. "The Psychology of Madness," in *Psycho-Analytic Explorations*, pp. 119–29, ed. Clare Winnicott. Cambridge, Mass.: Harvard University Press, 1989.

Yeats, W. B. "The Second Coming," in *The Faber Book of Modern Verse*, ed. Michael Roberts. London: Faber and Faber, 1936.

Yourcenar, Marguerite. *That Mighty Sculptor, Time*, trans. Walter Kaiser. New York: Farrar, Straus and Giroux, 1992.

Žižek, Slavoj. *The Parallax View*. Cambridge, Mass.: MIT Press, 2006.

Zornberg, Avivah. *The Beginning of Desire: Reflections on Genesis*. New York: Doubleday, 1996.

———. *The Particulars of Rapture: Reflections on Exodus*. New York: Doubleday, 2001.

PERMISSIONS

INDEX